The
RHETORIC
CANON

The
RHETORIC
CANON

Edited by

Brenda Deen Schildgen

WAYNE STATE UNIVERSITY PRESS

DETROIT

Manufactured in the United States of America.

01 00 99 98 97   5 4 3 2 1

Library of Congress Cataloging-in-Publication Data

The rhetoric canon / edited by Brenda Deen Schildgen.
    p.   cm.
    Includes bibliographical references and index.
    ISBN 0-8143-2632-3 (pbk. : alk. paper)
    1. Rhetoric.   2. Hermeneutics.   3. Canon (Literature)
I. Schildgen, Brenda Deen, 1942–
PN175.R47   1997
808—dc21   97-16334

CONTENTS

5

CONTENTS

CONTRIBUTORS

Gary P. Cestaro, professor of Italian at DePaul University, has published several essays on Dante and medieval rhetoric.

Thomas Cole, professor of classics at Yale University, is the author of *Democritus and the Sources of Greek Anthropology* (Scholars, 1990); *Pindar's Feasts, or the Music of Power* (Ateneo, 1992); *Epiploke: Rhythmical Continuity and Poetic Structure in Greek Lyric* (Harvard University Press, 1988); and *The Origins of Rhetoric in Ancient Greece* (Johns Hopkins University Press, 1990).

Kathy Eden, professor of English and comparative literature at Columbia University, is the author of *Poetic and Legal Fiction in Aristotelian Tradition* (Princeton University Press, 1986) and *Hermeneutics and the Rhetorical Tradition: Chapters in the Ancient Legacy and Its Humanistic Reception* (Yale University Press, 1997).

Stephen Halliwell, professor at the School of Greek, Latin, and Ancient History at St. Salvator's College, University of St. Andrews, includes among his books *Aristotle's Poetics* (Duckworth, 1986); *The Poetics of Aristotle*, translation and commentary (University of North Carolina Press, 1987); *Republic 5/Plato*, introduction, translation, and commentary (Warminster, 1993); *Poetics/Aristotle: Longinus, On the Sublime*, editing and translation (Harvard University Press, 1995).

William J. Kennedy is professor of comparative literature at Cornell University. His books include *Jacopo Sannazaro and the Uses of Pastoral* (University Press of New England, 1983), which was awarded the Howard R. Marraro prize; *Authorizing Petrarch* (Cornell University Press, 1994); and *Writing in the Disciplines*, 3rd ed. (Prentice-Hall, 1995).

The late Raymond Adolph Prier was an independent scholar. He wrote *Archaic Logic: Symbol and Structure in Heraclitus, Parmenides, and Empedocles*

(Mouton, 1976) and *Thauma Idesthai: The Phenomenology of Sight and Appearance in Archaic Greece* (Florida State University Press, 1989), and edited *Countercurrents: On the Primacy of Texts in Literary Criticism* (State University of New York Press, 1992).

BRUCE ROSENSTOCK has published on Plato and in Jewish studies. He teaches religious studies and classics at the University of California, Davis.

BRENDA DEEN SCHILDGEN, editor, teaches comparative literature, Italian, and medieval and religious studies at the University of California, Davis. She is the author of *Crisis and Continuity: Time in the Gospel of Mark* (Sheffield, 1997) and of several essays on Dante and Petrarch, ancient Christian rhetoric and its medieval uses, and composition and rhetorical theory. She is also coeditor of a forthcoming collection of essays on Boccaccio and the Canterbury Tales (Fairleigh Dickinson University Press), of a monograph on Dante's geography, and of a study of the reception of the Gospel of Mark.

THOMAS O. SLOANE, professor emeritus of rhetoric at the University of California, Berkeley, is the author of *Donne, Milton, and the End of Humanist Rhetoric* (University of California Press, 1985) and *On the Contrary: Studies in Rhetoric, Education, Erasmus, and Thomas Wilson* (Catholic University Press, 1997).

HAYDEN WHITE, professor emeritus of the history of consciousness at the University of California, Santa Cruz, is the author of *Metahistory: The Historical Imagination in Nineteenth-century Europe* (Johns Hopkins University Press, 1973); coeditor with Margaret Brose of *Representing Kenneth Burke* (Johns Hopkins University Press, 1982); and author of *Tropics of Discourse: Essays in Cultural Criticism* (Johns Hopkins University Press, 1978) and *The Content of the Form: Narrative Discourse and Historical Representation* (Johns Hopkins University Press, 1987).

ACKNOWLEDGMENTS

I WISH TO express my deep gratitude to all the contributors for their outstanding essays and for their conscientiousness and promptness throughout the long process of bringing this volume together. I am especially indebted to Hayden White, who wrote his essay for a conference ("Literacy and Literature") that I organized at the University of San Francisco in 1987. I also must express special gratitude to Ray Prier, now deceased, who has an essay in this collection and who encouraged me from the start to pursue this project. He introduced me to Tom Cole, who had directed his dissertation at Yale, and to Bill Kennedy, also a close friend of his, who both contributed to the volume on Ray's recommendation. I have special thanks for Tom Sloane for being a patient editor of my introduction and for many conversations about the importance and relevance of rhetoric.

Thanks go to Mary Beth O'Sullivan, who has shepherded this project through the various board meetings at Wayne State University Press, to the readers for their suggestions for improving the order and shape, as well as the content, of the collection, and to the editors at Wayne State University Press, especially Jennifer Backer, for their care and conscientiousness.

Finally, I must recognize the support of my family, and particularly my husband, who edits everything I write.

Introduction

BRENDA DEEN SCHILDGEN

Rhetoric is the science of speaking well on civil questions;
eloquence is the flow of words, designed to persuade people
to the just and good.

—ISIDORE OF SEVILLE, *ETYMOLOGIES* II[1]

T
HE TITLE OF this book refers to the rhetoric canon as if a list of canonical texts actually held authority in the discussion of rhetoric, but these essays make clear that differences about the nature and function of rhetoric throughout history have relegated some texts to obscurity, revived some, and peripheralized others, while consecrating new ones. The canon of rhetorical texts turns out to be far more flexible than is generally recognized. Consider the case of Plato, who is regarded as an enemy of rhetoric. His "canonical" status as an anti-rhetorician, and the assumption that he believed philosophy was the means to "the truth" while rhetoric was nothing more than a trope-wielding skill exploited by self-serving politicians, have obscured his interest in examining how rhetoric worked. Possibly because of his "canonical" status in philosophy and intellectual history, and because of his and Socrates' assumed scorn for rhetorical practice, his contribution to debates about rhetoric's vital role in education has been overlooked. Furthermore, because Plato chose to examine various forms of education and questioned what he considered the limitations of conventional rhetorical education, Gorgias and Isocrates, his contemporary rhetoricians, for example, despite their insights, have been marginalized. On the other hand, as Plato's intellectual heir, Aristotle was invested with an authority that contributed to the reverence accorded his rhetorical treatise and the arguments he developed in it, particularly when it was recovered in the Middle Ages. From then on, his treatise took on canonical and normative status.

The essays presented here argue collectively and polemically for re-consideration of rhetoric's historic role in humanistic practice and in the formation of citizens. The collection, which represents scholars in classics, rhetoric, and comparative literature, includes views on Homer, Longinus, Plato, Aristotle, Isocrates, Cicero, Augustine, Jerome, Dante, Boncompagno da Signa, Eberhard the German, Erasmus, Kant, and Adorno.

Although the essays range from the ancient Greeks and Romans to late antiquity and the Middle Ages, and from early modern to modern views, they reflect some consistent positions about rhetoric's function as an educational instrument. Whether the discussions focus on Isocrates, Augustine, Plato, or Erasmus, or whether or not they argue for original interpretations of rhetorical texts, all of the arguments are important to contemporary education. The contributors' interests and the rhetoricians they discuss vary radically— some rejecting the restrictions of canons upheld by rhetorical masters while simultaneously recognizing the canons' capacity to undermine their own limiting powers; others seeing rhetoric as a powerful instrument which codifies and upholds standards for imitation; some focusing on rhetoric as a philosophy, as a tool of propaganda, as the twin of hermeneutics, or as the intermediary between an oral prenominalistic culture and a culture in which literacy and writing dominate; others arguing that rhetoric, to be useful, must encourage self-criticism, and furthermore that training in rhetoric sustains a culture of live debate which is essential for the practice of responsible citizenship. But whatever the focus of the argument, all the contributors insist that rhetoric and its intellectual practices are crucial to education and therefore to the preparation of citizens.

The above quote from Isidore of Seville's *Etymologies* was chosen very purposefully, for the seventh-century late antique/early medieval author is the hinge between the ancient and medieval worlds. Isidore's link ensured that despite the massive cultural rupture that took place at the end of the ancient world, its educational practices would be carried forward in some form. Isidore "canonized" rhetoric for medieval education (from the seventh century to the fifteenth), ensuring that Roman educational methods, already appropriated to Christianity by the Latin fathers (Augustine and Jerome), would be continued in his own times. Testifying to the importance he ascribed to grammar, rhetoric, and dialectic, Isidore began his encyclopedia with a thorough discussion of the trivium, the basis of all learning. Ironically, though Isidore served as the central reference for medieval trivium education, few modern humanists delve into his encyclopedic text. He has long since been replaced by select authors within the canon to which he referred for his description of the purposes and methods of rhetoric. However, his definition of rhetoric offers an uncompromising start to our discussion of rhetorical texts and topics. He defined rhetoric as training in citizenship in which practice in eloquence and ethics are joined for the benefit of society. As canonizer and canonized, Isidore contributed to the history of rhetoric and rhetorical practice by restating and so disseminating in brief form what the "canonical" rhetoricians and rhetorical theorists of antiquity—Gorgias, Aristotle, Hermagoras, Cicero, and Quintilian—had earlier argued.

Isidore's interest in rhetoric reflects the conviction carried over from the ancient world that the foundation of education and performance in public life was the capacity to speak well, a skill that required training in the ancient discipline of rhetoric, from which the modern disciplines of literature, philosophy, and speech were born. Speech, thus, is not merely a skill but an art, training in which intellectually prepares its practitioners to argue persuasively and eloquently, to discern complexity and mediate differences, and to participate in the forums of public life. One of the most interesting aspects of Isidore's work on rhetoric is his reference to a canon of texts that he identifies with a discussion of rhetoric, a list he connects to the scope of rhetoric's purposes. He assigns the discovery of rhetoric to the Greeks, citing Gorgias, Aristotle, and Hermagoras, who he claims were translated into Latin by Cicero and Quintilian. In his discussion of dialectic, Isidore credits Plato with having divided rhetoric from dialectic, for Plato a subcategory of logic, a consequence of Plato having added logic and rational philosophy to moral philosophy.

Lists of Greek and Roman quotations from philosophers and rhetoricians and the authoritative Christian writers of late antiquity—Lactantius, Tertullian, Marius Victorinus, Jerome, Boethius, Cassiodorus, and, of course, Augustine—provided Isidore with examples of rhetorical tropes and arguments. Though his primary source for his discussion of rhetoric is Cassiodorus's *Institutions* (c. 480–575 C.E.), his rationale for ascribing such importance to the practice of grammar and rhetoric was provided by a late classical pagan encyclopedist, Martianus Capella, author of one of the most important rhetorical treatises in use in the Middle Ages, *De nuptiis Philologiae et Mercurii*. When he needed literary examples to demonstrate principles and rhetorical tropes, Isidore turned to his literary canon, giving equal place to Virgil, to Cicero, or to the Bible. By Isidore's time, the concept of "canon" in regard to scriptural texts and a list of Latin works deemed worthy of study and illustrative of stylistic principles had been established in the Latin West, and Isidore's encyclopedia, which emerged as a normative reference tool, canonized their authority.

The *Etymologies'* canonical status in education throughout the Middle Ages, shown by the quanity of its surviving manuscripts, is a provocative start to a discussion of the notion of a rhetorical canon. Isidore defined rhetoric, recorded its history, established a list of authors, identified its "studied eloquence" as the foundation of skill in speaking, connected rhetoric to legal cases and to syllogism, listed tropes, and reviewed "rational and legal status" and many-sided dispute. In essence, he "epitomized" and so preserved the known learning about the forms and practice of rhetoric in the ancient world and in so doing became an authoritative source for rhetorical practice along with his own Latin sources throughout the Middle Ages. What he defined as the essential features of rhetoric, summarized in his discussion, installed the terms of rhetoric's practice and the authorities to whom it deferred as a canon of exemplary texts. Isidore became an exclusive reference tool for rhetoric and rhetorical practice until the twelfth century, when Aristotle's *Rhetoric* reappeared in the Latin West.

As an encyclopedist and collector of information, Isidore confined his inquiry to identifying a canonical core of writers and texts associated with rhetoric, including Aristotle, Cicero, Quintilian, as reworked in Martianus Capella, Cassiodorus, Jerome, and Augustine. Furthermore, spelling out the intellectual concerns raised by these authors, as the traditional topics of rhetoric—the production of eloquent speech and its purposes, the interpretation of speeches and writing, the authors one might study to develop eloquence, the connection rather than the division between rhetoric and dialectic, and the function of rhetoric in the body politic—he did not raise the kinds of questions that are intrinsic to the practice of rhetoric. It is these questions—for example, what function do rhetorical canons serve, what makes a canon, who determines it and why, and why are canons constantly in flux—that launch the essays in this collection. Even more important, going to the center of rhetoric's dialectic mode, these essays probe the rhetoric of canonicity and the role specific speech-making and textual strategies play in overturning established methodologies and convictions about rhetorical practice.

To situate the contemporary revival of rhetoric historically, the collection begins with Hayden White's essay on the suppression of rhetoric in the nineteenth century, a development that he argues followed as a consequence of Kantian notions of aestheticism resulting in the division between "literature" and "literacy," or practical and factual writing which served the emerging capitalist economy versus poetic expression which lacked this practical application.

Following White's essay, to interrogate the role of canons, their definition and function, and why canons should be the focus of continued academic debate, essays by Tom Cole and Bill Kennedy take on arguments about canonicity and what rhetorical traditions have to contribute to the discussion. Both argue persuasively that canons, though appearing restrictive, have the capacity to undermine the very standards they purport to uphold. In other words, canons have the potential to be as provocative as the countercanons that oppose them, whether in stylistic or discursive matters.

Distinguishing between ancient "grammar-oriented" cultures and modern "text-oriented" cultures, Tom Cole in "Canonicity and Multivalence: The Case of Cicero," argues that synonymy is as much a master trope for ancient rhetoric as polysemy/multivalence is for modern. The ancients' art of saying the same thing in many ways has been replaced by the modern art of being many things to many people, a degraded use of rhetoric. Thus, the modern idea of the "fluid" personality, the person who can change himself or herself and his or her speech practices for whatever new circumstances arise, has replaced the ancient inflexible socially defined person, the product of rhetorical education, who nonetheless could write a poem, make a speech, present an argument, write history and poetry, and produce fiction and nonfiction without perceiving any epistemological difficulties with the transitions. The Ciceronian texts, partially oral in origin but merged into an enduring intellectual, political, and literary testament when their author collected and edited them for publication, are situated between oral practice and literary rule. Cicero's "pervasive ambiguity" mediates the contradictions that infuriated his contemporaries. Though Cicero's literary testament was designed to limit the range of potential debate, it has functioned throughout history both to challenge and to reinforce dominant intellectual, social, or political developments. Cicero's rhetorical canon, though revered, at least in the canon of classical texts, turns out to be, like Cicero himself, "an ambiguous tool," a potentially subversive instrument.

In his essay "Interest in the Canon: Kant in the Context of Longinus and Adorno," arguing that debates about the canon that reduce it to reading lists trivialize the issue, Bill Kennedy points out that the concept of canon originates in rhetorical theory, practice, and pedagogy, where it is defined as a standard or rule that students duplicate in their own writing. During late classical times, it came to refer to specific texts worthy to be imitated or emulated because of their depth and complexity, or, from the standpoint of a broad readership, worthy to be analyzed and interpreted because of their seminal cultural importance. Both Longinus and Kant regard the canon as a negative and constraining force in rhetorical practice because for Longinus it encourages a dull sort of competence (*Peri hupsous*, ch. 36) while for Kant it promotes mere rules that true genius should transcend (*Critique of Judgment*, l.l.17). Including "classical" texts or neglected texts representing marginalized people in canons may alter our literary knowledge, Kennedy argues, but the underlying goal of canon formation is more nearly the transformation of historical consciousness. Thus, mere "reshuffling of titles" may prove to be less effective in achieving the social-political goals that prompt the changes than intellectual dialogue about how canons function in education.

In order to frame the discussion of the practice of rhetoric as a discipline, there follows an essay on the Homeric corpus, in an era long before the discipline and its discursive methodologies were tentatively formalized. In "Achilles *Rheter?* Homer and Proto-rhetorical Truth" Raymond Prier argues that because Homeric language is poetic, that is, paratactic, distinctly antihypotactic, and prenominalistic, it lacks the rhetorical possibilities reflected in the later Classical-Greek distinctions. *Logos,* which appears but twice in the Homeric corpus and then only in very restricted, negative senses, is overshadowed by *mythos* in the Homeric *ergon* because sophistry in its Classical-Greek sense was linguistically proscribed. This essay describes the Homeric oral social ethos and how it translated into poetry, serving as the backdrop against which rhetoric developed, for one of the most important features of rhetoric is that it preserves the dialogic nature of spoken language. However, though rhetoric may use the poetic means of oral poetry and the spoken medium, it also employs the intellectual modes of writing, of hypotaxis, logic, and abstract thinking. Although Aristotelian and Ciceronian rhetorics preserved, to their benefit, the spoken aspects of discourse, which provide its contentious and negotiating features, they introduced abstract notions of a collective good to be discovered through argumentation and canonized for the benefit of the public, aspects of rhetoric that are developed in all the other essays here.

Bruce Rosenstock's "From Counter-rhetoric to *Askesis:* How the *Phaedo* Rewrites the *Gorgias*" examines Plato's special contribution to the history of rhetoric's purposes and methods, probing how Plato interrogates rhetoric's role in the formation of political leaders. Between the *Gorgias* and the *Phaedo*, Plato shifts from a view of philosophy as practice to philosophy as theory. Under close scrutiny, traditional readings of Plato are called into question as Plato's shifting views almost look like an abandonment of Socrates himself, for Socrates engaged actively in the public life of the city, confronting its foremost citizens with questions that sought to elicit from them a justification of their political practices that went beyond expedience, pragmatism, and tradition for its own sake. The "speech practice" of Socrates, represented in the "aporetic" dialogues, ran directly counter to that of the powerful leaders of his day. But with the new theoretical interests ushered in by the *Phaedo*, Plato made Socrates the spokesman for doctrines about the nature of reality that seem far removed from the pretensions of political leaders. By comparing the *Gorgias* with the *Phaedo*, linking Socrates the citizen with Socrates the theorist, the essay calls into question the long-standing split between rhetoric as public political practice and philosophy as theory, a contrast that grew out of the traditional reading of Plato, which Rosenstock challenges. Plato, the essay argues, was engaged in a battle with the standard rhetorical practices of his day while developing a "counter-rhetoric," for as the *Gorgias* shows, Socratic speech is not able to generate absolute knowledge of the good but has the less pretentious role of being able to dispel illusions. Rosenstock's iconoclastic essay concludes that Platonism, as presented in the *Gorgias* and the *Phaedo*, began as a rewriting of the agon between the Socratic counter-rhetoric and the demagogic rhetoric in civic practice, and that the goal of the Academy was to liberate the city from the illusions supported by this demagogic rhetorical practice. The essay itself functions as a challenge to canonical readings of Plato that have upheld the dichotomy between Plato as philosopher against the rhetoricians, showing that Plato himself was engaged in a counter-rhetoric that sought to dispel the power of the prevailing rhetorical canon whose methods of discourse and literary reference held coercive educational authority.

Stephen Halliwell's "Philosophical Rhetoric or Rhetorical Philosophy? The Strange Case of Isocrates" goes to the core of this rhetoric/philosophy debate to argue that Plato's and Aristotle's roles as canonical figures in the debate, which relegated Isocrates to rhetorician, shut out Isocrates' contribution to the linkage between philosophy and rhetoric. Halliwell's reinsertion of Isocrates into a discussion of rhetoric in fourth-century B.C.E. Greece forces a reconsideration of the relationship between rhetoric and philosophy as a live, contentious issue in the intellectual history of the period. Isocrates' work, written in the genre of speech, made the domain of common discourse a legitimate medium for the formation of ethical beliefs and values. Whereas for Aristotle and Plato philosophy is the ultimate framework of truth and a mode of understanding to which all other human pursuits, including rhetoric, must remain subordinate, for Isocrates rhetoric is the "logos in action," and philosophy is its mature mastery. Halliwell argues that despite the fact that Isocrates' influence on Western ideals of education and culture stem from his integration of ideas of language, reason, and practical wisdom, his mode for integrating these activities lacks the self-critical dimension central to Plato's and Aristotle's theories. Although some account is given of other figures, including Plato and Aristotle, the argument focuses on Isocrates' views of rhetoric in the context of his own culture, while suggesting that the argument between rhetoric and philosophy should be understood as a precursor of arguments that have proven permanently important in the history of controversies about the value of rhetoric. The study of Isocrates as a canonical figure in rhetoric is fruitful precisely because he lacks a dominant aspect of rhetoric, its capacity to be self-critical.

Turning to the relationship between rhetoric and hermeneutics as a consistent feature of rhetorical practice, Kathy Eden's "Hermeneutics and the Ancient Rhetorical Tradition" considers the rhetorical developments in the period between the fourth century B.C.E. and the first century C.E. to demonstrate Schleiermacher's claim that "every act of understanding is the obverse of an act of discourse." The essay ranges widely over ancient rhetorical practice, examining the contributions of Plato, Isocrates, Aristotle, Cicero, Quintilian, and Demetrius, arguing that between the fourth century B.C.E. and the first century C.E., rhetorical theory was not limited to questions of composition, or speech-making. Quite the contrary, it developed a specialized terminology to take up questions of interpretation, which drove apart legal and stylistic matters—rhetoric as hermeneutics versus rhetoric as literary terminology— a rift that hardened into an opposition through the Renaissance. The essay contributes to the ongoing discussion of the connection between rhetoric's twin activities of composition and interpretation, and how these supporting intellectual activities contributed to the development of modern interpretation theory or hermeneutics.

"Rhetoric and the Body of Christ: Augustine, Jerome, and the Classical *Paideia*" demonstrates St. Jerome's and St. Augustine's transformation of the ancient *paideia* and their application and revision of classical rhetorical treatises for Christian interpretive and teaching purposes, a transformation that would influence educational practices for well over a thousand years. Jerome and Augustine interrogated and evaluated the resources of ancient rhetorical education, scrutinizing their usefulness in debates about canonicity, interpretation, declamation, and orthodoxy, subjects at the heart of the Christian cultural program. In defining the common ground for discussion and debate with an inflexible canon of shared readings, methodologies for interpretation and declamation, and strict boundaries within which orthodoxy would be protected and heterodoxies could be confined, these Church fathers were intentionally transforming consciousness and ensuring the future power of the Church. Ever conscious of the importance of rhetoric to the survival and successful evangelization of Christianity, they sought rhetorical methods to make "the Word" living speech rather than a dead letter. In contrast to upholding rhetoric's tradition of the coexistence of differences to be mediated through dialogue and argument with consensus tentative at best, these Christian writers stressed a nonnegotiable Truth as the subject of rhetoric's practice. Despite the successful cultural transformation, Augustine and Jerome were haunted by a sense of the very contingencies that are intrinsic to Christian philosophy, contingencies that make any absolutes in human endeavors theologically suspect. Ultimately, these inhibitions delimit any effort to impose absolute interpretations on Christian texts, for only God is absolute, and human experience and knowledge are limited. This, however, does not prevent these fathers from appropriating ancient Roman rhetoric's methods and canonical texts to undergird Christian doctrine and to support Christian teaching. On the contrary, they adopt all the learning of the ancient world as necessary to support their Christian rhetorical practice.

In "Dante, Boncompagno da Signa, Eberhard the German, and the Rhetoric of the Maternal Body," Gary Cestaro applies contemporary theory to three important rhetorical texts of the later Middle Ages—Boncompagno da Signa's *Rhetorica novissima* (1235), Dante's *De Vulgari eloquentia* (c. 1304), and Eberhard the German's *Laborintus*. He argues that rhetoric's historical role as lawgiver is re-enforced in these texts, while grammar is relegated to the maternal role. Bringing the terms of these important late-medieval rhetorical discussions into a contemporary theoretical framework and applying a psychoanalytic vocabulary, the essay argues that by aligning grammar with the maternal semiotic (Kristeva), these texts strategically impose rhetoric's Oedipal authority (the Lacanian *nom-du-père*) and thus reinforce its traditional role as giver of rules within the patriarchal symbolic order.

In the final essay, "Never-Ending Dispute: A Proposal of Marriage," Tom Sloane uses Erasmus's letter to Lord Mountjoy urging him to marry, which Erasmus claimed was deeply misunderstood by Church authorities, in order to reconsider the value of training in argumentation. Erasmus incorporated the letter in his textbook on letter writing to drive home his point about the educational mission of two-sided argument, *disputatio in utramque partem*. Its purpose is, in sum, to counteract exactly the attitudes Church authorities displayed. Showing how much Erasmus enjoyed and exploited controversy and fractiousness, Sloane argues that Erasmus was a "thoroughgoing rhetorician," an educator without a classroom, who proposed educational and intellectual reform aimed at changing society's manner of thought. He lived in an age not unlike our own when the new was calling all the old into doubt, the sort of age, Sloane insists, in which rhetoric thrives. The humanistic value of two-sided argument and rhetoric's linkage to "fractiousness and turmoil" are the themes of this essay, which uses Erasmus as its prime example and closes by calling for a new emphasis on rhetorical education. The urgency of the final plea is impelled by the gradual disappearance of what used to be called "speech" in education and by the rise of new language philosophers who discount the profoundly oral and disputatious nature of language.

The essays in this collection deliberate on a canon of rhetorical texts and the many roles and functions of canonical rhetoric. With close scrutiny, it becomes clear that the diverse practices and functions of rhetoric and the catena of texts associated with it free rather than block its intellectual avenues. Instead of confining rhetoric to a narrow scope of practices and a limited set of authors, as a group, these essays argue for rhetoric's power to uphold interpretive principles and to promote canons while simultaneously calling them into question. This is the heart of rhetoric's purpose and strength as an epistemology.

When rhetoric was expunged from university curricula in the later nineteenth century, a powerful discipline for challenging received ideas was lost. Further, when the discipline of English literature was separated from freshman composition at the same time, this curricular development, which would sweep through higher education, ensured that in the present era rhetoric could only survive refashioned as the freshman composition requirement. Whatever benefits the nineteenth-century reform had, rhetoric's contemporary revival, while not seeking to undo the reforms, nonetheless aspires to reconsider rhetoric's academic and intellectual value.

Since all the works surveyed in this collection belong to a tradition of discussions about the uses and properties of language, the variety of themes is not surprising. Rhetoricians are persistent in supporting the necessity of contingencies and two-sided arguments (Sloane, Cole, Kennedy); in pairing philosophy or hermeneutics and rhetoric (Eden, Schildgen, Rosenstock, Halliwell, Cole); and in analyzing the power, purpose, and dangers of canonicity (Cole, Kennedy, Schildgen) as the foundation for a common discourse. The authors discussed in this collection were engaged in traditions of rhetorical discourse, and, like the essayists who interpret them, they were preoccupied by the philosophy and practice of education, because debates about canons, interpretation, argumentation, and eloquence inevitably have profound educational implications. They engage the philosophy/rhetoric squabble, argue against traditional intellectual divisions, address what students being trained as citizens should read in order to participate in democratic dialogue, discuss whether argumentation can ever be conclusive, and analyze the role of style and rhetorical tropes in public discourse. That is, as Plato's *Gorgias* argues, these essays discuss the "techne" of rhetoric rather than its "truth" content. Without taking up the topics of speech or writing, these issues go farther than the classroom, the school, and the university, for they underlie discussions about how citizens are to perform as decision makers and as critics of events directing all aspects of public life. Because rhetoric as a language study should not be separated from public issues, this collection and the "canonical" authors surveyed contend that it is an indispensable discipline because it develops the skills to argue, to dispute, and to reach consensus. The subjects and practices of rhetoric discussed in this volume—canons, standards of eloquence, rules of discourse, grammar, argumentation, ethics, and the relationship between interpreting and making speeches—are not mere matters of decorum but rather the essential means to debate critical issues in letters and science. At this time of continuing public controversy about the humanities curriculum, rhetoric provides the means for students, teachers, and citizens to debate not only its methods but its canons as well.

Notes

1. Isidorus Hispalensis, *Etymologiae* II, ed. and trans. P. K. Marshall (Paris: Les Belles Lettres, 1983), 22.

The Suppression of Rhetoric in the Nineteenth Century

HAYDEN WHITE

THE CONCEPT OF literature—as against stylized speech or writing in general—is a relatively recent invention. Moreover, the notion that literary writing is virtually unteachable is also a relatively recent idea. It was not always so. Prior to the early nineteenth century, what we call literature was called belles lettres. It was regarded as a branch of rhetoric, which was itself considered to be the science of speech and writing in all their aspects, and the principles of which could be taught because they were regarded as inherent in the general human capacity to speak. One important practical difference between the kind of rhetorical theory that developed between the Renaissance and the late eighteenth century and the various theories of composition that supplanted it in the nineteenth century turned on differences between the notions of the nature of language itself that informed them. Put most simply, pre-nineteenth-century rhetorics recognized the figurative and tropical nature of all linguistic conventions and made of this recognition the basis of a general theory of speech as discourse, of which the various kinds of speech and writing—prosaic and poetic; narrative and dissertative; factual, fictive, and mixed; communicative, expressive, and performative— were treated as instances, the relations among which were presumed to be identifiable, and the different possible uses of which in different situations could be specified.

This notion that all speech should be treated as discourse and that all discourse should be viewed as a function of the figurative and tropical nature of all linguistic conventions was what got lost sight of in the process of cultural reorganization that attended the transition from feudal to capitalist society in the early nineteenth century. It is this loss that explains both the mystification of "literature" and the peculiar idea of what basic "literacy" should consist

21

of, which inform the general ideology of writing and of which the presumed qualitative difference between them is the constituent element.

The term *literature* inhabits the semantic field constituted by the nineteenth-century ideology of aestheticism, one effect of which has been to so mystify art in general and literary art in particular as to render the idea of teaching students how to produce them virtually inconceivable. The process of literary production has been rendered so mysterious by the ideology of aestheticism that the idea that we might presume to teach its principles, in much the same way that we teach basic literacy skills, is often regarded—especially in the departments of literary studies that are the principal beneficiaries of this ideology—as little short of heresy, as the ghettoized status of most programs in "creative writing" amply attests.

Yet, prior to its sublimation by the ideology of aestheticism, the kind of writing that came to be called literary only in the nineteenth century was not regarded as particularly mysterious at all, its principles were not viewed as unfathomable, and the teaching of those principles was not unthinkable. For before the invention of "literature" in the nineteenth century, rhetoric effectively served as a science of speaking, writing, and reading on the basis of which instruction in their processes of production could be—and was—provided. This is why the suppression of rhetoric was a necessary precondition for the separation of literary from other kinds of writing, the constitution of "literature" as the virtual antithesis of mere literacy, and the establishment of the myth of the unteachability of the latter as against the teachability of the former. But any effort to lead students "from literacy to literature" presupposes the necessity of dissolving the presumed opposition between a writing that is merely literate and another that is distinctively literary. This project will entail the dissolution of the ideology of aestheticism that underwrites this opposition, the reconceptualization of literate and literary writing as simply different kinds of what is substantially the same activity, and the restoration of some version of rhetoric as the science of speaking, writing, and reading on the basis of which the teaching of both basic literacy and literary writing once again may be theorized and practiced.

It is no accident that the terms *literacy* and *literature* were coined and entered into general usage at about the same time, in the early nineteenth century, because they belong to the same process of a general reorganization of culture as that which attends the establishment and integration of the nation-state, the transition from an "estate" to a "class" organization of society, the advent of corporate capitalism, and the transformation of the masses from subjects into citizens capable of taking their place as functionaries in a system of production and exchange for profit rather than use. The separation of what had formerly been called belles lettres from the general domain of "discourse," of which it once had been considered to be a branch or department, and its elevation to a new status for the designation of which the term *literature* was coined, were effects of this process of cultural reorganization. From that point on, literature would be regarded as a kind of writing, the value of which lay in part precisely in its differentness not only from speech but also from the kind of writing that would henceforth be considered to be merely literate.

The ideology of aestheticism from now on will teach that the difference between literary and merely literate writing is only a special case of the more fundamental difference, amounting to a strict opposition, between beauty (or the beautiful) and utility (or the useful). Literature is beautiful writing—writing that appeals, even fascinates, by virtue of its form alone, irrespective of its content or subject matter. The value of a writing that is merely literate, by contrast, will be held to reside less in its form than in its function, specifically its communicative function, its usefulness in serving as a medium for the transmission of information, thought, and—perhaps more crucially—commands, within every department of social life organized for the realization of purely practical ends or purposes. The ideology of aestheticism has it, as a matter of pride, that society does not need literature in the way that it needs literacy. Literature is a luxury, as anything that is merely beautiful is a luxury, which is to say as a supplement or ornament. But literature, as thus envisaged, becomes disposable in any situation in which the interests of work and struggle are conceived to take precedence over play or the restful contemplation of things merely beautiful. Or so the ideology of aestheticism would have it.

In these convictions, of course, the ideology of aestheticism reveals its complicity with the ideology of utilitarianism that comes to serve as the dominant theoretical basis for the ascription of value to the various practices of our society and, by extension, of our pedagogical institutions. These two ideologies, aestheticism and utilitarianism, conspire to deprive art in general of any claim to a distinctively cognitive authority and therefore of any practical utility. They conspire especially in the relegation of literary art to the status of a luxury, the social value of which varies in direct proportion to its scarcity, on the one hand, and, on the other, its uselessness as measured against the presumed need that every member of society is supposed to have of basic literacy. This is one of the reasons training in basic literacy skills comes to consist not so much of an introduction to a general writing practice that will culminate in the achievement of a capacity to produce a distinctively literary kind of writing as well, as rather of a training in a kind of writing in which every evidence of literariness is suppressed in the interest of making it useful.

On this formulation, the relationship of literacy to literature directs our attention to a problem that is as much theoretical as practical. The theoretical problem has to do with the difference, apprehended as an opposition, between literacy and literature—where literacy is considered as consisting of basic writing skills to be used primarily for the efficient communication of practical information, a certain kind of thought, and commands; and literature is considered as the product of a writing practice, the creativity of which is thought to consist of its capacity to permit the expression of intuitions, feelings, and thoughts of a certain impractical nature by virtue of their individuality, subjectivity, or idiosyncrasy, on the one side, and their status as products of a rare, inborn talent, even genius, on the other.

It is a commonplace of our pedagogical ideology that "creative" writing cannot be taught in the ways used—and used effectively, I might add—in progams designed to teach basic writing skills to the general run-of-the-mill undergraduate student. Literary writing, it is held by many, cannot be taught because, the ideology has it, only a small number of the mass of students come provided with the talent requisite for the cultivation of a specifically literary language, just as only a small minority are supposed to come equipped with the kind of sensibility permitting the cultivation of a capacity to appreciate the classics of literature.

I forbear discussing at length the extent to which this notion of the inherently literary type of student participates in the nineteenth-century myth of a genius distinctly "poetical" in nature and of a sensibility effectively identified with the passivity ascribed to women in the psychological economy of Victorian society. The feminization of artistic work in general and of literary work in particular goes hand in hand with the masculinization of other kinds of practical work in Victorian society and has had the same pacifying effect on male writers that the domestication of women has had on females in our society. This process of pacification works through the seemingly benign, twofold operation of simultaneously idealizing and marginalizing the social roles assigned to both groups. For literary writers, the idealizing process consisted of the ascription to them of a genius limited to the expression of a sensibility wholly imaginative (neither rational nor practical) in nature, a sensibility that distinguished them from those "real men" to whom the well-being, protection, and provision of the necessities of life to their families had been consigned as a right both genetic and generic in nature. Needless to say, this literary sensibility was tacitly conceived to be of the same nature as that which women were supposed to possess by virtue of their lack of a fully rational soul and their endowment with a practical capacity limited to the bearing and care of children, the maintenance of the home, and the provision of love and support for their husbands, and as having nothing of value to contribute to the management of public affairs consigned, by a right more divine than natural, to men whose practical talents were manifested in their capacities to repress both their feelings and their imaginations—which was to say, any impulse identifiably poetic in nature. It was this twofold process—the domestication of women and the feminization of literature—that underwrote and determined the masculinist ideology of the literacy movement throughout the nineteenth century in western Europe and America.

24

This masculinist ideology explains why middle- and even upper-class women were for a long time denied access to literacy training while being allowed and even encouraged to cultivate their literary talents. The sexism of this ideology explains why training in grammar and logic would become established as the principal bases for literacy training, while poetic training in the techniques of literary writing would be excluded therefrom. Safely consigned to the preserve of literary writing, itself domesticated by its effective feminization, poetic, the art of linguistic figuration, could be left to the cultivation of those sensitive souls—male, female, and androgynous—who had no part to play in the real world of manufacture, business, politics, and war.

But this interpretation of the sociopolitical bases of what I have called the literacy system does not explain another exclusion required for its establishment in its nineteenth-century form. I refer to the progressive derogation of rhetoric in favor of the elevation of poetic to the status of the very principle of literarity, on the one side, and its effective repression, in favor of promoting grammar and logic as the twin components of training in basic literacy, on the other. What explains this subjugation or at least neutralization of the kind of knowledge that rhetoric provides for the understanding of principles of discourse production, exchange, and consumption, in a culture increasingly devoted to the promotion of both sciences and arts whose principal authority was thought to reside in their practical utility alone?

We know the reasons given in justification of this exclusion from the standpoint of the ideology of aestheticism: discourse composed on the basis of rhetorical principles of composition could be neither sincere (the touchstone of all genuinely poetic expression, according to Romanticist aestheticism), authentic (the ideal of post-Romanticist literary art down through Modernism), nor truthful (the principle of every Realism from Balzac's historicist version down to Lukacs's socialist variant). Rhetoric, whether considered to be the art of eloquence, the theory of representation and the composition of discourses, or the craft of persuasive speech and writing (a craft that specializes in the promotion of what Jakobson calls the "conative function" of language use), was officially condemned on ethical grounds by scientists, philosophers, theologians, and, above all, literary artists alike as the very principle of immoral speech.

Kant himself, in his *Critique of Judgment,* the founding text of the ideology of aestheticism, provided the ethico-economic justification for this condemnation. In comparison to scientific, philosophical, religious, and poetic discourse, Kant maintained, rhetoric (by which he meant oratory) produced nothing but fraudulent discourse. Rhetoric taught the art of appearing to be "serious" while actually engaging in a wordplay purely frivolous in nature. Unlike the poet, who pretended to be playing with words but was actually engaged in examining the most serious of matters, and who therefore always delivered much more than he had promised, the orator always delivered less than he promised. This was because the orator traded in form alone, while pretending to deal in pure content, real value. The orator's seriousness, Kant maintained, is always feigned, because he is never concerned with truth, goodness, or beauty as ends in themselves but only as means to the end of producing an immediate emotional effect on his audience or, failing that, of bludgeoning them into submission to his point of view, against all reason, logic, or truth, by verbal means alone.

Given this notion of rhetoric, the truth of which is presumed in the vehement rhetoric that Kant uses to condemn it, one might have expected that the ideologists of utilitarianism would have embraced it as the keystone of a training designed to endow students with a literacy intended to be primarily practical in its uses, especially within the context of a triumphant capitalism in which making a profit by whatever means was rapidly becoming the rule rather than the exception.

But no such luck for rhetoric. No less an authority than Jeremy Bentham, the founding father of utilitarianism, joined Kant in condemning rhetoric as the very antithesis of rational discourse, as the pseudo-art of substituting "sound" for "sense," and as the enemy of that morally neutral speech alone capable of reflecting reality as it truly was, on the one hand, and of representing a purely rational, by which he meant a purely logical, thought, on the other.

What Bentham called "neutral speech"—characterized by a diction concrete, definite, and specific, a grammar that had been "orthologized" (which is to say standardized) and presided over by a logic that bore no relation to that of living conversation or dialogue, a speech that could be produced only by the process of written composition or, if spoken, could only sound like writing being read, which is to say, a grammatico-logical speech—became the utopia of the literacy system set up in the nineteenth century in the United States to train a nation of rude farmers and foreigners in a comportment that would be proper in a political no less than a cultural sense. As Noah Webster put it, with his characteristic bluntness and "neutral" forcefulness: "our political *harmony* is concerned with a *uniformity* of language."[1] It is the ideal of the uniform that inspired the program for standardizing American English in the nineteenth century. This program entailed not only the elimination of dialectal variants and languages other than English but also the creation of a sociolect for that part of the citizenry whose social destiny was to serve as functionaries in the emerging manufacturing and business complex, whose political role was to be that of passively approving the policies decided on by the holders of power and wealth, and whose role in the cultural system was to be that of consumers only, never producers.

The poetic aspect of language was left to the cultivation of what would become a class faction of "literary writers," while the rhetorical aspect was domesticated into the principles of clear, concise, and sincere expository prose or those of forceful elocution appropriate for the kinds of mock debates carried out by lawyers, politicians, journalists, and what later became majors in departments of speech. There remained, to be sure, a rhetorical dimension to the kind of literacy that was to be provided for every child entering the public school system. It was the rhetoric of anti-rhetoric, which, while masking itself as plain speech and practical prose, was in reality the rhetoric required of subjectivities whose principal function was to collect and communicate information, limit themselves to the practice of commonsensical thought, and save the expression of their feelings for their diaries and private correspondence, both regarded primarily as feminine genres.

What was really behind the condemnation of rhetoric in general as an inherently immoral or at least duplicitous discursive practice? What prompted the suppression of training in rhetoric during the period of formation of mass democracies, the nation-state, capitalism, and imperialism, and its progressive exclusion from programs designed for training students in basic literacy in the public schools of the country?

Anyone who knows the history of rhetoric or is willing to look at it from beyond the perspective provided by Plato's misrepresentations of it in the *Gorgias* and the *Phaedrus,* will be able to answer this question easily enough.

First, rhetoric was born not so much as the art as rather the science (*techne*) of speech, language, and representation in general. It comes after the invention of artistic speech and writing and takes both these and their nonartistic counterparts as its object of study and analysis. As a general science of discourse, then, rhetoric purports to explain not only the principles of literary-artistic discourse but also those of all nonartistic, practical discourses, such as those of politics and the law, not to mention philosophy and history, and, more importantly, the relation of these to power—political, social, and economic. Rhetoric thus represents a kind of knowledge with a distinct social value insofar as it yields insights into the relation between political power and the control of language, speech, and discourse, which political elites always have recognized as a necessary basis for effective rule. If rhetoric always has been "the possession of the most highly literate" members of society, as Hoskins remarks, this is because the most highly literate members of society always have belonged to the most powerful classes.[2] If the relationship among rhetoric, literacy, and social class power is as intimate as the history of that relationship suggests, then the democratization of society in the nineteenth century should have been attended by the extension of training in rhetoric to all classes of society as a necessary component in their political empowerment to which their training in basic literacy was meant to contribute. The exclusion of rhetoric from such training can thus be seen as an aspect of a more general program of political domestication of the mass of the citizenry by the powerful classes, who never ceased, incidentally, to provide training of a kind in rhetoric for their own children in elite schools and universities.

Second, rhetoric—especially as cultivated by the Sophists, its first practitioners—was conceived as the study and practice of speech, not only in politics but also and above all as politics, as the politics of language use, for purposes both defensive (against the power of the state) and offensive (in the exercise of that power). Rhetoric studies speech and language in its active rather than passive aspects alone; traditionally, it has been treated as the study of speech and language as used in those practical situations in which there is not only no agreement on first principles or on the facts of the matter at hand but not even any agreement on what shall constitute the facts themselves, situations in which first principles have to be hammered out in an operation more dialectical than demonstrative—as Aristotle himself insisted. This is why—from the fifth century B.C.E. in Sicily, where, according to legend, rhetoric was born, to the end of the eighteenth century, rhetoric was regarded as a sine qua non for the training of politically active citizens in democracies and of elites in aristocracies. Neither poetic, grammar, nor logic directly addresses the question of the politics of language use, and therefore any training that takes these, to the exclusion of rhetorical training, as providing the fundamentals of a basic literacy effectively deprives students of access to a kind of practical knowledge without which they can never develop their political critical capacities fully.

Third, and most pertinently to our purposes, rhetoric served or intermittently aspired to be the science of figuration, a science not only of the figurative dimensions of discourse but of language understood as being figurative in its very nature, as being what speech act theorists call performative or illocutionary, constitutive of every form of meaning—and, as such, a science taking precedence over and laying claim to being able to mediate among all the various kinds of representational practices resembling speech and language and at all levels of articulation, from simple nomination to the most sophisticated and formalized representations of pure logic.

The claim of rhetoric to be a general science of verbal and visual representation hinges upon the perception of the inevitably tropical nature of all discourses at every level of their articulation, from the phonemic-morphemic level up to that most elusive of gross structures of discursivity, the paragraph. Rhetoric claims to know the secret of the mode of expression called poetical, and this is why, from the standpoint of the modern ideology of aestheticism, it had to be suppressed. It claims also to know the secret of practical speech, speech in its active, conative, and political uses, speech as an instrument of power and rule. And this is why, from the standpoint of political elites who want a citizenry literate enough to receive messages but not so savvy as to be able to read them, it was desirable to suppress the teaching of rhetoric to the masses while continuing to cultivate its principles, in an appropriately masked form, which is to say, as "the humanities," in the education of their own children.

But here it will be objected that the very principle of poetic or literary writing is figurative language, the cultivation of which distinguishes it from mere literacy, as it has become identified with the cultivation of "literalist" discourse and productive of a sensibility that seldom rises above "literal-mindedness." Indeed, it might well be asked, is not literary writing above all the kind of writing that rises above and becomes qualitatively superior to mere literacy by virtue of its expression of a figurative mode of thinking and a specifically metaphorical manner of expression?

This was the position taken by I. A. Richards some fifty years ago in his still influential call for a new rhetoric, centered on a reconsideration of metaphor as the very soul of creative thought in general and culminating in a celebration of Coleridge's theory of the symbol as a "translucent instance, which 'while it enunciates the whole, abides itself as the living part of that unity of which it is the representative.' "[3] Richards went on to desiderate the study of metaphor, considered the basis of that "skill in thought" which it alone made possible, into "discussable science."[4]

But while suggesting that metaphor should become the object of a science of our skill in thought, Richards concluded that "our reflective awareness of that skill" must inevitably be "very incomplete, distorted, fallacious, over-simplifying." Thus, the discussable science envisioned had as its business "not to replace practice, or to tell us how to do what we cannot do already; but to protect our natural skill from interferences of unnecessarily crude views about it." To be sure, he added that such a science should "above all . . . assist the imparting of that skill from mind to mind," but he qualified this recommendation by noting that "progress here, in translating our skill from observation and theory, comes chiefly from profitting from our mistakes."[5]

Richards anticipated modernist—semiotic, structuralist, and poststructuralist—rhetorical theory, which begins with the presumption of the figurative nature of all discourse, factual or realistic, historical or scientific, logical or poetic, narrative or analytical. But the notion of figuration that informs modernist rhetoric is utterly different from that proposed by Richards. Whereas he had regarded figuration as a mode of thought based on comparison, similitude, analogical thinking, the capacity of language to say one thing and mean another, and so on, modernist rhetorical theory, while presuming the figurativeness of all discursive practices, takes its rise in an apprehension of the utter arbitrariness of all figuration. Metaphor ceases to be the basis of figurative language and becomes once again, as it was in the seventeenth century, only one figure among many and by no means the essence of literary speech, as against merely literate or, for that matter, illiterate speech. If anything, it is the figure of *catachresis*, "abusio" or "mis-use," that is considered to be the secret, not only of both figurative speech and its literalist counterpart but also of the relation between them. Merely literate speech or writing becomes only a special case of the abusive relationship that obtains between words and those

29

other things in the world they are called upon to signify, but neither is less nor more abusive than its supposedly, qualitatively superior counterpart, literary speech.

The application of this fundamental rhetorical hypothesis—that all language use is figurative in nature—to the study and teaching of discursive practices would prescribe an approach to teaching basic literacy in which the differences between a merely literate and a distinctively literary writing were considered to be simply a matter of different uses of the strategies of figuration common to both. It would not exclude the teaching of grammar and logic as elements of composition, but it would introduce them as tropical strategies neither more nor less conventional than those informing the production of literary works. It would distinguish between literate expository prose and a literary work on the basis of the extent to which the latter kind, unlike the former, makes of figuration and troping an element of its explicit content and in so doing demands that we confront the problem of the relation between the form and the content of discourses in terms of a general theory of figuration. In terms of such a theory, grammar, logic, and what we conventionally think of as poetic would be represented as components of every discourse, the enabling feature of which is nothing other than language's capacity to figurate.

This capacity, in turn, would be presented as being in everyone pos-sessing the capacity to speak, not as some arcane gift of a talented few, those poets supposedly possessed of genius or a sensibility different from that possessed by everyone else. Literary writing would be presented as what it manifestly appears to be, merely a species of writing in which the act of figurating is presented as an element of its manifest content as well as the dominant characteristic of its form. A merely literate writing, by contrast, would be presented as only another species of writing, as a mode of writing in which figuration is no less present but is systematically masked, hidden, repressed, in the interest of producing a discourse seemingly governed by standardized rules of diction, grammar, and logic that produce their distinctive meaning-producing effects by the employment of strategies of selection and combination just as figurative, however formalized, as any poetic discourse.

This argues of course for the utility of introducing students to basic writ-ing by way of the study and imitation of the kinds of texts we conventionally call literary, not because such texts contain the moral and aesthetical wisdom of the ages (although some of them may do so) or because they incarnate a beauty or sublimity accessible only to poets endowed with a sensibility adequate to the apprehension thereof but rather because such texts take language's power to posit and trope as a part of their manifest content. A literary text, in short, is any in which figuration itself is an aspect of its content no less than of its form.

It is in the consideration of such texts from a specifically rhetorical perspective, which includes but is not exhausted by grammatical, logical, and poetical analyses of them, that our students can be introduced to, taught the principles of, and perhaps even encouraged to imitate the practices of figuration in general. On this basis, they might be able to comprehend what is really going on, both on and beneath the surfaces, not only in literary discourse but in the peculiar kind of exercise in repression and sublimation that we call merely literate writing.

Every verbal artifact that we might wish to call literary always can be shown to feature the problem of figuration as an element of its manifest content. The difference between literary and merely literate writing would not be presented as residing in the presence of figurative language and tropical strategies of combination in the one and their absence in the other. As Paul de Man put it, in a seminal article on "The Epistemology of Metaphor": "Contrary to common belief, literature is not the place where the unstable epistemology of metaphor is suspended by aesthetic pleasure, although this attempt is a constitutive moment of its system. It is rather the place where the possible convergence of rigor [in thought] and pleasure is shown to be a delusion."[6] And this is because with the suppression of rhetoric, the modern conception of literary writing, based on the ideology of aestheticism, which identifies literature with poetry and poetry itself with the expression of genius, effectively has denied that the processes of linguistic figuration ever can be the object of scientific study, one aim of rhetorical studies.

Notes

1. Keith Hoskins, "Making Cobwebs to Catch Flies With," (unpublished essay), 1.27. Emphasis added.
2. Hoskins, "Making Cobwebs," 14.
3. I. A. Richards, *The Philosophy of Rhetoric* (Oxford: Oxford University Press, 1936), 109.
4. Ibid., 94.
5. Ibid., 116.
6. Paul de Man, "The Epistemology of Metaphor," *Critical Inquiry* 5 (1978): 30.

Canonicity and Multivalence:
The Case of Cicero

THOMAS COLE

A CANONICAL TEXT in the modern world is, almost inevitably, a multivalent text: a verbal artifact, secular or religious, whose enduring value and continuing relevance to successive generations can be maintained only by means of a succession of different or even contradictory rereadings. It was not so—or, at any rate, not always so—in the ancient world. For the Augustan rhetorician Dionysius of Halicarnassus and, presumably, for most of his predecessors, a *kanôn* is not a text or a body of texts but an unvarying extratextual standard, a literary rule or set of rules—those governing the plain style or the Ionic dialect, for example—adherence to which makes a given author (Lysias is Dionysius's choice for the simple style, Herodotus [*Letter to Pompeius* 3] for the Ionic dialect) a valuable exemplification of the *kanôn* and so, secondarily, a *kanôn* (or quasi-*kanôn*) himself.[1] The number of names placed on a given list often corresponds to the number of evaluative criteria that must be applied. Thus, Varro's choice among authors of Roman comedy[2] (*Menippeae* fr. 399 Bücheler) falls on Plautus (for diction), Caecilius Statius (for plots), and Terence (for character drawing); and the *Iliad* and the *Odyssey* figure on all lists as supreme instances, respectively, of epic *pathos* and epic *êthos*.

Strictly applied, the concept would exclude textual canons in the modern sense—since it is always possible that more perfect exemplifications will come into being or to the *kanôn* applier's attention. Conversely, the modern, textual canon dispenses with the articulatable criteria for excellence assumed by the ancients. It is a canon for the benefit of readers, identified by the simple fact of provenance, and as such does not need or even, in many cases, allow the commentary of critic or teacher that is required if it is to function, in proper ancient fashion, as adjunct to a *kanôn* for students and prospective writers. Whatever appears within it is authoritative by virtue of location.

33

Thomas Cole

The ancient concept belongs to the world of "grammar-oriented" cultures: those "governed by a system of rules"; the modern, by contrast, presupposes a "text-oriented" culture or, in this instance, subculture, one "governed by a repertory of texts imposing models of behavior."[3] The *kanôn*/canon transfer in meaning is rather like that which converts the ancient *kharaktêr*, a stamp or stereotype imprinted with varying degrees of perfection on a coin or other material object, into the character of modern literary or psychological parlance, an irreducible individual entity which, if it reflects the imprint of any outside mold, does so only because the latter is one that nature broke after a single use.

A natural and obvious point of origin for the transformation of meaning is the one set of ancient texts in connection with which the word *kanôn* in the modern sense is attested: the *Septuagint* (4 *Maccabees* 7.21). Here the primacy of texts over grammar is obvious. Also obvious is the need for constant reinterpretation if the authoritative position of the canonical repertory is to be maintained, and the fact that the presence of such a repertory, whether in a Christian or Hellenized Jewish context, is a phenomenon essentially alien to the Greco-Roman tradition. Homer and Hesiod, though studied with biblical regularity and frequency, were never regarded by the ancients as having the exclusive claims to cosmological, theological, historical, and moral authority that were to be made for subsequent sets of sacred writings, whether Christian or Islamic.[4] And the debate over authenticity was a purely literary one. Texts deemed non-Homeric, unless seen as inferior forgeries, did not become less authoritative for that reason.[5] Apocrypha and Satanic verses are as foreign to the classical world as their genuiniely "inspired" authentic counterparts—and equally necessary prerequisites for the creation of the modern notion of literary canonicity. Indeed, the Latin literary canon ultimately derives from texts copied and edited in the course of the so-called Pagan revival of the fourth century C.E.—obviously in an effort to create some sort of secular counter-canon to set against the sacred one which was threatening to become a single repertory of proper thought and behavior that excluded all others.[6] It would be going too far, however, to maintain that the text-oriented reader's canon had no earlier analogues at all—as is evident from the case, and cases, to be considered here.

The Latin texts copied and edited in the fourth century were composed by and large in the hundred years between 80 B.C.E. and 20 C.E. and it is clear from reading them that for certain authors at any rate—if not always for their critics and expounders—something close to the modern notion of canonicity antedated by several centuries the alien notion of scripture and sacred texts.

Three aspects of the set of attitudes these texts reveal are of crucial importance. The texts are, first of all, the work of authors who wrote in the full expectation of coming to constitute what we now know as a canon. This is evident both in the Augustan poets' repeated proclamations of impending immortality[7] and in the consistent effort on the part of both Cicero and his

Augustan successors—to resume, recover, and replace for a Roman audience the achievement of their greatest predecessors, both Greek and Roman. Virgil will surpass the didactic, bucolic, and heroic (whether Iliadic or Odyssean) traditions in hexameter poetry, as will Horace those of lyric monody (Sapphic, Alcaic, and Anacreontic), Livy those of Roman historiography (both *Zeitgeschichte* as produced by Sisenna, Sallust, and Pollio and chronicle in the manner of annalists from Fabius Pictor to Aelius Tubero), and Cicero those of nonhistorical prose literature (oratory, philosophy, rhetorical theory).

The effort to outdistance all predecessors is an eloquent testimony to the canonical status that Cicero and the great Augustans foresaw for themselves, though no more striking than the second aspect of their work to be noted in this context. Canonicity is acquired through emulation, but once acquired it means exclusive rights to preeminence in the genre to which claim is laid. There is no triad or tetrad or Pleiad of luminaries here—merely the solitary splendors of the blazing sun at noon. Avoidance of competition when friends are involved is as striking as the elimination of one's competition in the case of enemies or predecessors: epic, bucolic, and didactic are reserved for Virgil; drama for Varius; invective, satire, and lyric for Horace, whose venture into the reflective verse of the second book of *Epistles* did not come until death ended Virgil's plans to devote his declining years to the study of philosophy. It was only disgrace (Gallus) and early death (Tibullus) that made it still possible for a third contender (Propertius) to aspire to the position of definitive preeminence in elegy; and Ovid's mischievous undercutting of the whole canon industry as developed in the generation previous to his own was the only thing that allowed the pretentions—largely ironic this time—of a fourth.

The obvious model for all such efforts at preeminence or monopoly came two generations earlier, in the form of Cicero's comprehensive Latinization of large areas of Greek philosophy and political theory, and of his related efforts, through a series of three dialogues, to establish himself as, first, the perfect synthesis of the two traditions of practical and "philosophical" oratory whose claims are debated by his predecessors M. Licinius Crassus and Marcus Antonius in the *De Oratore* (55 B.C.E.), then the culmination of the entire Greco-Roman oratorical tradition studied in the *Brutus* (46 B.C.E.), and finally the earthly embodiment of the Platonic form of the perfect orator whose existence is posited in the *Orator* (45 B.C.E.).

Monopoly and the power it brings are inevitably accompanied by responsibility; hence a third important aspect of the Latin proto-canon. A sense of responsibility makes it impossible for Virgil, Livy, Horace, and Propertius to be exemplars of a single excellence or a set of related excellences in the way their Greek predecessors had been. All tastes and expectations—or all "legitimate" tastes and expectations—must be accommodated, by the interweaving and alternating of *Musa severa* with *Musa iocosa* in Horace, for example, or of the etiological with the amorous in Propertius, or of the martial with the pathetic in Virgil, or—in Cicero—of the philosophical with the forensic or political and the dogmatic with the skeptical. In analyzing the phenomenon, it is customary to see a characteristically Roman broad-mindedness, dislike of ideology, and talent for adaptation and assimilation. But the practical needs of the canon maker at a much more down-to-earth level could have been just as significant a consideration. Sentimentalists and patriots alike must be moved by the fourth book of the *Aeneid,* just as both hedonists and moralists must find the content of the *Odes* attractive if either work is to qualify as the great Roman epic or lyric. Nor, since classics are regularly best-sellers as well, should one forget the effect of having an eye on the book trade—a persistent and self-confessed preoccupation of Roman men of letters.[8] Ovid's ability to make lengthy segments of the *Metamorphoses* read equally well as heroic narrative or heroic travesty is crucial to his success in composing—in a spirit of spoof—not merely the epic to end all epics, or the lyric to end all lyrics, but the long poem to end all long poems.

Cicero enjoys a position of primacy among these proto-canonizers—both chronologically and by virtue of the fact that attitudes that are more often than not implicit in the Augustans receive explicit and detailed presentation in Cicero. Though the essay specifically devoted to intimations of immortality and their justification, the *De gloria,* does not survive,[9] his preoccupation with the subject is evident enough from many passages in those works that do survive, as well as from the care he took to collect, revise, and edit his works for publication.[10]

Even more striking is Cicero's elaborate, painstakingly developed strategy for achieving the twin canonical goals of exclusiveness and multivalence. This is seen most easily in his philosophical corpus, ostensibly a panoramic survey designed to satisfy all tastes and expectations, but one that sacrifices comprehensiveness for canonicity by the skillful deployment of three techniques: (1) Reduction of the chorus or pandemonium of voices in Hellenistic and pre-Hellenistic philosophy to a dialogue between Stoics and the *veteres* or "ancients" (various permutations and combinations of Academics and Peripatetics). Of all the schools of thought that came into being in the three centuries following the death of Socrates, these are the only ones deemed truly worthy of being heard—a point reinforced by consistent vilification of other traditions (usually that represented by the Epicureans) as morally repugnant and intellectually inconsequential. (2) Minimization of the differences between these preferred interlocutors to the point of nonexistence or triviality—a matter of terminology in the case of Stoic and Academic disagreements on the nature of choice and free will,[11] for example, or of quibbling over whether *virtus* in and of itself is sufficient to make a person *beatissimus* (the Stoics) or merely, as the more hedonistically inclined Peripatetics were inclined to say, *beatus.* (3) Implying—when major, irreducible differences still remain—that the two views are not really in competition, because one of them represents merely a position advanced for the sake of argument,[12] or by way of polemical overreaction to the intransigence of an opponent,[13] or with a view to the demands of audiences and situations that for one reason or another did not allow a rigorously established standard of conduct or argumentation.[14]

What results from the application of these three techniques, sometimes simultaneously and sometimes separately, is an ambiguous product: part doxographical survey, part eclectic blend, and—since the material surveyed is more conspicuous for the range of the spectrum within which disagreement is excluded than for that within which it is permitted—part actual syncretization of large areas of Academic, Peripatetic, and Stoic doctrine. The contrary requirements of a successful canon— definitiveness and multivalence—require that the reader never be entirely certain which of the three ingredients, at any given moment, or over the whole philosophical corpus, is the most important.

Cicero figures in this synthesis as a definitive expounder rather than a definitive model of excellence, but the philosophical canon, dating from 44–43 B.C.E., postdated by a decade the earliest—and most elaborate—text of the oratorical canon (see above), in which his role was that of both expounder and model. In this text, Cicero's own oratorical manner—distinguished from that of his Roman predecessors and contemporaries by its ability to draw on wide reading in the work of both the practitioners and the theoreticians of Greek eloquence, as well as by a more thorough and conscientious mastery of the political, legal, and historical background of the situation being addressed on any given occasion—is presented anachronistically, as a fusion and perfection of two traditions exemplified by the two leading orators of the generation immediately preceding his own. In a long conversation imagined to have taken place in 91 B.C.E., Marcus Antonius, grandfather of the triumvir, defends the ideal of a practical, success-oriented discipline that scorns pretensions to learning, stylistic finery, or higher moral goals; and his views are countered by his contemporary and sometime opponent, M. Licinius Crassus, advocate of an ornate, refined manner of presentation that draws on the full resources of historiography, philosophy, and earlier eloquence.[15] Not unlike the Stoics and their more indulgent Peripatetic colleagues in the realm of ethics, Antonius and Crassus pursue the high and low roads of eloquence, united by a common contempt for the public-speaking manuals and crash courses in eloquence offered to upstart lawyers and politicians by unscrupulous Graeculi and their Latin imitators. The latter are the moral and intellectual equivalent of the Epicureans so contemptuously dismissed in the philosophical writings; and the intellectual basis for a common philosophical or rhetorical front against them is, in both instances, asserted and implied rather than demonstrated. To accept this basis as a reality, one must accept the intermittent suggestion that Antonius's scorn for learning is only partially sincere[16] (like the skeptical philosopher's insistence on withholding assent when it involves those doctrines

Cicero considers of crucial importance), or take the two orators' friendship and participation in three books of friendly discussion as symbolic of an underlying compatibility of approach, or recognize a kind of unity *in potentia* that will come to exist *in actu* only when the separate promises of their different oratorical manners are brought to a single fruition in the work of their common pupil Cicero.[17]

Significantly, however, the most unambiguous area of common ground between the two figures involves their joint espousal of textual canons—a natural counterpart to their joint rejection of *kanones* promulgated by writers of handbooks and teachers of public speaking in an effort to reduce the discipline to a set of easily mastered rules. An extreme instance of the effect of such *kanones* is found in an anonymous work—the so-called *Rhetorica ad Herennium*—roughly contemporary with Cicero's own initial assay in rhetorical theory (the *De Inventione*), begun (and left incomplete) thirty years before the *De Oratore*. The author of this work eschews the use of rhetorical examples taken from the works of established orators, offering instead (along with a lengthy defense of the practice) original examples of his own composition whenever he wants to illustrate the aspects of style and argumentation under discussion. The subordination of the text to grammar thus achieved is almost complete: grammatical *kanones* generate, in effect, a series of texts that are totally devoid of interest except insofar as they illustrate articulatable, extratextual rules.

Antonius and Crassus offer, by contrast, a pair of canons, oral on the one hand, written on the other. Antonius's rejection of any effort to bring erudition or theory into the practice of Roman oratory means that learning will take place through imitation of selected models: the actual speeches that the prospective orator will hear when he is serving his apprenticeship—the so-called *tirocinium fori*—in the entourage of a prominent older politician or lawyer. Some of these speeches, of course, might be remarkable enough (like Antonius's own defense of Norbanus against the charge of *perduellio* brought by his opponents in 96 B.C.E.) to persist in memory—but only in the form of an oral recreation or summary of their principal arguments.[18] What Crassus sets up by contrast with this is a written canon—the entire published heritage of major oratorical and, to a lesser degree, historical and philosophical discourse, which must be familiar, or at least available, to the *summus orator* if he is to achieve the *copia* that his preeminence requires.[19]

That Cicero saw the program he attributes to Crassus as involving a privileging of texts over grammar is clear from the way he has Crassus interpret his own role in an important episode in the history of Roman education. In 92 B.C.E., Crassus, acting in his capacity as censor, ordered the suppression of the first school of rhetorical instruction in Latin at Rome, a move he is made to defend at *De Oratore* 3.93–95—and perhaps did, in fact, defend—by reference to the superiority of Greek to Latin as a vehicle for teaching.[20]

What is denied in the Latin learner is access to the information (*rerum silva*), learning (*doctrina, prudentia*), and cultural tradition (*humanitas*) available in Greek. Greek instruction at Rome in 92 B.C.E. could draw on a rich corpus of oratorical, political, and philosophical texts in which there would be polished models for the treatment of almost any subject with which an orator might have occasion to deal; Latin instruction, on the other hand, given the meagerness of the then existing corpus of published Latin prose, would have to rely heavily on grammar-generated exemplars of the sort contained in the *Rhetorica ad Herennium*.[21]

Crassus's effort to put an end to the teaching of rhetoric in Latin is generally assumed to have been inspired less by pedagogical than by political considerations: a desire to make sure that the voices of the classes hitherto excluded from the decision-making process at Rome should continue to be unheard as well as unheeded.[22] But canon making and political censorship are closely interwoven, both in Cicero and, later, among the Augustans, as part of a single conservative agenda. Creation of a body of Roman "classics" that will match and partially replace their Greek progenitors is a means of minimizing the potentially subversive aspects of Greek learning and thought by integrating it as much as possible into the traditional pattern of Roman education. The latter was designed to ensure that political, religious, and linguistic expertise remained the monopoly of the aristocratic families with whom it had resided from time immemorial, and this meant, inevitably, an essentially private transmission of skills from father (or father's friends and associates) to son.[23] Unlike the rules taught by the rhetorical schoolmaster, education through familiarity with a textual canon requires leisure, learning, libraries— things not readily available outside the narrow circle of the governing class. And, more important still, the content of libraries can be controlled by official or unofficial censorship in a way that the content of oral discourse cannot.

Here, and only here, Cicero may fairly claim to have understood the lesson of his master Plato better than any other of the philosopher's later admirers. To find the earliest—if not the most continuously influential— ancient instance of a self-conscious, exclusive, encyclopedic reader's canon, one must go back well beyond the authors considered here to the dialogues of Plato—works clearly intended, as the author's ongoing polemic with poetry shows, to form a core curriculum that would replace the Homero-centric curriculum of earlier ages, and a core curriculum that, at least at its time of inception, envisioned no competition beyond what was contained in the texts Plato himself chose to preserve from, or ascribe to, certain favored predecessors, notably Parmenides and the Pythagoreans.

Comprehensive in style as well as subject matter, the dialogues run the full gamut from conversational to mythopoeic to dialectical to apodeictic;[24] and however much importance one attaches to the tradition of an esoteric,

unwritten Platonic doctrine or to the role of an authoritative, orally transmitted interpretration of the dialogues current among Plato's successors in the
Academy, they comprise a body of written texts that recommended themselves
to readers' attention by the simple fact of Platonic authorship (hence the later
disputes about the nature and extent of the true canon—in the modern sense—
of Platonic writings).[25]

Cicero has correctly understood Plato's purpose, but he largely ignores—
perhaps as a result of the process of Romanization and rendering harmless
already referred to—Plato's insistence[26] that written texts must exist alongside
a tradition of oral dialectic that constantly reexamines itself and subjects
any written document to the possibility of being rewritten, improved, or
replaced in the event that shortcomings are discovered in its argument.
Plato seeks to control the potentially destabilizing aspects of this insistence
by requiring that instruction in dialectic be confined to those who have
reached the age of thirty (*Republic* 7.537d) and have finished a program of
studies in higher mathematics or by producing—as in the *Laws*—a blueprint
for a commonwealth in which such instruction will not be available to all.
Cicero goes much farther, relegating the process of oral reexamination and
reformulation to the level of mere exercise—part of the process of sharpening
and improving the prospective orator's faculty for debate and improvisation.
As such, it belongs as much to the realm of rhetorical performance and delivery
(*actio*) as it does to that of devising and testing arguments (*inventio*).

Distrust of written texts on the part of Plato's immediate followers helps
account for the fact that the Platonic canon had to wait three centuries to
find a successor. But other factors were involved as well: the shortcomings
of most of those followers as literary artists and the continuing prestige
enjoyed by the poetic curriculum Plato had sought to displace. It was only
the *tabula rasa* (relatively speaking) of Roman intellectual culture, combined
with the ambitions and self-confidence of a Cicero, that made possible the
relaunching of the whole canon-construction enterprise in the early years of
the first century B.C.E. Once relaunched and confirmed by Ciceronian and
Augustan practice, however, textual canons play an increasingly important
role in Roman rhetorical theory, as does the accompanying scorn for those
who reject such canons in favor of a rhetorical grammar based on *kanones*. Both
are, for example, conspicuous in Quintilian whenever he must move beyond
his Greek sources in order to talk about matters Roman, with Latin writers far
more likely than Greek ones to be seen simply as models of achieved excellence
rather than as illustrations of how to go about achieving one or more of the
qualities that constitute it. (Virgil is characterized in purely Homeric terms—
as the number two epic writer, who, however, stands nearer to first place than
to third [*Quintilian* 10.1.85–86]; and Cicero is defined in terms that have
nothing to do with anyone but himself: the mere fact of liking him establishes
one's credentials as a judge of what is good and bad in rhetoric.)[27] Beginning

in the first century c.e., the contempt Cicero feels toward setters of *kanones* for taste and composition comes to embrace those who lay down rules for correct linguistic usage as well[28] and only disappears in late antiquity, as contemporary literary production declines into something so different from anything good enough to illustrate the workings of a *kanôn* that the Ciceronian and Augustan canon ceases to be simply a set of model texts and becomes in addition the only reliable basis for the generation of literary and rhetorical grammar.[29]

One naturally wonders how much the Ciceronian-Augustan proto-canon may have speeded the process of decline and transformation—by encouraging students, even before it was necessary, to abandon the active grammarian's role for the passive one of textual commentator, critic, or compiler; and it is easy enough, letting one's thoughts proceed along this line, to condemn the whole canon-building enterprise, particularly in its political and philosophical aspect, as an early—perhaps the earliest attested—example of what has come to be known in recent years as the "manufacture of consent."[30] The exchange of pleasantries between Roman nobles that passes for Socratic discussion in Cicero's philosophical corpus is thus a kind of sinister anticipation of the tête-à-tête between the center right and extreme right that now passes for public debate on important issues in the United States. "In an ideal oral society, where production and reception are indissolubly linked, canonization inevitably becomes censorship";[31] and so natural a link remains hard to dissolve, even in the most ideal of literate societies. Plato's creation of a new curriculum is—or would have been—inseparable from his burning of the books of his philosophical rival Democritus;[32] the *damnatio memoriae* that became the fate of Gallus and the removal of Ovid's books from imperial collections are simply the other side of the coin to patronage in the form of imperial subsidies for libraries, literature, and a favored few among those who produced it. That such additional steps should have been taken as well as contemplated is probably the result, in the first instance, of the accident that put the power of the Augustan state or, later, the church triumphant at the disposal of the canon makers in the event that they chose to enforce their whims. Yet the character of the canon or, better, of the medium in which it was couched is not totally irrelevant. A series of authoritative texts is ideally suited to the censor's aim. It makes the posing of fundamental doubts or questions far more difficult—even in those embarrassing situations when official policies are modified or reversed. The illusion of continuity that such situations demand is often achieved more easily and more effectively through exercise of the canon maker's prerogative of reinterpreting his texts than it would be through the rewriitng of history. It is unlikely that Cicero himself ever gave much thought to the precise mechanisms of such state control, but he clearly saw the creation of a philosophical and oratorical canon as the best way for a conservative intelligentsia simultaneously to limit competition from outside and police its own membership.

Unemployed cold warriors turned thought police of the New World Order can fairly be credited with carrying on the Ciceronian tradition when they defend the teaching of an unchanging core of subjects or authors as essential to maintaining what they regard as the civilized values of the Western tradition. But both parties to the contemporary debate would do well to bear in mind the sobering—or consoling—thought that Cicero's intellectual-literary testament reveals, for all its cleverness, a certain shortsightedness. Designed above all to close and constrict the range of potential debate, it has over the centuries, on occasion at any rate, aided those who wished to go against prevailing currents of thought and behavior more than those who sought to reinforce them—whether as one of the core items in a secular canon that served as a relaxing counterbalance to the dominant sacred canon of the Middle Ages, or as an island of relative sanity and benign indifference to nuance and logic in the early modern period when debate and dialogue threatened to degenerate into a fratricidal controntation between rival dogmatisms,[33] or as a populist rallying point in the era of revolution and reform, when catchwords such as *ius*, *libertas*, and *res publica* were removed from the oligarchical context for which they were originally intended and took on completely different meanings. Plato's reservations about the multivalence built into any written canon helped to ensure that his own efforts to establish one never had quite the success he might have on occasion envisaged; but it was the Greek philosopher who saw more clearly and in terms of ultimate rather than immediate consequences. The Roman rhetorician, by contrast, left behind an ambiguous tool which followers have used—and will doubtless continue to use—at their peril.

Notes

1. Thus, the desires of the "good" (*spoudaios*) man are not a *kanôn* of right and wrong at Aristotle, *Nichomachean Ethics*, 3.4. 1113a33: they merely function "as if" (*hôsper*) a *kanôn*. And Pliny the Elder is aware of the anomaly involved in speaking of a single statue (the Doryphoros or Diadymenos) as a *kanôn*: *Polyclitus . . . solus . . . hominum artem ipsam* (i.e., a set of *kanones* regulating the sculptor's art) *fecisse artis opere* (by means of a [particular] work of art) *iudicatur* (*Natural History*, 34.55).
2. Petronius Arbiter, *Petronii Saturae*, ed. Franciscus Büecheler (Berolini: Apud Weidmannos, 1958), fragment 399.
3. U. Eco, *A Theory of Semiotics* (Bloomington: Indiana University Press, 1976), 137–38, utilizing a distinction drawn by the Russian semiologist Juri Lotman.
4. What applies to Homer and Hesiod also applies, *a fortiori*, to the leading representatives of other literary genres—also selected for commentary and reading in schools but less intensely and less frequently.
5. They might even be considered non-Homeric because they lacked some of the characteristic excellences of the genuine article—and to reason in this fashion is to think in terms of *kanones*, not canons.
6. Though the fourth-century counter-canon had evolved by the middle of the following century into a kind of co-canon existing alongside rather than in

competition with its sacred counterpart, its basic content remained unchanged. See R. A. Markus, "Pagans, Christians and the Latin Classics," in J. W. Binns, ed., *Latin Literature in the 4th Century* (London: Routledge & Kegan Paul, 1974), 11–12.

7. Virgil, *Georgics,* 3.8–9, *Aeneid,* 9.446–49; Propertius, 3.1.9; Horace, *Carmina,* 2.20.9–20, 3.30; Ovid, *Metamorphoses,* 15.875, *Amores,* 1.15.41–42, 3.9.128, *Tristia,* 3.7.49–50, 4.10.122, 129–30, *Epistulae ex Ponto,* 2.9.62, 3.2.31–32. The motif, as Steele Commager was the first to point out in *Horace* (New Haven: Yale University Press, 1962), 310 n. 5, is characteristically Roman. Apart from "occasional and quite tentative assertions," Greek poetry's function is to confer immortality on its subject, not its maker.

8. See Horace, *Ars poetica,* 323–32; and Juvenal, 7.

9. See, on both topics, A. D. Leeman, "Gloria" (Ph.D. diss., Rotterdam, 1949).

10. *Ad Atticum,* 2.1.2. Included among them were self-laudatory compositions in Greek prose, Latin prose, and Latin verse—*ne quod genus a me ipso laudis meae praetermittatur* (1.19.20).

11. See *De Fato,* 44 (*verbis non re dissidere*) and, for similar phrases applied to other philosophical disagreements, *Academica,* 2.15; *De Finibus Bonorum et Malorum,* 2.20, 3.41, 4.60, 4.72; *De Natura Deorum,* 1.16; *De Officiis,* 3.83.

12. See *De Fin.,* 5.20, on Carneades' sponsorship (*non ille quidem auctor sed defensor disserendi causa*) of the view that morality is simply a means to achieving the *prôta kata physin* or *prima naturalia*—things such as physical comfort, sexual satisfaction, companionship, etc., which are the objects of the instinctual drives humans share with other animals.

13. The *studium contra Stoicos disserendi* whose dangerous consequences for established religious belief are noted at *De Divinatione,* 1.8. See *De Natura Deorum,* 1.4., and *Tusculanae Disputationes,* 5.84.

14. Thus, Cicero will reconcile Academic skepticism with the dogmatic position that he personally finds most attractive by having his Academic speaker accept the "probability" if not the ascertainable philosophical truth of that position. The most famous instance involves Cicero himself, speaking as an Academic at the end of the *De Natura Deorum* (3.95) and declaring that he finds the Stoic argument for divine providence (book 2 of the treatise) not "truer" (*verior*) than the Academic rebutal offered in book 3 but "more inclined to the likeness of truth" (*ad veritatis similitudinem . . . propensior*). The suggestion of P. Levine ("The Original Design and Publication of the *De Natura Deorum*," *Harvard Studies in Classical Philosophy* 62 [1957]: 20–22) that Cicero is simply refraining out of prudence from giving voice to what readers might see as a personal skepticism with regard to a central tenet of established religion is possible, but not necessary—given the studied ambiguity with which a kind of second-class citizenship is so often conferred on all manner of "noncanonical" candidates for admission into Cicero's intellectual Republic. Only in the *De Divinatione* is there a straightforward confrontation between admittedly incompatible positions, with Cicero's own preferences fairly clearly on the side of the skeptics.

15. That Cicero's picture is anachronistic emerges from the contrast between it and the (doubtless correct) impression that contemporaries had of Crassus and which

is recorded (and attacked) at the beginnning of book 2 (Crassus, it was generally believed, had no more general cultural knowledge than what he had acquired *prima . . . puerili institutione*). Note also the absence of any references to the quasi-encyclopedic learning of Crassus in the long passage (143–65) devoted to him and his contemporaries in the more circumstantial survey of the history of oratory found in the *Brutus*.

16. Antonius is made to say as much himself at 2.40, though the anti-intellectualism of the stance he had assumed in book I and disowns in his "palinode" reappears sporadically later in the dialogue and is in accord with the impression he left on his contemporaries; see, from the same passage cited in note 14 above, 2.1: *magna nobis pueris, Quinte frater, opinio fuit . . . M . . . Antonium omnino omnis eruditionis expertem atque ignarum fuisse.*

17. See Crassus's *vaticinatio ex eventu* (3.95) of a day when there shall be men sufficiently *eruditi* to equal and surpass the Greeks in transferring *veterem illam excellentemque prudentiam ad nostrum usum moremque.*

18. See the account, roughly two pages in the Oxford classical text, given at *De Oratore*, 2.199–201. Since Antonius never published any of his speeches (*Brutus*, 163), Cicero's report must be based ultimately on oral tradition.

19. Symptomatic of the distinctly literary approach favored by Crassus is the presence, both in his circle of friends (*De Oratore*, 1.265) and among the authorities he cites (1.193), of the philologian and legal scholar Aelius Stilo, one of the earliest collectors and editors of Latin poetic and oratorical texts.

20. A lost letter from Cicero to Titinius quoted by Suetonius (*On Grammarians and Rhetoricians*, 2) tells how he himself in his youth was dissuaded by learned friends (who may have included Crassus) from attending the school. The reason they gave was the same one given by Crassus in the *De Oratore: Graecis exercitationibus ali melius ingenia posse.*

21. It need not follow that the *Rhetorica ad Herennium*—as maintained by, e.g., Friedrich Marx in the Prolegomena to his famous edition ([Leipzig: B. G. Teubner, 1894], 147–53)—reflects the teaching of the particular group (Plotius Gallus and the so-called *Latini rhetores*) whom Crasssus suppressed. Subsequent efforts to deny this identification (see, for example, George Kennedy, *The Art of Rhetoric in the Roman World* [Princeton: Princeton University Press, 1972], 131) strike me as unconvincing, but the answer to the question does not affect the argument being advanced here.

22. See, most recently, P. L. Schmidt, "Die Anfänge der institutionellen Rhetorik in Rom," in E. Lefèvre, ed., *Monumentum Chiloniense* (Amsterdam: Adolf M. Hakkert, 1975), 209–11.

23. See, for oratory, the famous account in Tacitus, *Dialogus*, 28.

24. Holgar Thesleff's enumeration of ten distinct modes (*Studies in the Styles of Plato* [Helsinki: Suomolaisen Kirjalisuunden Kirjapaino, 1967]) is unlikely to win universal acceptance, but it gives a good idea of the richness and variety involved.

25. That the Platonic curriculum of later ages was intended to involve specific books rather than simply dialectic or the Socratic method is especially clear at *Laws*, 7.811c–12a, where that dialogue itself is named explicitly as a suitable text for teachers and students in the ideal commonwealth being described.

26. Most notable, of course, in the *Phaedrus* (274b–78e). See also *Protagoras*, 347e, and, from an early Academic, if not necessarily Platonic context, *Episteta*, 7.341b–42a.
27. *Ille se profecisse sciat cui Cicero placebit* (10.1.112).
28. See R. A. Kaster, *Guardians of Language: The Grammarian and Society in Late Antiquity* (Berkeley: University of California Press, 1988), 52–60.
29. Hence the paradox noted by Kaster, ibid., in discussing the *Saturnalia:* that "the grammarian's ethos and expertise stand at the center of the work, but the grammarian himself is at the margins: so thoroughly has grammar been engrossed by the learned amateurs of Macrobius' ideal."
30. The phrase seems to go back to Walter Lippmann, *Public Opinion* (New York: Harcourt Brace Jovanovich, 1922), 187–88; see Noam Chomsky and Edward S. Herman, *Manufacturing Consent: The Political Economy of the Mass Media* (New York: Pantheon, 1988), xi.
31. Glenn Most, "Canon Fathers: Literacy, Morality, Power," *Arion* 3rd series 1 (1990): 44.
32. Aristoxenus's story to this effect (quoted in *Diogenes Laertius* 9.40) is, at the very least, *ben trovato.*
33. The "single supreme being," acceptance of whom allowed so many believers and nonbelievers to avoid religious persecution while salving their consciences, need not be a direct descendant of the *aliquis praestans natura* recognized by skeptics (*De Natura Deorum*, 1.100, *De Divinatione*, 1.248) and dogmatists (*De Natura Deorum*, 2.46) alike in Cicero's pages, but the similarity of underlying attitudes that the two phrases reveal is very striking.

Interest in the Canon:
Kant in the Context of
Longinus and Adorno

William J. Kennedy

T HE CONCEPT OF canon originates in rhetorical theory, practice, and pedagogy. It refers to a standard or rule that students imitate and emulate
in their own writing. In late Classical times, it came to refer to specific texts
worthy to be imitated or emulated because of their depth and complexity
or, from the standpoint of a broad readership, worthy to be analyzed and
interpreted because of their seminal cultural importance. Not all critics or
theorists prize the concept. Both Longinus and Kant notably regard the canon
as a negative and constraining force in rhetorical practice. For the one, it
encourages a dull sort of competence (*Peri Hupsous* 36). For the other, it
promotes mere rules that true genius should surpass (*Critique of Judgment*,
section 17, 69–73), though Kant later emphasizes that genius itself cannot
dispense with definite rules:

> Although mechanical and beautiful art are very different, the first being
> a mere art of industry and learning and the second of genius, yet there is
> no beautiful art in which there is not a mechanical element that can be
> comprehended by rules and followed accordingly, and in which therefore
> there must be something *scholastic* as an essential condition.[1]

Longinus offers general advice about managing the rules so as to resist or
oppose any repressive compulsion to form a limited canon, while, from the
perspective of rules, Kant summons a "disinterested satisfaction" for similar
reasons—to enable an expansive canon that serves more than one set of
interests. Because "disinterested satisfaction" is a negative whose positive
implies a desire for, investment in, and fascination with the object of pleasure,

it calls upon us to examine the unstable relationship between disinterestedness on the one hand and desire, investment, and fascination on the other. No less than Longinus, Kant traces this relationship in a dynamic way to accommodate the workings of a broad and ever-changing canon.

For Kant, interest means satisfaction in the existence of the object artistically represented (section 4, 41–43). A person who experiences art displaces his or her interest from the empirical reality of the thing represented to an immediate apprehension of its subjective reality.[2] This response acknowledges a negative moment that defines the audience's interest in three ways: as a sublimated desire for the existence of the object represented in art; as a surplus earned in return on the intellectual capital invested in apprehending the art work; and as a fascination with artistic techniques that generate the aesthetic response. The audience's desire is sublimated when its immediate aim for the represented object (say, the desire that a person such as Hamlet should actually exist) yields to other aims that it values more highly, such as an expanded awareness, enlarged knowledge, and deeper understanding (about, say, Hamlet's predicament). The audience's investment is intellectual when it generates a thoughtful response oriented to the represented object. Finally, the audience's fascination with artistic technique is consequential when it engages with the work's meaning. A work's concrete application of its form prevents its style or technique from reaching any end in itself, so that style or technique functions as one component among many. The more complex this component, the more comprehensive the audience's appreciation may be.

In our own century, Theodor Adorno has illuminated Kantian aesthetics by foregrounding the idea of interest inherent in disinterestedness. Whereas Kant tries to integrate into an organic whole the cognitive and emotional faculties that apprehend the work, Adorno draws attention to fractures in the work that resist such integration. Adorno examines Kant's relationship to the eighteenth-century rationalist tradition that emphasizes "the effect a work of art has upon the viewer."[3] At the same time, Adorno submits Kant's aesthetics to a radical critique of "its attempt to salvage objectivity by means of an analysis of subjective moments" (14). For Adorno, one can salvage objectivity and at the same time acknowledge the audience's active role in interpreting art by examining the work's historicity. Aesthetic productions of relation embedded within forms comprise "sedimentations of social relations of production bearing the imprint of the latter" (7). The work's form best defines its relationship to society as the immanent problems of art express "unresolved antagonisms of reality" (8). All aesthetic interest is therefore historical: it reflects an interest in the subjective and objective forces that galvanize art's potential to inspire progress and emancipation. For Adorno, "there is no beauty without historical remembrance" (96), as art "reenacts the process through which the subject comes painfully into being" (163).

Kant approaches history from a similar angle as a constitutive basis for artistic production and critical reception. The historical sciences furnish supports for any productive canon. They include history, a knowledge of the antiquities, competence in foreign languages, and familiarity with earlier texts. Kant posits a historical canon not because he is promoting it as the dominant standard for imitation, and still less because he is associating it with any classical curriculum—that is, texts studied in the classroom, generally of Greco-Roman or Judeo-Christian origin and assumed to be indisputable. Instead, he posits a historical canon that corresponds to the historicity of art itself. Because it "furthers the culture of the mental powers in reference to social communication" (section 44, 148), art requires social and therefore historical knowledge for its appreciation. For the very same reason, it requires an understanding of change and the workings of change upon human interests. One concomitance of this understanding is that art may challenge the rules of the canon even as it finds itself compelled to respect them: "In order to accomplish a purpose, definite rules from which we cannot dispense ourselves are required" (section 48, 153). From a rational standpoint, every innovative art depends on such rules to distinguish it from free play: "Otherwise we could not ascribe the product to art at all; it would be a mere product of chance" (section 48, 153). The upshot is an aesthetics as contestatory as it is conscious of the canon.

Kant's interest in furthering historical knowledge, in challenging art's accepted rules, and in promoting art as a motor for human development finds earlier analogues in Longinus's treatise *Peri Hupsous* ("On the Sublime"; Rome? 40 C.E.?). Recovered by Robortello in the sixteenth century (Basle, 1554), it acquired fame in Europe after Boileau translated it in 1674. Formulated during an age of political oppression, *Peri Hupsous* takes irregular account of the classical canon, of the need for adjusting rules to accord with current interests, and of rhetoric's political consequences upon private and collective behavior.[4] One result is Longinus's expansion of the canon as represented by texts that he cites in the treatise: its author refers to standard Greek and Roman authors (Homer, Plato, Demosthenes, Cicero, Horace) but also to now lost authors; to the less popular plays of Aeschylus, Euripides, and Eupolis; and finally to the Septuagint Book of Genesis.[5] Another result is Longinus's apparent transgression of accepted convention despite his sharp rebuke of novelty and innovation for their own sake. A third is Longinus's placement of his argument about rhetoric in a social and political context that heightens his discussion of form. Kant shaped his own critique in the aftermath of Longinus.

Longinus foregrounds issues of acquired value and assigned prestige in his concluding discussion on political freedom. Here he refutes the topos of rhetoric's ascendance and prestige in a participatory democracy and its decline with the loss of a common voice in government. Freedom, he asserts, depends on no form of collective government but on one's own moral mastery of appetite and will. Political institutions matter less than personal integrity;

the enemy lies within: "Perhaps it is not the world's peace that corrupts great natures but much rather this endless warfare which besets our hearts" (44.6). If virtue based on self-knowledge begets the only freedom worth having, then the only polity worth having will promote this virtue. Democracy can in fact inhibit progress by giving way to mob rule and eventual chaos. A centralized monarchy—even an imperial or a tyrannical one—may on the other hand enable the good life by enforcing order and stability: "Nay, for such as we are perhaps it is better to have a master than to be free" (44.10). Figures of greed, unearned self-interest, and the purchase of luxury evoke from Longinus's earlier discussion a horrifying image of corrupted judgment and empowering bribery.

One might wish to conclude that in an era of Roman domination, Longinus is simply repressing his own political instincts for freedom, that he acquiesces to the status quo mindful of his own commercial success in the pedagogical institutions where he taught rhetoric. To enter this argument from the opposite perspective, however, we might trace the extraordinary development of Longinus's reasoning. The master trope of self-interest governs his discussion of the canon. When one's judgment reflects self-interest, its value becomes arbitrary and is based on appearances: "For the corrupt judge inevitably regards his own interest as fair and just" (44.9). When, on the other hand, one's judgment enables the greatest possible good, its value multiplies as interest earned on accumulated capital, "the honourable and admirable motive of doing good to the world" (44.11). The models proposed for such a canon, indeed the qualities imputed to them and to the canon itself, are flexible, expansive, growth-oriented, and high-yield.

Longinus's flexibility is especially prominent in a passage that refers to Polycleitus's statue, the *Doryphorus* ("Spearman"), called by the ancients the *canon* ("standard, rule, model") because they regarded it as a standard of perfection for other sculptors to emulate. The passage occurs in chapter 36 amid a discussion of whether quantity or abundance in the whole can compensate for flaws in the quality of some parts, or, mutatis mutandis, whether striking aspects of its parts can compensate for unevenness in the whole. Longinus argues that bursts of excellence, even if they violate the usual precepts, surpass a mere correctness that is maintained throughout: greatness compensates for breaking the rules. Yet he immediately counters his own argument with the example of Polycleitus. The mere size of a gigantic statue with some extraordinary parts—for example, the Colossus at Rhodes—is not necessarily better than the stunning accuracy of a completely perfect small statue—for example, the Spearman: "As to the statement that the faulty Colossus is no better than Polycleitus's Spearman, there are many obvious answers to that. In art we admire accuracy, in nature grandeur" (36.3). The difficulty here goes beyond Longinus's logical confusion of quantity (size, extension, grandeur, abundance) and quality (excellence, perfection, accuracy, correctness). It concerns the relationship of correctness to art, the determining role that correctness plays in relation to some real or imagined standard by which one judges art and, by implication, the canon of rules or models that one espouses for art.

How does Longinus accommodate these discordant ideas? At least initially, he argues that artistic correctness supplements nature's amplitude. Correctness is nonetheless finite. It has no foundational essence or existence of its own, but it functions only in relation to a model that conditions it and, moreover, to the way in which one perceives that model. The faculty of judgment emerges as a necessary component of this supplement. It affects not only one's notion of correctness but also the apparently unmediated experience of grandeur. A perception of size exceeds simple intuition. It occurs on a horizon or from a vantage point that the perceiver takes into account in measuring size or extension, and it accrues from the interest that one invests in both that horizon and the thing perceived. Quantitative size becomes important because of a qualitative judgment.

In the light of these qualifications, rhetoric would seem by its very nature to entail risk and risk-taking. The canon would seem only a norm that exists to be transgressed. Early on, however, Longinus disparages gratuitous novelty. The treatise's first chapters initiate a tirade against innovation. They associate unusual effects with "puerility," "the academic attitude," "the tinsel reefs of affectation" (3.4). They ridicule effects that sink into an "insatiable passion for starting strange conceits" (4.1), and they assert that "all these improprieties in literature are weeds sprung from the same seed, namely that passion for novel ideas which is the prevalent craze of the present day" (5.1). In each case, the problem stems from a defect of art, an ignorance of technical rules, a failure to honor some standard or model. It follows that a useful canon would be genuinely earned rather than conventionally accepted. It would be flexible, adaptable, far-ranging, and not at all conformable to "merely some such outward show of grandeur with a rich moulding of casual accretions" (7.1). But how might it remain so without being essentialized into some timeless universal, to which Longinus's own argument inadvertently leads him by the end of chapter 7?

Among all his examples of canonical excellence, Longinus quotes one text in its entirety, an ode by Sappho:

φαίνεταί μοι κῆνος ἴσος θεοῖσιν
ἔμμεν' ὠνήρ, ὅστις ἐναντίος τοι
ἰζάνει καὶ πλησίον ἀδὺ φωνεύ-
   σας ὑπακούει
καὶ γελαίσας ἰμερόεν, τό μοι μὰν
καρδίαν ἐν στήθεσιν ἐπτόασεν.
ὥς σε γὰρ ἴδω βροχέως με φώνας
   οὐδὲν ἔτ' εἴκει.

ἀλλὰ καμ μὲν γλῶσσα ἔαγε. λεπτὸν δ᾽
αὐτίκα χρῷ πῦρ ὑπαδεδρόμακεν.
ὀππάτεσσι δ᾽ οὐδὲν ὄρημ᾽, ἐπιρόμ-
βεισι δ᾽ ἄκουαι.
ἀ δέ μ᾽ ἰδρὼς κακχέεται, τρόμος δὲ
παῖσαν ἀγρεῖ, χλωροτέρα δὲ ποίας
ἔμμι. τεθνάκην δ᾽ ὀλίγω ᾽πιδεύης
φαίνομαι. . . .
†ἀλλὰ παντόλματον, ἐπεὶ καὶ πένητα†

I think him God's peer that sits near thee face to face, and listens to thy sweet speech and lovely laughter.

'Tis this that makes my heart flutter in my breast. If I see thee but for a little, my voice comes no more and my tongue is broken.

At once a delicate flame runs through my limbs; my eyes are blinded and my ears thunder.

The sweat pours down: shivers hunt me all over. I am grown paler than grass, and very near to death I feel.

Appearing in chapter 10, it offers a particularly intriguing model. As a female-authored text, it stands outside the male-dominated canon. Its woman's voice dramatizes her speaker's rivalry with a man, "that sits near thee face to face," for the love of an attractive addressee. Whether it challenges any real or imagined male-dominated heterosexual code is another matter. If we assume that both its speaker and its addressee are female, then we deduce a rivalry between the speaker and a young man for the addressee's attention. Nothing in the poem confirms these gendered identities, however, and one might as legitimately construe the speaker as male and the beloved as either female (and thereby understand a conventional heterosexual triangle) or male (and thereby understand a homosexual triangle). Sappho may be fashioning neither a female voice expressive of her love for another woman nor one expressive of her love for a man, but rather a voice that is wholly conventional, wholly normative, wholly exemplary, and wholly degendered. She would then be adopting as pure artifice the male-dominated topoi of amatory poetry in which the beloved is usually figured as female.[6]

An academic footnote to literary history bears out these implications. At least a century before *Peri Hupsous*, the Roman poet Catullus adapted this poem for the presumably male speaker of his carmen 51, *Ille me par esse deo videtur* ("He seems to me to be equal to a god").[7] Catullus's text comes to us only in a corrupted form, however, and a significant interpolation in line 8 registers at least its emender's surmise that the speaker's voice is a conventional artifact: *Nam simul te, / Lesbia, aspexi, nihil est super mi / [vocis in ore]* ("For whenever I see you, Lesbia, at once no sound of voice remains within my mouth"). Here the conjectural *[vocis in ore]* foregrounds the poem's concern with the speaker's voice. The romantic nostalgia that invites us to

52

associate this voice biographically with a man named Catullus—or with a woman named Sappho—yields to the rhetorical engendering of a voice that suits both genders. And this engenderment raises issues of gender that need resolution.

Longinus himself refuses to marginalize gender and sexuality in his own rhetoric. His argument describes the process of imitation in highly charged sexual figures. Chapter 13 presents at least four such figures.[8] The first two are female-gendered. No sooner does Longinus refer to those who "are carried away by the inspiration of another" (13.2) than he evokes a violent representation of rape and impregnation. The imitator resembles a prophetess who breathes a divine vigor that impregnates her, with a suggestion of seminal fluid originating in sacred precincts: "From the natural genius of those old writers there flows into the hearts of their admirers as it were an emanation from the mouth of holiness" (13.2). Next, Longinus praises Plato for assimilating so many fine models as an eager recipient of these fluids, drawing them into the uterine cavity from which they will reemerge as transacted forms, "with ten thousand runnels from the great Homeric spring" (13.3). In both cases, the maternal imitator nurtures seed into new life.

Two other figures are male-gendered. One represents a contest or agon in which the imitator struggles against a precursor. The other represents an act of witness or judgment through which the imitator earns a predecessor's approval. Both unfold upon a field of masculine action. The imitator enters the lists for first prize in contention with his model. Even if he fails to surpass the model, his valiant efforts merit recognition. Thus, Plato hardly would have succeeded so well "had he not striven, yea with heart and soul, to contest the prize with Homer, like a young antagonist with one who had already won his spurs" (13.4). Alternatively, the imitator presents himself for judgment by his model. The predecessor becomes an imagined judge and jury, and his approval offers testimony of the imitator's worth: "Great indeed is the ordeal, if we propose such a jury and audience as this to listen to your own utterances and make believe that we are submitting our work to the scrutiny of such superhuman witnesses and judges" (14.2).

Longinus's figures radiate sexual energy. Tὸ ἀγώνισμα ("ordeal") registers a contest between males who are γυμνόι ("naked, unarmed"), whether in wrestling or in running or in some other feat of endurance. The elder's testimony is a ὅρκος ("covenant" or "surety") that transmits a paternal inheritance. The word is related to the Greek ὄρχις ("testicle") with associations that are even richer in their Latin forms, *contestari* and *testis*. These words derive from the ancient Proto-Indo-European root *trei* ("three") compounded with *stà* ("stand") to imply a third person who mediates a dispute between two others in "an agonistic situation," a "con-test," to be adjudicated in favor of one or the other party.[9] Thus, *testis* also denotes the male sexual organ, a witness to anatomical male sexuality, the seed bed of future generations, and in antiquity

53

that portion of the body upon which the hand was placed when swearing testimony.

Longinus's figure of the model as a witness or judge raises the issue of interest in a heightened form. The canon acts as a third-party patriarch existing between (*inter-esse*) the imitating writer and his or her posterity. It bears witness to the latter's claims for excellence and authority, at once reassuring the writer of his or her abilities and commending them to a judgmental readership. It thereby assists as a paratextual guide for the writer who produces the text and as an intertextual guide for readers who interpret and evaluate it. It plays this role, moreover, as an allegedly disinterested third party. "Disinterested" here does not mean "uncaring about" or "aloof from" the writer's or reader's claims, as though the workings of the canon were simply mechanical or deterministic. This witness or judge is indeed "interested" in affording the best possible outcome that respects past relations and generates further ones. It is, however, not "interested" in the sense of being tendentious or prejudiced in favor of or against either claimant, for then it would no longer mediate between them as a third party but would rather join forces with one or the other side.

A corrupted judge can award the prize to an inferior work, of course, and bribery generated by powerful interests can result in such judgment. As an institution of rhetoric, the canon lies open to corruption. Longinus registers a sharp awareness of this weakness when he discusses rhetoric's propensity to dominate and deceive. As a disinterested skill, rhetoric may abet the perverse interests of its most skillful users. Even when good rhetoricians posit virtuous intentions, their art may enslave the audience; or the audience itself may be less than honest and upright or may lack the background and skills to understand precisely. Longinus proposes several techniques to allow the audience a degree of autonomy. One is for the rhetorician to project an appearance of spontaneity, so as to display honesty and unmediated ingenuity. The give-and-take of question-and-answer in self-dialogue contributes to this enlarged effect: "This way of questioning and answering one's self counterfeits spontaneous emotion" (18.2). In the end, however, even benign illusions confirm rhetoric's propensity toward domination and deception. How can the canon in its role as witness and judge avoid such postures?

This problem bedeviled classical rhetoric after as well as before Longinus addressed it. For Quintilian in *De Institutio Oratoria* (95 C.E.), for example, imitation acquires value only when it represents an improvement upon the original. Simply to follow a model is the mark of "a sluggish nature" (10.2.4), and the result "must necessarily be inferior to the object of its imitation" (10.2.11).[10] By surpassing the model in some important way, the copy earns interest upon it for investing its own initial labor in trying to understand the model. In *De Oratore* (55 B.C.E.), Cicero already had tried to escape the tyranny of imitating models in his own language by turning to those in a foreign language: "By rendering into Latin what I had read in Greek, I not only found myself using the best words—and yet quite familiar ones (already available in Latin)—but also fashioning by analogy certain expressions such as would be new" (1.34).[11] Translation, of course, presupposes not only the anteriority of a foreign canon but also its alien difference that requires the later writer to act out and work through its strangeness. An important by-product may be the formation of a rhetorical *I*, the result of confronting an alien identity inscribed in earlier texts. Cicero's advice to practice *disputatio in utramque partem* follows upon this recognition. In this exercise, a sense of heightened or augmented identity comes into play as the speaker tries on roles antithetical to his or her self-image. As Antonius explains in *De Oratore*, "In my own person, and with perfect impartiality, I play three characters, myself, my opponent, and the arbitrator" (2.24). The canon thus reproduces not itself but an antitype of itself, a surplus arising from the difference between an archetype and its imitation. It can be thought of as a surplus earned as a return on the work of forming a canon itself.

Longinus does not resolve the value of the canon, nor can he calculate the interest earned from it. He does, however, explore the matter of rhetorical technique in an attempt to confer relative value on some aspects of the canon. For Kant, on the other hand, rhetorical technique becomes an object of palpable distrust. In classifying the arts in sections 51 through 54, Kant opposes rhetoric to poetry on every count. It is entirely rule-bound and follows the narrow conventions of a strict canon. Because rules dominate, one can judge easily whether a speech is technically good or bad, but one can not judge so easily whether it advocates morally good or bad action: "Since it can be used equally well to beautify or to hide vice and error, it cannot quite kill the secret suspicion that one is being artfully overreached" (section 53, 172). A portentous footnote to this passage further disparages rhetoric as "a treacherous art which means to move men in important matters like machines," especially so when Kant refers to the "readiness and accuracy of speaking" that result from formulary rules and scholastic training (172). The provenance of rhetoric is entirely a matter of technical skill.

Art also depends on rules, but they by no means constitute art, nor do they determine the admittance of any given art work into the canon. Aesthetic value turns out to be relative in an absolute way as it depends on the gift of genius, but its relative nature leads early on to an *a poria* in Kant's argument:

> If now it is a natural gift which must prescribe its rule to art (as beautiful art), of what kind is this rule? It cannot be reduced to a formula and serve as a precept, for then the judgment upon the beautiful would be determinable according to concepts; but the rule must be abstracted from the fact, i.e. from the product, on which others may try their own talent by using it as a model, not to be *copied* but to be *imitated* [*nicht der Nachmachung, sondern der Nachahmung, dienen zu lassen*]. How this is possible is hard to explain. (section 47, 152; *Kritik,* 409)

55

To unravel distinctions crucial to this issue, Kant starts to clarify operations that are basic to critical reasoning and to determine what warrants our assent in critical judgment.[12] Aesthetic values appear to change from one epoch or locality to another, and arguments about them lead to mutually contradictory conclusions from the same premises. These antinomies require scrutiny, not so much that we might avoid them—for no culture can stabilize its aesthetic values for all time or for every other culture—but rather so that we might understand the power and scope of such values. The surprising result is that they only increase in value as they transact their original freedom and purposiveness.

In the third critique, Kant, like Longinus, raises the issue of the canon in a passage that refers to Polycleitus's Spearman. Like Longinus, moreover, Kant disparages it as a canon or "rule" for subsequent works of art. He recognizes that as the product of observation, a canonical model reflects the observer's experience, "the normal idea in the country where the comparison is instituted" (section 17, 71), and hence that "a Negro must have a different normal idea of the beauty of the [human figure] from a white man, a Chinaman a different normal idea from a European etc." (section 17, 71). The rule constitutes only an indeterminate norm, a provisional attempt toward universality that must forever undergo artistic revision.[13] It proposes nothing definite, nothing specifically characteristic, nothing that contradicts any general condition.

Kant's argument leads toward the privileging of genius and the violation of rules as a standard for art, but it equally implicates a universal understanding, common sense, and determinate purpose. As purpose itself motivates the idea of interest, and specifically interest in the existence of something represented, it entails a consideration of interest on several interlocking levels: as that which exists between (*inter-esse*) the artist and his or her own purpose; as that which exists between the receiving audience and its purpose; as that which exists between the thing represented and its purpose; and as that which exists between the work of art and any of its productive or receptive forces. Interest thus can be understood as anything that grows out of the representation of art, while its converse, disinterestedness, can be understood as anything immediately bound up with the representation itself.[14]

If we can separate interest from disinterestedness, the latter concerns material limits—that is, its relationship to a circumscribed representation. Interest, however, knows no logical or material limit, and hence frays out into indeterminacy of a special sort. Kant reasons that one's judgment of art is only subjective but that it is nonetheless assumed to be subjectively universal as it claims universal assent. The critic accepts that what is represented does not exist in actuality, but wishes that others may experience it as he or she has done, so that others may direct their subjectivity toward it with similar results. Because what is represented is not an objective concept, it cannot command everyone's assent: "It does not say that everyone *will* agree with my judgment, but that he *ought*" (section 22, 76). However, it can appeal to the possibility of common agreement, and hence of universal communicability.[15]

Kant's most remarkable example of an aesthetic judgment presupposes a concurrence of conscientiously formulated judgments. It informs the praise that he heaps upon a poem attributed to Frederick the Great.[16] Composed in French, it appears in section 49 of Kant's text in a German prose translation. Here are the respective French and German versions:

> Oui, finissons sans trouble et mourons sans regrets,
> En laissant l'univers comblé de nos bienfaits.
> Ainsi l'astre du jour au bout de sa carrière,
> Répand sur l'horizon une douce lumière;
> Et les derniers rayons qu'il darde dans les airs,
> Sont les derniers soupirs qu'il donne à l'univers.

> Yes, let us have done with perturbation and let us die without regrets, leaving the world filled with our good deeds. Thus the day star at the end of its course spreads over the horizon a soft light; and the final rays that it discharges in the air are the final sighs that it gives to the world.

> Laßt uns aus dem Leben ohne Murren weichen und ohne etwas zu bedauern, indem wir die Welt noch alsdann mit Wohltaten überhäuft zurücklassen. So verbreitet die Sonne, nachdem sie ihren Tageslauf vollendet hat, noch ein mildes Licht am Himmel; und die letzten Strahlen, die sie in die Lüfte schickt, sind ihre Seufzer für das Wohl der Welt. (416)

> Let us withdraw from life without grumbling and without regretting anything, in that we leave behind the world even afterwards heaped with good deeds. In this way, after the sun has completed its day's course, it still diffuses a soft light in heaven, and the final rays that it sends into the air are its final sighs for the well-being of the world.

This example prominently exposes the compulsions of binary thinking that dominate the formation of a canon. Why does Kant feature a translation rather than the original? Why the work of an occasional writer rather than an acknowledged master? Why prose rather than poetry? Why German rather than French?

Responding to the last question, we might answer that for his German readership, Kant is proffering his translation as an appropriate linguistic aid, except that Kant's audience of professional philosophers would have been able to deal with the French anyway. (Curiously, John Bernard's standard English translation of the *Critique* offers only the French version without any assistance in translation.) We might add that the patriotic force of using German alone counters the Prussian king's sentiment in using French. We might note finally, without confusing grammatical gender with biological gendering, that the example is not free from the binary opposition of gendered relationships. The

German translation elides the figure of the sun rendered by the masculine French noun as *l'astre du jour* ("day star"), and prefers instead the literal referent given in the feminine German noun, *die Sonne*. As the French original carries out the figure *au bout de sa carrière*, it concludes with the day star discharging into the air (*il darde dans les airs*) its final rays as sighs that it gives to the universe (*il donne à l'univers*). None of these quoted phrases makes its way exactly into the German translation, though that translation does transform the first of them into a dependent adverbial clause, *nachdem sie ihren Tageslauf vollendet hat*. The pronominal effect in each of these clauses is, first, to emphasize a personified action (*il darde, il donne, sie vollendet hat*) and, second, to cast its action into a gender-inflected role: the masculine *il* in French and feminine *sie* in German. Though Kant does not draw any radical implications from these features, he does praise the poem's author for "quicken[ing] his rational idea" with imaginative associations that excite "a number of sensations and secondary representations" (section 19, 159).

But which poem? The German translation is curiously flat, a noteworthy instance of the utter conventionality that Longinus ascribes to composition by rule. So, too, is the French original, even if it has the dubious distinction of personifying the sun as a day star. When Kant admits it into his argument about the canon, he strips from it any implication of a charged, much less sexually charged, energy that it may possess in *il darde* or *il donne*. The feminine gendering of *sie vollendet hat* is entirely neutralized by the plainness of the philosopher's prose. Figuration, it would seem, provides no motive or justification for its admission to the canon. In Kant's translation, as in his argument, the poem is admissible chiefly on other grounds—namely, that its author is Frederick II. The judgment that exalts this poem is an individual judgment, flawed in its evaluation by one's knowledge of the poet's identity. It is difficult for the philosopher to put the king's poem in analytic perspective. Based on this knowledge, the critic's investment in the poem's capital yields some return on the attention that the reader pays to it, though one can hardly accord it the fascination of artful technique.

Kant's contemporary Prussian readers might have made a similar judgment. Earlier, however, Kant tries to avoid such a conclusion by appealing to the "collective reason of humanity" (section 40, 136), something greater than a judgment of individual taste. If this collective reason is not an absolute *sensus communis*, a sense absolutely common to all, it is nonetheless a sense larger than that of the individual. It requires an individual to take account of how others think, to put oneself in the place of another in order to compare judgments. The result widens the field of evaluation beyond formal precision and technical brilliance as it enables one "to escape the illusion arising from the private conditions that could be so easily taken for objective, which would injuriously affect the judgment" (section 40, 136). This escape proves important for aesthetic values, including but not limited to those associated with artistic technique. It endows the work of art as a vehicle for enlightenment that promotes unprejudiced, enlarged, and consecutive thought. Above all, it mitigates the work's effect as something that occurs privately, anarchically, and relativistically, and shapes it instead as an experience modifying and modified by the audience's collective view of history. The interest that accrues from such a canonical work is a social one as it heightens and transforms the audience's understanding of itself and hence of its place in history.

How can we be sure that this privileging of the canon does not simply reinforce the prejudices of its collective audience and therefore reduce one's aesthetic judgment to a heteronomic judgment? Though Kant admits that subjective interest may err, he would like to believe that a collective interest can tend only toward betterment of the whole. When obstacles intervene, human beings unite to overcome them. The canon serves as teacher and guide in assigning values, much in the manner of Longinus's disinterested third-party witness or judge. It offers not a rule to replicate but an example to emulate. It requires technique, discipline, and skill that can be acquired through academic training as "its execution and its *form* require talent cultivated in the schools" (section 47, 153). The procedure for studying art, and hence for shaping a canon, sharply differs from that for studying science, and hence for compiling a body of scientific data. The latter follows the steps of earlier science, replicating its discoveries, corroborating its results, and adding to the body of knowledge so that "the greatest discoverer only differs in degree from his laborious imitator and pupil" (section 47, 152). What counts in poetry is not the duplication of method and result but an apprehension and transmutation of form. Given the first lines of a poem, no later poet could complete the text exactly as it had been written previously. The canon exists not to be reproduced but rather to be challenged and contested by those who receive it.

For Theodor Adorno, of course, form acquires value by articulating a rift between the aesthetic subject and society: "Forms go on exercising their say over the subject until a cleavage opens between them and the consistency of the poetic work. It is then that the subject explodes them, for the sake of consistency and because the objective situation demands it" (*Aesthetic Theory*, 288). The oppositional role of art calls attention to fissures that divide social forces and the relations of production: "This social deviance of art is the determinate negation of a determinate society" (321). By refusing to separate affirmation from critique, by refusing to become an easy commodity, art engineers a resistance to the totalizing aims of a totally administered modern society. Merely polished form is valueless in art.

On this score, Adorno agrees with Kant even while critiquing him in a highly qualified way. Kant challenges the merely correct rules in fashioning a canon, though he still insists on respect for rules in executing the art work. So, too, for Adorno, each successive art work presents a challenge to the canon by altering the formal purity of canonical models. This feature is particularly striking in lyric poetry, the most highly formalized of literary genres: "What we mean by lyric . . . has within it in its 'purest' form, the quality of a break or rupture."[17] The medium of this challenge proves to be language as a reflector of history: "This is accomplished by means of language. The specific paradox belonging to the lyric poem—this subjective personal element transforming itself into an objective one—is bound to that specific importance which poetry gives to linguistic *form*" (*Notes,* 1.43). These delicate negotiations between form and rupture depend as much upon a conscious recognition of rules as upon a conscious or unconscious transgression of them. Logically, then, Adorno's critique of Kant's formalism leads him to the critical limits of neoclassical aesthetics as much as to those of modern mass culture, for both cherish homogenizing norms as a standard of artistic value. In fact, as Adorno shows, modern mass culture is a creature of Western rationalism, as the culture industry reflects and reflects upon the power of capitalism and bourgeois society that are products of eighteenth-century enlightenment.

In all fairness to Kant's complexity, the *Critique of Judgment* anticipates this criticism. Kant's example of Frederick II's thoroughly mediocre, thoroughly commonplace poem endorses the primacy of neoclassical rules in art, but Kant blurs these rules by presenting the poem in a German prose translation rather than in its original French verse. He thus eclipses the power of rules even as he pays homage to it. If elementary forms of art—Kant gives the examples of domestic and personal adornment, flowers, body paint, specially crafted tools (section 41, 139)—function as commodified pleasantries designed to grace social relations among neighbors and coworkers, more advanced forms reflect these relations in more complex, perspicuous, and morally productive ways that resist commodification. Interest accrues from the interaction of these works with their environment—not only their sublimated environment of origin but that to which they are transmitted across space and time, their environment of reception. To the distant audience, the art work communicates its relationship to history, a palimpsest of social relations embedded even in the work's technical features, challenging them, and challenged by them.

The civilizing process thus prompts individuals to communicate their pleasure to others and to feel satisfaction in common with others. Interest occurs as a passage from sense enjoyment to moral feeling. It unfolds in a space between enjoyment and moral desire whenever aesthetic sensations become universally communicable. As Longinus implies, the canon of a given culture smoothes this passage as a paratextual guide for writers in producing their texts and as an intertextual guide for readers in interpreting them. Upon this view Kant projects a social process of unstable negotiation rather than the uncontested imposition of any a priori superiority or strength. The workings of the canon are pointedly economic as they register the social, distributive, and commutative priorities that a culture acts out and works through.

Debates about the canon, whether on a national or international scale, trivialize the issue whenever they reduce it to an argument about which texts should or should not be included in reading lists. They avoid a deeper problem when they suggest that the inclusion of texts favored by various constituencies can remedy problems of cultural inequality. The replacement of ancient or esteemed or prejudicially high-culture texts by hitherto neglected ones representing marginalized genders, races, or classes may alter literary knowledge to some extent, but it will not transform the historical consciousness of our literary knowledge unless it asks how readers use this canon. I would suggest that such a question defines Kant's interest better than any cultural or intellectual Darwinism that invites the new to replace the old at periodic intervals. Possible answers to it may uncover the gaps, fissures, silences, and inconsistencies of different ideologies and initiate a dialogue among them, a dialogue that interrogates the past and present availability of power, knowledge, culture, and other resources to privileged and disenfranchised groups. And this kind of dialogue may serve as a more effective motor for progress and enlightenment than any reshuffling of titles in the canonical Rolodex ever could. It is an ideal worthy of today.

Notes

1. Immanuel Kant, *Critique of Judgment*, trans. J. H. Bernard (New York: Hafner-Macmillan, 1951), section 47, 153; quotations from Kant in English refer to this edition; those in German refer to *Kritik der Urteilskraft*, vol. 5 of Immanuel Kant, *Werke*, ed. Wilhelm Weischedel, 6 vols. (Wiesbaden: Insel, 1957).

2. For Kant's intention in the third critique not to write about aesthetics for its own sake but to investigate knowledge claims about principles that cannot be justified by experience alone, see Dieter Henrich, *Aesthetic Judgment and the Moral Image of the World* (Stanford: Stanford University Press, 1992), 19–56. For recent efforts to relate Kantian epistemology to hermeneutics, see Hans-Georg Gadamer, *Truth and Method*, trans. Garret Barden and John Cumming (New York: Seabury, 1975), 39–51; and Richard Rorty, *Philosophy and the Mirror of Nature* (Princeton: Princeton University Press, 1979), 325, 357–65. For the adversarial relationship between science and rhetoric, see Hans-Georg Gadamer, "The Expressive Power of Language," *PMLA* 107 (1992): 345–52.

3. Quotations from Theodor Adorno, *Aesthetic Theory*, trans. C. Lenhardt (London: Routledge & Kegan Paul, 1984), 14; for relevant criticism, see Russell A. Berman, *Modern Culture and Critical Theory* (Madison: University of Wisconsin Press, 1989); and Andreas Huyssen, *After the Great Divide: Modernism, Mass Culture, Postmodernism* (Bloomington: Indiana University Press, 1986), 16–43.

4. For Longinus's irregularities as a critic, see Paul Fry, *The Reach of Criticism* (New Haven: Yale University Press, 1983), 47–86.

5. The Septuagint is cited in 9.9; all references are to Longinus, *On the Sublime*, trans. W. Hamilton Fyfe (London: Heinemann, 1927).

6. For the perception that "there are not enough indices to tell us the degree of Sappho's subjectivity," see Lowry Nelson, Jr., *Poetic Configurations* (University Park: Pennsylvania State University Press, 1991), 43.

7. Catullus, Tibullus, and *Pervigilium Veneris, Works,* trans. F. W. Cornish (London: Heinemann, 1913).

8. For analysis, see Thomas M. Greene, *The Light in Troy* (New Haven: Yale University Press, 1982), 78–80.

9. See Walter Ong, *Fighting for Life* (Ithaca: Cornell University Press, 1981), 47–49. For the relationship between play and agon in Socratic testimony, see Mihai Spariosu, *God of Many Names* (Durham: Duke University Press, 1991), 171–86.

10. Quintilian, *Institutio oratoria,* trans. H. E. Butler, 4 vols. (London: Heinemann, 1921).

11. Cicero, *De Oratore,* trans. E. W. Sutton and H. Rackham, 2 vols. (London: Heinemann, 1942).

12. See Salim Kemal, *Kant and Fine Art* (Oxford: Clarendon Press, 1986), 35–53. For a discussion of how the epistemological and moral concerns of the first two critiques are grounded in the supersensible faculty of aesthetic judgment, see Timothy J. Reiss, *The Meaning of Literature* (Ithaca: Cornell University Press, 1992), 319–22.

13. See Rudolf A. Makkreel, *Imagination and Interpretation in Kant* (Chicago: University of Chicago Press, 1990), 118.

14. For Kantian meanings of "interest," see René Wellek, *A History of Modern Criticism,* 8 vols. (New Haven: Yale University Press, 1955–92), 1.229–31. For the influence of this idea on Coleridge and English Romanticism, see René Wellek, *Immanuel Kant in England, 1793–1838* (Princeton: Princeton University Press, 1931), 110–12. For appropriations of Kant by such twentieth-century critics as Benjamin, Lukacs, and Thibaudet, see Wellek, *A History,* 7.183–84, 7.210, and 8.49–51, respectively.

15. See Paul Guyer, *Kant and the Claims of Taste* (Cambridge, Mass.: Harvard University Press, 1979), 310–26.

16. For Kant's relations with Frederick II, see John H. Zammito, *The Genesis of Kant's Critique of Judgment* (Chicago: University of Chicago Press, 1992), 21–34. For Kant's hostility to Sturm und Drang and its advocacy of throwing off the constraint of all rules, see Zammito, 137–42.

17. Theodor Adorno, *Notes to Literature,* ed. Rolf Tiedemann, trans. Shierry Weber Nicholsen, 2 vols. (New York: Columbia University Press, 1991), 1.40.

Achilles Rheter?
Homer and Proto-rhetorical Truth

Raymond Adolph Prier

he gar sophistike ouk en tei dynamei all' an tei proairesei. plen entautha men estai ho men kata ten epistemen ho de kata ten proairesin rhetor, ekei de sophistes men kata ten proairesin, dialektikos de ou kata ten proairesin alla kata ten dynamin.

For sophistry [is characterized] not by its ability but by its previous assumption [to any argument]; except in that, he will be a *rhetor* whether [he argue] by epistemological certainty or by a previous assumption. A man of dialectic [argues] not according to previous assumption but by his ability [alone?].[1]

Aristotle, *Rhetoric*, 1355b 17–21

THE TEXTS OF Aristotle and Homer are read most fruitfully in terms of their respective philological differences and their ensuing cultural implications. Differences, however, also imply some similarities, for instance, in the history and application of rhetoric, the lexical choices of Aristotle's *rhetor* and Homer's *rheter* to designate the man who speaks before men. But, ultimately, how did Aristotle relate the rhetorical value of Homer's archaic texts to the ethical, logical, and political system that informs his *Rhetoric?* In the Philosopher's suppression of Homer's paratactic, descriptive verse in order to stress his own logically reflective, hypotactically deductive and inductive prose, there arose a radical contingency of experience for which Aristotle was forced to employ a non-Homeric word: *proairesis,* a deliberate choice, a point of possible prejudice, and an a priori premise.

At this point, however, the modern reader might well be struck with the odd awareness that the Philosopher is undercutting the ethical value or any intrinsic claim to "truth" that his rhetorical treatise would elicit. But is the "difference" between the texts of Homer and Aristotle so universal and, thus, so absolute? What again of *rheter* and *rhetor*?

The important matter here lies in the way an audience recognizes the veracity of what the *rhetor* or *rheter* speaks, or, more precisely in the case of Homer's men, how they speak and how they use the epic language. By extension, of course, both terms imply the necessity of human discourse recognized as true. "Truth" beginning with the pre-Socratic Parmenides assumed some kind of at least proto-eidetic, nonimmediate, and reflected status in the Greek culture. This was not the case in Homer's texts, where how a statement "rang true" depended to a much greater extent on its traditional linguistic power than on the idiosyncratic, individual behavior of a specific character or some universalized sense of character that Aristotle was yet to create in the *Nicomachean Ethics*. Homeric truth lay in a factual *mythos* ("myth"), not a fictive *logos* ("argument"). The archaic *mythos* was defined in its factual, even artifactual, relationship to an immediately recognizable "deed" (*ergon*), not to an *ergon* that Aristotle might wish to judge, through a problematically narrated *logos*, "certainly" (*akribes*), "decorously" (*to prepon*), and ultimately universally or "absolutely" (*haplos*). Consequently, as Vico perceived in his *De Antiquissima*, for Homer fact implied truth (*verum-factum*). Vico was to attribute to the ancient Latins the different Aristotelian notion that only certainty implies truth (*verum-certum*). So arises yet another difference linked to a common source, in this instance "truth." Again, it suggests a shift or skew that is central to our rhetoric and its powers of interpretation, that is, its hermeneutics.

The key that unlocks Greek rhetoric must, then, be doubly philological and philosophical. What does "myth" mean in Homer? What is "true myth"? How is it recognized? Where and how does *logos* come to play in Homer's texts and those after his? Why as a term must *proairesis* enter the language and text of Aristotle, although it is neither present nor necessary in the language and texts of Homer? How do Plato's and Aristotle's philosophical hermeneutics color the latter's sense of a *rhetor*? How, in the end, might these hermeneutics be not only necessarily suppressing readings of Homer but more importantly the reason we are called upon to accept Aristotle's inherently self-contradictory *proairesis* for rhetorical theory and practice as a whole?

Philologically, the method to uncover the meaning of Achilles' seemingly distinctive claim of being a *rheter* is to compare how he speaks "true myth" with how other men similarly speak in Homer's texts, for instance Ajax and Odysseus. Here, however, one must not indulge in the blinkered reading that fell to Plato, to Aristotle, and even to Sophocles: Odysseus, although of "many wiles" (*polytropon* [*Odyssey*, 1.1]), cannot be torn from his traditional, philological context as some kind of entirely "separated hero." There is a distinction between Achilles and him, but it is not in any ability to "speak true myth" or to recognize it. Philosophically, however, Plato and Aristotle employed this putative distinction to reinterpret the Homeric text in such a way that "truth" could be judged as certain, instead of striking an audience as powerfully immediate fact. Thus, one must focus on Plato's and Aristotle's readings of Homer as a second, complementary way to uncover why *proairesis* appears so disturbingly in *Rhetoric* 1, section 1.

The term *rheter* occurs but once in the Homeric corpus and is used to describe an achieved desideratum in Achilles' education. Phoenix to his former charge:

> *touneka me proeeke didaskemenai tade panta,*
> *mython te rheter' emenai prektera te ergon.*

> On this account did he [Peleus] send me to teach you everything,
> To be a speaker of myths and a practitioner of deeds.

> *(Iliad, 9.442–43)*

Rheter is derived from the verb "to speak" (*eirein*)[2], specifically, as the lexical context of the above passage suggests, "to speak myths" (*mythoi*). What does this mean? *Iliad* 9, "The Embassy," in which the hapaxlegomenon *rheter* occurs, is a text rife with argument and attempts at persuasion that provides as a context for Achilles' rhetorical powers a surprisingly acceptable insight into his talents. The book is replete with what Achilles was taught to speak, that is *mythoi*, and the verb that literally means "to speak myth for oneself and another," *mytheisthai*. Both noun and verb, moreover, are well used throughout Homer's texts.[3]

Iliad 9 opens with the stark exigency of persuading Achilles to return to battle. Agamemnon and Diomedes reflect the general indecision about how anyone might proceed in realizing such a project. Diomedes, however, states the facts of the matter directly and without concern for Agamemnon's unmanly position: "You, Agamemnon, may hightail it back to Greece; we shall remain to destroy Troy" (34–49). Nestor dubs Diomedes' aggressive words a *mythos* and declares that he will deliver a powerful one of his own. Nestor's myth contravenes Agamemnon's self-serving rationale in the Briseis affair and advises persuasion (*pepithomen*, "let us persuade" [112]). In short, Nestor's myth advocates the admission of wrong and the purveying of some kind of verifiable truth that Achilles will accept. The embassy departs for Achilles' camp in whatever combination of friend and foe the scholars might deem exact[4] and sets itself physically in direct opposition to the recalcitrant Achilles.

Odysseus opens the negotiations, offers Agamemnon's bribe, pleads for pity for the Achaeans on the part of Achilles, and goads him with the rumor that Hector is bragging that he is the better man (300–306). Odysseus' words are not dubbed *mythoi* in this instance, but Achilles' response is:

chre men de ton mython apelegeos apoeipein

'Tis necessary, let me tell you, to speak out
the un-sugar-coated myth.

(Iliad, 9.309)

Achilles will make them confront the truth, that is the truth in what he means.[5] He excoriates Agamemnon and his deeds, declares he will not be persuaded (*oude me peisei* [345]), and enjoins that, with the exception of Phoenix, they should all exit posthaste. The embassy responds to Achilles' myth in wonder (*mython agassomenoi* [431]), that is anything but "in an appalled silence."[6] In an instance of hardly elevated American diction, the attitude is much more along the lines of "Well, I'll be damned." Thus does book 9 carefully establish the context of Achilles *rheter*, the *rheter mython*, and, immediately in the text, Achilles' "tirade" and his action are defined and approved didactically by Phoenix himself (*Iliad*, 9.442–43 above). Phoenix alleges that the host also speaks the direct truth (*mython* [522]) in their appeal to the man and adduces an example: the story of Meleager or, to be more exact, some vague attempt at its putative kernel of truth. Aristotle in *Rhetoric* 1 draws directly from Homer for this "line of argument," for he codifies an exemplum as the key characteristic of rhetorical induction. But what should interest us in Homer is not so much the use of an example as Achilles' reaction to it. The man dismisses Phoenix's argument, whether there is myth in the myth or not.

Ajax, typically laconic, advises his comrades to scuttle negotiations because their *mythos* will not find a fulfillment (625) and to return to the host with the naked truth of what has taken place, a *mythos* the Danaans will "not in any way deem good" (*mython Danaoisi kai ouk agathon per eonta* [627]). Achilles declares that Ajax apparently has "mythed" everything as Achilles himself has felt it (*panta ti moi kata thymon eeisao mythesasthai* [645]). The embassy returns. Odysseus recounts what happened, and the host as a whole marvels at Odysseus's true myth (*mython agassamenoi* [694]). Then, once again, as at the book's beginning, everyone admires the myth of Diomedes (*mython agassamenoi* [711]), who informs the assembly that all is lost at this point with Achilles and tomorrow they must return to war.

Thus, both Achilles and Odysseus "myth" the truth; that is, they "speak myth." But why does Homer never refer to Odysseus as a *rheter*? There is certainly nothing in Homer's traditional use of language—that is, the use of the *hemiepies mython te rheter*—that would preclude it from a verse referring directly to Odysseus. Quite to the contrary, if Homer or his epic men perceived Odysseus as a solid and upstanding *rheter mython*, the formulaic language lay ready at hand to claim such. Where lies the inherent distinction between the two men? Is it one of an absolute cultural discontinuity, or is it one of possibly multiple uses of the epic tongue that made Odysseus sometimes verifiable in his facts and sometimes not?

It has been suggested that *Iliad* 9 should be read against a subtext of a deeply resonating and, hence, culturally understandable hatred between Achilles and Odysseus.[7] The textual locus of the antagonism lies at *Odyssey* 8, line 75, where, in a fully formulaic hexameter, we are told of the *neikos Odysseos kai Peleideo Achileos* (the quarrel of Odysseus and Achilles, son of Peleus). Nagy is only partially correct in noting that in *Iliad* 9, when Achilles curses as an *echthros* ("enemy") *hos ch' heteron men keuthei eni phresin, allo de eipei* ("he who hides one thing inwardly and speaks another"), his attack must apply "to the epic behavior of Odysseus."[8] "Epic behavior" might be a good descriptive choice for a text, the language of which is more traditional than individualized. But the curse also applies to the epic behavior of Achilles, and it does so because it is lodged in a *mythos,* an epic language, directed point-blank against Odysseus:

> *diogenes Laertiade, polymechan'*
> *Odysseu, chre men de ton mython*
> *apelegeos apoeipein,*
> *hei per de phroneo te kai hos*
> *tetelesmenon estai*

> God-born son of Laertes, Odysseus, [you]
> multicontriver,
> 'Tis necessary, let me tell you, to speak out
> the un-sugar-coated myth,
> Just exactly the way I indeed instinctively
> sense it [in my *phren*] and as it will
> all come about in the end[9]
> (*Iliad,* 9.308–10)

Nagy employs this text to discuss a subtext that might explain the presence of the grammatical dual in the description of the embassy as a whole. But his philological sense here is somewhat misdirected, for what strikes the reader of Homer's text is not the presence of the grammatical choice of the dual elsewhere in the text so much as Achilles' insistence that *chre men de ton mython apelegeos apoeipein,* and that by the direct force of that full hexameter verse, Odysseus in this instance is under no such obligation. In short, it is not some divisively dramatic hatred between Achilles and Odysseus any more than it is some plot-fulfilling hatred between Achilles and Agamemnon that should lie behind our search of the Homeric *rheter mython.* If hatred be involved in Achilles' disbelief, it is only compounded by his hatred of Odysseus. It is defined by his hatred of Agamemnon. After all, Odysseus's

67

words are Agamemnon's (*Iliad*, 9.122–57 equals verbatim *Iliad*, 4.264–99). The philological point, however, is that Achilles sees no factual validity in Odysseus's attempt at persuasion. Odysseus does not proclaim that he is speaking "true myth," and his audience, including Achilles and ourselves, perceives or senses none. Odysseus does not "converse" with us; he is not overcome with a "passionate desire."[10]

After Odysseus delivers his unpersuasive harangue (*Iliad*, 9.225–307), Achilles evinces no amazement and refuses to enter into discourse, even though the "formulaic full verse" that contains the expected verb lies ready at hand. Why, as is the case a bit later with Ajax, does Achilles not accept Odysseus's harangue with a *panta ti moi kata thymon eeisao mythesasthai* ("you seem to myth me everything as I sense it" [645])? Why, on the contrary, does Peleus's son launch into a diatribe about true *mythos?* Once again, we need to reflect on the only place in *Iliad* 9 where Odysseus's words are accepted as myth and in wonder, that is, when he reports back to Agamemnon and the Achaean troops facts that are verifiable by others previously present:

> *mython agassamenoi. mala gar krateros*
> *agoreuse.*

> marveling at [the] myth; for indeed he
> addressed the assembly powerfully.
> (*Iliad*, 9.694)

Does his "power" arise from his persuasive "narration" of the event or from some kind of acknowledged factual truth of what he says? Did, moreover, his lack of myth in Achilles' ear devolve from the absence of such acknowledged truth, that is, of direct, unreflected, and sure meaning? Do Odysseus and the whole embassy, *paremenoi allothen allos* ("sitting [in contention?] one [side] against the other"), merely, as Achilles himself states, "coo like a dove" (*tryzete*, another interesting word that appears only once in Homer and, perhaps, in a slightly more individualizingly textual sense than is normally expected [311])?

There is another instance in Homer's text when another spurns a potentially significant dialogue with Odysseus, scornful Ajax at the bloody pit that opens to the underworld when he rejects Odysseus's following proposition:

> *all' age deuro, anax, hin' epos kai mython akouseis hemeteron . . .*

> But come here, prince, that you might hear the voiced word and myth
> that is ours [mine].
> (*Odyssey*, 11.561–62)

Ajax stands back aloof and in hatred, as Odysseus would have us believe, because of an affair over Achilles' arms, in which Odysseus had appeared the victor (*Odyssey*, 11.541–51). What leaps from the text, however, is that

Ajax distrusts how Odysseus might deal with the true facts in any *mythos* whatsoever. He rejects any discourse. Sophocles in the *Ajax* was to mark this difference in the two men as the distinction between the "character" of an archaic hero and the then modern sophist, but here in the Homeric text, the matter assumes a much more culturally interesting skew: whatever the facts of the matter about the loss of Achilles' shield might have been or are, Ajax dismisses any myth whatsoever about them in the mouth of the *polytropon*. His *mythos* could easily not "ring true" (*ouk . . . mythos etetymos* [*Odyssey*, 23.62; see *Hymn to Demeter*, 44]).

Ajax's response to Odysseus suggests that he rejects what Odysseus says because he does not trust his enemy's discourse. But why, in particular philological terms, is Odysseus's ability "to discourse" so much in doubt? Perhaps he is perceived through the merits or demerits of his epithet.

The problem with Odysseus, according to *Odyssey*, 1.1, is that he is *polytropon*. He is elsewhere also *polymetis, polymechanos, polytlas,* and *polyphron*. Whether these epithets be traditional, fixed, ornamental, and, hence, formulaic, or whether, as in the interesting case of *polytropon*, they are not,[11] the point of the matter is that Homer on one level of linguistic comprehension or another attributes to Odysseus a domain over "the many" that far excels that of any other man in his text. Whatever state of syntactical analogy might exist among the epithets cited above might be—and it is because of the possibility that I refrain from any specific lexical translation of each term—it is clear that Odysseus's problem with any act of persuasion he might perform lies in the multiplicities that obfuscate whatever truth his *mythos* might entail. In short, Odysseus is always at the mercy of the prefix that opens several of his epithets: *poly-*.

We need to understand Odysseus's relationship to *mythos* better and not fall into a Sophoclean error of perceiving the hero as a character somehow totally different from Achilles or Ajax and, therefore, potentially alien to the epic text. If the Homeric man is perceived as apart from the common ground of epic language, both he and hero become a closed and suspect quantity for any audience. Achilles and Odysseus are not different in what they and their audience seek on a proto-rhetorical level. There is no doubt whatsoever, as I indicated above in discussing *Iliad* 9, that at times Odysseus may be recognized as a true myth-sayer. Elsewhere, Alcinous touts him as such when he "myths" the woes of his life (*Odyssey*, 11.376), although, to be sure, it has been the case that Odysseus much earlier claimed himself capable of such an act (*Odyssey*, 7.213). One of the most touching instances of Odysseus's ability to speak directly and truthfully is attested to by Nestor when he compares Telemachus to his father:

> *sebas m'echei eisoroonta.*
> *e toi gar mythoi ge eoikotes, oude ke*

phaies andra neoteron hode eoikota
mythesasthai.

> Wonder
> holds me looking on you. For indeed 'tis true the
> very *mythoi* [you speak] are like [his], and you
> [one] would not aver that
> A younger man would speak *myth* thus similarly.
> <div align="right">(<i>Odyssey</i>, 3.123–25)</div>

Telemachus has made no bones of being Odysseus's son (*Odyssey*, 3.83–84), even though earlier he has queried Athena-Mentor about his ability to speak *mythoisi pykinoisin* ("with strong or deep myths" [*Odyssey*, 3.23]). Thus, like his son, Odysseus can speak true myth with the best of Homer's men: *Odyssey*, 9.16, in a verse linked to the revelation of Odysseus's name; 17.514, in a passage in which Eumaeus claims Odysseus's true myth, even when the husband is in disguise both from Penelope and from him; 18.342, when Odysseus threatens the lives of the wanton serving women; and, especially, 23.265, at the point where he tells Penelope of the clear symbol-sign (*sema ariphrades*)[12] that will appear to him at the point in time when Teiresias has foretold his death.

With archaic *semata*, however, we at last begin to focus more sharply on the "fact of myth," one that rests on immediate experience of recognition, just as much as does an audience's acceptance of Achilles as a *rheter mython*. It is important that in spite of a general reaction to the "truth" of symbol-signs in the forms of Zeus's thunderbolt or grave markers throughout the texts of Homer,[13] it is Odysseus, from his own view, who is continually drawn from his servants' recognition and particularly from Penelope's so that he and others may be involved with symbol-signs and the truth value of their immediate semiotic recognition. But, once again, that we might not tumble into Aristotle's view of the necessary components of a "reflecting judgment," a symbol-sign is neither a "viewed object" nor "abstract" in Homer but "made."[14] *Semata*, especially, have nothing to do with thought or thinking as Plato and Aristotle conceptualized that process.[15]

The guises that Odysseus assumes are strikingly ripped aside by a mutual recognition of signification that is one and the same with some wondrously created artifact: Odysseus's brooch, the bed created with the post of living olive, and especially the scar high on Odysseus's thigh, the "artful making" and wondrous properties of which necessitate the tale of Odysseus's youthful escapade and how it came to rest in the body of the man (19.392–468).[16] And it is from the last corporally entokened artifact that Odysseus himself will fear that "all the works might be made clear" (formulaic *hemiepes: amphada erga genoito* [19.391]). It is also this artifact that will help convince Penelope, as she searches for the *mythos etetymos* ("true myth" [23.62]), that Odysseus might well have destroyed the suitors, although Eurycleia's previous telling of their slaughter was not compelling (23.40–79). After Eurycleia announces the presence of the scar, however, Penelope will descend into the hall to see for herself the factual evidence of the dead suitors (*andras mnesteras tethneotas* [23.84]) and seek to establish the truth about her husband's presence *epei mega sema tetyktai / en lechei asketoi* ("since a great symbol-sign was fashioned / in the finely wrought bed [23.188–89]). Homer's texts reveal clearly a powerful relationship between *mythos* and a humanly worked ergon.

In the case of Odysseus as man, then, the truth of the matter lies in the mutual recognition of a making or doing that nothing in Odysseus's polytropaic manipulation can overcome. The details of the creation and perception become one in the recognition. The problem with Odysseus *polytropon* is never that he is outside the archaic "laws" of recognition of "truth." He simply makes them more difficult to apply because Homer's polytropaic lexis so oddly qualifies the way he speaks that his language requires further proof for an audience to recognize whatever myth he might assume or declare to possess. Such is Achilles' problem in *Iliad* 9 and Ajax's in *Odyssey* 11.

Therefore, true language in the Homeric texts assumes the property of immediate, somehow worked recognition. It is this that Achilles as a *mython te rheter . . . prektera te ergon* ("a speaker of myths and a practitioner of accomplished deeds" [*Iliad*, 9.443]) must be (*emenai* [*Iliad*, 9.443]). Far too little emphasis has been attached to this full, formulaic verse, for it reveals completely what kind of truth Homer and his language signify in all instances throughout his text.

Homer's truths are factual rather than fictive. Their truth quotient arises from verifiable deeds, not from some narrated or exemplary lies. As Otto noted, *"Es [mythos] ist das Wort der Tat und Wahrheit"* ("It is the word of deed and truth" [69]). A *mythos* must assuredly have taken place, be taking place, or take place in the future as verifiable fact in the human discourse into which a *rheter mython* enters. Whatever the language of truth in Homer might signify in its use in affirmative or negative response, for example, of *alethes*, *nemertes*, or *atrekes*, it must involve a "primary reference . . . to the transmission of information through [oral] discourse."[17] One replies to Homeric myth with a simple yes or no.[18] Instinct and not reflection lies at the base both of what is answered and of what is received. Homer's human myths "ring true," not because their language is "performed," "performative," or a "speech act,"[19] but because they do not partake in any way whatsoever of such mimetic and metaphorical representations on Aristotle's poetic and rhetorical stage. They are unreflected. Moreover, one special concern of the major classical Greek philosophers and their ancient and modern epigones cannot apply to Achilles, the *rheter mython:* Achilles simply "mythed" or asserted the instinctual nature in which we humans receive facts; Aristotle's *rhetor* had to narrate them.

A sense of a speaker's narrative veracity lies at the base of any difference between a Homeric *rheter* and an Aristotelian *rhetor*. Do we believe a man's

71

words are true because we sense a veracity in his words themselves or more indirectly simply agree with the narrated veracity of those words? There is a major cultural shift in perception in such a question that is more complex than might be admitted initially, for it must deal with philosophical readings of Homer's texts that were not executed in a broad philological sense, readings that, in the end, were to obscure truth in a mimetic objectivity that would distance an audience from fact as immediately experienced and, thus, perceived.

The first decisive blow against Homeric truth lay in Plato's reading the Bard's archaic texts for narrators and narration over any acknowledgment of an immediate, factual truth in nonwritten human discourse. The second blow came about with Aristotle's reinterpretation of Plato. Both involved a reading of Homer that substituted what was Hesiod's problematic use of *logos* for Homeric *mythos*.

Plato was obsessed by the "lying Homer," and although his inherent distrust of the Bard can be traced easily in several ways and in several dialogues, the most virulent attack in terms of how Homer uses language is in the *Republic*. The attack is couched in terms of *diegesis* ("narrative description") and *mimesis* ("imitation"), two abstract nouns in *-sis* not found in Homer's texts. At *Republic*, 392d–397c, Plato addresses the putative way Homer tells his tale. He declares that, first, all mythologues and poets speak a *diegesis* of things past, present, or future and that, second, all *diegesis* is of three types: unmixed, imitative (*dia mimeseos*), or both. He turns to *Iliad*, 1.1–67. The first sixteen verses, according to Plato, reveal Homer speaking in his own person in an unmixed, indirect discourse; but verses 17 through 67 show us a Homer falling into the pretense of speaking as if he were another in a mimetically direct discourse. Plato then has Socrates claim that the moral man will make use of very little mimesis indeed. In other words, in terms of ethical behavior, Homer was untrustworthy and a liar. He also did not write down his text in a dialogue form, which was for Plato, as we read at *Theaetetus*, 143b5–7, the philosophically acceptable way of arriving at Truth.[20] The last mode of communication that would have interested Achilles was a written dialogue.

Aristotle, receiving Plato's reading of the lying Homer in terms of the abstract notions of *diegesis* and *mimesis*, retained and developed narrative description and imitation with yet another twist of the philosophical dagger into the heart of Homer's text. The key Aristotelian text here is the *Poetics*.

Aristotle cannot separate *diegesis* from *mimesis*, either, and, like Plato, discovers both in epic (*Poetics*, 1459b26–27). The Philosopher, however, sets a greater value on *mimesis* itself, declaring that a poet should not speak in his own voice because such an act is not mimetic (*Poetics*, 1460a9). Aristotle is making the case here for drama on the stage over an orally transmitted epic. His reason becomes clear only if one considers the parallels between the ethical universals mouthed by an actor on a stage and, thus, visually separated from an audience and the objectification of universals in the Philosopher's epistemic method. To assume, however, the fictive role of a character in a play is not, perhaps, the most felicitous tack for a *rhetor* who must depend on his voice for a communication of truth somehow established in fact. In the end, Aristotle can attribute to Homer only the dubious honor of knowing how "to tell lies as they should be told" (*pseude legein hos dei* [*Poetics*, 1460a18; for further explanation, see all of 18 and 19]). All Aristotle establishes, in the end, is that "Lying comme il faut is a tolerated exception to the rule."[21]

What is central in all this to any discussion of rhetoric beginning with Aristotle is that it was the poetics of the represented and representing stage that the Philosopher used to shift from immediate truth in language to a reflected and reflecting notion of truth in what a man narrated: *diegesis* as a term in his legal *lexis* is "the statement of the case" (*Rhetoric*, 1416b–17b). From a purely theoretical or philosophical point of view, therefore, whatever truth might be, it has been abstracted away from any oral, experiential immediacy Homer's Achilles and Ajax knew, or, more to the point, from which they could know.

But what philologically cultural evidence might have suggested such a skew? How did this occur in the differentiating continuum of the Greek language? Once again, the focus must rest on how the philosophers read the Homeric texts, in this case how they particularized the character of the *polytropon* man, Odysseus, not as a *rheter mython* but as a *rhetor logon*.

Logos most probably entered the Greek language as a positively defined quasi-rational concept with Heraclitus,[22] but as a problematic choice of language, sometimes related to truth, sometimes to falsehood, it is in the texts of Hesiod that the term first arose with any clear-cut ambiguity. Yet, also in Hesiod's texts, "*logos* and *mythos* were . . . trapped within the same metaphysics,"[23] and truth, one expects concurrently, became "a notion of Truth" (*ein Wahrheitsbegriff*).[24] In short, once again, truth is seen shifting from fact to the objective fictions of philosophical certainty.

None of this rests easy within the Homeric texts, for although innumerable instances of *mythos* and *mytheisthai* are scattered throughout the *Iliad* and the *Odyssey*, and although the verb *legein* (oddly sharing forms from two roots, *leg-* and *lex-*, and signifying "to enumerate, tell, select," and "to lay") is also common, the plural noun *logoi* appears only twice, once in *Iliad* 15 in a scene where Eurypylus diverts Patroclus's attention from the war with pleasant chit-chat (*kai ton eterpe logois* [*Iliad*, 15.393]), and more ominously in *Odyssey* 1, where Circe is described as overcoming Odysseus's desire to return home: *aiei de malakoisi kai haimylioisi logoisin* ("and always with soft and wheedling words" [*Odyssey*, 1.56]). The adjective *haimylios* appears only once in Homer and is perhaps related to the adjective *haimon* ("cunningly"), another hapaxlegomenon found in a possibly formulaic phrase at *Iliad* 5.49: *haimiona theres* ("cunning in the hunt").[25] It is highly doubtful, because of the traditional nature of Homer's texts, that these were reflectively constructed neologisms of an individual poet. Both instances of these plural uses of *logos*, however, bespeak deceit; both easily could have focused the ethical attentions of both Hesiod and Plato and, consequently, suggest to the latter a "lying Homer" lodged someplace in the telling of tales.

Nevertheless, it is possible to anchor Plato's reading even more solidly in the *polytropon*'s putative narrative technique. The philological clue most probably rests in the verb *mythologeuein*, which Ebling, among others, dutifully translates as *loquor, narro* ("I speak," "I narrate").[26] Yet this verb occurs only twice in Homer within the space of four verses and at a point where Odysseus addresses Alcinous and his court about how he has delivered the multiple tales of his adventures.

Odysseus finishes by declaring again his arrival on Calypso's isle and asks:

> *ti toi tade mythologeuo;*
> *ede gar toi chthizos emytheomen eni oikoi*
> *soi kai iphthimei alochoi. echthron de moi estin*
> *autis arizelos [hapaxlegomenon] eiremena mythologeuein.*

> Why indeed do I myth-speak selectively these things?
> For 'twas no doubt just yesterday I mythed in your house
> And also to your powerful wife; to me 'tis detestable to myth-speak
> selectively again things spoken clearly.

> (*Odyssey*, 12.450–53)

In four hexameter verses lies the connection among Odysseus, Plato's "mythologue," Aristotle's *mythos* as "plot" rather than "factually verified speech," and, perhaps, the Philosopher's *rhetor* (from *eirein*, "to say," note *eiremena* [*Odyssey*, 12.453]). From these verses, too, one easily perceives why Plato's reading of the lines might well have identified, because of their proximity, *mytheisthai* with *mythologeuein* and have turned Western critics toward narrative in some putatively Odyssean vein.[27] Our preoccupations with truth, narrative, and rhetoric are inextricably intertwined. The same holds true for Aristotle.

But what of Homer? Do his texts bear out Plato and the contemporary critics, especially in a discussion of some kind of proto-rhetoric? First, whether Alcinous and his court accepted Odysseus's *mythos* as true or not—and there is no indication from the text that they do not—Odysseus intends his "collection and enumeration of myth" to be received as such. His only claim is that to retell events before the same audience could well be boring, not because of some vice of repetition—repetition, after all, is a central characteristic of Homer's traditional language at all grammatical levels—but because Odysseus, the "mythologue," has completed in full his tale and, as we see from the beginning of book 13, now wishes to expedite his return to Ithaca. Of course, he could have spoken a shorter catalogue of events, just as the books of the

Iliad could have been shorter or those of the *Odyssey* longer. Such is the case with the catalogue he speaks to Penelope as they delight each other with their verifiable experiences (*mythoisi* [*Odyssey*, 23.301]). His abbreviated response to his wife's equally brief *mythos* is a full catalogue of the facts without descriptive amplification, a bare-bones catalogue set loosely about the repetition of the beginning line marked ὡς (*Odyssey*, 23.310–43). Linguistically, it is not the length of what a man says but the clear, factual, repetitive cataloguing or enumeration of language that suggests the truth.

To Alcinous and to Penelope, Odysseus, the epic man, has spoken "true myths." Insofar as he has "mythologued" his language, he has simultaneously "mythed" it, and, indeed, the use of *mythologeuein* in the above passage indicates that he is aware of how he has performed his task "truly." The root sense of *-logeuein* lies in choosing fully and truthfully, as is the case with a similarly rooted verb *katalegein* ("to enumerate," "to catalogue") as it deals with Homeric "myth" (*mythos*), "truth" (*aletheie*), and "symbol-signs" (*semata*): *mython d' . . . epistamenos katelexas* ("you have catalogued myth in a knowing way" [*Odyssey*, 11.368]); *per aletheien katelexa* ("indeed I catalogued the truth" [*Odyssey*, 7.297]); and *ede semat' ariphrdea katelexas* ("you catalogued indeed clear and evident symbol-signs" [*Odyssey*, 23.225]). Odysseus has catalogued his language to enumerate the facts.[28] There is no indication whatsoever, as Plato and subsequently Aristotle would have us believe, that Odysseus in the Homeric texts is an inveterate liar, alienated from the culturally proscribed value of factual truth, or that his language similarly alienated him from a community that understood his polytropaic nature only too well. It was, however, through the philosophers' blinkered readings of Homer's text that Odysseus has come to be suspect, rather than simply acknowledged as "the man of many devices," that Socrates, the seeker of Plato's eidetic "truth," could never be identified with this particular epic hero, and why, especially, Aristotle was forced to select the non-Homeric term *proairesis* to somehow reformulate the rhetorical "problem" that Plato himself had created in his attempt to reinterpret communal values in terms of an eidetic premise.

Thus again, we arrive at Aristotle's *proairesis*, and, in conclusion, it is necessary to suggest why he plucked this non-Homeric word as the a priori value on which his whole science of rhetoric became contingent. The reasons are philological, cultural, and, ultimately, philosophical.

Language became for the Philosopher a self-fulfilling prophecy of the way he viewed the world. If, as Snell asserts, language from Homer through the Hellenistics exhibited a growing tendency toward abstraction, it was Aristotle's overriding ambition to codify the fact, whether or not the Greek for his process was drawn from Homer and whether or not his quest for universals based on "certain facts" might make human participation in events more difficult. His penchant for non-Homeric abstract nouns ending in *-sis* is everywhere prevalent. One could adduce *aisthesis, poiesis, anamnesis, diegesis, mimesis,* and so on. The present issue, however, is *proairesis*, what the term implies and what it does not.

Proairesis signifies literally "the abstraction of the act of drawing before." If some form of the related verb had existed in the texts of Homer, *pro-airein* would probably have meant simply "to draw" some phenomenon "before" another. Whatever the action or its participants, however, it would have been clear to an archaic man's immediate view, just as Homeric *pro-phainesthai* indicates "to shine forth" or "to be visible for oneself and another," and in the much vexed verse that deals with Homer's sense of time, the meaning of *pro* involves Calchas's sure knowledge (*eide*, "he knew") of the *pro t' eonta* ("and [what] it was before" [*Iliad*, 1.70]). In a rare case of an abstraction in *-sis*, Homeric *prophasis* appears twice as an adverb in the accusative case and signifies "ostensibly" in the sense of some legitimate and present appearance that could be applied to some other feeling or act: the women's grief for Patroclus (*Patroklon prophasin*) that each could apply to her own sorrow (*Iliad*, 19.302) or the pressingly present claim to make love (*eunes prophasin*), which Agamemnon swears he forswore in the case of Achilles' Briseis (*Iliad*, 19.262). There is no ethical ambiguity in the context of either usage, no calculated choice to speak and act truly or not. What one says in Homer often appears without reflection and is received as an immediate wonder.[29]

Aristotle's *proairesis*, then, reflects a hypotactic philology and philosophy that shift away from what might be characterized as Homer's view of the world, but this shift did not deny the necessity of truth as facts so much as it suppressed the issue. What Aristotle accomplished—and I make no judgment either upon its ultimate effectiveness or upon its unequivocal success—was to subvert the immediate, paratactic experienced fact of Homeric truth into a "certain truth" in the mimetic and objective rhetoric of the narrated poetic image.[30] As the philological nexus transformed itself from *mythos-ergon* into a *logos-ergon*, the philologically established *verum-factum* assumed the much more philosophical tone of a *verum-certum*, the judgment of truth over and above the instinctual, human recognition of present, sometimes clearly artifactual truth in what a man said. Homer speaks of "true myth" as *atrekes* ("not turning"); Aristotle seeks facts that may be "judged certain," that are *akribes* (from *akros*, "sharp," and *krinein*, "to judge").[31] In Homer, *akros* signifies a position that is "highest" or "at the top," and is never found in an adverbial context or compounded with the Homeric verb *krinein*.

In short, Aristotle's judgmental search for truth as absolutely (*haplos*) certain threw both philosophy and its narrating handmaiden, rhetoric, into a dilemma, recently characterized as "a distinction between the excellence of the object [read in this case "truth"] to be represented and the accuracy [*akribeia*, Aristotle's "rigid discipline"] with which the mind may know the object."[32] The concurrent necessity to turn truth into an object of philosophical investigation and hence rhetorical contingency in the name of a convincing narrative immediately opened to question the positive value of Aristotle's "art of rhetoric" and suppressed the audience's instinctual sense of what was "true language" in the unending questioning of what might be a "true argument" from an orator, whose *proairesis* might always be opened to doubt.

But just because Aristotle could not elevate as a narrative ploy the non-narrative sense of *verum-factum* in Homer, so could he not rid his speaker of an audience's instinctual support of his claim to truth, and it is on the surety of the Homeric reaction that Aristotle's art must depend if his particular brand of rhetorical hermeneutics is to convince any circle of perceiving human beings, even us. While in classical Greek the tools of rhetoric might well be lodged in a speaker (*rhetor*) or in the written treatises or the dicta of a *sophistes* (a "teacher of rhetoric," used more negatively in philosophy as an unethical "sophist"), the truth of rhetoric must always lie in the speaker's voice, not the teacher's or writer's arguments.

In Latin, the *rhetor* was the teacher and the *orator* was the speaker. Both terms are derived from the same root and reflect a shift away from the negative connotation of the classical Greek sophist. In this we see not only the cultural continuity always implied in any radical contingency of truth but, more important, the specific continuity Homer's texts supply in the discussion and practice of "true" rhetoric in the West. A Latin *rhetor* and a Latin *orator* must hold their constituencies' sense of recognized, archaic trust. The Latin recognizes clearly that the Aristotelian *proairesis* can lose its intellectually problematic appearance only in the recognition of instant, paratactic truth. Even though Homeric truth was suppressed in the method by which Aristotle dictated we achieve truth's knowledge, it reasserts itself through rhetoric's modes for human communication and discourse.

Aeneas in *Aeneid* 7 commands *centum oratores augusta ad moenia regis / ire* ("one hundred orator-ambassadors to go to the august ramparts of the king [Latinus]" [*Aeneid*, 7.153–54]) that his arrival might be known. The king *veteris Fauni voluit sub pectore sortem* ("revolves in his chest [Homeric *phren*?] the cast prophecy of ancient Faunis" [*Aeneid*, 7.254]) and recognizes Aeneas. The king declares:

> "hunc illum poscere fata
> et reor et, si quid veri mens augurat, opto."

> "that this is the man whom the fates call
> I both believe and [him], if my mind [Homeric *noos*?] instinctively augurs
> anything of truth, I choose."

> (*Aeneid*, 7.272–73)

Virgil's verses suggest much more than a flair for imitation; they prove that the factual kernel of Achilles' human communication is not suppressed but alive and well, a fact with which rhetoric since Aristotle must deal, if any kind of human knowledge is to be discovered in practice and in the art.

Notes

1. All translations are my own.
2. H. Frisk, *Griechisches Etymologisches Wörterbuch.* 2 vols. (Heidelberg: Carl Winter, 1955–70), II.654.
3. *Lexicon Homericum,* ed. H. Ebeling, 2 vols. (Hildesheim: Olms, 1963), I.1121–22. For the links among myth, epic songs (*epea*), and formulaic style, see Raymond Prier, *Thauma Idesthai: The Phenomenology of Sight and Appearance in Archaic Greek* (Tallahassee: Florida State University Press, 1989), 235–41.
4. See Prier, *Thauma,* 237; for summaries of various positions, M. W. Edwards, *Homer: Poet of the Iliad* (Baltimore: Johns Hopkins University Press, 1987), 218–19.
5. B. Snell, *Der Weg zum Denken und zur Wahrheit: Studien zur frühgriechischen Sprache* (Göttingen: Vandenhoeck & Ruprecht, 1978), 81.
6. Edwards, *Homer,* 224.
7. G. Nagy, *The Best of the Achaeans: Concepts of the Hero in Archaic Greek Poetry* (Baltimore: Johns Hopkins University Press, 1979), 42–58.
8. Ibid., 53.
9. It is important here not to confuse the Homeric *phren* with the Euripidean variety that may remain "unsworn"—*he gloss' omomoch', he de phren anomotos* ("the tongue had sworn, and the *phren* [was] unsworn" [*Hippolytus,* 612]). Whatever takes place in the Homeric *phren* does not designate what, by Euripides' time, came to mean "to think." Snell quite early on established the Homeric term in a sense beyond any Cartesian division of the mind and body: *phren* in Homer never assumes the meaning of a spiritual or mental activity (Snell, *Der Weg,* 54–55). He argued, to the contrary, that the *phren* deals with shock and some kind of "inner" reaction to it (59), never with a mental "reflection" (76). Snell adduced *Iliad,* 9.308–310, to illustrate his point and argued specifically, as does Achilles more generally at *Iliad,* 9.608, that the truth of the hero's assertions lie with his "apportionment from Zeus" (*Dios aisei* [80–81]). My sense here is that Snell grasped too quickly a simplistic explanation of events that points more to Achilles' character than to his language. Consequently, the audience is forced outside, rather than inside, the process he otherwise so admirably suggests and describes. As is the case with the Homeric *thymos* (*Iliad,* 14.195–96, 18.426–27), so is it with the *phren:* both intend a "fulfillment" (formulaic: *kai* [*ei* or *hos*] *telesmenon* [*estin* or *estai*]; compare *Iliad,* 9.310, 14.196, and 18.427). It is important that Snell translates *telesai* as *in die Realitat umzusetzen* ("to convert into reality" [79]), for it is what is "real" to Achilles that lies at the crux of his ability to speak and will eventually broach Aristotle's problematic grasp of the language of Homer.
10. See É. Boisacq, *Dictionnaire étymologique de la langue grecque,* 4th ed. (Heidelberg/Paris: Carl Winter/C. Klincksieck, 1986), 264–65.
11. Milman Parry, *The Making of Homeric Verse: The Collected Papers of Milman Parry,* ed. Adam Parry (Oxford: Oxford University Press, 1971), 154, 156. A word or two must be said generally about the problem of verifiably traditional and nontraditional language in Homer and particularly of the multitude of "poly-epithets" that cling to Odysseus. Milman Parry's work is useful in that he collected evidence of a poetic language that deals more with syntax, versification, and

sound than with specific lexical meanings and choices. Parry's explanation of his material was, for the most part, inconclusive, for it never could transcend the very Aristotelian dependence on individuals and universals that his collected evidence sharply refutes. In the case of the poly-epithets, however, he provides ample evidence that they apply to Odysseus overwhelmingly. (Compare Parry, *The Making of Homeric Verse,* 11–16, 39, 51–53, 95–96, 141–44, 154–56, 180–81.) The poly-epithets are neither particular in their meaning nor universal, but they are suggestive of a reaction Achilles, Ajax, and the audience (read in this case also "the reader") might possess toward the way language and its use might sharpen a difference between how Achilles and Ajax express truth and how Odysseus sometimes does not. Not one of the above poly-epithets is ever found linked to Achilles or Ajax, although metrical possibilities are not wanting, e.g., *polymetis Achilleus* or *polymechanos Aiae.*

12. Prier, *Thauma,* 199–201.
13. Ibid., 108–11.
14. Ibid., 112–14.
15. The contrary has been argued recently by Nagy in chapter 8 of his *Greek Mythology and Poetics* (Ithaca: Cornell University Press, 1990), 202–22. Adducing Indic *dhya-* ("think"), Nagy illustrates an "interpretive" and hence "cognitive" function between *sema* and *nous* ("mind") which he expresses in terms of "coding" and "decoding." The skew of his argument is much more Platonic than he openly admits, in that the intellectual activity and consciousness he adduces from a comparison of *noos, sema* as "sign" and "tomb," and *psyche* ("a conveyer of identity") differ little except in metaphor from Plato's antiscientific etymology which links *sema* to *soma* ("body") and asserts that the human body is a "seen tomb" or envisioned "memorial of the soul" (*Cratylus,* 400b–c). But we need more contextualization of the early Indic *dhya-* to prove that Homer's "thinking" is Plato's, let alone Aristotle's; an incorporation into the argument of Homeric *noema,* usually translated as "thought," but linked not to ponderous reflection but to "swiftness" (*Odyssey,* 7.36); and finally consideration of Hofmann's somewhat renegade linkage of *dhya-* to *dhi-* to *dhau-* and, hence, to *thauma* ("wonder"). See J. B. Hofmann, *Etymologisches Wörterbuch* (Munich: Oldenbourg, 1949), 310–11. Etymologically and contextually, *sema* is thereby bound to unreflected and immediate perception and action. The *noos* assumes the characteristics of *phren* (see note 7 above); *sema,* the characteristics of *thauma.* Homer's "semantic nexus" of experience becomes lodged in the language of *sema, erga* ("works," "deeds"), *thauma, phainesthai* ("to appear for oneself and another"), *idesthai* ("to see for oneself and another"), and *tetyktai* ("he made for himself and another") (Prier, *Thauma,* 157–91).
16. Prier, *Thauma,* 179–201.
17. A. T. Cole, "Archaic Truth," *Quaderni Urbinati* 42 (1983): 13–14.
18. Snell, *Der Weg,* 91–100. *Der Weg* is an important collection of those essays that most clearly reveal Snell's insights into the idiosyncratic properties of Homeric experience. Chapter 5 ("The Development of the Notion of Truth among the Greeks") was written specifically against Heidegger's false notion of archaic "Truth" and, as such, succeeds in dismissing any putative "onto-theological" essence of "Truth" from the Homeric treasure house of nonrepresentational

mental activity. The chapter is a shortened version of an earlier essay entitled "ALETHEIA" (*Festschrift Ernst Siegmann* [Würzburg: Schoningh, 1975], 9–17), which should be read by those interested in more Homeric examples to bolster the argument. In both pieces, as is the case in Snell's most popular work, *Die Entdeckung des Geistes*, 4th ed. (Göttingen: Vandenhoeck & Ruprecht, 1975), there lies an Aristotelian differentiation that too easily skews the cultural continuity of Homeric experience, with which we all must deal. If indeed, as Snell argues generally, mental activity moves from the concrete sense of Homeric experience to an abstract reflection of the philosophical sort, two reservations must always apply to any statement about how the Greeks or we "think": (1) the opposition concrete/abstract is purely an Aristotelian formulation designed by him, along with his notion of particulars and universals, to arrive at a "proper judgment," and (2) the philosophical penchant for an abstract lexis does not in any way minimize the continual operation of Homeric perception to the present day.

Snell defines "the three significant aspects, under which Homer sees what one later named the truth." Here, too, it is necessary to identify the Aristotelian, philosophical lexis that tends to creep into Snell's modern German prose:

alethes is that consistent, solid surety in memory (that in its fullness can be enumerated). ["Memory" in any functional sense is not found in the Homeric texts; *mnemosyne* appears as a hapaxlegomenon at *Iliad*, 8.181, with an imperative: *mnemosyne tis epeita pyros deioio genestho* ("then let some memory of blazing fire come about"). "Fullness" and "enumeration" are, however, characteristically Homeric perceptions of experience, especially when linked to "cataloguing."]

eteon is the factual [*Tatsächliche*], an objective Being [*ein objektiv Seiendes*] (that as such draws necessarily specific consequences, in sharp antithesis [*Gegensatz*] to Not-Being [*NichtSeienden*]). ["Objective Being" suggests too strongly the *De Anima*, and Snell's argument is not convincing that at *Iliad*, 2.299–300, when Odysseus asks the host to wait *ophra daomen / e eteon Kalchas manteuetai, ee kai ouki* ("that we may learn whether what Calchas foretells is true, or whether indeed it is not"), there arises the question of objective Being and Not-Being (Snell, *Der Weg*, 95–96). "Antithesis" or "opposition," moreover, too easily falls into some Aristotelian reading of a pre-Socratic, not entirely Homeric structure of thought. It is the relationship between *eteon* and the factual that is the insight here.]

nemertes is the Not-Failing [*Nicht-Verfehlende*] in especially the replying word (the "*Ant-Wort*"), that something factual [*ein Tatsächliches*] (*eteon*), at last comes about [*trifft*], when one makes inquiries about it.

(Snell, *Der Weg*, 100)

It is Snell's understanding of *nemertes* as "truth" that forms a common definition of all lexical choices in Homer that attempt to express the force of the human experience. Snell's attempt to color *alethes* with a "subjective" tone over an "objective" one (*Der Weg*, 109) is probably best explained by a zeal to crush Heidegger's "objective" fiction. Unfortunately, the philosophical debate tends to blur the central issue of language and human discourse that the root sense of all "truth" in Homer suggests

(Cole, "Archaic Truth," 27). (For distinctions among *nemertes, atrekes,* and *alethes* that Snell is unwilling to draw [*Der Weg*, 98], see Cole, "Archaic Truth," 17).

19. G. Nagy, *Pindar's Homer: The Lyric Possession of an Epic Past* (Baltimore: Johns Hopkins University Press, 1990), 32.

20. Prier, *Thauma*, 202, 275.

21. G. F. Else, *Aristotle's Poetics: The Argument* (Cambridge, Mass.: Harvard University Press, 1967), 632; see also G. F. Else, *Plato and Aristotle on Poetry* (Chapel Hill: North Carolina University Press, 1986), 163–84. The above three paragraphs are reductions from Prier, *Thauma*, 163–66, 201–2. I shift the facts here from a more general discussion of Homer's proto-narrative style to a context of rhetorical truth.

22. R. A. Prier, *Archaic Logic: Symbol and Structure in Heraclitus, Parmenides, and Euripedes* (The Hague and Paris: Mouton, 1976), 57–89.

23. P. Pucci, *Hesiod and the Language of Poetry* (Baltimore: Johns Hopkins University Press, 1977), 44.

24. Snell, *Der Weg*, 102.

25. See H. Frisk, *Griechisches Etymologisches Wörterbuch*, I.40; and Hofmann, *Etymologisches Wörterbuch*, 7; but also Boisacq, *Dictionnaire étymologique*, 25.

26. Ebeling, *Lexicon Homericum*, I.1122.

27. Recent critics of this ilk include M. Foucault, T. Todorov, G. Genette; see Prier, *Thauma*, 201–9.

28. Prier, *Thauma*, 210–11.

29. Ibid., 56–64.

30. K. Eden, *Poetic and Legal Fiction in the Aristotelian Tradition* (Princeton: Princeton University Press, 1986), 62–111.

31. Hofmann, *Etymologisches Wörterbuch*, 11; Boisacq, *Dictionnaire étymologique*, 39.

32. W. Trimpi, *Muses of One Mind: The Literary Analysis of Experience and Its Continuity* (Princeton: Princeton University Press, 1983), 97.

From Counter-rhetoric to Askesis: How the Phaedo Rewrites the Gorgias

BRUCE ROSENSTOCK

From Philosophic Practice to Philosophic Theory

In the "aporetic" dialogues (those that seem to end without arriving at firm conclusions) such as the *Euthyphro,* the *Laches,* or the *Lysis,* philosophy as it is practiced by Socrates seems to be a way of life much more than a theoretical pursuit.[1] To be sure, philosophy in those dialogues is the thoughtful investigation of what constitutes the excellences (*aretai*) of the individual, but it is an investigation with performative force: it both seeks to define and helps to produce those excellences, or so Socrates is made to insist. Examining one's beliefs about the nature of the human excellences is essential for the acquisition of those excellences. In the words of what is probably the best-known line in Plato: "An unexamined life is not worth living" (*Apology,* 38a5–6).

Reading the aporetic dialogues, one might forget that Socratic philosophizing was only one option among many for "doing" philosophy in classical Greece. Plato seems to be simply oblivious to the philosophic speculation of Heraclitus, Parmenides, and to the post-Parmenidean thinkers Empedocles, Anaxagoras, and Zeno. It is true that "theoretical questions" become prominent in some dialogues where Plato shows Socrates in confrontation with sophists (*Euthydemus, Hippias Major, Protagoras, Gorgias,* and, because Meno is represented as a student of Gorgias, the *Meno*), but these questions have mainly to do with the relationship between teaching and the excellences of the individual, and they emerge naturally from the conflicting practices of the sophists and Socrates.

It is first in the *Phaedo* that Socrates is made to expound views directly related to the theories of Heraclitus, Parmenides, and the post-Parmenideans.[2] Most of the dialogues that follow the *Phaedo* (especially the *Cratylus, Republic,*

Timaeus, Parmenides, Theaetetus, Sophist, and *Philebus*) reveal Plato's continuing interest in the metaphysical and epistemological issues of the philosophy that had preceded Socrates. It certainly would be wrong to say that these issues became the sole focus of his philosophizing, since the *Republic,* the *Phaedrus,* the *Statesman,* and the *Laws* continue to envision philosophy as a practice that holds the promise of producing human excellence. But it seems that Plato has altered his focus from that of the earlier dialogues. To put it most straightforwardly, Plato seems to have shifted from a view of philosophy as practice to a view of philosophy as theory.

There is a certain sense in which this shift looks like an abandonment of Socrates himself. Socrates engaged in the real life of the city, confronting its foremost citizens with questions that sought to elicit from them a justification of their political practice that went beyond mere popularity. The "speech practice" of Socrates ran directly counter to that of the powerful leaders of his day. He eschewed the set speech, the lengthy harangue, designed to elicit the right emotion with the most fitting words. In other words, Socrates quite deliberately refused to practice rhetoric, at least in its typical forms. Instead, he spoke in questions, directed at a single individual. For all that, his speech was powerfully effective. It is that speech practice, the so-called *elenchos,* that is represented in the aporetic dialogues.[3] But with the new theoretical interests ushered in by the *Phaedo,* Plato makes Socrates the spokesman for doctrines about the nature of reality that seem to have little to do with debunking the pretensions of political leaders.[4] Has Plato forsaken the Socratic engagement with the real life of the city? Has he abandoned what might be called Socratic counter-rhetoric for a theory-oriented philosophic discourse?

Those are the questions to which this essay is addressed.[5] I hope not to answer them in all of their ramifications but to look closely at two dialogues in which the shift from Socratic counter-rhetoric to theoretical discourse seems quite marked. If by comparing the *Gorgias* with the *Phaedo* we might be able to find some underlying pattern that links Socrates the citizen with Socrates the theorist, then perhaps the long-standing contrast between rhetoric as engaged with the realm of practice and philosophy as engaged with theory, a contrast that owes much to a certain reading of Plato, might be called into question. What I am proposing, then, is to return to the scene of the rhetoric/philosophy divide and examine how this divide is marked out. I hope to show that Plato's apparent rejection of Socratic counter-rhetoric, the method of *elenchos,* in favor of theory is really another way of engaging in battle with the standard rhetorical practices of the day. And if this is true, then we might continue to describe Platonic philosophy, even when it seems most theoretical in its aims, as a form of counter-rhetoric. We therefore can see how Platonic philosophical theory remains rooted to the Socratic way of life, which, as the *Gorgias* most clearly shows, is an embodiment of what I have called a counter-rhetoric.

The *Phaedo*: Ontology of Human Desire

WHAT EXACTLY IS the nature of the change in Plato's conception of philosophizing that is marked in the *Phaedo*?[6] Let us, first of all, be somewhat more precise about how Plato brings pre-Socratic speculation within the compass of the dialogue. Very briefly, Plato describes the world in terms inherited from, on the one hand, Heraclitus and, on the other, Parmenides. In the *Cratylus* (see 440c1–3) and again in the *Sophist* ("It seems that there has been a sort of battle of the giants in the debate about being" [246a4–5]), Plato will state very clearly that in the past there have been essentially only two alternative versions proposed concerning the nature of reality: that everything is in movement and a thing's stable identity through time is only apparent, or that whatever is is unchanging and all movement is illusory. The first version he associates with Heraclitus and his followers, the second with Parmenides and the Eleatic school. (Plato is not, and has no pretension of being, a historian of philosophy, and so his representations of Heracliteanism and Eleaticism should not be taken as faithful portraits of these two very complex movements.) In the *Phaedo* and indeed in all his later reflection on these issues, Plato will attempt to fit both Heracliteanism and Eleaticism within his own version of the nature of reality. In the *Phaedo,* the realm of the body and sensation is given over to something approaching a Heraclitean flux (his several descriptions of the physical world make it hard to know how much stability he really grants it), while the realm of the soul and intellect possess an Eleatic-like permanence. In some way deliberately left vague, the Heraclitean physical world participates in the Eleatic intelligible world and stands in a relation of dependence on it.[7]

Plato's "two-world ontology," as his fusion of Heraclitean and Eleatic views has sometimes been called, is first introduced in the *Phaedo* in order to explain why the soul of the philosopher seeks to free itself as much as possible from its association with the body. The philosopher seeks above all to acquire *phronêsis,* "intellectual discernment." In the dialogues preceding the *Phaedo, phronêsis* had been the knowledge of the good that should guide the soul in all its actions, because it is only with *phronêsis* that "all the soul's efforts and exertions end in happiness" (*Meno,* 88c1–3). The acquisition of *phronêsis* could begin only when the individual had been led into *aporia* about all that he previously had thought was good, just, fair, and so on, but there was hardly a suggestion that one needed to free oneself from the deceptive reports of sight and hearing in order to have a clear mental grasp of the good and the just. In the earlier dialogues, the obstacle to *phronêsis* was the false belief that one already knows what the good is; in the *Phaedo,* that obstacle is the body. More precisely, pleasure, pain, sight, and hearing are the obstacles to *phronêsis*: "It [the soul] reasons best when it does not suffer from these things, neither from sight nor hearing, nor pain, nor pleasure, but rather when it comes to be just as it is in itself as much as possible and leaves the body behind, and, to the extent that it is able to have nothing to do with it and to hold itself distant from it, the soul longs for what is [*to on*]" (65c5–9).

Plato offers several reasons in the *Phaedo* for condemning the body as the obstacle to *phronêsis*. The first has to do with the inaccuracy of the reports of the senses: "Does the combination of sight and hearing give men the truth, or is what the poets are always telling us really the case, that we neither hear nor see anything accurately?" (65b1–4)[8] The inaccuracy of sight and hearing, however, cannot be the most significant reason for the philosopher's flight from the body, because the objects in which the philosopher is interested (the good and the just, for example) are unlikely ever to be sought for among the visible and audible objects, and it is hard to understand how inaccurate reports about sensible objects could cause one to lose track in one's thinking about the good.

The more telling reason for the philosopher's rejection of the body has to do with the body's desires or, as we might more accurately express it, the desires of the human that have to do with the satisfaction of bodily needs. While even the basic desire for nourishment can interrupt the philosopher's contemplation, more dangerous and disturbing are desires for objects that are not necessary for simple survival. Plato explains (*Phaedo*, 66b7–67a6) that the body fills us with "passions and desires and fears and all sorts of imaginings and a multitude of vanities," and that the body even brings on wars because it is the source of the desire for property. Only by distancing ourselves from the body and its desires, Plato concludes, can we hope to come close to acquiring knowledge.

Plato will explain later how the deceptiveness of the senses is related to bodily desire. The link is to be found in the nature of pleasure and pain. Intense pleasure or pain, he says, makes us judge its cause to be most true and clear (see 83c5–8), "and when the soul is companion to the body and serves it and loves it, it is deceived by it and its desires and pleasures into believing nothing is true but what is corporeal, what it can touch and see and drink and eat and make love to" (81b2–6).

The real culprit in this tale is the desire for pleasure and not the inaccuracy of the senses or, what is related to it, the unstable nature of the objects of sense perception. In fact, the very language Plato uses to describe the effect of the senses upon the soul more appropriately describes the effect upon it of powerful desire. In one passage (79c2–8), Plato declares that "when the soul makes use of the body in investigating something, either by means of sight or hearing or some other sense . . . the soul wanders lost [*planatai*] and is distressed and dizzy as if it were drunk." In a passage (81a4–8) just a little beyond this, however, Plato describes the postmortem condition of the pure (*kathara*) soul as being "completely released from wandering [*planê*] and senselessness and fears and wild passions." It seems very clear that Plato is attempting to fuse into a single account a Heraclitean analysis of the nature of the physical world and a description of the soul's enslavement to bodily desire.

Similarly, Plato's account of the soul's purification from the body and its corrupting passions is tied to a newly adopted Eleatic portrayal of the objects of the soul's contemplation when it is "just by itself" (*autê kath' hautên*). Such objects (Plato mentions as examples the just, the fair, the good, magnitude, health, and strength in a first listing at 65d4–13, and later adds the equal, the greater, the less, and the holy at 78c9–d1) cannot be apprehended through the senses, are not composed of parts, and never suffer any change or alteration. These objects, Plato has Socrates inform us, are the very same objects about which Socrates and his interlocutors had been "asking questions and giving answers" (75d2–3) all along, each of which they had labeled "the very thing which is" (*auto ho esti*, 75d2); they are the things "we have always been harping about" (76d8). In all those discussions as they are represented in Plato's early dialogues, there is no indication that the objects, often called forms, about which Socrates is asking have a special ontological status, namely, that of being wholly immune to any kind of change and possessing no parts. It went without saying that Socrates was not interested in something physical, but it does not take an Eleatic philosopher to understand that not everything we talk about can be looked at, or heard, or felt, or weighed upon a scale. And, of course, if one agreed to engage in a discussion about justice or piety, one believed quite naturally that any answers that might be forthcoming would not require revision the next day because justice or piety in the meantime had suffered some alteration in its identity. Believing this certainly did not commit one to Eleaticism regarding justice and piety. It would appear that just as Plato has imposed a Heracliteanism upon an already worked-out theory of desire, so he has formulated the presuppositions of the earlier dialogues' questions and answers about forms in terms derived from Eleaticism.

What has led Plato to adopt the two-world ontology of the *Phaedo* as a framework within which to describe the soul's enslavement to desires that are alien to its true nature and its subsequent release from this enslavement through the practice of philosophy? The traditional form that most answers to this question have taken is that given by Plato's pupil Aristotle: Plato was persuaded by the Heraclitean philosopher Cratylus to consider all sensible objects as in flux and, seeking to legitimize the Socratic quest for unchanging definitions of the moral virtues, posited a realm of nonsensible forms to serve as the objects of such definitions. There is no question that Plato in the *Phaedo* sees his "theory of forms" as unpacking the unspoken "ontological commitments" behind the Socratic *elenchos*, but this is not its major function. The intellection of the forms is the object of the soul's desire (66e1–4); the physical world provides the objects of bodily desire. The soul desires what is eternal, the body what is transitory. The theory of forms is, in the *Phaedo*, primarily the ontology of desire.

The question we face, then, is this: Why has Plato chosen to offer an ontology of desire, and why does he use a mixture of Heracliteanism and Eleaticism in order to do so? What has led Plato into this realm of philosophic speculation and apparently away from the dramatic recreation of Socrates in conflict with the accepted beliefs of the city? What has led Plato apparently to reject Socratic counter-rhetoric for a clearly un-Socratic doctrine that calls for world-renouncing *askesis*?

The *Gorgias*: Philosophy Confronts Rhetoric

IF WE ARE adequately to understand why Plato found it important to offer a Heraclitean/Eleatic ontology of desire, we must look at a dialogue whose principal focus is the nature of human desire, the *Gorgias*. The *Gorgias's* analysis of the two objects—the good and the pleasant—which each define two types of desire, and of the corresponding two instruments by means of which desires can be satisfied—knowledge and flattery—lies behind the two-world ontology of the *Phaedo*, as I hope to show. In order to answer the question of why Plato has adopted Heraclitean and Eleatic terms to describe an ontology of desire, we must chart the course that leads from the *Gorgias* to the *Phaedo*.

As briefly stated above, Plato's representation of Socrates in some of the aporetic dialogues has as one of its aims the dramatization of how Socratic *elenchos* could unveil the contradictions that obtain within the moral discourse of the city. Those individuals (such as Miletus and Anytus) whose power or (such as Protagoras) whose livelihood lay in their ability to master the rhetorical resources of the city's moral discourse were unmasked by the *elenchos* as being unable to answer without contradicting themselves the simplest questions about the meaning of the terms of that discourse. In the *Gorgias* more than any other dialogue of Plato's early period, Plato shows us a Socrates engaged in a battle with the power at the heart of the city.

The battle in which Socrates is engaged is one in the human sphere which, in the much later *Timaeus*, Plato describes as being at the heart of the cosmos itself: the battle between Reason (*Nous*) and Compulsion (*Anagkê*) (*Timaeus*, 48a1). The power of the democratic city, as it is revealed in the figures of Thrasymachus (in *Republic* 1) and Callicles (in the *Gorgias*), is wielded by those who know how to use speech as an instrument of Compulsion in the achievement of what they take to be their self-interest. Such speech is the disguise the demagogue assumes in order to conceal the fact that his power is no less brutal than that of a tyrant. Plato in the *Gorgias* is not primarily interested in this disguised tyrant, nor even in the deceived *dêmos*, but in the power of speech to generate illusions that can enslave the city, tyrant and *dêmos* alike. This is not a simple problem of mass psychology but one that must be phrased in terms that go far beyond politics or sociology. Plato sees the battle between the speech of Socrates and the speech of the democratic city as a battle waged for the soul of man.

Plato in the *Gorgias* thematizes this battle within the framework of his analysis of the nature of rhetoric. Rhetoric was the art of persuasion taught by sophists such as Protagoras and Gorgias and, in Plato's day, by Gorgias's pupil Isocrates, who also ran in Athens a school of what he called *philosophia.* Plato's analysis of rhetoric and its relation to philosophy begins with the *Gorgias,* a dialogue probably composed not long before the *Phaedo,* continues throughout his middle period (in the *Republic,* for example, especially in book 6's discussion of the corruption of the philosophic temperament), and culminates in the *Phaedrus.*

As I have said, the *Gorgias* more than any other dialogue of the early period shows us Socrates engaged in combat on behalf of philosophy against the power that rules within the democratic city. One might say that the combat is a mortal one: the dialogue has to do with nothing less than how one should lead one's life, two views being pitted against each other, each claiming that the other, if followed, will lead to the loss of one's life. Callicles, at whose house Gorgias, a native of Sicily, is visiting, tells Socrates that philosophy renders one helpless before those who would bring one, though innocent of all wrongdoing, to trial for one's life. Socrates responds by representing rhetoric as being of no avail to one who stands before the judge of the netherworld, the marks of one's previous injustice visible upon one's naked soul. There is no neutral ground between Callicles and Socrates; the reader is made to feel that, like Prodicus's Heracles before the paths of Vice and Virtue, he stands at a crossroads where he must make a choice, and that this choice, if he believes Socrates, will determine into which path his judge in the afterlife will direct him, either to his punishment in Tartaros or to his reward on the Isles of the Blest.[9] The life-and-death combat at the heart of the dialogue is suggested by its first words, "war and battle" (*polemou kai machēs*).

Socrates vs. Gorgias: Is Rhetoric an *Epistêmê*?

THE BATTLE IS pitched with Socrates' first question to Gorgias after he has ascertained that Gorgias claimed to have knowledge of the skill (*technê*) of rhetoric. He asks, "With what of the things which are does rhetoric happen to be concerned?" (499d1–2). Eventually, Gorgias and Socrates will agree that rhetoric's whole concern is with persuasion (453a2–3) and that the arena in which it seeks to effect its persuasion is that of public deliberations about what is and is not just (454b5–7). Gorgias admits that persuasion produces belief (*pistis*) and not knowledge (*epistêmê*), the former being fallible, the latter not (454e3–455a2). But he claims that the persuasive power of rhetoric is greater than that of knowledge, since a rhetorician could convince a crowd to heed his advice over that of one who had knowledge but lacked the skills of rhetoric

(456a7–c8). Because rhetoric has such extraordinary power, it is proper that the one who employs it do so for just ends; if he does not, however, one should find fault with the rhetorician and not with rhetoric (456c8–457c3).

Socrates agrees with Gorgias's claim that rhetoric can create belief in an audience that does not itself have the relevant knowledge, and, Socrates gets Gorgias to concede, one of the beliefs it creates is that the rhetorician addressing the audience possesses knowledge about the matter at hand. Socrates then wants to know whether Gorgias would say that the rhetorician really knows or only seems to know what is just and what is not—the subject with which Gorgias had said rhetoric specifically dealt. Gorgias explains that the rhetorician possesses a knowledge not only of justice but also of what is good and bad, noble and shameful.

In one portion of the latter interchange between Socrates and Gorgias, we find Plato using language resembling that of the *Phaedo*. He has Socrates ask: "So this is how the rhetorician and his rhetoric are related to all the other skills: it isn't necessary for him to know the things themselves [*auta ta pragmata*], how they are [*hopôs echei*], but he must discover some means of persuasion whereby he will to a greater extent seem (to those who lack knowledge) to possess knowledge than those who in fact have knowledge" (459b6–c2). Here "the things themselves" are the objects of the various kinds of knowledge. The rhetorician does not have knowledge, but he uses his persuasive skill to make himself appear to have knowledge. In the *Phaedo*, Socrates refers to "the things themselves" as the objects of "unpolluted" knowing, when the soul is freed from the body: "It has been truly shown by us that, if we are ever going to know anything unpollutedly, the soul must be freed from the body and it must view the things themselves" (66d7–e2). The *Phaedo* distinguishes things like the just itself and the good itself from the objects of sensation, but in the *Gorgias,* knowledge of the just, the good, the fair, and so on are distinguished from the conviction (*peithô*) about them that it is in the rhetorician's power to produce. The rhetorician can create through the power of his speech the illusion of knowledge in cases where he has none. It is certainly not the case that Plato in the *Gorgias* would say that either the rhetorician's or his audience's false beliefs have sensible particulars as their objects, as in the *Phaedo*'s analysis. One way of characterizing the change from the *Gorgias* to the *Phaedo* is to say that in the *Phaedo,* the senses have assumed the function that the rhetorician possesses in the *Gorgias.*

But we are running ahead of ourselves. Let us return to the argument of the *Gorgias.* As I have mentioned, Gorgias claims that the rhetorician actually will know the just and the good. Socrates finishes his discussion with Gorgias by getting him to acknowledge that his previous remarks about how one should blame the rhetorician and not rhetoric for the misuse of his skill implicitly contradict his ultimate claim about the rhetorician's knowledge of the just. For how can one who knows what is just and good deliberately do what is contrary to what he knows is best?

Socrates vs. Polus: Rhetoric as Mere Flattery

GORGIAS AND SOCRATES do not pursue this question, because it is at this point that Polus breaks into the discussion and, angry at Socrates for never risking an opinion of his own, asks him what he believes rhetoric is. Socrates is ready with an answer, one, in fact, derived from Polus's own handbook on rhetoric:

> *Polus:* What do you think rhetoric is?
> *Socrates:* Something which you yourself make it out to be in your book which I have just read.
> *Pol.:* What are you referring to?
> *Soc.:* I call it a kind of "knack" [*empeiria*].
> *Pol.:* Rhetoric, you think, is a knack?
> *Soc.:* I do, unless you call it something else.
> *Pol.:* And a knack for what?
> *Soc.:* For showing favor [*charis*] and producing pleasure. (462b10–c7)

By defining rhetoric as a knack, Socrates is denying that there is a set of strictly defined rules that can be followed and that will guarantee the production of persuasive speech. We know that Isocrates, too, believed that the best a teacher could do was to provide a repertoire of standard approaches (he called them forms) to basic situations which, through practice, would become more and more easily reworked into extemporaneously produced variations. To call rhetoric a knack, therefore, is not in itself derogatory. The attack on rhetoric depends more on its association with pleasure than with the manner in which one learns it.

Socrates will go on to explain that rhetoric, lacking a clearly defined set of rules, is not a skill (*technê*) at all, but, because it has to do with the production of pleasure, it is a kind of flattery (*kolakeia* [463b1]). For every kind of flattery there is a corresponding skill; the flattery is an image (*eidôlon* [463d2]) of the skill. The kinds of skill and, similarly, the kinds of flattery fall under two large classifications: those that relate to the soul and those that relate to the body. The whole domain of skills that relate to the soul Socrates calls "political" (464b3); the domain of skills that relate to the body does not have a single name. Rhetoric is an image of one part of the domain of political skills (463d1–2). "Bodily" skills are divided into two kinds: gymnastics and medicine. Political skills, likewise, are divided into two kinds: legislation and justice. Legislation is related to the soul as gymnastics is to the body; justice in respect of the soul corresponds to medicine in respect of the body. The skills of legislation and gymnastics maintain the condition of their objects so that they function well; the skills of justice and medicine correct the dysfunctioning of their objects and restore them to their proper condition. All four skills serve their objects with an eye to what their best condition is (*pro to beltiston therapeusai* [464c3]). Having laid out the structure of the domain of skills and their several functions, Socrates proceeds at last to describe the realm of flattery and rhetoric's place within it. He speaks of flattery as if it possessed a will of its own:

> Flattery, having perceived [the structure of the four skills]—it doesn't have knowledge but it only makes guesses—divides itself into four, and slides beneath each of the parts [of the domain of skill], and pretends to be that very part beneath which it has slid. It doesn't give a thought for what is best, but by means of what is immediately most pleasant it hunts its prey, senselessness, and deceives it, so that it comes to seem to be something of great worth. (464c5–d3)

Of the domain of flattery related to the body, one part, cookery, slides beneath the domain of medicine; another, cosmetics, beneath gymnastics. Of the domain related to the soul, one part, sophistry, pretends to be legislation, and the other, rhetoric, passes itself off as justice (465b1–c3).

The manner in which sophistry and rhetoric work their flattery upon the soul will involve, if it is to parallel that of cooking and cosmetics, the existence of certain pleasures whose gratification provides the incentive for the soul's critical judgment to let itself be persuaded that the rhetorician and the sophist are truly exercising political skills aimed at what is best. Those who are taken in by the sophist and the rhetorician will believe of them that they know what is just and good and noble, and they will believe of themselves that they are just and good and noble, when they are, in fact, quite the opposite.

Socrates vs. Polus: Rhetoric as the Instrument of Tyranny

BUT WHAT EXACTLY are these pleasures that the false belief in one's own justice (and the *rhetor*'s knowledge) permit one to enjoy? It is possible, of course, that this false belief is, in itself, a source of pleasure for those who hold it. The rhetorician and the sophist, then, would only be serving the crowd's need to see itself in the best possible light. But what aim does the rhetorician have in flattering the crowd? Here the story Plato wants to tell gets more complicated and more sinister. Unlike the cook and the cosmetician who are only trying to make a living from their flattery, the sophist and the rhetorician are using their flattery to gain power. Far more serious than the crowd's false belief that it is just when it is not, is the rhetorician's belief that the power he is seeking within the city is the most desirable object for a human to pursue.

This is precisely the claim with which Polus counters Socrates' condemnation of rhetoric. Polus retorts that "rhetoricians have the greatest power in cities" (466b4–5), and "like tyrants, they kill whomever they wish, they confiscate property, and they banish whomever they like from their cities"

92

(466b11–c2). The pleasure the rhetorician is seeking is not that of being thought of as a just man; it is the pleasure he believes limitless power might afford him.

We must further ask how any man could come to believe that tyrannical power is eminently desirable. As we pursue this question, we will find that the rhetorician and the crowd are not at all different in their fundamental desires and that both, without knowing it, are enslaved to an illusion about what happiness is, namely, that it consists in fulfilling all of one's desires, whatever they may be. The pleasure of such total gratification is, for those who are taken in by this illusory ideal, *the* human good. We must wait for Callicles to make this claim explicitly about the nature of the human good, but we may detect hints of it already in what Polus says.

Polus believes that the rhetorician, like the tyrant, is able to achieve all he wants from the power he wields in the city. Polus is quite ready to admit that the rhetorician often will use this power unjustly in the service of what he takes to be his personal good. Socrates will argue that no unjust act can serve the good of the agent, and, since no one wants to do that which does not lead to his good, the rhetorician is not really achieving what he wants. His power, therefore, turns out to be impotence, since what he gains by it is not really what he seeks, namely, his own good.

This argument depends on Polus's acceptance of Socrates' claim that injustice, the means the tyrant employs to achieve his ends, is shameful (*aischron*) and justice noble (*kalon*). Given this admission, Socrates can force Polus to admit that, since no one willingly does what is shameful, the tyrant does not act willingly and in full knowledge of what is good for him when he commits an injustice. It might seem strange that one who finds ruthless tyranny enviable would accept Socrates' characterization of injustice as shameful, but Polus has not gone at all beyond conventional morality. In fact, he is portrayed as its spokesman. Like the crowd whose judgments he simply mirrors, Polus finds the tyrant's ability to satisfy his every whim enticing and desirable, but the method whereby this power is exercised he sees as base and ignoble. The crowd finds the great criminal an alluring figure but condemns him for his crime nonetheless.

Socrates vs. Callicles: Rhetoric Creates
the Tyranny of Illusion and the Illusion of Tyranny

It is only Callicles who will be bold enough to reject conventional morality's condemnation of the tyrant's injustice. He claims that the crowd mouths its praise of justice because it fears the tyrant's strength. The tyrant, he says, is the only man who has the courage to seek what all men desire, though most are too cowardly to risk their lives in pursuit of it. They would rather mask their cowardice with the fine language of justice's nobility. Surrounded by the crowd, the individual, previously cowardly and weak, now finds strength and even a superiority over the would-be tyrant. Callicles declares real justice to be the ascendancy of that individual who has the strength and the courage to be what all others secretly wish to be. In the democratic city, such an individual must rely on the subtle violence of rhetoric to achieve his purposes. The crowd will become this man's willing servant, not because he makes them believe themselves to be just when they are not (although he does do this) but because he gives them (at least partial) satisfaction of their own rapacious desires. He satisfies the crowd's desires by offering them victims, and these are precisely such men as Socrates, who have never learned how to defend themselves against the machinations of power. Men like Socrates, Callicles says, are naive enough to believe sincerely that justice is noble and good and spend their days in the leisured pursuit of wisdom ("philosophy") apart from what they see as the madness of practical life. Callicles explains that the tyrannical rule of others is desirable because it allows the ruler to "permit his desires to grow as large as possible," and, since "luxuriance and indulgence" constitute true happiness, only the tyrant is truly happy (*Gorgias*, 491e5–492c8). Socrates responds: "Your candor in coming forth with this argument is not ill-bred, for you express in clear language what all other men think, but are unwilling to say" (491e5–492c8). We have reached the heart of the illusion that rules within the city. Everyone, be he demagogic rhetorician or one of the crowd swayed by his speech, believes that the unbridled pursuit of pleasure constitutes human happiness. But the crowd, unlike the demagogue, will not admit to this belief and seeks to flatter itself about its justice and temperance. The crowd is as rapacious as the demagogue, but, unlike the demagogue who seeks tyranny, it also wants to be on the side of justice. Those who make up the crowd are too afraid to let their rapaciousness have free rein.

If Callicles is right and pleasure is the human good, then Socrates' distinction between the skills that tend the soul with an eye to what is best and the knacks or flatteries that merely make the soul seem good, although they make it "feel good," cannot stand. If Callicles is correct, what is best would not be different from what is pleasant, and so the whole domain of soul-directed skill must be rejected as illusory, as false images (*eidōla*) of the knacks of sophistry and rhetoric. And what would be the consequence of this? We could not describe rhetoric and sophistry in any other way than to say that they would be the illusion of an illusion, because it would remain their object to mimic those skills that, however, do not really exist. The rhetorician can never simply declare himself to be a flatterer; he must assume the trappings of the statesman and legislator. And, further, the most real thing about the soul would be its desires for pleasure, and these desires, once satisfied, need to be fed by ever new objects. In other words, the soul, on Callicles' rendering, would inhabit a universe of ever-shifting illusions. Although Callicles finds such a universe a fitting backdrop for the cunning ruthlessness of his hero, the tyrant, Socrates sees it as nothing less than hellish. But despite their differing attitudes toward it, both men agree that one place in particular is the embodiment of a world given over to the reign of flattery. That place is Athens.

Later in the *Gorgias,* Socrates will describe the city of Athens as a place where the quest for pleasure has become the sole reality. The policies of Athens, he will say, are motivated by nothing less than the crowd's rapacious needs, abetted by their politicians' readiness to discover new ways to serve those needs. Socrates describes all of Athens's past leaders as men

> who laid out a feast before them [the Athenians] and catered to their desires. People say that they were responsible for making the city great, but they don't realize that the city has become swollen and bloated because of these "elder statesmen." For they filled the city with harbors and dockyards and walls and revenues and other such rubbish, but they left it vacant of temperance and justice. And when its inner weakness will bring the city's collapse, men will blame those who had offered counsel, but they will continue to honor Themistocles and Kimon and Pericles, who are truly responsible for their ills. (518e2–519a7)

The democratic city, Athens being its prime representative, lives wholly by its illusory strength and security which its demagogues maintain for it. Indeed, the city is nothing less than a theatrical spectacle in which stagecraft has usurped the place of statecraft. Socrates speaks of the theater as rhetoric with a musical dress, and by implication the city is a theater where the players and the audience no longer can be distinguished.

If Callicles is right and it turns out that political skill exists only as a false image projected by rhetoric, its front, so to speak, within the spectacle of the city, if, in other words, Callicles is right about pleasure being the human good, then there would be no hope that the spell cast by rhetoric upon the city might be broken.

Socratic Counter-rhetoric:
The True Statesman as True Rhetorician

But Socrates will not admit that pleasure is the human good, and he brings a very reluctant Callicles to concur. The good being different from pleasure, there must be a skill that serves it. It is not essential for our purposes that we trace the course of Socrates' argument to show that pleasure is not the good (495a–500a). More significant is Socrates' reformulation of the dichotomy between political skill and mere flattery. In this reformulation, we find him describing the method whereby any skill functions in executing its proper task, and the description includes a reference to the "form." He says (503d6–504a1) that craftsmen do not "set about their several tasks by a random application of procedures, but they seek to invest whatever they produce with form [*eidos*]" so that the resultant product is an "arranged and ordered [*kekosmenon*] object." Working like a craftsman, the true statesman, "the skillful and good rhetorician" (504b6), will direct his gaze to that which will invest the soul with order (*kosmos*) and arrangement, and this is justice and temperance. Until the soul comes to acquire justice and temperance, the good rhetorician will chasten its desires (505b1–5) and attempt to bring them into conformity with law (504d2). When the good rhetorician, who himself has knowledge of what justice is (508c2), has given order (*kosmos*) to the individual soul and to the city, both will resemble the cosmos itself.

Whereas Callicles stressed the tyrant's deliberate indulgence of limitless desire, Socrates emphasizes the statesman's commitment to order, limit, and form. Against Callicles' vision of soul, city, and world ruled by force and torn by enmity, Socrates proposes that all three should be bound together by friendship and order. But this can be so only if the speech of the demagogue is replaced by the speech of the statesman. Plato does not tell us in the *Gorgias* how this might take place or precisely what the just city would look like. Plato is only intent on demonstrating that the Calliclean man is a miserable and pitiable creature, and that the Calliclean city is not unredeemable because statecraft does, indeed, exist. Until the city is redeemed, however, demagogic rhetoric will continue to hold the crowd in its thrall.

Opposed to the rhetoric of illusions is a rhetoric guided by a knowledge of the good. We may well ask whether Plato wants us to think that Socrates possesses this rhetorical skill. I believe that the answer cannot be unqualifiedly affirmative. Socrates as Plato represents him in the *Gorgias* does not possess a knowledge of the good. His knowledge is negative: he knows the inadequacy of the claims of Gorgias, Polus, and Callicles. So what is the relation between Socratic speech practice (the *elenchos*) and true rhetoric? Socratic speech is not able to generate knowledge of the good, but it is able to dispel illusions. It is in direct conflict with the illusion-creating rhetoric of the city, and it prepares the ground for the eventual establishment of the true statesman within the city. Or, better, it would prepare the ground if its adversaries did not wield the power of life and death in the city. But Plato will argue in the *Gorgias* that the city is deceived even about what life and death really are.

Rhetoric and the Soul's Damnation

IN THE *GORGIAS*, Plato seems to be suggesting that there is a part of the soul in which the desires for pleasure have their seat and that rhetoric's illusions appeal somehow to this part of the soul. (At 493a3, for example, Socrates refers to "that part of the soul in which desires exist and which is such as to be persuaded and swayed back and forth.") It is perhaps not difficult to see that a false belief about justice, one that flattered one's self-image, could facilitate the satisfaction of desires that, seen for what they really were, might bring on shame and even self-loathing. But one surely would want to know how and why the soul possesses such desires and how such tenacious false beliefs about justice and the good ever come to be held by the judging faculty of the soul.

Plato does not provide an answer to these questions in the *Gorgias*. However, he does offer a sort of mythology by which one might imagine the origin and nature of the soul's bondage to illusion. He suggests that the soul falls prey to the demagogue because it has forgotten its immortal nature, its kinship and fellowship with the divine. Even though it has forgotten this, the soul's desire to recover its immortal blessedness remains. Without knowing its true object, however, this desire is led astray by objects that are in truth alien to the soul. The spell of forgetfulness can be broken only if the soul recognizes that what it took to be its happiness is, in fact, a shameful slavery. Within this eschatological framework, the soul would possess only desires for objects that are other than its true good because it has come to be linked with a mortal body and has, in the process, forgotten its origin. In its true nature, the soul would not possess any other desire than to be as like to the divine as possible.

Such is the mythic biography of the soul at work in Socrates' analogy of the soul and the pitcher, narrated immediately after Callicles had revealed so "candidly" his views about the happiness of the sybarite's life. He introduces it with the suggestion, which he has heard from "wise men," that this life is a postmortem existence, and our true life will be found only after our death, which is really our birth. Those who had been "initiated" in their previous existence lead temperate and just lives here; those who were not initiated are filled with insatiable desires. Socrates says that a certain clever Sicilian or Italian Greek (probably a Pythagorean) had called the soul a jug (*pithos*) and had said that the "soul of the senseless" (the uninitiated soul) was full of holes, "unable to be sated because of its lack of conviction and its forgetfulness" (*di' apistian te kai lêthên* [492b3–c3]). Socrates asks Callicles (493c7–d2) if he has persuaded him that a life spent in trying to fill unchastened desires is truly wretched: "Am I persuading you [*peithô ti se*] in any way to reverse your judgment and declare those who lead ordered lives to be happier than the unchastened?" Callicles says he is unpersuaded, and Socrates offers a second analogy, almost identical to the first (493e8–494a5). The temperate man is like one who has many sound and undamaged pitchers holding milk, wine, and honey which he has gathered from streams that flow with these substances. The unchastened man is like one who has many rotting and punctured vessels "and is continually compelled, both day and night, to fill them, [and] the pains he suffers are the most extreme." And again Socrates asks Callicles: "Am I persuading you a little with my narratives to agree that the well-ordered life is better than the unchastened one, or am I not persuading you?" Callicles responds, "You are not persuading me, Socrates."

97

Callicles is represented in this interchange as a perfect example of one who cannot be initiated because of his "lack of conviction" (*apistia*), his inability to be persuaded by the truth. Later in the dialogue, he will be chastised by Socrates for the fact that the power of geometric equality, the proportionality at the heart of the cosmos, has "escaped your notice" (*lelêthen se* [508a5]), a construction whose verbal root is related to "forgetfulness" (*lêthê*). We thus are made to see that, in some sense, Callicles' "lack of conviction and forgetfulness" are responsible for his false belief that the life of unchastened, "proportionless" desires is most happy. Callicles in this way becomes the dramatic embodiment of the mythic biography of a soul that has lost its one saving power, the memory of its kinship with the divine.

We may complete our picture of the fates of the initiated and the uninitiated souls with an image drawn from the close of the *Meno*. Socrates is telling Meno what relation the true statesman bears to the city: "[H]e could be described as being such among the living as Homer says Teiresias was among the dead. Homer says that Teiresias 'alone possessed the power of intellect' among those in Hades, 'who flitted about like shades.' Such a man here would be just like that man there—in respect to excellence he would be the genuine article, and all the others would be its shadows" (100a3–7). The *Meno*'s analogy of the statesman to Teiresias in Hades provides a civic setting for the *Gorgias*'s characterization of this life as the true Hades. We certainly may find in these separate but nonetheless fundamentally coherent analogies the adumbration of Plato's most famous analogy, that of the cave, found in the opening of the seventh book of the *Republic*. Indeed, in one passage in the *Republic*, Plato speaks of the ascent from the cave as like one "out of Hades up toward the gods" (521c3).

The *Phaedo*: Translating the Critique of Rhetoric into Theory and *Askesis*

PLATO IS ALWAYS aware that to illuminate a philosophic issue with a myth, however dramatically forceful, cannot alone bring an individual to choose to commit his life to philosophy and justice, which is the stated goal of the *Gorgias*. In the *Republic*, for example, the analogy of the cave is followed by an exposition of its meaning in terms of the ontology and epistemology of the divided line. What Plato attempts to do in this exposition is translate a temporal narrative about the soul's enslavement to the illusions of the city and its subsequent release and return to its true abode (the obvious significance of the allegory of the cave on a first reading) into a static structure in which the stages of the soul's progress will correspond somehow to different ontological levels. The shift from biography into topography, as it were, produces serious problems. Specifically, the fit between the soul's enchainment and its initial condition of release is not at all adequately rendered by the first two ontological levels, namely, that of shadows and that of the physical objects that cast them. In what sense, except perhaps metaphorically, do the illusions of the city possess the ontological status of shadows?

I refer to the *Republic*'s translation of the analogy of the cave into the ontology of the divided line because it provides a clear example of what I take Plato to be doing in the *Phaedo*. He is taking the *Gorgias*'s dichotomy between political skill and flattery, the first possessed by the initiated soul of the true statesman, the second wielding its power among the uninitiated, and rendering it in terms of a two-level ontology. The objects that are known by the *Gorgias*'s "good" rhetorician—the just, the good, the noble, the temperate—become the partless and unchanging forms of the *Phaedo*, whereas the imitations of these same objects produced by the flattering rhetorician become the constantly changing pluralities of sensible particulars of the *Phaedo*. Of course, all skills, and not just political skill, will have their appropriate forms, so that we find the *Phaedo* referring to health (for medicine) and magnitude (for geometry). Just as we saw very briefly in the case of the *Republic*'s analogy of the cave, the ontological reconstruction of the *Gorgias*'s skill/flattery distinction produces some peculiar problems. Plato continues to want to condemn the desire for pleasure because it is the source of the soul's enslavement to the illusory goods of this world, but at the same time his ontology compels him to bring blame against the senses and physical particulars. One way Plato seems to slip from a condemnation of the desire for pleasure to an attack upon the senses is to attribute the desire for pleasure, which in the *Gorgias* is an aspect of both the soul and the body, to the body only. It is as if he had declared that all flattery was directed toward the body. Locating the desire for pleasure within the body permits him to move from an attack on the organs of the body as the seat of pleasure to an attack on these organs as the seat of sensation. According to the final words of the *Meno*, the city is a Hades where the knowledge of how to produce virtuous citizens is wholly absent. In the *Phaedo*, it is not the city that is the habitat of "shades" but the physical world and, more specifically, the entombing body in which the soul dwells. The relationship between the soul and the body in the *Phaedo* is paralleled by that between the soul and the city or, more accurately, between the soul and the power that rules in the city, as I will explain.

Throughout the first half of the *Phaedo*, Plato uses metaphors that suggest that the body is a close companion of the soul, the soul's lover. The soul is said to be able to "share in the life of the body" (80e3–4), hold intimate converse (*homilia*) with it, or "cultivate its ways" (81e3). This intimate association of the soul with the body brings it about that the soul becomes more and more like the body in its fundamental nature, "heavy, earthy and visible," so that after death "it is weighted down and drawn back to what is visible and . . . it haunts graveyards and tombs where certain shadowy *phantasmata* of souls have been seen, the sorts of images such souls produce" (80b4–81d3).

99

The condition of such corrupted souls is really no different from that of those souls that while they inhabit a body come to adopt its habits and nature. Indeed, each pleasure and pain that the soul shares with the body "nails the soul to the body, pinning it there and making it like the body so that it comes to believe that whatever the body declares to be true is true. And as a result of this unanimity of belief and sharing of pleasures [*tois autois chairein*], the soul, I think, is compelled to become both like in character to the body and like in breeding" (83d4–8).

In the *Gorgias*, it is not the body's character that comes to dominate the corrupted personality but the character of the city. Socrates persuades Callicles that no one can find security in the city without imitating the one (or the many) who holds power in the city, thus becoming his friend. For example, in a city ruled by a tyrant who is "vicious and brutish," his friend is "one who has a similar character, who censures and praises the same things" and who must "habituate himself to share in the same pleasures [*tois autois chairein*] and pains as the ruler, and so to see to it that he comes to resemble him as much as possible" if he wants to gain power and be free from injury (510c7–d8). Of course, this imitation of the ruler (*mimêsis tou despotou* [511a2]) also will bring it about that the young man will become as unjust as the ruler. Or, if the city is ruled by the *dêmos*, the one who would achieve security against its power to do him injustice must become as like to the *dêmos* as he can. What renders one able to imitate the *dêmos* is rhetoric, and this "skill" does not merely make one's words mirror the *dêmos*'s words, but makes one's very being mirror the *dêmos*'s being: "If you think that such a skill, one which can indeed give you great power in this city, will not transform you so that you resemble the city's polity—regardless of whether that transformation would be for the better or, as I think, the worse, if you think this, Callicles, your planning is off track. For the demand is not to become the *dêmos*'s mimic, but to instinctively identify with it" (513a7–b4).

Just as in the *Phaedo* the soul's intimacy with the body renders it like the body, so also in the *Gorgias* does the rhetorician's love for the *dêmos* (*ho dêmou erôs* [513c7]) maim his soul (*tên psychên lelôbesthai* [511a2]). And just as the soul's attachment to the body causes it to leave traces of itself in the vicinity of tombs, so, according to the eschatological myth of the *Gorgias*, does injustice leave traces visible on the "naked" soul as it stands before its judge in the underworld. (I take Plato to be offering in both cases allegorical renderings of the corruptive power of a certain way of life.)

If, as we have clearly seen, it is the city that in the *Gorgias* is the metaphoric land of the dead, and in the *Phaedo* it is the realm of the body that plays this role, and if in the *Gorgias* it is rhetoric that enchains and enchants the soul, whereas in the *Phaedo* it is sense perception, then we may understand better how the *Phaedo*'s two-world ontology is meant to function. Let me explain.

100

Although it does not directly assault the ideology of the city, Plato's condemnation of the realm of the senses nonetheless is aimed at the philosophic equivalent of that ideology, namely, the belief that things are really like what they are generally perceived to be. This belief might be summed up best in the words of the sophist Protagaras: "Man is the measure of all things." If most men think that the goal of life is pleasure, then so it is. When Plato attacks the reliablity of the senses, he is attacking the foundation of what might be called Protagorean humanism. And because Plato understands Protagorean humanism to be nothing more than popular belief turned into philosophic jargon (as we may surmise from his representation of the sophist and his teaching in both the *Protagoras* and the *Theaetetus*), when he attacks the trustworthiness of the senses and, by implication, Protagorean humanism, he attacks the very basis of the city's ideology. Furthermore, Plato's postulation of a realm of intelligible forms characterized in Eleatic terms is the philosophic equivalent of the claim that the knowledge of the human good is the reality of which the city's beliefs are but the appearance. To translate the war between philosophy and rhetoric in the *Gorgias* (whose first word is "war," *polemou*) onto this new plane, casting it as a war against the sensible world, is, I would argue, a significant new strategic move in philosophy's battle with the city.

In the *Phaedo,* Plato is offering an account of how the philosopher can withdraw from politics and the city and still remain true to the Socratic tradition of combative engagement with the city. The philosopher will practice a counterpolitics at the very heart of the city (as Socrates continues, against the wishes of his jailers, to practice philosophy within his prison cell) by seeking to live in commonality in a realm where true virtue can be practiced, not "demotic" virtue, which is but the shadowgraph of true virtue (see *Phaedo,* 69b6). The philosopher alone exercises the authentic political virtues—courage, temperance, and justice—because he has been persuaded that authentic life requires that one die to all that the city holds dear, the pleasures of wealth and honor. (The philosopher is contrasted at *Phaedo* 68c2 and 82c5–8 with "lovers of wealth" and "lovers of honor," prefiguring the tripartite characterology of the *Republic.*) The city condemned Socrates to death, but philosophy judges the city to be already dead and ruled, like the souls that cling to gravestones, "by the fear of what it cannot see, the god of Death," because all of the city's virtues are motivated by nothing but the fear of death: "Is this not a significant indication that a man is not a philosopher but a lover of the body, if you see him agonizing when he is about to die? This very same man is, I would hazard, both a lover of wealth and a lover of honor" (68b8–c2). This man's courage is nothing but a cowardly aversion from the imaginary evils of death, just as his temperance is only a self-indulgent yielding up of some pleasures out of the fear that others, more desired, might be lost (see 68d).

If the lover of the body fears what is invisible (*aïdios*), the philosopher desires it and yearns to commune with it. He alone is courageous, because he does not fear death, and temperate, because he scorns all sensual pleasures. Plato says that the philosopher alone is just, though he does not say how the philosopher's justice differs from that of the lover of the body. (This will be the task of the *Republic*.) But, unlike the historical Socrates, the philosopher as he is portrayed in the *Phaedo* does not directly confront the city so as to reveal to it the truth about its so-called virtues.

In condemning Socrates, the city has put philosophy under a ban of death, and all philosophers must consider themselves as leading what the city would deem to be a condemned prisoner's existence ("most people would think that it is well said about philosophers that they are really putting themselves to death [*thanatôsi*] and that they always deserve this fate" [*Phaedo*, 64b2–6]), although it is the city that stands so condemned. The philosopher must "bid farewell" (64c1) to the city's illusions about who is dead and who alive and, like Socrates within his prison, find freedom in converse with those for whom philosophy provides an antidote for the poison of the city. (We are told early in the dialogue that talking may heal Socrates' body and necessitate a triple dose of poison: philosophizing counters the death-dealing power of the poison.) Although the philosopher does not face the city and declare it dead, his withdrawal to an alternative community is a symbolic negation of the city. I believe that we may identify this alternative community with Plato's Academy. Although certainty cannot be had on this topic, it is not unlikely that the *Phaedo* was composed around the time of the founding of the Academy, after Plato had encounted Archytas, a Pythagorean philosopher who also was a statesman and general in the Italian city of Tarentum.[10] (The *Phaedo* is full of Pythagorean themes, and Socrates' interlocutors Cebes and Simmias are Pythagoreans.) The *Phaedo* is not, like the *Gorgias*, a declaration of war between philosophy and the city but rather an announcement that philosophy is withdrawing from the battle because the enemy is already perishing from a fatal disease. If the enemy reads the withdrawal as its own victory, philosophy knows that such an illusion is but a symptom of the disease.

I am proposing, then, that we read the *Phaedo* as Plato's "foundation charter" for the Academy, the site within the city where philosophy can find safety from the reigning powers of the city. Within the Academy, philosophy will await its opportunity to reenter the city and provide it with the guidance that "true rhetoric" alone can offer. Within the Academy, philosophy will pursue its assault on the city's illusions, but this time on a plane that does not bring it into direct conflict (and possibly mortal conflict) with the city. Plato and those gathered within the Academy will engage in "theoretical" pursuits, but the "subtext" of these pursuits is a highly political one.

Conclusion: Platonism and Its Legacy

EARLIER, I ASKED what motivates Plato's adoption of a Heraclitean description of the physical world and an Eleatic description of the forms in the *Phaedo*. I have argued that this two-world ontology should be understood as heralding a new strategy in philosophy's conflict with the city. In the *Gorgias,* Plato makes Socrates attack the ideology of the city head-on, with the intimation that this may lead to his death; in the *Phaedo,* Socrates is condemned to death by the city, although in philosophy's perspective it is the city that is the realm of the dead. The philosopher's withdrawal from the city is described as a withdrawal from the realm of death and mutability which contains all that the city holds dear and believes to be real. Rather than attack the citizens who condemned Socrates to death, Plato chooses to attack the entire realm of the senses, the realm that nurtures the false beliefs of the citizens.

The *Phaedo* ushers in the philosophic tradition that may aptly be named Platonism. We may characterize Platonism broadly as resting upon the dichotomy between appearance and reality, with appearance understood to be the realm of change and the senses, and reality the realm of eternity and the intellect. Within Platonism, rhetoric falls squarely in the realm of appearance.

But if my analysis of the relationship between the *Gorgias* and the *Phaedo* is right, then Platonism is in its inception a rewriting of the *agon* between Socratic counter-rhetoric and the rhetorical practice of demagogues such as Callicles. This places rhetoric in the foreground of Plato's concerns. Plato's two-world ontology sets up the theoretical defense of a rhetoric that would persuade citizens of what is true and good. It may be true that Plato never really offered an example of what such a rhetoric might look like (although a case could be made that the preamble to the legal code in the *Laws* [715c7–718a6] comes very close), but it remains true that the legacy of Platonism with its denigration of rhetoric is a betrayal of its origins. One might even say that the goal of the Academy was the creation of a new rhetoric as envisioned in the *Gorgias,* one whose forms and tropes would be patterned upon the immutable and intelligible order of the cosmos and whose goal would be the liberation of the city from its reigning illusions.

Notes

1. Jean Laborderie, *Le dialogue platonicien de la maturité* (Paris: Les Belles Lettres, 1978), 251, puts it this way: "Tout se passe comme si chacun de ces dialogues nous présentait à ce sujet une partie du *philosophikos bios.*"
2. It is true that the *Gorgias* and the *Meno* show evidence of the influence of Pythagoreanism, but the Pythagoreanism they reflect is, like the philosophy of the early dialogues, a way of life grounded in a certain conception of the soul and its place in the order of things. We get nothing like the Pythagorean speculations

of the *Philebus,* where the principles of the limited and the unlimited are invoked to explain "all there is."

3. For a discussion of how the *elenchos* functioned, see Gregory Vlastos, "The Socratic Elenchus," *Oxford Studies in Ancient Philosophy* 1 (1983): 27–58. For the fullest recent discussion of the Socratic *elenchos,* see Thomas C. Brickhouse and Nicholas D. Smith, *Plato's Socrates* (Oxford: Oxford University Press, 1994), chapter 1.

4. For the best description of the differences between the Socrates represented in the aporetic dialogues and the Socrates represented in the more theoretical dialogues, see Gregory Vlastos, *Socrates: Ironist and Moral Philosopher* (Ithaca: Cornell University Press, 1991), chapter 2. For a critique of the use of these differences as evidence of a profound change in Plato's philosophical aims, see my "Socrates as Revenant: A Reading of the *Menexenus,*" *Phoenix* 48, no. 4 (1994): 331–47.

5. These are also the questions to which a recent study of the *Phaedo* is addressed. Paul Stern, in *Socratic Rationalism and Political Philosophy: An Interpretation of Plato's* Phaedo (Albany: State University of New York Press, 1993), argues that the *Phaedo* continues to challenge the reigning political ideology through its scrutiny of the nature of human desire. I would agree, but I do not share Stern's view of the almost existentialist message that the *Phaedo* allegedly advances ("human existence is characterized by an awareness of incompleteness," 145).

6. For an important recent discussion of the motivation of the change from the "early" to the "middle" dialogues that sees the *Gorgias* to be pivotal in the transition, see Gregory Vlastos, "Elenchus and Mathematics: A Turning Point in Plato's Development," *American Journal of Philology* 109 (1988): 362–96; chapter 4 in Gregory Vlastos, *Socrates: Ironist and Moral Philosopher.* Vlastos argues that Plato's dissatisfaction with the *elenchos* as a method for grounding moral judgments (that injustice is never in the agent's interest, for example) led him to seek an alternative model of how the truth of moral judgments might be known and demonstrated.

7. I am aware of the complex debate on the origins and interpretation of what has come to be known as Plato's two-world ontology. Recently, the "standard" approach to subject has been challenged by Terry Penner in *The Ascent from Nominalism: Some Existence Arguments in Plato's Middle Dialogues* (Dordrecht: D. Reidel, 1987). Penner argues that Plato's "theory of ideas" should be seen as part of a polemic against the nominalist claim that "what we are talking about when we use general words like 'beauty,' 'equality,' 'the shuttle,' or 'cut'" can be explained "*without referring to anything other than* particular spatio-temporally locatable objects (beautiful sights and sounds, equal sticks and stones, particular material shuttles or acts of cutting at particular spatio-temporal locations)" (ix, emphasis added). I am sympathetic with Penner's general approach, although I will argue that the polemic against nominalism is motivated by the threat to both individual and city which Plato recognizes in the "metaphysics" (I will call it Protagorean humanism and not nominalism, though I would not argue about such labels) underlying the discourse of rhetoric in the city. Penner seems not to be interested in explaining the seriousness Plato gives to his polemic against nominalism (but see 120–121, 334 n. 25, 344, n. 40, for some idea about how he

would relate Socrates' ethical concern to defeat relativism with Plato's interest in nominalism).

Besides reviewing the relevant Platonic passages, Penner also discusses the "standard" interpretation of the "theory of forms," esp. 43–65 and 181–231, and provides a useful bibliography. For a detailed commentary on the two-world ontology of the *Phaedo* in particular, see David Bostock, *Plato's Phaedo* (Oxford: Clarendon Press, 1986).

8. Translations, unless otherwise indicated, are my own.

9. In a recent article, "Plato's *Gorgias* and Euripides' *Antiope*: A Study in Generic Transformation," *Classical Antiquity* 11.1 (1992): 121–140, Andrea Nightingale argues that the *agon* between Socrates and Callicles is a reworking of the tragic *agon* between Zethus and Amphion in the Euripidean version of the myth. Plato is certainly using every device at his disposal to convey the profound dimensions of the dichotomy of lives at stake in the *Gorgias.*

10. For an assessment of the evidence about the date of the founding of the Academy, G. C. Field's work, *Plato and His Contemporaries: A Study in Fourth-Century Life and Thought,* 2nd ed. (London: Methuen, 1948), remains the most useful treatment. Field rightly understands that Plato's theorizing is a continuation of the Socratic practice of engagement with the city. At around the time of Plato's foundation of the Academy, Field writes, "the conviction [was] gradually strengthening itself in his mind that the mere study of practical politics by itself can never bring about what is needed. It is necessary to go beyond this to a systematic study of the foundations of conduct. But not even here is it possible to stop short. For the principles of conduct themselves seem to demand, before they can be regarded as established, that they should be followed back to something more fundamental still. Ethics and Politics demand a metaphysic" (16).

Philosophical Rhetoric or Rhetorical Philosophy? The Strange Case of Isocrates

Stephen Halliwell

Despite his substantial and acknowledged influence on the history of rhetoric, particularly on Cicero and (partly through Cicero) on Renaissance humanists, Isocrates in recent times has become one of the least keenly discussed figures in the rhetorical canon. Although some scholarly energy continues to be devoted to the reconstruction of his polemical relationship to Plato, Aristotle, and other contemporary thinkers, more general interest in his writings has not been widely sustained by intellectual historians.[1] In part, this no doubt has much to do with features of Isocrates' work that strike a jaded modern palate as especially unprepossessing: a stylistic fullness that can easily be found cloying; a conservatism of mentality that is too often hospitable to platitudes; an outlook so seemingly static as to make it possible for the author, when justifying his career in the *Antidosis* of 353, to quote a passage from *Against the Sophists* (of almost forty years earlier) as evidence of his stable and persistent principles of education;[2] and, last but not least, consistent suspicion (and a correspondingly successful avoidance) of most kinds of intellectual subtlety. The purpose of this essay, I should say at once, certainly is not to be a general defense or rehabilitation of Isocrates against complaints of the kind just cited. One of my aims, in fact, will be to argue that beneath some of the faults mentioned, there lies a more disturbing weakness which goes to the very roots of his thinking. But those aspects of his writing that now may seem so unexciting do not, I believe, vindicate what is close to becoming a consensus about the clarity and comfortableness of Isocrates' place within the history of rhetoric. It may well be, indeed, that the uniformity of his style and self-presentation actually impedes proper recognition of the ways in which his guiding motivation eludes stable evaluation. I shall be trying, in what follows, to develop an account of why Isocrates ought to be regarded as a much more problematic thinker than most historians of ideas currently take him to be.

If Isocrates' historical status can and should be found problematic, one reason for this is his paradoxical relationship to the categories of rhetoric and philosophy. There can be, however, no question of bringing these categories to bear on his work as given, ready-made divisions of intellectual activity or analysis. Concepts of rhetoric and philosophy were recent and still evolving developments in the culture of fourth-century Greece in which Isocrates practiced as a teacher and publicist. The term *rhêtorikê* almost certainly was coined in Isocrates' own lifetime, probably close to the end of the fifth century B.C.E.[3] This is no mere terminological detail but a reflection of the increasingly explicit and systematic spirit in which precepts and procedures of (oratorical) persuasion were being articulated in this period. Although the terms *philosophos* and *philosophia* were older, their use, too, was a matter of a good deal of debate, redefinition, and refinement at the time. These cultural circumstances form something much more than pieces of the background to Isocrates' own career; they provide, to a considerable extent, the very material out of which he chooses to forge his own identity as both thinker and teacher. It is, therefore, to the ongoing process of self-definition of both rhetoric and philosophy throughout Isocrates' lifetime that we must look for the primary historical perspective on his writings.

The development of rhetoric as a conscious and self-defining art of public speech or discourse in classical Greece is intimately related not only to the political conditions and ideologies of the cities in which this development took place but also to the emergence of philosophy as an intellectual discipline, or range of disciplines, with which rhetoric soon acquired, and was long to keep, a relationship of mutual and sometimes hostile rivalry. In the cultural setting of late fifth and fourth century B.C.E. Athens, where discussion of the nature and aspirations of both rhetoric and philosophy was brought to its sharpest focus, three individual figures now stand out as particularly important for their contributions to the debate about the potential antagonism between the two pursuits. Two of these three figures, Plato and Aristotle, erected frameworks of thought within which philosophy and rhetoric could be confidently defined and distinguished. In doing so, they laid substantial parts of the foundations for a configuration of intellectual history that has survived and indeed remained dominant in the Western tradition ever since, at any rate until the radical questioning of inherited categories pursued by various branches of poststructuralist criticism. One implication of this influence is that the demarcation of philosophy from rhetoric on which Plato and Aristotle broadly agreed has come virtually to erase the notably different views propounded by their contemporary and rival Isocrates—views that make the relationship of philosophy and rhetoric a very much less clear-cut and more ambiguous matter. In consequence, Isocrates himself has been assigned a securely acknowledged position in the history of rhetoric, yet he has been almost entirely written out of a history of philosophy that owes so much to Plato and Aristotle. Is this, as many have judged it, purely a triumph of definitional clarity and cogency over mediocre looseness of ideas? Is Isocrates no more than "a bundle of contradictions"?[4] Or are there more telling things to be said about Isocrates' own deployment of the categories of rhetoric and philosophy?

At the prima facie level of his own claims, it is doubly paradoxical that Isocrates has come to be so readily regarded as a rhetorician and not a philosopher. Throughout his surviving writings, Isocrates uses the Greek word group *philosophia, philosophein* (verb), and so on, to describe his own teaching program and his intellectual posture. At the same time, not only was he personally unable (because of physical weaknesses) to practice oratory in Athenian public life, but he frequently criticizes the ideas and methods of those who claimed unequivocally to be teachers of rhetoric. These paradoxes are matched by other anomalies within Isocrates' life and self-presentation. He was a professional educator who derided what he saw as the excessive pedagogical pretensions of several schools and schemes of education. He was an intellectual who, as we shall see, was well capable of identifying with the anti-intellectualist cynicism of some strains of popular opinion in Athens. And he was a believer in the essential importance for human communities of "political speech/argument" (*politikos logos*),[5] even though many of his contributions to the political debates of Athens and of Greece as a whole were couched in the form of fictional enactments of public oratory and were thus at one remove from the practical.[6] It will, I hope, be worth asking how deeply rooted these paradoxes lie in Isocrates' ways of thinking and whether they should be treated as anything more than the symptoms of an imperfectly clarified set of educational aims and cultural ideals.

Answers to those questions need to start from a recognition of the unsettled and contentious nature of many basic intellectual categories in the culture of fourth century B.C.E. Athens within which Isocrates, as well as Plato and Aristotle, worked. Isocrates' entire career is animated by a context of competition and controversy which frequently involved the definition of particular disciplines or "arts." Far from being purely abstract, such conceptual issues impinged directly on the training of those who aspired to political activity and leadership: Isocrates himself educated a number of figures who became highly prominent in Greek politics, including the Athenian general-politician Timotheus, the orator Hyperides, and the Cypriot king Nicocles. Some idea of the contours of this context of intellectual controversy, as well as of Isocrates' entry into it as a formal educationalist, can be gathered from his early and now fragmentary work *Against the Sophists*, which was probably written around 390 B.C.E. and within a year or two of the opening of his school at Athens. The work's function is an explicitly programmatic statement of the agenda of Isocrates' school, though this is realized, so far as the surviving sections go, by polemically negative means. While, like so many other Isocratean compositions, *Against the Sophists* is a written "pamphlet" circulated for reading,[7] its tone deliberately borrows something from the ethos of personal animosity that played a recurrent part in so much contemporary Athenian oratory, both political and forensic. This reflects the more general fact that Isocrates' works embody in the written word a manner and tone that are consciously reminiscent of public speech. In many aspects of form, style, and "voice," Isocrates conspicuously adopts and adapts the postures of oratory, and that is a quality of his authorial persona intended to impress would-be students by its links with the rhetoric of political institutions. In this salient respect, as in many others, the impression created by an Isocratean pamphlet is very far from either a Platonic dialogue or an Aristotelian lecture-treatise. Yet *Against the Sophists* would have confronted its fourth century B.C.E. readers, and continues to confront us, with arguments and suggestions that leave it highly debatable in what sense its author can be regarded as a rhetorician.

Isocrates approaches his task of announcing and defining his own school of education by means of an attack on two other groups of teachers. It is significant that in doing so he assumes, at the outset (13.1, see 13.11), that "philosophy" is the aim of all (advanced) education: "If all those who undertake to educate were prepared to speak the truth, and not to make promises which outrun what they are likely to achieve, they would not have such a bad reputation with ordinary citizens. As it is, those with the temerity to boast so irresponsibly have made it appear that even people who choose an idle existence can make better deliberations than the students of philosophy." This is, in itself, no merely terminological quirk but a conceptually purposeful move which preserves a wide, open-ended, and perhaps partly popular status for a term that was beginning to be given a much tighter and more specific sense by various Greek thinkers. Isocrates' use of *philosophia*, here as in many other passages, is a calculated eschewal of any notion of philosophy as an esoteric discipline that requires admission into a special way of life or an exclusive domain of theory. It intimates the idea of a broad human understanding that cannot be readily circumscribed or technically demarcated—a capacity for insight or sagacity akin, perhaps, to traditional conceptions of *sophia*, "wisdom." Some such implication is developed by the double attack on two groups of rivals which Isocrates proceeds to launch, first (13.1–8) against those he calls dealers in "eristics" or "disputations," then (13.9–13) against teachers of public oratory. The former are criticized not simply for a (quasi-Socratic) method of argument that attends too fastidiously to verbal distinctions (13.7) but also and more importantly for laying claim to practical/ethical principles of conduct that arrogate the status of knowledge and purport to guarantee happiness or well-being (*eudaimonia* [13.3]). The rhetoricians, too, are censured for professing a "knowledge" that they cannot validate—in their case, a knowledge of "speeches"/"arguments" (*logoi*) which they offer to transmit to their students, according to Isocrates, with a technical self-confidence that transcends both experience and individual ability.[8]

This critique of both eristic philosophers and formal rhetoricians is far from being a sustained argument. It is discursive, somewhat anecdotal, and carpingly ad hominem, though also oddly coy about identifying its opponents explicitly. But the work does nonetheless convey some essential aspects of the position Isocrates took up early in his career as an educator, which he was scarcely to modify during the rest of his long life. While the two sets of opponents are evidently envisaged as different kinds of people, Isocrates' disapproval of them depends on an effectively single point of view. In both cases, the allegation of unjustified pretensions to knowledge depends principally on considerations of contingency as a defining factor in human life. A sense of contingency was an old and deeply embedded constituent of traditional Greek patterns of thought; it was an idea important, in different ways, for religious feeling, for the historical outlook of Thucydides, and for Greek tragedy. Isocrates is clearly indebted here, as so often, to the wider traditions of Greek thought: he invokes contingency in the readily comprehensible form of human ignorance of the future, and he cites Homer as a witness to the point (13.2). But Isocrates makes distinctive use of the concept of contingency by building on it his rejection of what he sees as specious claims to knowledge by certain types of teachers. If the conditions of life are irredeemably contingent, then there is no possibility, according to Isocrates, of discerning practical or ethical principles that will have prior validity for all possible situations.[9] And if that is so, then it follows that, among much else, there can be no substantially codifiable or wholly teachable rules of rhetoric, given rhetoric's need to guide deliberations about the actual and the feasible.[10] The existence of contingency leads Isocrates, then, to rule out the attainability of either ethical knowledge or, in the strongest sense, rhetorical art.

We need to ask, as his critics have so often done, where this leaves Isocrates' own program or principles of education. The question is awkward, not simply because of lacunae in our knowledge of his positive claims or methods but because there appears to be something intrinsic to Isocrates' position that militates against a definitive statement. In *Against the Sophists*, Isocrates shows some self-consciousness about this point (13.22), and our understanding of his response to it is not helped by the fact that the text is cut off at just this juncture. But nonetheless we can see a number of factors that are germane to his stance. It is important, in the first place, to recognize that contingency is not randomness, and Isocrates' repudiation of excessive claims to ethical and rhetorical certainty does not commit him to anything like a radical relativism.[11] If knowledge is not available in many crucial human contexts, then at least the possibility of better or worse "judgment" or "opinion" (*doxa*) remains: ordinary people sometimes must observe, according to Isocrates, that "those who use their judgment are more consistent and have greater success than those who profess to have knowledge."[12] This is one of a number of passages, in both *Against the Sophists* and elsewhere, where Isocrates allows his argument to converge with somewhat skeptical and even cynical popular attitudes toward philosophers and teachers. This is not simply, in the vulgar sense, a rhetorical ploy in the denigration of his rivals. It serves to underscore a point of view that implicitly relies on the broad acceptability of at least some prevailing cultural norms. In the present instance, the point has a double force: first, that standards of ethical and deliberative judgment (and therefore, in part, of rhetorical cogency) can be established, even though these realms do not allow of secure or permanent knowledge; second, that these standards are inextricable from publicly recognizable criteria of practical effectiveness. Throughout his work, Isocrates' reliance on criteria that he maintains to be grounded in widely shared values represents a conscious attempt to align his arguments with strong social currents of feeling: other teachers may "call their students to a type of virtue and intelligence which is unknown to other people, and disputed even by themselves; but I call mine to the type which is agreed on by all" (15.84).

Contingency; the principle that practical decisions and rhetorical persuasion can rest on good judgment but not on knowledge; and a willingness to appeal to popular notions of success in deliberation and action—these are all fundamental and recurrent markers of the position Isocrates attempts to stake out for himself as a teacher and a participant in political discourse. In *Against the Sophists,* this position is perhaps most strikingly encapsulated in the passage that denies the status of a "codified art" to rhetoric but ascribes to it that of a "productive/creative enterprise" (13.12): "something said by one person is not equally useful to the next speaker; the most artful impression is created by one who speaks in a way which befits the subject, and yet is able to find something different to say from the rest." Hence, as Isocrates argues, the vital importance in rhetoric of recognizing and adapting oneself to *kairos*—the "moment" or "opportunity" which is also the principle of "the right time." Contingency means that the past cannot provide an infallible guide to the future; every context is in some way new, and the success of rhetorical deliberation requires an ability and flexibility to respond aptly yet inventively to each situation. Isocrates maintains that experience is a crucial prerequisite for being able to recognize and meet the salient features of a fresh context; it is precisely because experience is, *ex hypothesi,* of the contingent, that it does not yield codifiable principles and therefore cannot be replaced by methodical teaching or doctrine. Experience, practicality, and contingency are interlocked: they provide the resolutely pragmatic Isocratean alternative to acceptance of any master art that can give access to an absolute framework of truth.

Isocrates' pragmatic program, sketched out in *Against the Sophists*, rejects ethical and rhetorical systems. Yet it is itself implicitly concerned with both ethics and rhetorical persuasion: the first, because it aims, however vaguely, at fostering a sense of an apt human responsiveness, in the interests of a common good,[13] to the conditions of social existence; the second, because it frames this responsiveness in terms of a capacity to use and deploy public and political speech(es). Isocrates sums up his educational philosophy as a "cultivation of political discourse(s)" (13.21); and while he suggests, if somewhat nervously (and perhaps self-defensively, given his own noninvolvement in practical politics), that its results may be more evident in ethical than in rhetorical qualities (13.21), his goal is one that makes the two things hard to separate. Another way of putting this point is to say that Isocrates' philosophy, his guiding insight, depends on conjoint concepts of *logos* and of a political life. The term *logos* has a semantic range that encompasses "speech," "reason," and "argument." Isocrates has a penchant for using it in the plural, in phrases such as *politikoi logoi*, to denote the discourse that finds expression either in the public speech of oratory on which most Greek political institutions depended or, in Isocrates' own case, on its written equivalent. But it will now repay us to take a slightly closer look at two particular passages which illustrate, in a suitably programmatic way, the breadth of connotations Isocrates tries to keep for the concept of *logos*.

In the *Panegyricus*, the first major statement of combined pleas for Greek unity and a Panhellenic war against Persia that were to remain central to his political stance, Isocrates argues for an Athenian entitlement to hegemony which is based on Athens's outstanding historical contribution to the civilization and culture of the Greek world. After surveying something of the range of Athens's achievement, in terms that embrace religion, law, economics, festivals, and "contests of speeches and intelligence" (4.45), Isocrates contends that the unifying factor and creative force behind all these things was "philosophy." Athens has revealed philosophy to the world, and for the same reasons has "honored speeches [*logoi*], which all men desire though they feel resentment toward those adept at them."[14] Isocrates' account of Athenian culture is thus not only tinged with considerable chauvinism; it also has, tacitly but unmistakably, a self-referential element. The *Panegyricus* itself is explicitly presented as a display of philosophical intelligence, expressed through command of *logoi* (4.6, 10). But 4.47–50 makes it clear that Isocrates intends the significance of *logoi* to be much freer than that of "speeches" in a strictly oratorical sense. Indeed, it is striking that he allows a kind of elision to occur between the oratorical and the wider senses of the word. The ability to use *logoi* is "the one natural endowment which distinguishes us from all animals" (48), which indicates that Isocrates is referring to a compound capacity for *logos* as reason and as language: hence the close conjunction he makes between intelligence (*phronein*) and speech (*legein*). Given the stress on contingency that elsewhere, as we have seen, leads Isocrates to reject any idea of systematic deliberative knowledge, it is significant that he here holds up *logos*, and the rational intelligence it embodies, as a partial human protection against contingency. Chance may make success or failure often utterly unstable in other areas, but the link between intelligence or practical wisdom and effective *logoi* is something that cannot, he suggests, be broken (4.48–9). If contingency removes any possibility of grounding deliberation or persuasion on firm knowledge, it also makes the need for the secure rationality of deliberation all the greater.

A further point of importance for Isocrates' intellectual position is that this passage of the *Panegyricus* displays faith in a philosophy whose roots can be regarded as potentially universalist. Neither here nor anywhere else does Isocrates present *logos* as anything other than a fundamental human endowment, albeit one that requires appropriate social and educational conditions for its nurturing and development. It is precisely the achievement of Athens, on his account, to have created such conditions to an exceptional and paradigmatic degree. But as a result, so Isocrates claims in a very famous passage, there has arisen a set of cultural forms that more truly define the possibility of a common "Greek" identity than do racial factors: "Our city has so far outstripped all mankind in intelligence [*phronein*] and speech [*legein*] that its pupils have become the teachers of others, and it has made the name of "Greeks" no longer belong to a race but to a way of thinking, so that the name is sooner given to those who share our education than to those who have the same [ethnic] nature" (4.50). The passage is heavily marked by chauvinistic hyperbole, and part of its purpose may well be an implicit denigration of Athens's traditional political enemy, Sparta.[15] But this statement of cultural Hellenism nevertheless attests to a universalist tendency present in Isocrates' ideal of a nonspecialized prudence that stems from the exercise of a common human *logos*.

This tendency can be similarly discerned in another much-noted statement on the nature of *logos* which occurs first in the *Nicocles* of the mid-360s B.C.E. (3.5–9; the speaker is, fictionally, Nicocles himself) and is subsequently reused in the *Antidosis* of 354/3 (15.253–7). Here *logos* is once more perceived not as a technical discipline or specialized accomplishment but as a faculty inherent in human nature; and it is glossed as the capacity "to persuade one another and to communicate our meanings to one another on whatever matters we wish" (3.6; 15.254). It need not immediately concern us that Isocrates writes here, as often, with highly generalizing sentiments; the level of generalization is entirely of a piece with the spirit of the claims he implicitly makes for his own teaching: "It is this [*logos*] which decreed laws about justice and injustice, about honor and shame; without order in these things, we would be unable to live with one another. . . . Through this we educate the ignorant and esteem the prudent: for we regard the ability to speak [*legein*] appropriately as the most reliable sign of fine intelligence" (3.7; 15.255). *Logos*, then, is the foundation of political communities, not only because it has made progress possible but also because it is the basis of ethical and legal standards. Yet the practical and the ethical seem here, as elsewhere in Isocrates, to be virtually indissoluble; ethical values are but an expression of the deliberative intelligence that allows communities to prosper. Moreover, as I noted in commenting on *Panegyricus* 47–50, Isocrates is ready—and his Greek terminology allows him—to elide the distinction between *logos* as a ratiocinative and deliberative faculty and its use in public speaking (*legein*). This assimilation accentuates his refusal to treat rhetoric as a technically demarcated discipline rather than as a heightened development of a human faculty whose basic operations are prior to, and independent of, formal oratory. *Logos*, as rational and ethical intelligence, underlies the arguments of public discourse; but we lose Isocrates' deliberate play on the wide resonance of the term if we flatten its significance into that of "speech" as such.[16] Nothing makes this clearer than the statement at 3.8 (15.256) that "we use the same convictions [*pisteis*] when deliberating [on our own behalf] as we do when persuading others by our speech, and while we call rhetoricians those with the ability to speak before the multitude, we count as prudent all those who debate excellently with themselves on practical matters." There is continuity, and indeed identity (in a sense) of *logos*, between private and public deliberations. This means that Isocratean education concerns itself indistinguishably with personal and with political prudence, as confirmed by passages such as 12.30–32. It is an education that aspires to the integrated cultivation of rationality and persuasiveness.

It is instructive to regard Isocrates as having responded in his own way to a division of thought that Cicero was later to characterize, in a famous (and highly Isocratean) passage of *De Oratore*, as part of the legacy of Socratic philosophy:[17] a division between wisdom and eloquence, between "tongue and mind," which introduced a fissure into what had supposedly once been a unified and harmonious form of culture. Isocrates certainly can be deemed to have fought against what he implicitly saw as the separation of "wisdom" (*sophia*) from the eloquence that was definable in terms of mastery of public discourse. In striving to preserve the ideal of philosophy, the pursuit of wisdom, for his own composite educational agenda, he tried harder than anyone else to resist its restriction to specially refined types of thought and argument which were, at the very least, inimical to quasi-oratorical modes of presentation. In terms I have explored above, we could say that Isocrates' resistance focused on the concept of *logos* and amounted to an attempt to maintain a conjunction of *logos* as rationality and *logos* as public speech.

But his resistance was in vain. The separation of philosophy and rhetoric did indeed become an institutionalized fact in the Greek world, with immense and lasting consequences for educational practice and the demarcation of intellectual activity. The history of that separation has generated the near-unanimous conclusion that Isocrates' rightful status can be unambiguously judged to lie on the rhetorical side of the division. This conclusion, with its paradoxical contradiction of Isocrates' own ostensible claims to the contrary, has been partly sustained by philosophical upholders of the division who—on the basis of conceptions of the subject stemming from Plato and Aristotle—can find no appropriate place for Isocrates within the domain of philosophy. It will be worthwhile to rehearse, with extreme brevity, three possible reasons for this exclusion of Isocrates from the (self-defining) history of philosophy.[18]

The first is Isocrates' explicitly stated antipathy to anything like a general, let alone comprehensive, interpretation of reality. Although he repudiates the charge, leveled against him during his own lifetime, of spurning all forms of philosophy other than his own (12.19), his insistence on a tightly practical test of the value of philosophy has obvious implications for a conception of the subject. Put most stringently, nothing merits the name of philosophy, on Isocrates' premises, that does not bear directly on speech or action in the present (15.266). This principle clearly devalues the entire pursuit of physics or natural philosophy (*phusiologia*) in the Greek tradition, and still more precludes the validity of metaphysical arguments.[19] But however severely narrow such a conception of philosophy may be thought to be, and however hostile to both pre-Socratic inquiry and the thinking of Plato and Aristotle, it is not without partial parallels in the later history of the subject, above all in certain aspects of positivism and linguistic philosophy. It is, in any case, obscure why an exclusive focus on philosophy as a force for the shaping of practical living should count as no philosophy at all. Equally inconclusive, and on related grounds, would be the suggestion that Isocrates disqualifies himself as genuinely philosophical by virtue of his opposition to systematic theorizing. That he is so opposed is undoubtedly true, as we saw earlier. But his opposition falls well within the bounds of positions that have been, and still are, occupied in philosophy, especially by pragmatist and conventionalist points of view.

In short, Isocrates cannot be denied the rank of philosopher purely by reference to his views on the limits of the legitimate subject matter or the authentic aspirations of philosophy. This leaves us, I believe, with only one substantive reason for the well-entrenched exclusion of him from the history of philosophy; but it is, I shall maintain, a decisive and compelling reason. We can state it perhaps most simply by saying that while Isocrates' working principles and general intellectual commitments are philosophically conceivable and arguably defensible, he himself neither mounts a real defense of them nor even, more troublingly, sees any need for their defense. Put from a slightly different angle, this amounts to the claim that Isocratean *logos*—whether construed as speech, argument, or rationality—operates only within the construction of specific pieces of deliberation, the application of ethical and political principles to particular situations, and, at most, the highly generalized statement of those principles. But this conception of *logos* does not, except in the most cosmetic manner, undertake to provide any analysis, still less a critical justification, of its own workings. It is not merely that Isocrates dismisses one particular kind of analysis or method of inquiry—the kind he denotes as "eristic" and which he may well have meant to include all forms of quasi-Socratic dialectic. He recognizes no special or distinctive method or any style of argument that has a peculiarly philosophical status. And this appears to leave him without either the inclination or the equipment to engage in anything more than first-order discourse—or, as it would be more apt to say, the "common discourse," the practical employment of *logos,* which he himself perceives as the essential constituent and medium of culture.

The principal difficulty,[20] then, in giving Isocrates more than tangential and anomalous recognition within the history of philosophy stems not from his antipathy either to systematic theorizing or to the search for an overarching account of reality, nor even from his effective conviction that the *logos* that truly matters is the *logos* of common discourse. It stems, rather, from his self-imposed refusal to subject this conviction to any critical questioning, any internal investigation, at all. Even so, it is important to see that providing reasons for the philosophical inadequacy of Isocratean "philosophy" does not warrant the automatic inference that the status of his program of political discourse is, in any uncontroversial sense, rhetorical. In fact, it is sometimes philosophers who reach unsustainably clear-cut and historically misleading verdicts on this point. Terence Irwin, for example, has written that in classical Greece, "rhetoricians concerned themselves primarily with techniques of persuasion, and not with the general moral and political education promised by the sophists"; yet he has no hesitation in calling Isocrates "one of the most influential rhetoricians among Plato's contemporaries."[21] This judgment effectively inverts the claims made by Isocrates himself in his surviving writings, where practically no reference to "techniques of persuasion" is to be found, where, moreover, the possibility of treating rhetoric as a technically precise discipline (*technē*) is explicitly denied (13.12), and where the concept of effective public discourse (and hence of Isocratean education) is inescapably "moral and political" in its implications.[22]

The question of whether or how far Isocrates deserves to count as a rhetorician can be explored appropriately by a reading of his avowed educational principles in the light of both Plato's and Aristotle's views on rhetoric. Only the bare bones of such a comparative exercise can be sketched here, but a fuller examination of details would confirm, I believe, that the results are hardly straightforward. Between Isocrates' denial of the possibility of ethical knowledge and the Platonic insistence that rhetoric must be subordinated to, and ideally informed by, the higher-order principles of a philosophical "science of politics" (*politikē*), there is evidently an unbridgeable gulf. But

Isocrates' conception of *logos* is nonetheless far from a paradigmatic case of the kind of rhetoric that Plato has in his sights in the *Gorgias,* the *Phaedrus,* and elsewhere. As we have seen, Isocrates does not, in the first place, accept the view of rhetoric as an "art" (*technê*), a body of rationally coordinated principles, which comes particularly under attack in the *Gorgias.* Accordingly, he does not espouse anything like a purely formal notion of rhetoric—one that makes it a subject-neutral and value-free capacity to speak on any and every subject.[23] There may be some obscurity attaching to the Isocratean goal of an educated experience which allows a speaker to match his "judgment" (*doxa*) to the needs of circumstance and "occasion" (*kairos*),[24] but it is indubitably a rather different goal from the standard rhetorical aim of cultivating an ability to speak with equal effect on either side of any question. Isocrates fails to give any space in his program to such thinking, and that is because of his commitment to an ideal of *logos* in which argument and practical ethics are intertwined. An educator who asserts, however cautiously, that his teaching is more likely to result in moral decency than in verbal facility (13.21) adopts a stance that is ostensibly inhospitable to the technical aims advertised by many Greek proponents of rhetoric.[25] It is no surprise, therefore, to find Isocrates specifically disowning the Protagorean principle of a rhetoric that can "make the weaker argument into the stronger" (15.15).

If Isocrates does not affiliate himself to a purely formal and value-free conception of rhetoric, neither does he ever voice ideas comparable to Gorgias's imagery of the druglike, magical power of persuasion over the mind.[26] The only general thesis about the force or nature of persuasion to be found in his work occurs in one of the accounts of *logos* I cited earlier. The human capacity "to persuade one another"—that is, to persuade and *be* persuaded— is picked out as an entailment of the shared possession of *logos,* the *logos* of both reason and speech (3.6; 15.254). Viewed in this light, persuasion is not a malignly manipulative instrument, and being persuaded need not involve submitting to irrational pressures, whether from without or within. In this respect, too, therefore, Isocrates' canon of "speaking well" (e.g., 15.275) does not simply correspond to the kinds of rhetoric against which Plato's critique was chiefly directed. While it is far from satisfying Plato's positive requirements for a rhetoric that can be responsive to philosophical standards of truth and goodness, it nonetheless sets itself decisively apart both from technical amoralism and from seductive irrationalism.

When we turn to a comparison of Isocrates' views with Aristotle's conception of rhetoric, the absence of outright antipathy turns, arguably, into a fair degree of common ground. Both thinkers accept the essentially rational potential of public persuasion. The availability to it of types of argument that are reasonable, respectable, and reliable is something with which much of Aristotle's treatise on rhetoric is concerned, and it is underlined by his principle that rhetoric is an offshoot of dialectic (i.e., a general facility in forms of argumentation).[27] Isocrates' rejection of a systematized rhetorical art and his treatment of "forms of discourse" as mere rudiments of a capacity for speaking well open up a serious difference of method between himself and Aristotle, but this does not erase their shared acceptance of a rhetoric that is properly rational in its capacity to engage with, rather than merely playing upon, the beliefs of audiences. Moreover, both men regard rhetoric as chiefly (or most importantly) concerned with matters of ethical and political deliberation: Aristotle counts rhetoric as an offshoot of *politikê*, as well as of dialectic; Isocrates builds his own program around the use of *politikoi logoi*, "political discourses." This represents, on both sides, not only a perception of symbouleutic oratory as the highest of the three canonical kinds, but a broader recognition of the function of public speech as a force for both the shaping and the expression of attitudes that have major structural significance within a culture. Aristotle, unlike Plato, is able to converge with Isocrates' position in this respect, because he regards the domain of common discourse as a legitimate medium for the working out of ethical beliefs and values.[28]

But the convergence is incomplete, and the reasons for this are foundational for both thinkers. Aristotelian *politikê* is not, in short, coterminous with Isocrates' political discourse(s). In the *Nicomachean Ethics* (10.10, 1181a12–15), Aristotle complains of "sophists" who erroneously regard *politikê* and rhetoric as one and the same thing. He may not have had Isocrates in mind, and it is certain that Isocrates does not describe his own commitments by either term, rhetoric or *politikê*. But the Isocratean position nonetheless amounts to a collapsing of any such distinction, since it presents the practiced use of persuasive discourse as the only medium in which ethico-political understanding can express itself. Aristotelian philosophy, by contrast, though it aims to keep *politikê* in touch with the goals of ethical practice, nonetheless conceives of it as a distinct theoretical discipline, and one whose pursuit involves analytical, critical, and at least partly systematic methods of reasoning. The complexity of this Aristotelian enterprise is not my immediate concern.[29] What matters here is that it can help to accentuate what is absent, and designedly absent, from Isocrates' own program. Aristotle believes that only a philosophical inquiry, not rhetoric, can achieve a grasp of "first principles" of ethics and politics.[30] Isocrates does not accept that there *are* such things as first principles to be worked back to, or reasoned down from, in a theoretical and systematic manner, since his entire project eschews a commitment to either theory or system. For Aristotle, as for Plato, philosophy represents an ultimate framework of truth and a mode of understanding to which all other human pursuits, including rhetoric, are subordinate. For Isocrates, philosophy is the most finely articulated level of thought that human wisdom can achieve, but this is not to be sharply distinguished from the direct application of reason and speech, through the medium of persuasive discourse, to the ordering of individual and communal lives. On this view, there is only the first-order discourse of *logos* in action, and "philosophy" is the name for its mature mastery.

In comparing Isocrates' ideas to both Plato's and Aristotle's views of rhetoric, we have been brought, I hope, to the point where we can see how Isocrates dissolves any distinction between philosophy and rhetoric of the kind elaborated by his two contemporaries and rivals. This bears out the conclusion reached by Alasdair MacIntyre, one of the few recent philosophers to have found any noteworthy implications in the writings of Isocrates, that the latter's importance lies in his having offered "an alternative to philosophy understood as Socrates, Plato, and Aristotle had defined it."[31] In rejecting dialectical inquiry, and relying on ethical teaching by examples, Isocrates represents, for MacIntyre, a continuation of "the sophistic alternative"—at root, the denial of anything more than de facto standards of justice and truth—to which Plato's quest for a definitive system of ethics had been opposed. If the sophistic alternative prevails, "disagreement about those de facto standards," according to MacIntyre, "can only be resolved by means of nonrational persuasion; and the most effective means of nonrational persuasion is the type of rhetoric taught and practiced by Isocrates." These further elements in MacIntyre's verdict on Isocrates are, however, wide of the mark. As I have already argued, Isocrates does not espouse a concept of "nonrational persuasion"; his view of persuasion is entirely intertwined with his ideal of practical wisdom in action.[32] And it is a further sign of the elusiveness of Isocrates' position that the assimilation of him to general sophistic relativism is, as I wish to suggest, far from convincing.

About Isocrates' rejection of a certain kind of claim to knowledge in ethics and politics, and hence in the techniques of rhetoric, we have seen that there can be no doubt. But he does not himself perceive this skepticism as entailing relativism of the sort ascribed to him by MacIntyre and many others. Among the intellectual targets of the preamble to his *Helen* (a showpiece [epideictic] encomium of the mythological heroine) are two very different groups: those who deny the possibility of falsehood or contradiction[33] and those who propound the idea that all virtue is one and dependent on unitary ethical knowledge (10.1). Isocrates regards both types of thesis as exhibiting an attachment to the "absurd and paradoxical," as well as illustrating the consequences of divorcing intellectual arguments from productive practice (see 10.4–6). Repudiating all such counterintuitive quibbling, Isocrates advocates a commitment to "pursuing the truth" and to educating his associates "in the actions by which we conduct our political lives": in characteristic fashion, he insists that "it is far superior to have decent opinions/judgments about useful matters, than to have precise knowledge about useless things" (4–5).

This section of the *Helen* complements other polemical and programmatic passages in Isocrates' writings, while supplying perhaps the clearest indication that he anywhere gives us of a desire to distance himself from a relativistic view of truth, the standards of practical deliberation, or (accordingly) the function of public persuasion. By definition, as I have emphasized, Isocrates' stance is not theoretically explicit, and it is therefore dangerous to elaborate it too strongly on his behalf. At the same time, it is feasible to make basic sense of this passage without resorting to the "bundle of contradictions" view of the author. Nothing here supports the picture of Isocrates as a relativist. He effectively excludes a strong cognitive relativism (including Protagorean subjectivism [10.2]) by his criticism of those who deny the possibility of falsehood or contradiction. Equally, there is no sign of cultural relativism either here or elsewhere; as I have already argued, everything in Isocrates' writings points to a belief in a single standard of human *logos* or rationality. Finally, neither his rejection of unitary ethical knowledge nor his suggestion that practical morality requires "decent judgments" rather than precise knowledge commits him to moral relativism. On the contrary, it commits him to a standard of acceptability or reasonableness ("decency") of moral judgment which, though not knowledge-based, should be compatible with the general aim of "pursuing the truth."[34] What this amounts to, I suggest, is that Isocrates neither conceives of nor presents himself as in any way a relativist, and is right not to do so. The position he stakes out for himself is much closer to a thoroughgoing pragmatism—a pragmatism, however, so much at ease with itself that it possesses, as I have been at pains to suggest, no scope for effective interrogation of its own principles or practice.

The lack of any conceptual provision for intellectually open self-criticism is, if I am right, the besetting and crippling weakness of the Isocratean agenda. It is here, not in any tendency to relativism (which might, indeed, have had the opposite result), that Isocrates repudiates the central element in the Socratic paradigm of philosophy.[35] A program of education, of ethical deliberation, and of active citizenship which sets itself to operate so comfortably within the parameters of a common discourse may in principle make substantial and wide-ranging claims for its own value. But it cannot incorporate into its conception of *logos,* and is therefore denied inside its practice, too, a serious capacity to scrutinize, regulate, and where necessary revise its own guiding principles. In stark contrast to the philosophies of Plato and Aristotle,[36] Isocrates' writings employ such concepts as contingency, nature, and judgment in ways that take their significance entirely for granted. The movements of an Isocratean mind are destined, where it matters most, to lead an unexamined life. If this is so, it might well be thought inauspicious that Isocrates should ever have been regarded, as he sometimes has been, as a prototypical humanist. His influence on Western ideals of culture and education has depended above all on his ostensible integration of ideas of language, reason, and practical wisdom.[37] But the analysis presented in this essay encourages the conclusion that such integration is achieved at the level of a rationality whose pragmatic character leaves it unable to explore, justify, or even comprehend its own intellectual allegiances. If, then, a case is to be made for the continuing inclusion of Isocrates in anything that might merit the description of a rhetorical canon, it can do no better than start from the suggestion that the study of his works could fruitfully, if obliquely, contribute to a history of rhetoric that cultivates self-criticism as an indispensable virtue.

Notes

1. The fullest modern discussion of Isocrates' relationship to his contemporaries is C. Eucken, *Isokrates: Seine Positionen in der Auseinandersetzung mit den zeitgenössischen Philosophen* (Berlin and New York: De Gruyter, 1983). As with some nineteenth-century treatments of the same material, Eucken's conclusions often have a speculative confidence that outruns the nature of the evidence. My own approach in this essay places no reliance on the discernment of implicit references to one another by Isocrates and his intellectual rivals or on secondary evidence for personal hostility between them.

2. See 15.193–5, quoting 13.14–18: Isocrates himself, of course, makes a virtue out of the consistency he claims between the beginning and end of his career. (Note that all my textual references to Isocrates' works use their standard modern numbers; the Loeb edition gives these numbers only in square brackets in its list of contents: on this system, 3 = *Nicocles*, 4 = *Panegyricus*, 5 = *Philip*, 10 = *Helen*, 12 = *Panathenaicus*, 13 = *Against the Sophists*, 15 = *Antidosis*. All translations are my own.)

3. Plato, *Gorgias*, 448d9 (where Socrates refers to "so-called *rhêtorikê*"), whether or not it is the earliest surviving occurrence of the term, shows that it was a newish coinage in the early fourth century B.C.E. See N. O'Sullivan, "Plato and Kaloumene—Rhetorike (Comments on Recent Works by Schiappa and Cole)," *Mnemosyne* 46 (1993): 87–89. Isocrates himself uses the adjective *rhêtorikos* at 3.8 (15.256), but he nowhere applies any member of the word family to his own program.

4. N. H. Baynes, "Isocrates," in *Byzantine Studies and Other Essays* (London: University of London, Athlone Press, 1955), 160. Baynes's polemical piece was a reaction to the excessive estimate of Isocrates' intellectual stature in W. Jaeger, *Paideia* (Oxford: Oxford University Press, 1945), 3: chapters 2–6.

5. Isocrates normally uses the phrase in the plural; see, e.g., 13.21, 15.46, 260. On the concept of *logos* see p. 113.

6. In the *Panegyricus,* which is a paradigmatic case of a work with a fictionalized setting (a Panhellenic gathering at the Olympic games), Isocrates describes himself as one of those who have "kept back from [practical] politics" (4.171); see, e.g., 5.81, 12.10, 15.34, 144–45.

7. See 15.193 for a reference to the "publication" of this work, that is, its release, by means we cannot fully reconstruct, to interested readers.

8. The forthright rejection of any concept of rhetoric as an "ordered/codified art [*technê*]" at 13.12 represents Isocrates' fundamental position; see 15.184, 271. The element of rhetorical *technê* implied in passages such as 4.48, 9.73, and 15.205–6 must be construed in a weaker or more limited sense; see below.

9. The argument, if it is to hold, requires what Isocrates anyhow took for granted:

a very close connection between the ethical and the feasible. Isocratean thought leaves no room for an idealistic ethics that might be partly unfulfillable in practical terms.

10. Isocrates does, however, allow that some parts of rhetoric may have stable principles: he refers, at 13.16, to certain "forms of discourse" (e.g., 10.11, 12.2, 15.183) that are of general validity and apparently teachable. There has been debate about the nature of these forms, but all that matters for my case is that Isocrates evidently regards them as mere rudiments, not sufficient principles, for speaking or reasoning well.

11. Two details help to reinforce this point: one is Isocrates' willingness to invoke the notion of truth in many contexts (e.g., 10.4, 13.9, 15.11); the other is his attack on philosophers who deny the possibility of falsehood or contradiction (10.1). See p. 120.

12. 13.8; for the sentiment, see 10.5, 12.9, 15.184. It is unfortunate that George Norlin, in the Loeb edition of Isocrates' works, (Cambridge, Mass.: Harvard University Press, 1929), 2:291, should have translated *doxa* highly misleadingly as "theory"; this serious error is reproduced without correction by Brian Vickers, *In Defense of Rhetoric* (Oxford: Oxford University Press, 1988), 150.

13. For this specific avowal, see, e.g., 4.1.

14. 4.47: "adept" translates Isocrates' use of the verb *epistamai* ("know how to"), which occurs in similar contexts at, e.g., 4.10, 186; see the cognate noun at 15.187. Such passages seem to contradict the insistence elsewhere that rhetoric is not a knowledge-based discipline, but they are to be understood as implying a looser claim of expertise—a consistent knack rather than a grasp of propositional principles. This is particularly clear in the transition from 15.184–87.

15. See J. Jüthner, "Isokrates und die Menschheitsidee," *Wiener Studien* 47 (1929): 26–31 (reprinted in F. Seck, ed., *Isokrates* [Darmstadt, 1976], 122–27), who contests the view that Isocrates genuinely proclaimed a dissemination of Hellenism.

16. Norlin's Loeb translation has a strong tendency to do this. When, for example, he translates the adverb *alogôs* ("without *logos*," hence "irrationally") as "without the help of speech" (2: 329), he produces a peculiar statement that blunts Isocrates' concept of practical wisdom.

17. *De Oratore,* 3.54–61; the division is described at 60–61.

18. Not all historians of philosophy would defend the exclusion. Alexander Nehamas, "Eristic, Antilogic, Sophistic, Dialectic: Plato's Demarcation of Philosophy from Sophistry," *History of Philosophy Quarterly* 7 (1990): 3–16, argues that it is not possible to adjudicate between rival conceptions of philosophy and concludes, with ironic generosity, that "philosophy can include even the garrulous Isocrates: one can always count against him his garrulity, that is, his dialectical incompetence" (14).

19. Isocrates allows the "preparatory" function of such things as geometry, astronomy, and dialectic at 12.26, 15.261–65 (see 11.23); these are usually taken to be slightly compromising references to studies pursued in Plato's Academy. His disdain for pre-Socratic "physics" is abundantly clear at 15.268–69.

20. At the level, of course, of conceptual definition. I take it for granted that most philosophers would be dismissive of Isocrates' philosophical status on grounds

of, from their point of view, the poor quality of his thinking; but being a bad philosopher is a different matter from not being a philosopher at all.

21. T. Irwin, "Plato: The Intellectual Background," in R. Kraut, ed., *The Cambridge Companion to Plato* (Cambridge: Cambridge University Press , 1992), 66. Irwin's distinction between rhetoricians and sophists is questionable on wider grounds which are not directly pertinent to my argument.

22. Irwin, ibid., 68, perhaps tries to cover this last point with his statement that Isocrates "presented rhetoric as a sufficient moral education"; even this could mislead, if it obscured the fact that Isocrates erases any distinction between speaking well and being morally educated.

23. Gorgias is shown to make such a claim at Plato, *Gorgias,* 457a5–6, though the dialogue suggests that he also wishes to lay claim to ethico-political knowledge; for the tension here, see Stephen Halliwell, "Philosophy and Rhetoric," in I. Worthington, ed., *Persuasion: Greek Rhetoric in Action* (London: Routledge, 1994), 228–29.

24. E.g., 15.184.

25. The nearest Isocrates comes to proclaiming such technical facility is probably at 4.8, but this passage is treated too readily as an admission of sophistry by Baynes, "Isocrates," 147–48, who also cites 15.15 in a way that is itself rhetorical. Baynes's larger imputations of bad faith against Isocrates may or may not be justified (I suspect they are partially so), but their concern with his sincerity and consistency of practice is distinct from my own analysis of his explicit pronouncements on the principles of rhetoric.

26. Gorgias, *Helen* (fragment, 11), 10–14.

27. Aristotle, *Rhetoric,* 1.2, 1356a25–27.

28. In Aristotle's terms, it is in common discourse that many "reputable" moral views (*endoxa*) come into being and can consequently be discerned.

29. I have tried to suggest some tensions within it in "Popular Morality, Philosophical Ethics, and the *Rhetoric,*" in D. Furley and A. Nehamas, eds., *Aristotle's Rhetoric: Philosophical Essays* (Princeton: Princeton University Press, 1994), 211–30, reprinted in slightly abridged form as "The Challenge of Rhetoric to Political and Ethical Theory in Aristotle," in A. O. Rorty, ed., *Essays on Aristotle's Rhetoric* (Berkeley: University of California Press, 1996), 175–90.

30. See especially the idea that if rhetoric does reach first principles, it will cease to be rhetoric (*Rhetoric,* 1.2, 1358a25–26).

31. A. MacIntyre, *Whose Justice? Which Rationality?* (Notre Dame: University of Notre Dame Press, 1988), 86.

32. Irwin, "Plato," 68, likewise links Isocratean rhetoric to "nonrational manipulation."

33. He ascribes views of this sort to a number of fifth century B.C.E. thinkers, including his own reported teacher, Gorgias, and at least one other figure, Protagoras, now standardly classed as a sophist.

34. The criticism of those who deny "that we have any [of the virtues] by nature" (10.1) implies that Isocrates takes morality to be partly natural; the same seems to be entailed by such general reflections as at, e.g., 13.14.

35. Isocrates' relationship to Socrates is an obscure and vexed subject which cannot be discussed here. But it is necessary to say that there is no evidence in Isocrates'

own writings to support the claim of (e.g.) George Kennedy, *The Art of Persuasion in Greece* (Princeton: Princeton University Press, 1963), 179, that he "regarded himself as a follower of Socrates." The only reference to Socrates occurs at 11.4–6.

36. The contrast is a matter of structural commitments within entire modes of thought and argument; its validity is not undermined by the flawed execution of those commitments in particular instances.

37. Isocrates' influence should not, however, be exaggerated. The attempt of M. I. Finley, "The Heritage of Isocrates," in *The Use and Abuse of History* (London: Chatto and Windus, 1975), 193–214, to connect him with the failings of liberal arts education on the broadest scale, is misguided. Of the three main factors in Finley's "ancient heritage" (202), the idea of "training the mind" and the aim of a "fundamentally literary education" are hardly integral to Isocrates' program, while the notion of "high culture" for an elite owes little to him. It is ironic, moreover, that Finley should link the ancient heritage with excessive educational specialization (203)—something utterly unisocratean.

Hermeneutics and the Ancient Rhetorical Tradition

KATHY EDEN

SCHLEIERMACHER, OFTEN CONSIDERED the father of modern hermeneutics, notes in his "Outline for the 1819 Lectures" (4.2) that "The unity of hermeneutics and rhetoric results from the fact that every act of understanding is the obverse of an act of discourse, in that one must come to grasp the thought that was at the base of the discourse."[1] While Schleiermacher unquestionably means to grant universal application to this relation between rhetoric and hermeneutics, it is the intention of this essay to examine his claim as something other than a universal truth.

More precisely, I hope to demonstrate the validity of Schleiermacher's claim with some specificity in the historical development of ancient rhetoric, by outlining what I take to be the influence of ancient rhetorical theory on the development of interpretation theory or hermeneutics. With good reason, moreover, I have confined my outline to the period between the fourth century B.C.E. and the first century C.E. So far as I know, we have no substantial evidence for the theoretical discussions of either rhetorical or interpretive strategies before the fourth century B.C.E. And while the narrative certainly continues beyond the first century C.E., the plot is complicated considerably by the abundant evidence concerning the grammatical tradition.

This evidence not only demands and deserves equal attention in the continuing history of hermeneutics, but it also records the long-standing interaction between the grammatical and rhetorical traditions—an interaction that well predates the evidence itself. As Dio Chrysostom reminds us (53.1), Aristotle inaugurates a long line not only of rhetorical theorists but also of grammarians (*grammatikoi*), then called critics (*kritikoi*), who worked at interpreting poetic intention (*ten dianoian exegoumenoi*). We should not be surprised, then, to find substantial overlapping between chapter 25 of the

127

Poetics, where Aristotle addresses the problems of literary interpretation, and portions of his *Rhetoric.* In ascribing these principles of interpretation to rhetoric, therefore, I do not mean to overlook their early grammatical affiliations. Nevertheless, there is good reason to believe—and I hope to show—that the earliest critics or interpreters not only used rhetorical strategies in their exegetical exercises but actually discussed the interpretive act in these same terms.

Both the strategies and the terminology that describes these exercises, moreover, are of two fundamentally different kinds, and the difference is clearly preserved in the actual plans of the earliest rhetorical manuals. These manuals, or *technai,* as is well known, regularly separate questions of style (*lexis, elocutio*) from questions of proof (*pistis, probatio*). Perhaps less well known but equally true, the principles of proof applied, as early as Aristotle, to all three different kinds of oratory—forensic or legal, deliberative, and epideictic— belonged originally to one of them, the legal.[2] There is, in other words, a fundamental split in the art of rhetoric between legal and stylistic strategies; and this split, as I will argue, is also central to the development of hermeneutics, reflected in two of its oldest and most persistent terms: *dianoia* and *hyponoia.*

Dianoia and *Hyponoia* in Isocrates and Plato

ONE OF OUR earliest interpreters and theorists of interpretation—and one who conveniently introduces the long-standing association between rhetoric and hermeneutics—is the fictitious exegete in Isocrates' *Panathenaicus* (339 B.C.E.). Toward the end of this oration (233), the famed teacher of rhetoric claims to have assembled his students to hear his completed speech in praise of Athens.[3] Among these students is the young man who had defended the Spartans earlier in this same work against Isocrates' allegations (202–3). In this second encounter, however, the young man completely changes his strategy, and instead of disputing Isocrates' arguments, he undertakes to explain just what Isocrates meant by organizing his encomium as a comparison between Athens and Sparta—especially one so uncompromisingly favorable to the Athenians.

According to this exegete, Isocrates' intentions both in summoning his audience and in delivering this particular speech are disingenuous (*ouch haplos* [236]). Having praised Sparta in the past and faced with the present task of praising Athens, Isocrates needs to discover a device that will at once please his fellow Athenians, preserve the integrity of his previous statements about Sparta—thus protecting him against the charge of sophism—and challenge the interpretive acumen of his listeners (236–41). To accomplish these several ends, Isocrates deliberately chooses to employ ambiguous statements or *logoi amphiboloi*—statements capable of a double meaning (240).

128

What appears on the surface as censure, in other words, is really just the opposite. To casual readers, Isocrates' discourse will seem straightforward, ingenuous (*haplous* [246]), and easily comprehended, while those who scan this same discourse more rigorously (*akribos*) will discover that it is difficult and obscure, full of *poikiliai* and *pseudologiai* (246).

Although Isocrates, according to his interpreter, is anxious to conceal his real meaning (*dianoia* [247, 249]), his interpreter is equally anxious to clarify this meaning, even at the risk of decreasing its worth. For as the interpreter himself admits (247), "by implanting understanding in those who are without knowledge I render the discourse naked and strip it of the honor which would otherwise attach to it through those who study hard and are willing to take pains." On the other hand, however, by bringing to light Isocrates' covert praise of the Spartans, the interpreter assures Sparta of the public recognition that it deserves and, no less importantly, Isocrates of the public acclaim that he deserves (260–61) for composing so fitting an epideixis of these two great cities. At the conclusion of the interpreter's own highly encomiastic exegesis, Isocrates, so he himself says, joined the others in commending the interpreter's efforts but offered no comment on just how far this interpretation had correctly or mistakenly judged the *hyponoiai* of his *dianoia* (*tais hyponoiais tes emes dianoias* [265]).

Isocrates, in other words, chooses to leave open the question of his intentions, offering in addition no explicit reasons for including in this oration an instance of its interpretation.[4] In view of the fact that he does include such an instance, however, it is worth noting the principles of interpretation that emerge from it.

There are, we learn, two ways of understanding a text, simply (*haplos*) and precisely or rigorously (*akribos*).[5] Some texts are obscure, even intentionally obscure through the use of ambiguity. These are full of *hyponoiai* which totally confound the simple reader. Whether these *hyponoiai* are the strategies for enclosing meaning (*dianoia*) or the hidden meanings that are themselves enclosed cannot be satisfactorily determined by Isocrates' brief remark (265).[6] Nevertheless, it is clear that by concealing his intention or *dianoia*, the author not only protects himself against possible reproach but also makes even the precise reader work for his pleasure and profit and so value them all the more. As a consequence of the obscurity and ambiguity of these same texts, however, there is the constant danger to the exegete of committing an error of interpretation—a *hamartia*, or misreading.

The hermeneutics briefly set forth in the *Panathenaicus* shares several key principles with the theory of interpretation that emerges from the Platonic dialogues. Like Isocrates' fictitious exegete, Socrates, too, recognizes the danger of misinterpreting another's discourse, even when the method of discussion is dialectic. As a consequence of this recognition, Socrates insists that those participating in the dialogue proceed according to clearly and fully articulated arguments—even at the risk of stating the obvious. Otherwise, they run the even greater risk of finding in their opponents' words *hyponoiai* that were never intended (*Gorgias*, 454B–C).[7] And this danger to dialectic presents an even greater threat to all written discourse (*Phaedrus*, 275D–E; see *Protagoras*, 329A), particularly poetry. The *hyponoiai* of the poets render their compositions obscure and so unfit for educational purposes. Whatever Homer may have really meant in those episodes where the gods behave irrationally and immorally, the young cannot be expected to recognize, much less interpret, these *hyponoiai*.

Whereas Isocrates' reference to the *hyponoiai* of his *dianoia* raises its own ambiguity, the *hyponoiai* of Plato's poets seem to refer more straightforwardly to the stylistic devices fashioned (*pepoiemenas*) to cover meaning as opposed to the meaning so enclosed (*Republic*, 378D):

> But Hera's fetterings by her son and the hurling out of heaven of Hephaestus by his father when he was trying to save his mother from a beating, and the battles of the gods in Homer's verse are things that we must not admit into our city either wrought [*pepoiemenas*] in *hyponoiai* or without *hyponoiai*. For the young are not able to distinguish what is and what is not a *hyponoia*, but whatever opinions are taken into the mind at that age are wont to prove indelible and unalterable.[8]

Such poetic *hyponoiai*, moreover, serve the same function as the *proschemata* of sophist and poet discussed earlier in the *Protagoras* (316D–317A). These *proschemata*, employed by, among others, Homer, Hesiod, and Simonides, are similarly fashioned (*poieisthai*) to conceal the writer's meaning. Like Isocrates' fictitious exegete, Protagoras divides the audiences of this kind of discourse into two groups: the politically astute, who can recognize and interpret these devices, and the multitude, who cannot. Sometimes, however, even the clever interpreter fails to explicate a difficult passage successfully—even one as clever as Protagoras himself.

In fact, during one round of the agon between Socrates and Protagoras, the sophist temporarily turns from disputation on the larger ethical issues at hand to the interpretation of poetry, defending this maneuver on two grounds (338E): first, to be well educated is to be *deinos* or skillful in understanding and judging poetry; and, second, the few verses of Simonides that Protagoras has in mind treat the same topic now under debate, namely the nature of virtue.[9] Simonides writes, "For a man, indeed, to become truly good is hard" (339B) and so on. Without actually interpreting these lines, Protagoras, after eliciting Socrates' favorable judgment on them, proposes instead that they contradict other lines in the same poem. Referring to Simonides' quotation of Pittacus—"Hard quoth he, to be good" (339C)—Protagoras maintains that Simonides rejects Pittacus's words even though their meaning is identical to his own. In view of this contradiction, Protagoras argues, Simonides' poem cannot be "finely and correctly composed" (339B), as Socrates had judged it. It is in response to this apparent literary *problema*, then, that Socrates offers Plato's most elaborate and "sophisticated" discussion of literary interpretation. In the course of it, as we will see, Socrates, like Isocrates, advances a certain kind of interpretation, even while he calls the whole activity into question. In doing so, moreover, Socrates borrows his interpretive strategies not only from the art of rhetoric but from legal or forensic oratory, on the one hand, and from the elements of style, on the other.

Confronted with an apparent error or *hamartema* (340D) in the text, Socrates (not unlike the legal judge) looks to correct the error and provide a fair and just reading (*epanorthoma* [340A]; see 340D)—one that will sustain the judgment (*gnome* [340B]) of others. To do this, he brings to bear on the case in question all of the available proof (*tekmeria, martyria*), including historical and philological evidence and the testimony of passages from the same text and of analogous passages from other texts. The verse immediately following the passage under consideration, for instance, offers clear evidence (*mega tekmerion* [341E]) that the word *difficult* [*chalepon*], is not meant to be taken here in a pejorative sense. Similarly, Socrates calls to witness (*martyrei* [344A]; *martyreitai* [344D]) both the remainder of Simonides' poem and the verse of another poem to confirm his interpretation of the lines in question. With these various corroborating proofs and testimonies, moreover, the argument as a whole works to discover the poet's intention, his *dianoia* (*dianoeisthai, dianooumenos*)—much as the legal investigation does. This, Socrates repeats several times, is the single aim of the interpreter's inquiry (341E, 347A; see 344B).

In this particular case, however, Socrates identifies the *dianoia* of the poet with a secret meaning or intention—namely, to outdo or refute (*elenchein*) Pittacus, whose saying he quotes and rejects. Moreover, Pittacus's meanings or intentions in the lines quoted are, in their own turn, equally obscure to the outsider—intentionally obscure. In an effort to hide their wisdom from the rest of the world, Socrates contends, the Spartans and the seven sages, including Pittacus, resorted to stylistic strategies, to the use of *schemata* (*schematidzontai* [342B]). Among them is *brachylogia*, or aphoristic statement. Pittacus's saying employs this particular *schema*, designed for the private transmission of knowledge. By undertaking to controvert this saying, Socrates argues, Simonides is contriving secretly to overthrow Pittacus and win fame for himself (343C).

Although Socrates' case in support of this interpretation is wholly incredible, the interpreter's own secret intention in framing his interpretation is not so obscure. The agonistic aim that Socrates finds hidden in Simonides' ode characterizes equally Socrates' interpretation of that ode.[10] While openly intending to overturn Protagoras's claim that Simonides' poem contradicts itself, Socrates' more overt refutation is in fact a pretext for another thinly disguised intention—namely to refute the entire enterprise of literary interpretation. Under cover of a parody so subtle that both Hippias and Prodicus misinterpret it, Socrates undermines this special kind of sophistic discourse even while he practices it.

However, Socrates does not rely exclusively on this particular strategy to overthrow his opponent. Early in his refutation, he disparages—only slightly covertly—the sophist's position on the importance of understanding and judging poetry. Protagoras's view (339A) that the consummately educated man is one *deinos* in matters poetical is soon undercut by Socrates' choice of this very word to support the philological argument in his case against Protagoras. Socrates recalls that *deinos* properly refers to something bad or blameworthy, such as poverty, war, and disease, and not to something good or praiseworthy, as Socrates himself (like Protagoras) often uses it (341A–B).

Elsewhere in the Platonic dialogues, it is worth noting, the term *deinos* refers specifically to literary matters, often qualifying in particular the exegetical activity. In the *Phaedrus,* for instance, Socrates rejects both Lysias's and his own first speech as being clever or *deinos* rather than true (242D), holding that it is even better to be ridiculous than clever (260C). Similarly, Socrates warns Phaedrus against the ingenious or clever interpretations of the rationalists of their own day on the grounds that these interpreters cannot possibly correct (*epanorthousthai*)—that is, explain—all the myths of the gods and giants (229D). In the *Cratylus,* moreover, Socrates identifies the many Homeric exegetes (*hoi polloi exegoumenoi ton poieten*) as those who are clever on the subject of Homer (*hoi nun peri Homeron deinoi* [407A–B]); and he questions Ion to see if the rhapsode is *deinos* in the exegesis of Hesiod or whether his cleverness pertains to Homeric questions only (531A–C).

These judgments on literary interpretation throughout the dialogues are completely in line with Socrates' position in the *Protagoras.* In conclusion and almost as a kind of palinode to his own exegetical exercise (347E–348A), Socrates maintains that the wisest men avoid just this kind of debate because, in the poet's absence, it is impossible finally to ascribe truth to any one among the various contending interpretations. Debarred from reaching the truth, those who participate in such debates actually are trying only to enhance their own reputations.

In the *Protagoras,* then, Socrates first schematizes his intention through parody (and irony) and then openly states it. Nevertheless, his defense of a coherent meaning in Simonides' ode, like the interpretation of Isocrates' fictitious exegete, is remarkable in the history of hermeneutics, insofar as it preserves in outline a method or *techne*—perhaps already standard among the sophists—for solving literary *problemata.* This *techne,* moreover, includes both legal and stylistic principles. On the one hand, it shares its procedures and its aims with the law courts. Through an examination of corroborating evidence from the same text or from other texts, the exegete seeks to discover

132

the intention of the agent as speaker or writer. Not infrequently, however, this agent has so fashioned his discourse to avoid discovery, except, perhaps, to a select few. On the other hand, then, the exegete must learn to recognize and interpret the *hyponoiai* or *proschemata* of poet and sophist, designed to conceal their meaning. It is in his efforts to uncover the poet's intention that Socrates charges Simonides with schematizing—that is, relying on a strategy of style—in a conspiratorial effort to degrade and so overthrow his adversary, Pittacus (343C), who had, before him, schematized in an effort to conceal his own meaning.

Plato's discussions of interpretation, defined as the recovery of the speaker's or writer's intention, consider the problems raised not only by an entire discourse but also by the individual word. And these considerations add an element crucial to Platonic hermeneutics. For it is while exploring the nature of words that Plato addresses the important relation between what we will call *dianoetic* and *semantic* meaning—a relation that forms the basis of ancient interpretation theory. Later to become the focus of the modern science of semiotics or the study of signs, semantic meaning in Plato refers specifically to the capacity of language to indicate or make known some nonlinguistic reality. In the *Cratylus,* Plato introduces the crucial distinction between semantic and dianoetic meaning in an effort to investigate how far the relativism of the sophists pertains to language. At issue is the nature of the correspondence between words and things—that is, between linguistic entities and nonlinguistic entities. Is the bond a product of nature or, as the sophists claim, of convention?

In the earlier part of this dialogue, Socrates argues both that speech or *logos* signifies all things (*to pan semainei* [408C]), and that the relation between *logos* and the things it signifies is not arbitrary. This is not, however, because one thing can be signified by one word and one word only. As Socrates explains, "whether the same meaning [*to auto semainei*] is expressed in one set of syllables or another makes no difference; and if a letter is added or subtracted, that does not matter either, so long as the essence of the thing named remains in force and is made plain in the name" (393D).[11] So for those who understand the nature of words, he adds, there is nothing strange about the fact that the names of Astyanax and Hector share a single meaning (*tauton semainei*)—"ruler of men"—even though they have only one letter in common (393A).

In this as in all cases, however, the semantic meaning is referred to the intention or *dianoia* of the name giver (*ho ta onomata themenos*)—here Homer (393A). And the same holds true of the namer of Hestia; Socrates asks Hermogenes what that man had in mind (*dianooumenon*) when giving the goddess her name (401B). As the material of *logos,* in other words, *onomata* possess a semantic meaning that, at least in the early part of this dialogue, finds its validation not in social convention or common usage but rather in some prior dianoetic meaning. Consequently, Socrates concludes, the ancient usage of a particular word is more likely to be correct than its modern usage (418E–419A; see 421D). "Only the ancient word [*to archaion onoma*]" he maintains, "discloses the intention [*ten dianoian*] of the name giver" (418C; see 407A–B). In the course of his fanciful etymology of the beautiful, Socrates even goes so far as to elevate *dianoia*—identified with *to kalon* (i.e., *to kaloun*)—as the name-giving power (416C).

In the second part of this dialogue, Socrates reverses his position on the arbitrary relation between words and things; nevertheless, he preserves the crucial role of *dianoia* in verbal communication. Instead of focusing on the name giver, however, Socrates now shifts his focus to the individual speaker, who represents his intention (*dianooumai*) in words so that the listener will recognize that intention (434E; see 435B). Even when Socrates accounts for the role of convention in language, in other words, he refers it to a higher standard—that of *dianoia*. And this standard operates not only in cases of spontaneous private discourse but also in more public recitation.

So it is that Socrates in conversation with Ion distinguishes between the poet's thought, his *dianoia,* and his words, his *epe* (530B–C), "since a man can never be a good rhapsode without understanding what the poet says. For the rhapsode ought to make himself an interpreter [*hermenea*] of the poet's thought [*dianoias*] to his audience."[12] And so it is that Phaedrus prefaces his recitation of Lysias's speech on the advantages of the beloved's giving himself to a nonlover rather than to a lover with the (admittedly false) declaration that having failed to memorize it word for word (that is, the *rhemata*), he will repeat the general sense, the *dianoia,* of the whole (288D)—if not exactly what the poet said, at least more or less what he meant. In both cases, then, the orator's or poet's intention (*dianoia*) exists somewhat independently of his actual words—his *epe* or *rhemata*—which, Socrates and Phaedrus would seem to agree, can vary without radically changing the *dianoia* itself.

The distinction between dianoetic and semantic meaning, which informs the various arguments of the *Cratylus,* proves to be equally fundamental to Aristotelian hermeneutics as developed in the *Rhetoric* and the *Poetics.* Together, these two manuals provide the first fully theoretical discussions of both the legal and the stylistic principles that we have already seen practiced by our two earlier interpreters. First, as we will see, the *Rhetoric* and *Poetics* firmly establish the crucial role of intention or *dianoia* as a legal principle (and as the basis of dianoetic meaning) not only in acting but, more important for our purposes, in speaking and writing. Second, these two works address the nature and function of signs or *semeia* (as the basis of semantic meaning), not only as the nonlinguistic elements of rhetorical persuasion and tragic recognition but, more to the point here, as the linguistic elements that, in combination, constitute style or *lexis.* And third and finally, Aristotle places

134

under considerations of style the *hyponoiai* so important, as we have seen, to the interpretation theory of both Isocrates and Plato.

Legal and Stylistic Strategies in Aristotelian Hermeneutics

THE ROLE OF meticulous literary critic that Socrates assigned to Protagoras coincides, in fact, with Aristotle's depiction of the sophist in the *Poetics*, where Aristotle himself defends Homer against Protagoras's charge that the poet has erred (*hemartesthai*) in the opening line of the *Iliad* (19.8). Whereas the sophist accuses Homer of giving a command, rather than uttering a prayer, with the words "Sing, goddess, the wrath?" Aristotle insists that such distinctions do not properly belong to the art of poetry. Distinguishing this art from the other arts, Aristotle then goes on in chapter 25 to refute just the kind of literary problem that Protagoras posed for Socrates.

Unlike the argument of the *Poetics* as a whole—which addresses Plato's more philosophical objections to poetry as one of the mimetic arts—chapter 25 in particular defends poetry against the more technical problems raised by literary criticism. Aristotle broadly categorizes the various charges (*epitimemata*) of the critics under five general headings; their refutation (*lusis, elenchos*), in turn, relies on twelve rules of interpretation (25.32). These include, generally speaking, many of the same historical, philological, textual, and contextual rules that Socrates invoked to refute Protagoras. Following Socrates, moreover, Aristotle formulates his defense in language familiar to forensic debate. When the poet is accused of contradicting himself, for instance, Aristotle (recalling Socrates' answer to Protagoras) suggests that the contradiction be examined (25.30–31) "in the same way as an opponent's refutations in argument, to see whether the poet refers to the same thing in the same relation and in the same sense, and has contradicted either what he expressly says himself or what an intelligent person would take to be his meaning." The method of refutation in matters of literary interpretation, in other words, overlaps with the method of refutation in rhetoric and dialectic.[13]

The aim of interpretation, as Aristotle understands it, moreover, is to establish a fair and equitable reading, one comparable to Socrates' "corrected reading" or *epanorthoma*—the very word Aristotle uses to describe equity in the *Nicomachean Ethics* (5.10.3, 6). Literary interpretation, the work of the *kritikoi*, is a matter of judgment (*krisis*), and the equitable literary judgment, Aristotle maintains, must distinguish the essential from the accidental error of poetry. Not surprisingly, only a consideration of poetic intention can determine the nature of the error (*hamartia*). The poet commits an essential error when he fails to carry out some aspect of his poetic intention. "If a man meant to represent something [*proeileto mimesasthai*] and failed," Aristotle contends, "that is an essential error. But if his error is due to his original conception being wrong . . . that is then a technical error in some special branch of knowledge" (25.6).[14] In spite of the accidental error, in other words, the poet still carries out his original artistic intention.[15] Following Glaucon, moreover, Aristotle contrasts the equitable literary judgment of these errors with one based on irrational prejudice. Some literary critics, imagining the poet to disagree with their own prejudgments, vote to condemn (*katapsephisamenoi*) his errors and then contrive arguments to support their verdicts (25.23–25). Aristotle agrees with Glaucon that this kind of judgment must be avoided.

Although prominent in the *Poetics* as a whole, as one of the three most important constituent parts of tragedy, the term *dianoia* does not occur in chapter 25. Instead, Aristotle refers to poetic intention with a verbal form of *prohairesis* (*proeileto, proelesthai* [25.6]), another term crucial to Aristotle's legal and ethical theory and closely associated with *dianoia* throughout the *Poetics*, the *Rhetoric*, and the *Nicomachean Ethics*. Both terms convey the notion of intention. *Prohairesis*, however, belongs to the context of action—what one intends or means to do—while *dianoia* seems on the whole more familiar to the context of verbal or written statement—what one intends or means to say.[16]

In his discussion of equity in the *Rhetoric*, for instance, Aristotle identifies the intention of the agent (an intention culminating in some action to be judged) by *prohairesis* and the intention of the legislator (an intention culminating in a written statement to be interpreted) by *dianoia* (1.13.17): "And it is equitable to pardon human weaknesses, and to look, not to the law but to the legislator; not to the letter of the law [*pros ton logon*] but to the intention [*dianoia*] of the legislator; not to the action itself but to the moral purpose [*prohairesin*]."[17] For the same reason, Aristotle insists that the wrongdoing in perjury—the crime of making false statements under oath—consists in the intention or *dianoia* of the speaker's words and not in what he actually says (1.15.32–33). On the same grounds, moreover, Aristotle attributes *dianoia* to both the periodic sentence and the enthymeme (3.9.3–4, 3.10.4). It is, then, fully in keeping with his definition of mimesis as an activity that Aristotle refers to poetic intention in chapter 25 as *prohairesis*.[18] And it is equally appropriate that he sends the aspiring dramatist to the *Rhetoric* to learn about *dianoia* (6.22, 19.2–4). Adept in the art of persuasive speaking, the dramatist can endow his tragic characters with varying capacities both to say what they mean and to convince their audiences that they mean what they say.

Crucial as a whole to the poet's understanding of *dianoia*, the *Rhetoric* also provides more specifically a set of guidelines for interpreting written texts, not unlike those under consideration in chapter 25 of the *Poetics*. Although for the orator these include the various written statements that bear on one's case, such as the laws and contracts that number among Aristotle's inartificial proofs, they nevertheless must be examined according to many of the same principles as the text of a tragedy. Both, for instance, are subject to real or apparent ambiguities and contradictions (*Rhetoric*, 1.15.9–11, 3.5.4; see *Poetics*, 25.20–25); and both can be read with more or less emphasis on the strictly literal statement as opposed to the broader meaning. That is, both can be read more or less equitably.[19] While recognizing that the advocate often must argue for strict construction in order to advance his position, Aristotle nevertheless favors, here as elsewhere, the more liberal judgment, which takes into full account the various ways that words can signify (*posachos semainein*).[20]

Both in the *Rhetoric* and in the *Poetics*, in fact, Aristotle gives careful consideration not only to dianoetic meaning but also to semantic meaning, recognizing the linguistic as well as the nonlinguistic nature of signs or *semeia*. Outside language, the sign or *semeion* is thoroughly familiar both to oratory, particularly legal oratory, and to tragedy. As palpable proof— the bloody knife, the torn cloak, the scar—the *semeion* is especially useful in arousing the emotions of the audience, bringing the physical reality of the deed right before their eyes (*Rhetoric*, 2.8.6). When brought within the compass of logical argumentation, on the other hand, the *semeion* provides the raw material of the rhetorical syllogism and in this way further contributes to the orator's powers of demonstration (*Rhetoric*, 1.2.14, 1.3.7). That Aristotle considers both functions of the sign equally indispensable to tragedy is clear, moreover, from chapter 16 of the *Poetics*, where he sets out the more and less dramatic uses of *semeia* in tragic scenes of recognition.[21] In its more complex linguistic relations, however, the sign, in conjunction with other linguistic signs, constitutes style or *lexis*.

The interaction or combination (*synthesis, synthete*) of linguistic signs— that is, style—is so fundamental to oratory and poetry that Aristotle devotes nearly the whole of the third book of the *Rhetoric* and chapters 19 through 22 of the *Poetics* to examining it. Together, these two discussions cover a full range from the smallest unit of sound, incapable on its own of signifying anything (*asemos*), to the most intricate statements, capable of signifying in more than one way.

The syllable, for instance, Aristotle defines as "a sound [*phone*] without meaning [*asemos*], composed [*synthete*] of a mute and a letter that has sound" (*Poetics*, 20.5). *Logos* or statement, at the other extreme, "is a composite sound with a meaning [*phone synthete semantike*], some parts of which mean something [*semainei ti*] by themselves" (*Poetics*, 20.11–12; see *On Interpretation*, 4, 16b27–28).[22] And metaphor, appropriate to both oratory and poetry (*Rhetoric*, 3.2.6), entails the application or transferral of composite significant sounds from a familiar (*oikeios, kyrios*) to an unfamiliar (*xenikos;* compare *glotta*) context, that is, from literal to figurative statement (*Poetics*, 21.7–15). This foreign or unfamiliar aspect, according to Aristotle, elevates or dignifies one's style (*Rhetoric*, 3.2.1–3; *Poetics*, 22.3–4).

Metaphor, in fact, lies at the very center of Aristotle's theory of style, which, in its commitment to clarity or perspicuity (*Rhetoric*, 3.2.1), aims above all at the appropriate combination of familiar (or literal) and unfamiliar (or figurative) elements.[23] When properly constructed, moreover, metaphorical statement actually clarifies what would otherwise remain unknown to the listener; and this new knowledge, painlessly won, gives him pleasure (3.10.2–3). When improperly constructed, on the other hand—that is to say, when the application is inappropriate or far-fetched (*porrothen*)—metaphor degenerates into riddle (*ainigma*) and thus renders the style obscure.[24] While obscurity results from the abuse or overuse of foreign or unfamiliar elements, including metaphor, it also may result from ambiguity (*amphibolia*), caused by the inherent capacity of words to signify in more than one way (*Rhetoric*, 3.18.5). Not infrequently, Aristotle notes, a speaker will intentionally exploit ambiguous terms in an effort to conceal the fact that he has nothing substantial to say (*Rhetoric*, 3.5.4). Aristotle considers this and all obscurity a vice of style.[25]

While condemning stylistic obscurity, however, Aristotle nevertheless recognizes the power of indirect statement, particularly in legal accusation and defense. In the third book of the *Rhetoric*, which treats matters of style, he refers to this strategy as *hypolepsis* and advises ways both to combat it (3.15.1, 6) and to exploit it (3.16.10). In the *Nicomachean Ethics*, on the other hand, Aristotle actually uses the term *hyponoia* in reference to the *schema* characteristic of New Comedy, contrasting it to the crude obscenities that characterize Old Comedy (4.8.6): "and the civilized person's amusement differs from the slavish person's, and the educated person's from the uneducated person's. This can also be seen from old and new comedies; for what people used to find funny was shameful abuse, but what they now find funny instead is *hyponoia*, which constitutes no small stylistic or *schematic* refinement [*pros euschemosynen*]."[26] Here as in the *Protagoras*, then, *hyponoia* belongs to the arsenal of *schemata* available to poet and rhetorician alike. As a feature of style, it depends on the inherent capacity of words to signify in more than one way, that is, to move between familiar and unfamiliar contexts, between literal and figurative statement. Like Isocrates and Socrates, Aristotle recognizes the political and legal advantages of schematizing in this way; and like them, he takes into account the presence of this device in all kinds of discourse, including poetic discourse.

After Aristotle, the rhetorical tradition between the first century B.C.E. and the first century C.E. preserves and even enlarges the division between legal and stylistic strategies. That is to say, in the tradition after Aristotle, the split between *dianoia* and *hyponoia* widens. The rhetorical works of Cicero, Quintilian, and Demetrius will serve here to demonstrate both this and two further related developments: on the one hand, the increasing prominence of stylistic matters and, on the other, the changing trend in the stylistic strategies most in fashion. Whereas Cicero and Quintilian lament the change, Demetrius finds stylistic virtue in an Aristotelian vice.

Hermeneutics and the Later Rhetorical Tradition

CICERO, AS FREQUENTLY noted, follows Aristotle on many of the most important questions concerning the literary arts. On the particular question of *interpretatio scripti,* the interpretation of written texts, Cicero in fact elaborates those rules outlined in Aristotle's *Rhetoric.* The usual context of his discussions is, like Aristotle's, the law court; and the texts under consideration are for the most part either the laws themselves, which must be applied to the events demanding adjudication, or last wills and testaments that have come under dispute. Although his early work, the *De Inventione,* identifies five ways in which the written word (*scriptum*) engenders controversy (1.13.17–18, 2.40.116–2.41.154), his later works reduce this list to the first three only (*De Oratore,* 1.31.140, 2.26.110; *Topics,* 95–96): contradiction, ambiguity, and discrepancy between the writer's words (his *scriptum*) and intentions (his *voluntas*).[27] Frequently, the means of resolving these controversies overlap.[28]

When, for instance, conflict arises from a contradiction (*ex contrariis*) between two written statements, such as two laws, the advocate will assess their relative reliability and applicability by comparing their individual integrity. A written statement containing either of the other two flaws, namely ambiguities or discrepancies between what its author says and what he intends, is arguably less reliable than one that avoids these problems (*De Inventione,* 2.49.144–47). In turn, a controversy arises from ambiguity (*ex ambiguo*) "when what the writer meant is obscure [*cum quid senserit scriptor obscurum est*] because the written statement can have two or more significations [*quod scriptum duas pluresque res significat*]" (2.40.116, see 1.13.17).[29]

Ambiguity, in other words, results here as in Aristotle from the inherent capacity of words as verbal *signa*—Aristotle's *semeia*—to signify in more than one way. And the consequence of ambiguity is obscurity. Like Aristotle, Cicero condemns obscurity as the chief vice of style; and like Aristotle, he attributes it in large part to the abuse of metaphor (*translatio*).

For Cicero, as for Aristotle, in fact, metaphor occupies the center of stylistic theory. Words can carry both a literal (*propria*) and a nonliteral (*translata*) sense. Used metaphorically, they can combine with other words used literally, or they can form part of a continuous metaphorical statement. In the second case—that of continuous metaphor—something other than what is said has to be understood (*De Oratore,* 3.41.166). While the Greeks now call this stylistic strategy *allegory,* Cicero explains, he will retain the name *metaphor* or *translatio,* preferring to stand by Aristotle on the question of terminology (*Orator,* 94).

When skillfully constructed, metaphorical or figurative statement surpasses the literal in its greater power not only to please the listener (*De Oratore,* 3.39.159) but also to instruct him (*De Oratore,* 3.39.155–56). When artlessly

139

constructed, on the other hand, metaphorical statement degenerates into riddle or enigma (*aenigma*), providing neither pleasure nor instruction (*De Oratore*, 3.42.167). When confronted with an equivocal or enigmatic word or passage, the interpreter must try to resolve the ambiguity by examining it in light of the common usage of words, the context, other passages by the same writer, and even apposite details of that writer's life and habits (*De Inventione*, 2.116–17).[30]

Even as it pertains to the interpretation of legal texts, then, ambiguity is a matter of style—the combination of linguistic *signa* or *verba*, used literally or metaphorically. The discrepancy between the writer's written words and his intention, in contrast, constitutes a legal rather than a stylistic matter. Sometimes the conflict is stated in terms of the familiar opposition between *verba* and *res* or *sententia;* but more often it takes the form of *scriptum* versus *voluntas.* In this case, *voluntas* translates Aristotle's *dianoia* and indicates that the will of an agent has found expression, either in speech or in action.[31]

In addition, the argument for interpreting word or deed on the basis of intention continues to bear the closest affinity with the legal arguments for equity.[32] In the *De Inventione* (2.46.136), Cicero advises that anyone speaking against the letter (*contra scriptum*) must do so by adducing the principle of equity (*aequitas*). And Crassus follows this advice, as it were, when he defends Manius Curius with the argument that the protection of equity depends on upholding the "last wills and the intentions [*voluntatis*] of dead men" (*De Oratore*, 1.57.242).[33] The legal judge, moreover, is an interpreter, an *interpres voluntatis*, who reads the lawgiver's intentions as preserved in his words (*De Inventione*, 2.47.139). It is for this reason alone, in fact, that the laws are so revered and "not because of their words [*non propter litteras*], which are only faint and obscure indications of intention [*quae tenues et obscurae notae sint voluntatis*]" (*De Inventione*, 2.48.141).[34]

Although enlisted above to defend the equitable reading, this particular argument is made equally to serve the advocates of the opposing position, who call for a more literal interpretation. Whereas the defenders of *voluntas* emphasize the feebleness of words as *obscurae notae*, their opponents, the advocates of *scriptum*, far from disregarding the writer's will, insist, on the contrary, that his words are the very image of that will and that these words alone can preserve his intentions (*De Inventione*, 2.44.128):

> Therefore, if the aim is to carry out the writer's intention [*voluntas scriptoris*], it is we and not our opponents who do this. For the one who interprets a writer's intention from his own writing approaches it more closely than the interpreter who does not look for that intention in the writer's own words, which he left as an image, as it were, of his intention [*sententiam*], but examines those words rather for hidden meanings [*suspicionibus*], to which the interpreter alone has access.

The defenders of *scriptum,* in other words, fight to preserve the authority of the literal text as a public image of the writer's meaning in contrast to what they see as the private, unverifiable *suspiciones*—or, in the Greek, *hyponoiai*— discovered by their opponents. Both sides, then, pursue the same end. Whereas the defenders of *voluntas* attack their opponents, the defenders of *scriptum,* for relying on the obscurity of words, the defenders of *scriptum* in turn accuse their attackers of upholding not the *dianoia* of the writer, to which they lay claim through the literal sense of his words, but rather some ingeniously conceived *hyponoiai*—not *voluntas* but *suspiciones.*[35]

This opposition between *dianoia* and *hyponoia*—or *voluntas* and *suspicio*—gains further ground with Quintilian. In the *Institutio Oratoria,* Quintilian follows Cicero in enumerating the kinds of controversy that can arise over a written text (e.g., 8 Preface 10–11); and like Cicero, he locates this discussion within his fuller treatment of legal oratory. More precisely, Quintilian brings the problems of *interpretatio scripti* under the larger rubric of the legal question (*quaestio legalis*) as part of the very specialized and by this time rigidified status system.[36]

On the other hand, Quintilian does not restrict the notion of *voluntas* to legal *scriptum.* On the contrary, he extends it to discourse or *sermo* in general and explains further that any *sermo* expressing purpose or *voluntas* will consist of *res* and *verba* (3.2.2). *Res* he defines as that which is expressed (*quae significantur*) and *verba* as that which expresses (*quae significant*) (3.5.1). The relation of *res* to *verba,* in other words, is that of signified to signifier.

On most questions concerning signification or, more simply, style, Quintilian follows both Aristotle and Cicero. Perspicuity is still the chief virtue of style and metaphor (*translatio*) or metaphorical expression (*verba translata*), the preeminent device for instructing, delighting, and moving an audience (8.6.4). Metaphor in a continuous series—Quintilian notes, accepting the un-Aristotelian designation rejected by Cicero—becomes an allegory. Generally speaking, allegory consists in "saying one thing, while intending something else to be understood" (*aliud dicere aliud intelligi velle* [9.2.92]).[37] As we might expect, an abuse or overuse of this figure renders one's style enigmatic and obscure (8.6.14).

Quintilian, in fact, laments the contemporary trend away from clarity toward obscurity and away from a striving for direct speech toward a reliance on allusiveness—that is, intending one's words to signify more than they say (*pleraque significare melius putamus quam dicere* [8 Preface 24]). Although this fashion includes the use of various figures such as *emphasis* and *aposiopesis,* the most fashionable of the many kinds of allusion practiced in the first century C.E. is *suspicio.*[38]

The "hidden meaning" that Cicero's interpreters were accused of finding, in other words, has become a regular feature of style in Quintilian's day. Through the use of *suspicio,* Quintilian explains, the speaker intends his

KATHY EDEN

listener to infer from his words what has not actually been said (*per quandam suspicionem quod non dicimus accipi volumus* [9.2.65]). This figure differs from irony, he continues, in that the meaning intended is not contrary to what the words actually signify but is rather hidden (*latens*) so that the hearer is left to discover it. *Suspicio* is so pervasive, Quintilian notes, that many contemporary rhetoricians simply refer to it by the more generic term *schema*. While he admits its special usefulness in cases where straightforwardness is either unsafe or unseemly (9.2.65–66)—before a tyrant, for instance, or a powerful adversary in court—he locates its special power in the "perverse" pleasure it gives the listener who, detecting the hidden meaning, "applauds his own penetration and regards another man's eloquence as a compliment to himself" (9.2.78–79). This perverse pleasure must be distinguished, it seems, from the true pleasure of instruction that results from the proper interpretation of metaphor.[39]

Quintilian's concern with the new vogue of an allusive style, and in particular with the increased popularity of *suspicio* or *hyponoia*, is further corroborated by another, probably contemporary, discussion of style, Demetrius's *Peri Hermeneias*, the so-called *On Style*. Whereas Quintilian speaks out against this new allusiveness, however, Demetrius approves it—at least in certain circumstances. Its special appropriateness to some kinds of statement, in fact, fosters in Demetrius's manual a new character of style. Although Demetrius is often and not without reason located among the theorists of Peripatetic rhetoric, the addition of this new style and its peculiar relation to stylistic obscurity locate a crucial shift away from Aristotelian rhetorical principles.[40]

In his *Peri Hermeneias*, Demetrius considers the place of both *dianoia* and *hyponoia* in rational expression. His concept of *dianoia* is derived more or less from Aristotle, who, as we have seen, treats dianoetic meaning in his *Rhetoric* and *Poetics*. Following Aristotle, Demetrius defines the *kolon*—the topic that begins the treatise—as the smallest unit of a completed meaning or *dianoia*.[41] With composition (*synthesis*) and diction (*lexis*), moreover, *dianoia* determines the character of expression (35) as either elevated (*megaloprepes*), elegant (*glaphyros*), plain (*ischnos*), or forcible (*deinos*) (38, 132–36, 139, 179, 187–89, 236–37).[42] These characters of style then occupy Demetrius's attention for the remainder of the manual.

Hyponoia, on the other hand, qualifies more specifically two of the four kinds of expression—the elevated and even more so the forcible. An addition to the traditional three characters of style—grand, middle, and plain—this fourth character, the *deinos*, distinguishes itself, in fact, by its indirect (*en schemati* [288]), allusive, allegorical (*allegorikos* [99, 100, 101, 151, 243, 282, 283, 285, 296]) nature, regularly using such *schemata* as *aposiopesis*, *eschematismenon* or covert allusion, *emphasis* or innuendo, allegory, and ambiguity.[43] The special province of this added style, in other words, is the expression of the *hyponoiai* characteristic of threats, criticisms, religious mysteries, and all symbolic expressions (*symbola*). Particularly in this last case,

Demetrius maintains (243), "We are left to infer [*hyponoesai*] the chief of the meaning, as though it were a sort of riddle [*ton symbolon*]. Thus, the saying 'your cicadas shall chirp from the ground' is more forcible in this figurative form [*allegorikos*] than if the sentence had simply [*haplos*] run 'your trees shall be hewed down.'"[44]

While Demetrius here and earlier (at 99–100) borrows his example from Aristotle's discussion in the *Rhetoric* of apothegms and riddles, Demetrius's emphasis in both passages differs significantly from Aristotle's. Whereas Aristotle is pointing out the effectiveness of these verbal puzzles as instruments of instruction—even contending that they serve no purpose at all unless the listener gradually apprehends their meaning—Demetrius, on the other hand, draws attention to the forcible quality of obscurity in its own right, with full awareness of how un-Aristotelian his position is (254): "And (strange though it may seem) even obscurity [*asapheia*] often produces force, since what is distantly hinted [*hyponooumenon*] is more forcible, while what is plainly stated [*exhaplothen*] is held cheap."[45]

One of the more common motives for obscure expression or allusiveness—and one that Demetrius discusses in some detail (289–94; see Quintilian, 9.2.65–66)—is fear of political reprisal. Not only under despotic but sometimes even under democratic rule, a man must follow the mean of indirection between the extremes of base flattery and overt criticism (294). We might remember here Isocrates' encomium on Athens in the *Panathenaicus*. The other motive, stated above, also recalls the conviction of Isocrates' fictitious exegete, namely, that the interpreter values less what he has gained with little labor. While it departs from the Aristotelian commitment to clarity, Demetrius's so-called forcible style nevertheless advances a position preserved—and maybe even practiced—not only by Isocrates but also by Plato.

In the *Protagoras,* as we have seen, Socrates points out the ambiguity of the very term that characterizes Demetrius's fourth style, responding to Protagoras's claim that it is the ultimate mark of the educated man to be clever or *deinos* in interpreting poetry by reminding him that the word *deinos* referred originally to something that inspires terror—to something terrible.[46] In Demetrius, the character of expression called *deinos* preserves its association with both aspects of the term, and with the older meaning through the regular presence of *hyponoia.* "Any darkly hinting expression [*to hyponooumenon*]," Demetrius says, "is more terror striking [*phoberoteron*]" (100); and he gives as an instance the mysteries that, revealed in allegories (*en allegoriais*), inspire fear and trembling (*pros ekplexin kai phriken*) (101; see 283).

But the forcible style is also noted for its cleverness or ingenuity. In the *Panathenaicus,* we recall, Isocrates has his fictitious exegete contrast two kinds of reading—*haplos* and *akribos*—and associates the latter with those discourses that include *hyponoiai,* in contrast to the discourse that is itself straightforward (*haplous*). Demetrius's so-called forcible style clearly characterizes Isocrates' second kind of discourse—the one that demands to be read *akribos*. As the style currently in fashion (245), the forcible rejects not only the simple, nonperiodic composition of the ancients but also the simple, naive state of mind that this composition reflects (244): "In this [forcible] style the periods should be brought to a definite point at the end. The periodic form is forcible [*deinon*], while looseness of structure is more naive [*haplousteron*] and betokens an innocent nature. This is true of all old-fashioned style [*hermeneia*], the ancients being distinguished by naïveté [*haploikoi*]." While this simple style—as Demetrius and the Isocratean exegete agree—is held cheap, the forcible style, in contrast, gains in value through its obscure and figurative or allegorical expression—through the presence of *hyponoia*.[47]

In his well-known essay on how the young man should study poetry—an essay concerned with the correction (*epanorthosis*) of both texts and young moral characters—Plutarch records for the first century C.E. an important shift in hermeneutical terminology. Whereas the interpreters bent on distorting poetic intention used to refer to their interpretive strategies as *hyponoiai*, they now call them *allegories* (*Moralia*, 19E–F). Plutarch's observation, coupled with his disapproval, not only coincides with Quintilian's contemporary judgment on the trend in rhetorical composition, but it also serves as a forceful reminder of the coincidence between the concerns of the ancient rhetor and interpreter.

Between the fourth century B.C.E. and the first century C.E., as we have seen, rhetorical theory did not confine itself to questions of composition. On the contrary, it regularly extended its field of inquiry to the problems of interpretation, which it defined according to a specialized terminology. This terminology, moreover, reflects the fundamental split in the rhetorical tradition between legal and stylistic matters. On the one hand, the spoken word or written text, like the consequence of any other act, must be understood with reference to the intention (*dianoia, voluntas*) of the agent—a legal consideration. As a special kind of act, on the other hand, speech or writing uses verbal signs (*semeia, signa*), which operate according to their own laws of signification. When these laws are neglected, the result is ambiguity (*amphibolia, ambiguitas*) and obscurity (*asapheia, obscuritas*); when they are manipulated, the result is style (*lexis, elocutio*). When the ambiguity and obscurity are intentional, the result is a style characterized by *hyponoiai* or *suspiciones*. Texts so constructed demand a special method of interpretation.

Both Quintilian and Plutarch raise objections to this kind of interpretation; but their objections are by no means universal. In the period that follows them, in fact, allegorical interpretation, largely neglecting its rhetorical affiliation, becomes increasingly more fashionable. It does not follow, however, that the position articulated by Quintilian and Plutarch lacks later proponents. Quite on the contrary, the division between the legal and stylistic strategies of ancient rhetoric and hermeneutics will develop into an opposition; and this opposition will shape the history of interpretation theory through the Renaissance.

Notes

A draft of this paper was first delivered to the Classical Civilization Seminar of Columbia University. I am grateful to William Race, Carey Ramos, Ann Van Sant, and James Zetzel for their helpful criticisms on this and subsequent occasions. I also wish to thank the readers at *Rhetorica* for their very useful suggestions. This essay is reprinted from *Rhetorica* 5.1 (1987): 59–86.

1. "*The Hermeneutics:* Outline for the 1819 Lectures," trans. Jan Wojcik and Roland Haas, *New Literary History* 10 (1978): 1–16.

2. See Kathy Eden, *Poetic and Legal Fiction in the Aristotelian Tradition* (Princeton: Princeton University Press, 1986), 9–19.

3. All references to this text are from the second volume of *Isocrates*, trans. George Norlin (London: Heinemann, 1929). On this oration, see Gunther Heilbrunn, "Isocrates on Rhetoric and Power," *Hermes* 103 (1975): 153–78; Hans-Otto Kroner, "Dialog und Rede: Zur Deutung des Isokrateischen Panathenaikos," *Antike und Abendland* 14 (1968): 102–21; and William H. Race, "*Panathenaicus* 74–90: The Rhetoric of Isocrates' Digression on Agamemnon," *TAPA* 108 (1978): 175–85. Race's comment, 175 n. 1, that scholars have found in Isocrates' reference to Agamemnon a covert allusion (that is, a *hyponoia*) to Philip is suggestive in light of the discussion that follows.

4. On this question, see Christoph Schäublin, "Selbstinterpretation im 'Panathenai-kos' des Isokrates?" *Museum Helveticum* 39 (1982): 165–78.

5. See *Panegyricus*, 11–12. And for the important role of these two contrasting terms in philosophical and literary matters more generally, see Wesley Trimpi, *Muses of One Mind: The Literary Analysis of Experience and Its Continuity* (Princeton: Princeton University Press, 1983), 116–43, 235–40.

6. Norlin's translation—"on the contrary, I praised both his native ability and his training, although beyond that I uttered not a word about the sentiments which he had expressed, *as to how far his conjecture had hit upon my purpose or missed the mark*" (italics added)—does not help to clarify the technical language at issue.

7. I am translating *hyponoountes* here as the condition of believing that some statement contains *hyponoiai*.

8. All references to this text, unless otherwise cited, are to Plato, *Republic*, trans. Paul Shorey (London: Heinemann, 1930). While I have preferred to retain *hyponoia* as a technical term in this passage, it is worth noting that Shorey translates it as "allegory," perhaps following Plutarch's well-known observations on this matter (*Moralia*, 19E–F). See *Republic*, 332B–C.

9. All references to this dialogue are to *Protagoras*, trans. W. R. M. Lamb (Cambridge, Mass.: Harvard University Press, 1924).

10. For a discussion of Socrates' interpretation, see Hermann Gundert, "Die Simon-ides-Interpretation in Platons Protagoras," in *EPMHNEIA: Festschrift Otto Regenbogen* (Heidelberg: C. Winter, 1952), 71–93.

11. Plato, *Cratylus,* trans. H. N. Fowler (London: Heinemann, 1926). All references are to this edition. On this matter, see T. W. Bestor, "Plato's Semantics and Plato's *Cratylus,*" *Phronesis* 25 (1980): 306–30; G. Fine, "Plato on Naming," *Philosophical Quarterly* 27 (1977): 289–301; R. J. Ketchum, "Names, Forms and Conventionalism: Cratylus 383–95," *Phronesis* 24 (1979): 133–47; Norman Kretzmann, "The History of Semantics," *The Encyclopedia of Philosophy* VII: 359–62.

12. Plato, *Ion,* trans. W. R. M. Lamb (London: Heinemann, 1925).

13. Aristotle describes these methods at *Rhetoric,* 3.17.13. While Else dismisses chapter 25 as not integral to the *Poetics* as a whole, his observation that its "point of view" is "that of an attorney working up a brief" is to the point (Aristotle, *Poetics,* trans. Gerald F. Else [Ann Arbor: University of Michigan Press, 1969], 112 n. 168). See also Gerald F. Else, *Aristotle's Poetics: The Argument* (Cambridge, Mass.: Harvard University Press, 1957), 632.

14. Aristotle, *Poetics,* trans. W. Hamilton Fyfe (London: Heinemann, 1927). All references, unless otherwise indicated, are to this edition.

15. See on this matter *Nicomachean Ethics,* 6.5.7; and Trimpi, *Muses of One Mind,* 382–90.

16. On the further distinction between *dianoia* and *prohairesis,* see *Rhetoric,* 3.16.9, and also *Poetics,* 6.23. See also A. M. Dale, "Ethos and Dianoia: 'Character' and 'Thought' in Aristotle's *Poetics,*" in *Collected Papers,* ed. T. B. L. Webster and E. G. Turner (Cambridge: Cambridge University Press, 1969), 139–55, esp. 145.

17. Aristotle, *Rhetoric,* trans. John Henry Freese (London: Heinemann, 1926). All references, unless otherwise indicated, are to this edition.

18. On mimesis as an activity, see Else, *Aristotle's Poetics,* 8–9.

19. See *Rhetoric,* 1.15.4–6, 12, and 1.13.17, quoted above.

20. See *Rhetoric,* 2.23.9; *Poetics,* 25.22; *Topica,* 1.15; and also *Topica,* 5.2, 129b30; *Sophistical Refutations,* 165a10; and *Metaphysics,* 1006a29. See also George L. Kustas, *Studies in Byzantine Rhetoric* (Thessaloniki: Patriarchikon Hidryma Paterikon, 1973), 64–65.

21. See Eden, *Poetic and Legal Fiction,* 9–24.

22. The first four chapters of Aristotle's *On Interpretation* are relevant to this discussion. There Aristotle also treats the units of meaning from the simplest to the most complex. In addition, he distinguishes the linguistic from the psychological aspect of interpretation (3.16b19–22)—a distinction so important to the *Rhetoric* and the *Poetics.* The former he refers to with *semainein,* the latter with *dianoia.* Semantic meaning—that is, the relation between signifier and signified—is wholly conventional or arbitrary (2.16a20–28), while dianoetic meaning—the relation between the thought, intention, or meaning of the individual speaker and the words he chooses—is emphatically not arbitrary and accounts for why the semantic meaning in the very act of communicating can and will express the dianoetic meaning more and less accurately. The case of contraries discussed at 14.23a32–38 is suggestive in this regard. In this passage, Aristotle argues that we cannot interpret whether a speaker means when he says, "Callias is the contrary of just," that Callias is unjust or not just; and the ambiguity results from the distinction between the verbal proposition as spoken (*en tei phonei*) and the speaker's intended meaning (*en tei dianoiai*). Although all discourse relies on semantics or the rules

of language, it finds its ultimate validation, here as in Plato, in the individual speaker's intention. On the difficulties of chapter 14, see Aristotle's *Categories and De Interpretatione,* trans. J. L. Ackrill (Oxford: Clarendon, 1963, rpt. 1978), 153–54.

On the distinction in Aristotle between meaning and signification—or what I have called dianoetic and semantic meaning—see T. H. Irwin, "Aristotle's Concept of Signification," in Malcolm Schofield and Martha Craven Nussbaum, eds., *Language and Logos: Studies in Ancient Greek Philosophy Presented to G. E. L. Owen* (Cambridge: Cambridge University Press, 1982), 241–66, esp. 253: "Aristotle, however, does not use 'signify' as we might use 'mean.' He does not think that what someone signifies is what he means; the speaker signifies what the word he uses signifies. Since '*proprium*' signifies what belongs always to a subject, that is also what the speaker 'signifies by his speech' (*Topica,* 134a9) in using '*proprium*' (134a5–7)."

See also Richard McKeon, "Aristotle's Conception of Language and the Arts of Language," in R. S. Crane, ed., *Critics and Criticism* (Chicago: University of Chicago Press, 1952), 176–231, esp. 204.

23. See on this matter *Poetics,* 22.1, 22.16–17; and *Rhetoric,* 3.2.8. And for the different status of metaphor in dialectic, see *Topica,* 4.3.123a33 and 6.2.139b33.

24. See *Rhetoric,* 3.2.12, 3.3.4; and *Poetics,* 22.5. And on the *ainigma* and *apophthegma,* see *Rhetoric,* 3.11.6.

25. On this judgment and its subsequent history, see Kustas, *Studies in Byzantine Rhetoric,* 63–100.

26. Aristotle, *Nicomachean Ethics,* trans. Terence Irwin (Indianapolis: Hackett Pub. Co., 1985), 4.8, 1128a20–25. I have modified this translation slightly for my particular emphasis.

27. To this list, the *De Inventione* adds (1) analogy (*ratiocinatio*) and (2) definition (*vis verbi*). For a nearly contemporary discussion, see *Rhetoric Ad Herennium,* 1.11.19, whose list of the types of controversy coincides with that of the *De Inventione,* with the addition of a sixth, namely *translatio,* or, in the Greek, *metalepsis.*

On the opposition between *scriptum* and *voluntas* in the ancient rhetorical treatises, see Heinrich Lausberg, *Handbuch der Literarischen Rhetorik* (Munich: M. Hueber, 1960), 118–19; and Trimpi, *Muses of One Mind,* 278–82.

28. The discussion in the *Orator* (trans. H. M. Hubbell [London: Heinemann, 1939]) clarifies this overlapping (121): "For he will clearly recognize that there can be no dispute in which the controversy does not arise either about fact [*res*] or about words [*verba*]: in the case of fact the dispute is about the truth of the charge, its justification or its definition; in the case of words whether they are ambiguous [*de ambiguo*], or contradictory [*de contrario*]. For if there is ever a case in which one thing is meant and another expressed [*aliud in sententia videtur esse aliud in verbo*], this is a kind of ambiguity which usually arises from the omission of a word [*ex praeterito verbo*]; in this case we see that there are two meanings [*res duas significari*], and that is the characteristic of ambiguity." See *De Oratore,* 2.26.110–12.

29. Unless otherwise indicated, translations of the *De Inventione* are my own. For the place of ambiguity in jesting and for the clear association of ambiguity with stylistic matters, see *De Oratore,* 2.61.250–2.65.261.

30. *De Inventione,* trans. H. M. Hubbell (London: Heinemann, 1949), 2.117: "In the next place, one ought to estimate what the writer meant from his other writings, acts, words, disposition and in fact his whole life, and to examine the whole document which contains the ambiguity in question in all its parts, to see if any thing is apposite to our interpretation or opposed to the sense in which our opponent understands it. For it is easy to estimate what it is likely that the writer intended from the complete context and from the character of the writer, and from the qualities which are associated with certain characters."

31. On *voluntas* as a translation of *dianoia,* see Albrecht Dihle, *The Theory of Will in Classical Antiquity* (Berkeley: University of California Press, 1982), 135–38, 241–42; and Lausberg, *Handbuch der Literarischen Rhetorik,* 109, 118.

32. On this matter, see Dihle, *The Theory of Will,* 136–38; Trimpi, *Muses of One Mind,* 266–75; and Eden, *Poetic and Legal Fiction,* 40.

33. See also 1.57.243–44 and *Brutus,* 144–46.

34. See Cicero, *Topica,* 8.35–36; and see *Rhetoric,* 3.15.9 and 3.16.10.

35. See *Brutus,* 131 and 144; and see *De Officiis,* 1.33. See also *Ad Herennium,* 4.53.67, on *significatio.*

36. See 3.6.29–104 and *De Oratore,* 1.31.139–40. For Quintilian on ambiguity, see 7.9.1–15, esp. 7.9.15 (*Institutio Oratoria,* trans. H. E. Butler [London: Heinemann, 1921], 4 vols. Unless otherwise indicated, all references are to this edition): "In cases of ambiguity [*amphiboliae*] the only questions which confront us will be sometimes which of the two interpretations [*sermo*] is most natural, and always which interpretation is most equitable [*aequius*], and what was the intention of the person who wrote or uttered the words."

    For recent discussions of the status system, see Otto Alvin Loeb Dieter, "Stasis," *Speech Monographs* 17, 4 (1950): 345–69; Ray Nadeau, "Classical Systems of Stases in Greek: Hermagoras to Hermogenes," *Greek, Roman and Byzantine Studies* 2, 1 (1959): 51–71, and "Hermogenes' *On Stases:* A Translation with an Introduction and Notes," *Speech Monographs* 31 (1964): 361–424; Wayne N. Thomson, "Stasis in Aristotle's *Rhetoric,*" *Quarterly Journal of Speech* 58 (1972): 134–41.

37. There are, however, two kinds of allegory under this general description: one presents one thing in words and another in meaning; the other presents something contrary to the words.

38. On *aposiopesis,* see 9.2.54–57; and on *emphasis,* see 9.1.3, where Quintilian defines it as "the gift of signifying more than we say" (*plus quam dixeris significationem*), and 9.2.64, where he says it is nearly identical to *suspicio.* At 8.2.11, however, *emphasis* is an aid to clarity.

    See on this matter Erich Auerbach, "Figura," in *Scenes from the Drama of European Literature* (Minneapolis: University of Minnesota Press, 1984), 25–28; and Kustas, *Studies in Byzantine Literature,* 159–99.

    Also interesting in this context is Quintilian's description of the Greek figure *adianoeta* (8.2.20–21): "Worst of all are the phrases which the Greeks call ἀδιανόητα that is to say, expressions which though their meaning is obvious enough on the surface, have a secret meaning. . . . Such expressions are regarded as ingenious, daring and eloquent, simply because of their ambiguity, and quite a number of persons have become infected by the belief that a passage that requires a commentator [*quod interpretandum sit*] must for that very reason be a masterpiece of eloquence. Nay, there is even a class of hearer who find a special pleasure in such passages; for the fact that they can provide an answer to the riddle fills them with an ecstasy of self-congratulation, as if they had not merely read the phrase, but invented it."

39. Quintilian's observations and judgments on the stylistic trends of the first century c.e. are substantiated by Longinus and, perhaps more surprisingly, by Seneca. Although Longinus approves of reading Homer allegorically (9.7), he nevertheless condemns the excessive use of metaphor, which inevitably degenerates into allegorical bombast (32.6–7). In addition, he warns against the overuse of *schemata*, which leads both despot and judge to suspect the speaker's words of *hyponoia* (17.1–2).

　　Seneca's advice to Lucilius on matters of style decries the same excess. At the other extreme from those who make a too frequent use of bold metaphors, Seneca condemns those who say too little rather than too much. These seek to please their listeners by fashioning some *suspicio* for them to discover (*sunt qui sensus praecidant et hoc gratiam sperent, si sententia pependerit et audienti suspicionem sui fecerit* [*Epistulae* 114.10–11; see 114.1, and Quintilian, 9.2.78–79]).

　　On the other hand, however, both Longinus (7.3) and Seneca (*Epistulae* 59.5) recognize the virtue of a style that is so full of significance that the words cannot be fully comprehended at first encounter. So does Cicero (*Orator*, 139), quoted by Quintilian, 9.1.45.

40. On Demetrius's relation to earlier Peripatetics, including Aristotle, see G. M. A. Grube, *A Greek Critic: Demetrius on Style* (Toronto: University of Toronto Press, 1961), 32–39; W. Rhys Roberts, *Greek Rhetoric and Literary Criticism* (New York: Longmans Green, 1963), 48–70; Dirk Marie Schenkeveld, *Studies in Demetrius on Style* (Amsterdam: A. M. Hakkert, 1964), 28–33, 80–106. On the question of dating, see Grube, *A Greek Critic*, 39–56, 133–55; and Schenkeveld, *Studies in Demetrius*, 120–22, 135–48.

41. For the *dianoia* of the enthymeme, see 30. For a thorough discussion of Demetrius on the *kolon*, see Schenkeveld, *Studies in Demetrius*, 23–50.

42. The opposition between *dianoia* and *lexis*, as two of the three parts of expression, recalls the familiar opposition between the *schemata dianoias* and the *schemata lexeos*—the figures of thought and speech—to which Demetrius refers at 184 and 267 (see also 133, 136). On the obscure origins of this division, see Schenkeveld, *Studies in Demetrius*, 132–34. While Aristotle does not in his *Rhetoric* juxtapose two kinds of *schemata*, he does nevertheless distinguish matters of *dianoia* from matters of *lexis* (*Rhetoric*, 3.1.7). In this regard, several things are worth noting: that between Aristotle and Demetrius, the concerns of style have become predominant; that the *schemata dianoias* come under the treatment of style; and that *hyponoia*, as we will see, is created by the *schemata dianoias* and not by the *schemata lexeos*.

　　For the place of these *schemata*, the *figurae sententiarum et verborum*, in the Latin tradition, see Quintilian, 9.1.10–18; and Lausberg, *Handbuch der Literarischen Rhetorik*, 308–9.

　　On the relation between *lexis* and *hermeneia* as technical terms, see Grube, *A Greek Critic*, 139–41; W. Rhys Roberts, "The Greek Words for 'Style,'" *Classical Review* 15 (1901): 252–55; and Schenkeveld, *Studies in Demetrius*, 66–68.

43. On the traditional three characters of style, see G. L. Hendrickson, "The Peripatetic Mean of Style and the Three Stylistic Characters," *AJP* 25 (1904): 125–46, and "The Origin and Meaning of the Ancient Characters of Style," *AJP* 26 (1905): 249–90. On Demetrius's addition of a fourth character, see Schenkeveld, *Studies in Demetrius*, 66–87. On Demetrius's treatment of these particular *schemata* in the forcible style, see 282–95 and also 103; Grube, *A Greek Critic*, 124–25, 134–35; Kustas, *Studies in Byzantine Literature*, 68–72; and Schenkeveld, *Studies in Demetrius*, 101–6, 120–22, 129–31.
44. Demetrius, *On Style*, trans. W. Rhys Roberts (London: Heinemann, 1927). All references, unless otherwise indicated, are to this edition. Although Roberts uses the English *infer* to translate both *hyponoesai* at 243 and *logizesthai* at 222, the two responses indicated here are not at all identical. Demetrius's advice in the latter case (borrowed from Theophrastus) that the speaker of the plain style encourage his listener to draw the necessary inferences echoes rather Aristotle's own position on how best to instruct and please one's listeners. In this way, Demetrius adds, the speaker makes the listener a witness (*martus*) to his words and avoids insulting his intelligence. It is in the context of instructing and pleasing the listener, in fact, that Aristotle uses the example of the cicadas which Demetrius appropriates (*Rhetoric*, 3.11.6; see *Poetics*, 4.5–6).
45. On the other hand, Demetrius does recognize that one can overdo it, not only in the plain style (102) but even in the forcible style (287).
46. On the use of this term to designate the fourth style, see Grube, *A Greek Critic*, 136–37; and Roberts, "The Greek Words," 266 n. 6.
47. For the contrast between *haplous* and *allegorikos* in discourse, see 100 and 243, quoted above.

Rhetoric and the Body of Christ: Augustine, Jerome, and the Classical Paideia

BRENDA DEEN SCHILDGEN

THE ROLE OF classical rhetoric in the Patristic period has been well docu-
mented.[1] Of the eight most prominent Latin fathers of the Church, five
(Tertullian, Cyprian, Arnobius, Lactantius, and Augustine) were professional
rhetoricians before they converted to Christianity, while Ambrose, Jerome,
and Hilary were trained in the rhetorical schools.[2] The specific character and
consequences of the adoption of classical rhetoric have been the subject of
recent explorations into Christian discourse. Averil Cameron has suggested
that Christianity's "special relationship to textuality" was a dynamic factor in
the growth and development of the religion rather than being secondary to
economic and institutional forces.[3] Peter Brown has argued that the adoption
of the classical *paideia* by the Christian leadership in late antiquity to Christian
structures of authority played no small role in the political ascendancy of
the Church. Thus, the classical *paideia* as "the common ground among all
members of the upper classes" provided codes of civic behavior and self-
control to support a generous and cultivated exercise of authority.[4] Pagan
rhetoric (declamation, argumentation, and hermeneutics) and a canon of texts
that came down to the Church fathers as its companion, the trademarks of
late antique education,[5] became the property and the power of the newly
emerging Christian ecclesiastical structure of the times. Because of the importance of the Bible, which had emerged as the canonical normative text
in Christianity,[6] rhetorical issues (in the form of hermeneutics, canonical
debates, proclamation, and argumentation) formed the central matrix around
which all other theological and ecclesiastical concerns were to be discussed
(dogmas, doctrines, canon law, and general teachings).

Plato's conviction that "true" rhetoric would truly "serve" the state and
Cicero's methods for rhetorical performance and delivery, ultimately in the

service of the state,[7] are appropriated to "the body of Christ" in the most profound way. The central text of this religion, its Bible, which would be used to uphold orthodox teachings, was translated into Latin by a skilled Ciceronian rhetorician. The most influential figure of the early Western Church, Augustine, whose intellectual authority would hold steady for more than a thousand years, adapted the methods of Ciceronian rhetoric for interpreting and understanding this central text as well as for proclaiming its mysteries. Though the contribution of Augustine's *De Doctrina Christiana* to the history of rhetoric is well recognized, particularly by medieval scholars, Jerome's contribution has not received comparable attention.[8] The *De Doctrina* was widely distributed during the Middle Ages, but scholars have tended to overlook Jerome's hermeneutical contributions in his prefaces to the Bible which appeared in many Bibles during the Middle Ages.[9] Pairing Jerome and Augustine to discuss their roles in institutionalizing the sacred texts and methods for interpreting them and the Christian compromise they negotiated with the canon of pagan Latin literature highlights the unique approach to rhetoric and rhetorical methods handed over to Western Christendom.[10] For both Jerome and Augustine, despite Jerome's occasional denials,[11] the canon of Latin letters, beginning as the concubine of the Christian Church, became its lawful handmaiden. However, despite this successful cultural transformation,[12] contingencies haunt the rhetorical activities of the two leading figures in this literary movement in Western Christendom, whose awareness of the vulnerability of their work undermines any certainties they sought to uphold. Because the Christian belief about human humility before an ineffable divinity is fundamentally opposed to the purposes of pagan rhetoric,[13] rather than triumphantly taking antique learning captive, their efforts reveal their awareness of the fragility of their rhetorical practices. There is in Jerome and Augustine an unresolved tension between what Augustine calls a *dispensatio temporalis* ("temporal dispensation" [*De Doctrina Christiana*, 1.35.39]), or all human interactions with language, and the single enjoyment of God. This is not just an addendum to the cultural project of late antique Christianity; it flows through every action and purpose contemplated or performed. For the Church fathers, the eschatological hope that the Incarnation provided calls all humans to attention as Augustine expresses it in the *Confessions:* "None of this is contained in the Platonists' books. Their pages have not the mien of the true love of God. They make no mention of the tears of confession or of the sacrifice that you will never disdain, a broken spirit, a heart that is humble and contrite, nor do they speak of the salvation of your people, the city adorned like a bride, the foretaste of your Spirit, or the chalice of our redemption."[14] Nonetheless, despite their knowledge of the vulnerability of their literary work, both Jerome and Augustine recognized that the rhetorical program of studies they had inherited and which they transformed for Christian use was the primary means for comprehending Scriptures and thus the process by which they and their fellow believers might come to know the Word of God. In assigning to rhetoric this central importance, that is, the salvation of one's eternal soul, they gave it an eschatological relevance that far surpassed its erstwhile role in Roman education.

In this discussion of Jerome's and Augustine's rhetorical philosophy, I will focus particularly on Augustine's *De Doctrina Christiana*, Jerome's prefaces to the Bible, Jerome's letter 57, the letter to Pammachius, letter 53 to Paulinus of Nola, and the correspondence between Augustine and Jerome,[15] examining their theories of hermeneutics (the mirror of rhetoric)[16] and translation and the role of the pagan and sacred canons in their literary theories. Despite their efforts to "close down" the open-ended interpretive possibilities intrinsic to all language-related activities, both recognized the tentativeness in rhetorical exercises. In this respect, while reflecting ongoing concerns of the rhetorical tradition firmly established in the West by the fourth century C.E., both Jerome and Augustine share in attitudes made popular in recent times by such new philosophical rhetoricians as Jacques Derrida and Hans-Georg Gadamer,[17] though they, like Derrida and Gadamer, have their own means to address the inevitable contingencies of language.

Jerome and Augustine must be credited as the Western fathers who conferred Christian approval on the pagan Roman canon of classical letters. Jerome possessed unreserved admiration for Cicero, "Tullius is inspired with the spirit of rhetoric . . . and translated,"[18] despite his occasional professions about secular letters which may at first glance seem to represent a more severe breach between his early rhetorical training and his adoption of the Christian life. This dichotomy is most vividly dramatized in his famous quote from the letter to Eustochium (22), where he admits that when he had moved to Jerusalem, he had taken his precious library with him, and Virgil, Cicero, Horace, and Plautus seemed stylistically more pleasing to him than the Bible.[19] When it came to his major literary project, the editing and translating of the Bible, it was Jerome's pagan rhetorical training that provided him with the tools for this monumental task, and he did not fail to inform his readers of this fact. For example, in his letter to his friend Pammachius (57), he defended his principles of translation on the grounds that he had followed the authority of Cicero and Horace to render the Greek into Latin *sensum de sensu* rather than *verbum e verbo* on the grounds not only of sense but also of rhetorical grace.[20] He writes, "Yes, as for me, I do not only confess, but I profess freely: when I translate the Greeks—except the holy Scriptures, where even the order of the words is also a mystery—I render not word for word, but sense from sense. In this, I have as teacher Cicero, who translated."[21] As he points out, it was the Ciceronian theory to translate *sensum de sensu* rather than *verbum e verbo*, and he follows in this tradition, and despite his insistence to the contrary in this letter, he invariably translated sense from sense in the Bible, too. His literary methodology unfolded in his numerous letters, particularly his correspondence with Augustine and other colleagues about problems with translating the Bible, and his prefaces to the biblical texts reflect this Ciceronian education, a humanistic approach to rhetoric and all language-related activities, which combined philosophy, the study (that is, interpretation) of revered secular literary texts, and ethics. Jerome reveals both his enamorment with classical letters and the impact his rhetorical studies had on him as he constructed his theory of translation and interpretation, based on Cicero, Horace, and, of course, Origen, whom he credits with inspiring his biblical translation activity: "Origen, who, assembled the old translation of Theodotius, prompted my studies . . . and he clarified what formerly was confusing."[22]

In letter 112, Jerome, referring Augustine to his prefaces to the various texts of the Bible and to letter 57, defends a multifaceted interpretation theory for the Bible similar to the kind applied to translating and interpreting secular literature,[23] and in letter 115, he asks his friend to "play together in the field of Scriptures without doing harm to one another."[24] One of Jerome's most careful defenses of Christian scholarship appears in letter 70, written to a Roman orator named Magnus. Magnus had asked him to defend his use of secular literature which polluted the "whiteness of the Church" with the "stain of the pagans."[25] He methodically pointed out to his correspondent that his habit of using nonreligious texts had precedents in Hebrew, Greek, and Latin religious writings, citing Paul (who quoted Callimachus and Menander), Josephus, Philo, Clement of Alexandria, Origen, Tertullian, Minucius Felix, Arnobius, and Lactantius. The language of his defense burns with the same passion that characterized his earlier promise to abandon Ciceronianism in letter 22. Speaking of Paul's domestication of classical learning to Christianity, Jerome argued:

> Is it so surprising that, taking possession of secular knowledge because of its elegant style, that is, the beauty of its parts, I wish to take it from captivity and slavery and make it an Israelite; if all that she has is cankered whether by idolatry, voluptuousness, errors, passions, I should cut it off or shave it away, and so with this body become pure, I will take her to myself to procreate servants born in this house for the Lord Sabaoth. My work profits Christ's family . . . my adultery with a stranger increases the number of my companions in service.[26]

Combining family, reproduction, sexual congress, and gender metaphors to describe the relationship of Christians to classical eloquence, Jerome makes an impassioned argument to legitimize this "sexual" liaison, so that the children of concubinage, that is, the wisdom wrought in the pleasure of classical letters, will be mated to Christianity. He argues to retain the learning and the rhetorical training of his pagan education and to match it with the Christian message, and in doing so to enrich Christian truth and increase Christian numbers.

Augustine's distinction between *uti* and *frui* (the "useful" and the "enjoyable") in the *De Doctrina*, in fact, a Christian revision of Horace's *utile/dulce* dichotomy,[27] successfully adapted classical rhetoric to the terms of late antique Christian humanism. The *De Doctrina Christiana* justifies all human knowledge as useful so long as it leads to the single enjoyment of the divinity. Though he gave up his professional relationship with these secular words to take up the cause of the single Word, he nevertheless never renounced the potential value of Latin letters. By 394, the year before he became bishop, Augustine argued in *Contra Adamantum* that classical authors should be deferred to only in matters of style, but in the *De Doctrina Christiana*, his dichotomy between *uti* and *frui* opened the possibility for all learning to prove useful in one's Christian development, depending, of course, on one's motive for pursuing it. In fact, in book 2, he specifically probes the place of "human institutions" in Christian learning, urging that what was to be learned in "pagan" education might prove useful.[28] Augustine's frequent references to the works of Latin authors, especially Virgil, Horace, and Cicero, testify to his enduring romance with classical letters.[29]

For both Jerome and Augustine, however, the reality of the Incarnation had changed everything (Jerome, "Prologue"; Augustine, *Confessions*),[30] and all Christian rhetorical activities had to be ruled by this new economy of salvation. All scriptural interpretive activities could not lead to a contradiction to this foundation. But although Jerome shared theological convictions with Augustine, on questions of interpretation, as the problematics of "meaning" emerged in the translation of the Bible, they frequently differed, with Jerome invariably supporting grammatical interpretations, what he would call the literal level of the text, over the allegorical possibilities.[31] Jerome was assigned the Bible project because of his philological and linguistic erudition, and as a consequence he was regarded as the most intelligent commentator on the literal level of the Bible.[32] A skilled linguist, following in the footsteps of the great early commentator and editor of the Bible, Origen, Jerome advanced a threefold hermeneutic theory (literal, historical, and allegorical)[33] also modeled on Origen's exegetical studies[34] in contrast to Augustine's multifaceted theory advanced in the *De Doctrina*. Jerome insisted that readers must have an accurate text, must understand the words and their sense, that is, their literal and historical meaning, and, finally, must comprehend their spiritual significance. Nevertheless, aware as they both were of the difficulties in interpretation and, from a theological perspective, the dangers, they share some important attitudes about how to harness written words.

For both Augustine and Jerome, spontaneous insight (or revelation), as experienced by Anthony, the perfect Egyptian monk, who had memorized sacred Scriptures simply by hearing them (*De Doctrina*, prologue, 4), or experienced by the apostles is rare (Jerome, letter 53), because it is brought about by direct spoken contact. These examples are unusual because for most people experience with the Word of God is mediated through written language (even if the Word is heard when read or recited), a medium that is flawed both because it is what Augustine labeled a "human utility" (words "are things used to signify something" (*On Christian Doctrine*, 1.2.2)[35] and also because it requires human intervention for clarification. Therefore, for both Augustine and Jerome, a teacher and a method are essential before "intelligent" interpretation can occur, and also interpretation is a science, or a sophisticated method. Both also want to exercise authority over the potentially anarchical reading or interpreting public by presenting systematic methods for understanding. These methods, systems, and guidelines are all intended to control the reading and interpreting activities of those less prepared for these activities than they themselves. What other reason did Augustine have for writing the *De Doctrina*, or Jerome for arguing for teachers in his prefaces to the Bible? Both recognized and feared the inherently fluid nature of the inscribed word and wanted to exercise authority over this inscription.

For Jerome and Augustine, the distinction between prophecy and interpretation, or between spontaneous insight and mediation, is the foundation for their discussion of hermeneutical methods. Augustine begins the *De Doctrina Christiana*, his most elaborate discussion of interpretive methods, with a reference to St. Anthony, who "without any training in reading" came to understand sacred Scriptures "through prudent thinking" (*On Christian Doctrine*, Prologue, 4).[36] Jerome, in letter 53 (parts of which appeared in prefaces to the Bible), remarks about how astonished the Pharisees were that Peter and John could know the Law though they were unlettered: "the Holy Spirit suggested to them what comes to others through daily meditation on the Law."[37] In both these examples, Jerome and Augustine distinguish between direct insight (unmediated), in which the open-endedness of language is overcome because the difference or alienation between God and humans has been erased, and their own hermeneutical activities which require the intervention of interpreters or translators.[38]

But in the absence of such a direct communication of the Word, as Augustine points out, the case for most of us (see *De Doctrina*, prologue), we must have recourse to a science of reading, a method mediated by men that will facilitate the interpretation of the words. Augustine, in fact, is impatient with those who would claim that they understand through direct communion with God, for these same enlightened ones would then proclaim their learning to other men: whoever "glories in his understanding of whatever is obscure in the Scriptures through a divine gift, believes correctly in thinking that his ability does not come from himself but is divinely given, so that he seeks the glory of God and not his own. But when he reads and understands without the explanantions of men, why does he presume to explain to others?" (*On Christian Doctrine*, prologue, 8).[39]

156

While Jerome argued that the disciples Peter and John, because of the differences between spoken and written words, had not needed to study because they learned directly from the Holy Spirit, in letter 53, he makes a spirited argument reaching back to the most revered figures of classical and religious tradition for teachers as mediators for those who want to understand Scriptures. He cites the journeys of Pythagoras to Memphis and Plato to Archytas of Tarentum, of nobles who visited Titus Livy, and Paul who went to Jerusalem to learn from Peter, because spoken words possess a latent power, and what passes directly from the mouth of the speaker to the ears of the learners sounds more strongly.[40]

About written words, particularly those in Holy Scriptures, on the other hand, and in contrast to unmediated logocentric communication, Jerome realized their inherent openness to multiple interpretations, thus requiring specialists because everyone thinks he or she can be an interpreter of Scripture. Arguing with his correspondent, Paulinus, that he could not progress in scriptural knowledge without a guide to show the way, he also insisted that like every other professional skill, understanding the Bible required teaching, method, and proficiency (letter 53, 14–15).

Knowing the dangers in the free operation of the inquiring interpreter, Jerome, like his colleague Augustine, sought a method or means to restrict a totally free exercise in interpretation, particularly with regard to Scriptures. In discussing his own translation project, he relied on the revelations of the New Testament to translate the Old Testament, not because he did not trust the seventy translators of the Septuagint but because they, unlike the apostles, did not experience direct revelation of the Word: "or for example the books of the Seventy translators, the Holy Spirit joins with the testimony of the Apostles. . . . Do we condemn the old? By no means. But we are able to work after the former in the house of the Lord. They interpreted [translated] before the coming of Christ and they did not know how to convey what was doubtful sense, but we write after his passion and resurrection."[41]

Testifying to the difficulties of biblical interpretation as well as the need for a process for interpreting, Jerome emphasized the need for specialized guidance before entering into the meaning of these most subtle texts. The capacity to understand these Scriptures, Jerome wrote, is a craft requiring a teacher (letter 53). Thus, in the absence of unmediated revelation, Jerome argued for intellectual mediation which is essential for penetrating the meaning of Scriptures. He promoted the means, if not to provide closure, at least to control arbitrary misreadings of Scripture.

But finally, Jerome knew that the learned and the unlearned understand according to their own intellectual capacities: "The Scriptures are the only art that everyone claims for themselves . . . the old chattery woman, the doting old man, the wordy sophist—this art—they all pride themselves in, bungling it and teaching it before having learned it."[42] His emphasis on self- consciousness in interpretation sought to recognize prejudice in the interpretive act,[43] and he focused on the necessary mediation of teachers who approach the Bible with an interpretive method and a "universal" understanding, formed from the transforming significance conferred by the Incarnation. This universal outlook, Jerome's "legitimate prejudice," ruled his translation of the Old Testament, for while he chose not to defame the work of the seventy translators, he argued that a radical new understanding of the Scriptures was made possible by the "coming of Christ." Both tradition and the unveiling of its doubtfulness by the redemption are measures by which he judged his own understanding.

Though Jerome sought, like Augustine, to close down the interpretive possibilities in the biblical texts, at the same time he admitted there are many who will "shape" Scriptures to their own will and interpret them for their own service, particularly those trained in secular letters:

> I say nothing of those people like me, who came to the Holy Scriptures after having been cultivated by secular literature. They charm the ears of people with their artistic language, and imagine that all their words are the Law just as God's and do not deign to inform themselves of the opinion of the prophets and apostles, but adapt conflicting texts to their own sense as if it were a method of magnificent expression rather than a great fault to alter the sense of the sentences and to do violence to Scriptures according to their own desires.[44]

While arguing against these free interpretive activities, he revealed his awareness of all the contingencies that written words, even Scripture itself, evoke.

Jerome's recognition that spontaneous insight (or revelation) as experienced by the apostles is rare and that the "meaning" of inscribed words is inherently fluid empowered "written words" as "signifiers" in themselves. This status for written words of necessity invests readers with the power, if not the authority, to read the words with whatever freedom the words inspire. Sounding somewhat like Hans-Georg Gadamer, Jerome, conscious of the role of personal prejudices in the act of interpreting, argued for a means to circumscribe their anarchy. In valorizing the authority of tradition and continuity, however, he restricted the authority of an interpreter and questioned the ideology of unbiased reading, noting the "immediacy" of reading. Making an analogy between working with wax and interpreting, he writes: "Wax is soft and easy to form even where the hand of the artist and modeler stops—and perhaps, it is all that it can potentially become."[45] Since wax can be shaped to whatever one chooses, he writes, "It is not what you find, but what you search for, that we consider" (*Non quid invenias, sed quid quaeras, consideramus* [letter 53, 10]), suggesting that the reader make intellectual provisions for what he or she may be looking for rather than merely responding to what he or she is able to "form" spontaneously. In this respect, Jerome agrees with Augustine that the text must be made to conform to Christian teaching (*De Doctrina*, 2.9.14, 3.2.5).

In expounding on the difficulty of interpretation in his letters and the prefaces to the Bible, Jerome drew attention to the subjective interests and attitudes of audiences who will advance personal interpretations, reflecting, of course, their own presuppositions, education, and interests in the act of interpretation. Such sophistication about biblical interpretation shows both his awareness of the necessity for interpretive method and his preoccupation with the openness of the texts to diverse meanings. The trained may have brought a systematic self-reflexiveness to the act of interpretation, but not all readers and audiences, as Jerome points out, had such sophistication. Jerome reveals a notable tension about the problem of the inscribed word, making efforts to "close the text," while at the same time making clear the difficulties in such a proposition. Biblical listeners and readers, just as today, had a habit of imposing their personal presuppositions onto sacred texts.

Augustine's *De Doctrina Christiana,* besides its many other features, is a systematic defense of a science of reading, or hermeneutics, which Augustine argues is essential to understand Scriptures. While Augustine does not reject revelation as a means to understanding the Bible, he does recognize how uncommon it is, and therefore spends the first three books of the *De Doctrina Christiana* developing a theory for how to read Scriptures in the absence of spontaneous, Anthony-style, divinely inspired, unmediated insight.

Augustine's discussion of how to read Scriptures distinguishes between kinds of reading. On the one hand is the ability to pronounce and decipher words, and on the other, and more important, the ability to understand them: "he who explains to listeners what he understands in the Scriptures is like a reader who pronounces the words he knows, but he who teaches how the Scriptures are to be understood is like a teacher who advises how the words are to be read" (prologue, 9).[46] Critical distinctions among basic literacy, reading as an interpretive act, and direct unmediated insight form the foundation for his discussion on Christian teaching. As a consequence, instead of considering the *De Doctrina Christiana* an adaptation of Ciceronian rhetoric and interpretive method, though it is influenced by it, we might see it as advancing a methodical approach to Christian intellectual activity or how to read as a Christian, particularly as applied to biblical interpretation.[47] Augustine's doctrine of signs, as advanced primarily in books 2 and 3, presents a method to harness the meaning of ambiguous (*ambigua*) or unknown (*ignota*) signs, both problematic areas for accuracy in interpretation (2.10.15). Though "unknown" signs can be made known through translations (2.11.16) or knowledge of disciplines (2.27–40), ambiguous signs which are made so by grammar problems or figurative language are more difficult to decipher (3). Augustine's theory of how to render these ambiguous or unknown signs finds parallels in both Hans-Georg Gadamer and Jacques Derrida. Like Gadamer, Augustine would like to provide a method for circumscribing the infinite number of interpretive possibilities anarchical reading allows, but like Derrida, he also recognized that because Scripture is mediated through written words, ultimately it can be circumscribed only by a reader's willful act of intrusive intervention.

For Augustine, all Scripture is intentional, because it is God's present Word as written. As Mark Jordan argues, "In Augustine's thinking, any method of reading the Scriptures is fundamentally a reflection on words as analogous to Christ the Word. It is not only that they convey the Word, it is that they are *like* the Word."[48] Augustine nevertheless recognized that understanding this present Word was not available to everyone. But anyone who understands in the Scriptures something other than that intended by them is deceived, although they do not lie (1.36.41).[49] For Augustine, despite "the ambiguities of figurative words" (*verborum translatorum ambiguitates* [*De Doctrina*, 3.5.9) in Scriptures, all interpretation must lead back and forward to the realization of the "double love of God and our neighbor" (*istam geminam caritatem dei et proximi*), or the Scripture has been misunderstood (1.36.40). This is the fundamental religio-cultural arena in which scriptural interpretation must operate. Augustine, therefore, like Jerome, by enlisting the existence of an infinite being in his discussion, disciplines his own interpretive activity. For Augustine, this is the uncontingent boundary that girds the territory of interpretive possibilities. To move outside these perameters is to move into the locale of possible error, as far as understanding the Bible is concerned, for, Augustine writes, if someone is deceived in an interpretation "which builds up charity, which is the end of the commandments, he is deceived in the same way as a man who leaves a road by mistake but passes through a field to the same place toward which the road itself leads" (1.36.41).[50] Although the interpreter has found the right end, he has deviated in the path to that end, which Augustine applauds but nevertheless warns against, for it is "more useful not to leave the road" (*quam sit utilius viam non deserere* [1.36.41]).

Augustine set out to write the *De Doctrina Christiana* precisely because he recognized the inherent interpretive problems of the Bible (prologue) and, by implication, of written texts in general. But for Augustine, despite the apparent absence of the Word due to the ambiguities of words, the Word might be made present, so to speak, through hearing or listening to the "spirit which gives life to the letter" (Paul, 2 Corinthians 3:6), for, as Augustine says, quoting Paul, "For the letter killeth, but the spirit quickeneth" (*Littera occidit, spiritus autem vivificat* [*De Doctrina*, 3.5.9). Because of the ambiguous meaning in signs, the signified (*signa* for Augustine) is open to the possibility of diverse interpretations. But despite the ambiguities of words, words in sacred Scripture, at least, link back to the originating Word. Augustine advances a method to interpret written "signs" on the grounds that they are social utilities and are intended to communicate: the meaning of verbal signs can be bridled by context, tradition, and history with which they are aligned; words belong to communities of linguistic and symbolic signification; as a consequence, words can be interpreted incorrectly. For Augustine, because only God the immutable and eternal is enjoyable (*frui*), and all other things are useful (*uti*) (1.22.20), words are a useful means to lead to this joy. Also, because of the seriousness of the interpretive enterprise, for Augustine humility is a necessary constituent of the act of interpretation. Most important for Augustine, language is a temporal dispensation (*dispensatio temporalis*) and therefore a vulnerable, fragile, and transitory human utility in contrast to God, who is the permanent, immutable, ineffable enjoyment. Words may lead toward this ineffability, but they can never fully express it. Thus, Augustine dismisses the metaphysics of the *logos* as an actual presence in words.

Having made the distinction between "thing" (*res*) and "sign" (*signa* [1.2.2]) and set the terms for words as signs that reach back to the single Word, Augustine accepts that the written text deploys ambiguous signs which are open to numerous interpretations and as a consequence that all a text's significations are in some sense potentially viable, that is, if they are taken outside Augustine's limiting context for understanding: the aim of all interpretation is to support the double love of God and neighbor. Because of his insistence on a method of interpretation for reading words, it is clear that he understands the text as a "signifier" and not as "signified." Augustine recognizes that as a "trace"[51] which offers numerous ambiguous meanings, the Bible invites readers to indulge in what Mark Jordan has called "over-construction"[52] of these figural potentialities: "Distinctions in interpretation of this kind may be made at the will of the reader "[53] (book 3, 2.5), again so long as the "reader" does not step outside the limiting boundaries of the double love.

Augustine, in *De Magistro, Confessions,* and *De Doctrina Christiana,* confronts the dichotomy between speech and writing and the alienation of the spoken word from the written which for modern deconstructive thinkers makes the word absent. For Augustine, as Kenneth Burke wrote, Word was "the spoken word; the spoken word silently conceived as spoken . . . the preparatory attitude guided by experience, that precedes human action; the word of God in the sense of religious doctrine transmitted by Scriptures and preachers; the Word of God as Wisdom, second person of the Trinity; the Word of God made flesh."[54] The Word of God, as represented in the Bible, was a single communication from God to man, which nonetheless required a theory of signs for its interpretation.

But this interpretation is not so fluid as mere translation from one system of signs to another as in the deconstructive formula. At the root of Augustine's theology of signs is a verbal principle that understands God as speaking to man, and man in his turn listening to God, or failing to listen. This "inscription" is the rare case of unmediated insight, God's writing, which eludes most of us. Since the Fall, according to the Christian *schema,* mediated communication substitutes for direct exchanges between man and God. The rupture between

God and mankind accounts for the flaws in language. For Augustine, there is God, who is immutable and from whom mankind was separated at the Fall. This separation makes all "human things," including writing, mutable. For Augustine, all writing, because it uses language, is a human utility and therefore ambiguous and subject to decay and corruption.

For Augustine, however, this equivocalness is the starting point for interpretation. Augustine's theory of signs is a systematic method for providing meaning or access to the presence of the Word, which he accepts as the essence of scriptural rendition, despite the ambiguities of the language used by the men who wrote Holy Scripture: "Nor is there any other reason for signifying, or for giving signs, except for bringing forth and transferring to another mind the action of the mind in the person who makes the sign. We propose to consider and discuss this class of signs insofar as men are concerned with it, for even signs given by God and contained in the Holy Scriptures are of this type also, since they were presented to us by men who wrote them" (2.2.3).[55]

In his discussion of how to understand both ambiguous and unknown signs, Augustine presents a series of means to establish their intended meanings. These include applying the central underlying conviction as outlined above, that what is gleaned from the text must teach love of God and neighbor, or the interpretation is certainly wrong. He also advances a scientific and intellectual methodology. The fact that God's Word as represented in the Bible speaks obliquely is for Augustine a challenge, because what is discovered with difficulty provides greater pleasure (2.6.8). Augustine's absolute commitment to the interpretive presupposition that words in Scriptures link back to the Word is the context through which the equivocalness or ambiguity of the texts or, by association, God's revelation must be understood. Since all the teachings that involve faith are said openly, obscure things should be interpreted only according to these clear communications (2.9.14). The equivocalness of the word conveyed through unknown (*ignota*) or ambiguous (*ambigua*) written language, furthermore, does not make meaning absent. Rather, he insisted that signs exist within a context of understanding that provides the clue to their meaning. This context embraces human history, textual traditions, human communications as represented through language, as well as the larger context of central Christian teachings.

This argument for language as an essentially social instrument, a traditional rhetorical position, together with his idea that signs open themselves to meanings within a "context," one might say "community" of communication, bridles arbitrary constructions of meaning. The context for clarification may be within the text itself, for which he recommends consulting translations that are *verbum e verbo*, not because they are better but because they help to sort out obscurities (2.13.19). Also, following Cicero, he places great emphasis on scrutinizing the "preceding and following parts" (*praecedentibus et consequentibus partibus* [3.2.2, 3.3.6]) to clarify a text. Because textual traditions also help establish context, it is important for Augustine to identify what books in the Bible are "canonical," which he does early in book 2 (8.13). This second context of other biblical texts (2.6.8, 2.8.12, 2.9.14, 3.27.38) where similar ambiguities occur, he recommends examining on the grounds that "Hardly anything may be found in these obscure places which is not found plainly said elsewhere" (2.6.8).[56] Thus, he argues that ambiguous signs make sense because of their connection to a community of related texts belonging to a continuous culture. For Augustine, meaning moves outward from the sign itself to the immediate social context of tacit agreement on what it might mean, to the local textual context in which it is written (the biblical words themselves), to the larger textual context (other related texts, for example, New Testament texts), to an enlarged textual context (the entire Bible), and finally to the largest context of all, the central teachings of Christianity, the "rule of faith" (*regulis fidei* [3.3.6]), for "Scripture teaches nothing but charity" (*Non autem praecipit scriptura nisi caritatem* [3.10.15]).

Aware that ignorance may lead interpreters to think that texts or words (*signa*) and things (*res*) are ambiguous (2.16.24), Augustine argues for the necessity of a knowledge of languages, history, geography, zoology, geology, logic, and math in order to clarify interpretations (2.16, 28, 32–40). To determine what is figurative or literal before the work of interpretation can begin, it is necessary to have a knowledge of things (2.16.23–24). With numerous examples, he demonstrates that what may appear obscure may be clarified by knowledge, whether of languages, translations, history, or any other discipline suggested by an ambiguous sign. Here also, where conflicts in interpretation may occur, he admits human vulnerability and emphasizes the usefulness of consensus and context to clarify conflicts in meaning that stem from translation. Recalling the number and variety of Latin translations of the Bible,[57] in themselves both an embarassment to Christians and a demonstration of the corruptibility of words used to convey the Word, Augustine, in contrast to Jerome for whom linguistic accuracy takes precedence in interpretive exercises,[58] considers this an opportunity for greater clarity rather than an impediment: "For an inspection of various translations frequently makes obscure passages clear" (2.12.17).[59] Also, defending pagan culture, he argues that knowledge from outside the Church may prove useful in interpretation: "Thus whatever evidence we have of past times in that which is called history helps us a great deal in the understanding of the sacred books, even if we learn it outside of the Church as part of our childhood education" (2.28.42).

This obliqueness in the meaning intended by signs, however, opens up the possibility of "wrong readings," for Augustine "carnal" understanding. Augustine sets out to harness these potentially carnal interpretations of the Bible ("That is, when that which is said figuratively is taken as though it were literal, it is understood carnally" [3.5.9])[60] by systematically presenting guidelines to moor readings within the central understanding, "the double love of God and of our neighbor" (*istam geminam caritatem dei et proximi* [1.36.40]). One might argue, in fact, that the *De Doctrina Christiana*'s particular purpose is to offer a guard against individualistic readings, that is, interpretations exiled from literary and cultural contexts, whether within a single text or in relationship to a text's "textual community"[61] or historical and social context.

Furthermore, for Augustine, there is no point in signs if they are not directed to signify something, in fact, intended to make contact with other people—so for Augustine, words, whether figural or literal, are a human means to facilitate communication between people: "For no one uses words except for the purpose of signifying something. From this may be understood what we call 'signs'; they are things used to signify something" (1.2.2).[62] They are not an end in themselves but move back and forth from persons to persons, from the historical past to the present and into the future—pointing to the beginning Word and to the final Word.

Thus, on a number of fronts, Augustine had prethought the deconstructive critique of the metaphysical aims of interpretation. If we put aside his central Christian convictions, that these "tentative" and ambiguous words lead ultimately back to the Word, the heart of the doctrine of the idealized text, Augustine nevertheless has much to offer to help clarify ambiguous textual communication. Though he is intellectually and emotionally sensitive to the difference between unmediated insight or experience of presence and the silence of the inscribed word, he rejects the idea that because the words are written on the page that their communication is therefore absent, insisting instead that no one uses signs unless he or she intends to communicate with them (2.2.3). Writing (that is, letters) replaces sounds which have no durability at all beyond the moment when the vibrations pass away in the air (2.4.5). Writing is an attempt to retain contact with those it addresses when sound has disappeared, because for Augustine, writing substitutes for the absence that follows silenced sounds. Augustine's grounds for a science of hermeneutics do not only rest on his faith formulations, but, as I have discussed, he spends the largest portion of the treatise elaborating a variety of means whereby ambiguous or obscure signs can be interpreted. These include using the resources of a number of ancient versions of disciplines, including history, grammar, mathematics, zoology, rhetoric, and logic. Also he argues persuasively for the notion of the cultural and linguistic continuity, despite the differences of languages, time, and social context, to which the biblical texts belong. This textual and cultural continuity, he shows, will help to unveil both unknown and ambiguous signs.

His deference to the model of revelation experienced by St. Anthony recalled at the beginning of the *De Doctrina Christiana* serves to expose this type of unmediated understanding as rare. In other words, right from the beginning in his discussion of interpretation, he sets out to distinguish unmediated revelation from the work of interpretation. It is not incidental, either, that in his discussion of his conversion in *Confessions* (8.12), Augustine mentions some other famous conversion scenes, including Anthony's and Paul's, but he contrasts his own conversion to Anthony's and Paul's, for both experiences were theophanies. Augustine distinguishes his own "reading" conversion, which came after arduous scriptural study and his early rejection of what he could not understand in his reading (*Confessions*, 3.5, 8.12) from Anthony's, whose conversion was an epiphany, a moment of spiritual intersection between the hearing and understanding of divinely spoken words.

The connection Augustine makes between his conversion and the work of interpretation emphasizes the relevance he assigns to this activity. But as an intellectual activity, it may lead one into arrogance, against which Augustine warns throughout the text (1.37), particularly for those who love disputation for its own sake (2.31.48). To counter this intellectual temptation, so that "knowledge cannot puff [him] up" (*scientia inflare non possit* [2.42.63]), he recommends that this work be approached with "a meek and humble heart" (*mitem et humilem corde* [1.40.44, 2.41.62, 2.42.63]). Making one of his most important contributions to hermeneutical theory, Augustine warns against captiousness, recommending that humility and purity of heart should rule the interpretive exercise (1.37.41, 2.31.48).

Finally, despite their earnest attention to hermeneutical theory and method, both Jerome's and Augustine's position on the contingent status of human language and language-related activities ties a knot in their efforts which makes their convictions tentative at best. Jerome's recognition that words can be molded like wax and his invitation to Augustine to "play in the field of Scriptures," like Augustine's knowledge that language is a flawed human utility, undermine certainty in their methods. Furthermore, in Augustine's formulation, God's "ineffability" makes it impossible to say anything about his presence, for it is not possible to express God's ineffability. Augustine writes: Whence do I know this, except because God is ineffable? If what I said were ineffable, it would not be said. And for this reason God would not be said to be ineffable, for when this is said something is said. And a contradiction in terms is created, since if that is ineffable which cannot be spoken, then that is not ineffable which can be called ineffable" (1.6.6).[63] God's ineffability, that is, the impossibility of actually "speaking" of God, makes God's presence in human words tentative at best.[64] Such an admission openly declares the vulnerability not only of words but of the metaphysical foundation of presence even in "sacred words." Since for Augustine God is beyond all mutable things (1.7.7), and not only man but his medium of experience, language, are transitory (2.4.5), then also sacred Scripture possesses this same ultimately fleeting character: We propose to consider and to discuss this class of signs insofar as men are concerned with it, for even signs given by God and contained in Holy Scriptures are of this type also, since they were presented to us by the men who wrote them" (2.2.3).[65] Scripture is a means whose end is "the love of a Being which is to be enjoyed and of a being that can share that enjoyment with us" (1.35.39).[66] It is a "temporal dispensation" (*dispensatio temporalis* [1.35.39]) which we should use, and it is like those things "by which we are carried along for the sake of that toward which we are carried" (1.35.39).[67] These assertions place the whole concept of the presence of the Word in sacred Scripture in a contingent status, because they admit of the fragility and tentativeness of both the Scriptures themselves and the capacity of language to express the presence whereof they hint. This is an essential agreement with the deconstructive proposition that language is vulnerable to uncertainties and that the sign may signify randomly and therefore be open to various constructions. But for Augustine this is the humble starting place for interpreters. However, because of his exceptional language abilities, Jerome possessed a confidence when dealing with the words of the Bible that Augustine, with his poor Greek and nonexistent Hebrew, lacked. Jerome knew precisely how words could be molded, but despite his *pius labor, sed periculosa praesumptio* ("pious labor but dangerous presumption" ["Praefatio"]), he trusted in his abilities. Augustine, on the other hand, is less certain both about his grammar skills and about his capacity to know exactly what is intended in the Scriptures. Writing to God in the *Confessions*, he declares this uncertainty and confesses the isolation scriptural reading entails:

> O my God, Light of my eyes in darkness, since I believe in these commandments and confess them to be true with all my heart, how can it harm me that it should be possible to interpret these words in several ways, all of which may yet be true? How can it harm me if I understand the writer's meaning in a different sense from that in which another understands it? All of us who read his words do our best to discover and understand what he had in mind, and since we believe that he wrote the truth, we are not so rash as to suppose that he wrote anything which we know or think to be false. Provided, therefore, that each of us tries as best he can to understand in the Holy Scriptures what the writer meant by them, what harm is there if a reader believes what you, the Light of all truthful minds, shows him to be the true meaning? It may not even be the meaning the writer had in mind, and yet he too saw in them a true meaning, different though it may have been from this. (*Confessions*, book 12, chapter 18)[68]

The Church fathers were engaged in a systematic transformation of the Roman *paideia* and Ciceronian discourse which they adapted to Christian purpose, but their triumph lies uneasily with their knowledge of the fluidity of language, the medium in which Scriptures are preserved. This knowledge, itself a construction of the rhetorical tradition, accepts discourse as a simultaneously fragile and powerful social utility which, while providing pleasure and learning, also can be corrupted or lead its listeners astray. Even more, the Church fathers plant their rhetorical methods of polemic and interpretation in the field of a universe where the presence of an immutable and omniscient eternal divinity makes all human acts, the human status, and human structures vulnerable and humbled before its awesomeness. Thus, along with their political triumph over the pagan world, they replaced the power of the empire with the power of the divinity, setting up an irresolvable tension between this world and the eschatological future world, between God and mankind. But despite their recognition of their limitations, both Jerome and Augustine argue that rhetorical methods provide the key to understanding and reconciling the two worlds. Thus, Jerome and Augustine confer on rhetoric the loftiest aims imagined in the history of its practice.

Notes

1. Averil Cameron, *Christianity and the Rhetoric of Empire: The Development of Christian Discourse* (Berkeley: University of California Press, 1991); E. Auerbach, *Literary Language and Its Public in Late Latin Antiquity and in the Middle Ages,* trans. R. Mannheim (Princeton: Princeton University Press, 1965); George Kennedy, *Classical Rhetoric and Its Christian and Secular Tradition from Ancient to Modern Times* (Chapel Hill: University of North Carolina Press, 1980); Rita Copeland, *Rhetoric, Hermeneutics and Translation in the Middle Ages* (Cambridge: Cambridge University Press, 1991); W. H. C. Frend, *The Rise of Christianity* (London: Darton, Longman & Todd, 1984), 604–5; Harald Hagendahl, *Augustine and the Latin Classics, Vol. II Testimonia* (Stockholm: Almquist & Wiksell, 1967), for a thorough discussion of Augustine's knowledge and appreciation of classical literature. For a substantial bibliography on Augustine and Cicero, see Gerald A. Press, "The Subject and Structure of Augustine's *De Doctrina Christiana,*" *Augustinian Studies* 11 (1980): 99–124. Robert A. Kaster, *Guardians of Language: The Grammarian and Society in Late Antiquity* (Berkeley: University of California Press, 1988), discusses rhetoric and grammar and the Christian leadership of the late empire. Also essential reading on Augustine's Ciceronianism is Joseph Mazzeo, "St. Augustine's Rhetoric of Silence: Truth vs. Eloquence and Things vs. Signs," in *Renaissance and Seventeenth-Century Studies* (New York: Columbia University Press and London: Routledge & Kegan Paul, 1964), 1–28. For a recent survey of Cicero's contribution to Western humanistic studies, see C. Jan Swearingen, "Cicero: Defining the Value of Literacy," in *Rhetoric and Irony: Western Literacy and Western Lies* (New York: Oxford University Press, 1991), 132–74; Michel Banniard, "Jérôme et l'elegantia d'après le *De optimo genere interpretandi,*" in Yves-Marie Duval, ed., *Jérôme entre l'Occident et l'Orient* (Paris: Études Augustiniennes, 1988), 305–22.
2. Kennedy, *Classical Rhetoric,* 146.
3. Cameron, *Christianity and the Rhetoric of Empire,* 3–6.
4. Peter Brown, *Power and Persuasion in Late Antiquity: Towards a Christian Empire* (Madison: University of Wisconsin Press, 1992), 4, 35–158.
5. Henri-Irénée Marrou, *A History of Education in Antiquity,* trans. George Lamb (New York: Sheed and Ward, 1964).
6. Bruce M. Metzger, *The Canon of the New Testament* (Oxford: Clarendon Press, 1987). See no. 40 in Charles Joseph Hefele, *Histoire des Conciles* II (Paris: Letouzey

et Ané, 1908), which records that at the Council of Hippo (393), the canonical books are listed as all the texts in the Septuagint and the same New Testament texts as appear in the United Bible Societies Greek New Testament (1975) (89).

7. See Thomas Cole's and Bruce Rosenstock's essays in this collection.

8. Rita Copeland's *Rhetoric, Hermeneutics and Translation*, 9–62, is obviously an exception. Copeland discusses Cicero's theories of rhetoric, hermeneutics, and translation and Jerome's transformation of Latin theories for his own intellectual purposes.

9. Joseph Martin, ed., "De Doctrina Christiana," in Corpus Christianorum Series Latina ed. in *Aurelii Augustini Opera, Corpus Christianorum* 32 (Turnhout: Brepols, 1962), 1–167. I will use D. W. Robertson, Jr.'s, translation, *On Christian Doctrine* (New York: Macmillan, 1958); "Prologus Sancti Hieronymi Presbyteri in Pentateucho," in *Biblia Sacra: Iuxta Vulgatam Versionem* I (Stuttgart: Württembergische Bibelanstalt, 1975); "Praefatio Sancti Hieronymi Presbyteri in Evangelio," in *Biblia Sacra: Iuxta Vulgatam Versionem* II (Stuttgart: Württembergische Bibelanstalt, 1975); *The Church Fathers and the Bible*, ed. Frank Sadowski (New York: Alba House, 1987), for translations of "Praefatio." Some of the material in this essay has appeared before in one of the following three essays which deal with Jerome's and Augustine's rhetorical and hermeneutical theories: "Jerome's Prefatory Epistles to the *Bible* and the *Canterbury Tales*," *Studies in the Age of Chaucer* 15 (1993): 111–30; "Petrarch's Defense of Secular Letters, the Latin Fathers, and Ancient Roman Rhetoric," *Rhetorica* 11, 2 (Spring 1993): 119–34; and "St. Augustine's Answer to Jacques Derrida in the *De Doctrina Christiana*," *New Literary History* 25, 2 (Spring 1994): 383–97.

10. Press, "The Subject and Structure."

11. See letter 22, "Ad Eustochium," in Saint Jérôme, *Lettres* 1, ed. and trans. into French by Jérôme Labourt (Paris: Société d'Édition Les Belles Lettres, 1949), 110–60.

12. What T. S. Kuhn, *The Structure of Scientific Revolutions*, 2nd ed. (Chicago: University of Chicago Press, 1970), would call a historical paradigm shift.

13. See Sancti Augustini, *Confessionum Libri XIII*, ed. Lucas Verheijen (Turnhout: Typographi Brepols, 1981): "Deus, deus meus, quas ibi miserias expertus sum et ludificationes, quandoquidem recte mihi vivere puero id proponebatur, obtemperare monentibus, ut in hoc saeculo florerem, et excellerem linguosis artibus, ad honorem hominum et falsas divitias famulantibus" (book 1, chapter 9). ("But O God my God, I now went through a period of suffering and humiliation. I was told that it was right and proper for me as a boy to pay attention to my teachers, so that I should do well at my study of grammar and get on in the world. This was the way to gain the respect of others and win for myself what passes for wealth in this world" [*Confessions*, trans. and intro. by R. S. Pine-Coffin (Middlesex: Penguin, 1961), book 1, chapter 9, 29–30]). See Brian Stock, *Augustine the Reader: Meditation, Self-Knowledge, and the Ethics of Interpretation* (Cambridge, Mass.: Harvard University Press, 1996) for this distinguishing feature of Augustine's practice of rhetoric. Or Jerome in letter 22, recounting his feverish visions: "Interrogatus condicionem, Christianum me esse respondi. Et ille qui residebat: 'mentiris,' ait, 'Ciceronianus es, non Christianus; ubi thesaurus tuus, ibi

est cor tuum.'" ("He asked me my condition: 'I am a Christian,' I responded. But this other responded, 'You lie,' he said; 'You are a Ciceronian, not a Christian; where your treasure is there is your heart.'") In *Saint Jérôme: Lettres* 1, 145 (110–60). (My translation.)

14. *Confessions,* 156. *Confessionum* 7.21.27: "Hoc illae litterae non habent. Non habent illae paginae vultum pietatis huius, lacrimas confessionis, sacrificium tuum, spiritum contribulatum, cor contritum et humiliatum, populi salutem, sponsam civitatem, arram spiritus sancti, poculum pretii nostri."

15. Martin, ed., "De Doctrina Christiana"; "Prologus Sancti Hieronymi Presbyteri in Pentateucho" and "Praefatio Sancti Hieronymi Presbyteri in Evangelio"; Saint Jérôme, *Lettres* 1–8, trans. into French and ed. Jérôme Labourt (Paris: Société d'Édition Les Belles Lettres, 1949–63); letter 53, "Ad Paulinum Presbyterum," in *Lettres* 3 (Paris: Société d'Édition les Belles Lettres, 1953), 1–25; and letter 57, "Ad Pammachium de Optimo Genere Interpretandi," in *Lettres* 3, 55–73. St. Augustine letters 28, 40, 71, 73, and 82, and Jerome 102, 105, 112, and 115 in Carolinne White, *The Correspondence (394–419) between Jerome and Augustine of Hippo* (Lewiston, N.Y.: Edward Mellen Press, 1990). All translations from Jerome are mine.

16. See Paul Ricoeur, *The Rule of Metaphor,* trans. Robert Czerny, Kathleen McLaughlin, and John Costello (Toronto: University of Toronto Press, 1977); Ernesto Grassi, *Rhetoric as Philosophy: The Humanist Tradition* (University Park: Pennsylvania State University Press, 1980); Hans Georg-Gadamer, *Reason in the Age of Science,* trans. Frederick G. Lawrence (Cambridge, Mass.: MIT Press, 1981); and Hans-Georg Gadamer, *Rhetorik und Hermeneutik* (Göttingen: Vandenhoeck, 1976), for the connection between hermeneutics and rhetoric.

17. Jacques Derrida, *De la grammatologie* (Paris: Les Éditions de Minuit, 1967); Hans-Georg Gadamer, *Truth and Method* (New York: Crossroad, 1986); see Schildgen, "St. Augustine's Answer to Jacques Derrida."

18. "Tullius . . . afflatus rethorico spiritu transtulisse" ("Prologus," ll.31–32).

19. See "Ad Eustochium" in *Lettres* 1, 144 (110–60).

20. See letter 57, "Ad Pammachium de Optimo Genere Interpretandi," in *Lettres* 3, 55–73.

21. "Ego enim non solum fateor, sed libera voce profiteor me in interpretatione Graecorum absque scripturis sanctis, ubi et verborum ordo mysterium est, non verbum e verbo, sed sensum exprimere de sensu. Habeoque huius rei magistrum Tullium, qui . . . transtulit." "Ad Pammachium," in *Lettres* 3, 59.

22. "Origenis me studium provocavit, qui editioni antiquae translationem Theodotionis miscuit, . . . dum aut inlucescere facit quae minus ante fuerant aut superflua quaeque iugulat et confodit." "Prologus," ll.8–11. Also see "Praefatio"; "Ad Pammachium," in *Lettres* 3, for the influence of Cicero and Origen in Jerome's theories of translation.

23. Letter 112, *Lettres* 6 (Paris: Société d'Édition Les Belles Lettres, 1958), 40–41 (18–43).

24. "In scripturarum si placet campo sine nostro invicem dolore ludamus." Letter 15, ibid., 46.

25. "[E]t candorem ecclesiae ethnicorum sordibus polluamus." Letter 70, "Ad Magnum," *Lettres* 3, 209–15 (209).

26. "Quid ergo mirum, si et ego sapientiam saecularem, propter eloquii venustatem et membrorum pulchritudinem, de ancilla atque captiva Israhelitin facere cupio, si quidquid in ea mortuum est idolatriae, voluptatis, erroris, libidinum, vel praecido vel rado, et mixtus purissimo corpori vernaculos ex ea genero Domino sabaoth? Labor meus in familiam Christi proficit, stuprum in alienam auget numerum conservorum." Ibid., 210–11. (My translation.)

27. Horace, "The Ars Poetica," in C. O. Brink, ed., *Horace on Poetry* (Cambridge: Cambridge University Press, 1971), ll. 333–34; for Augustine's *uti/frui* distinction, see *De Doctrina*, 1.3–5.

28. *De Doctrina*, 2.25–28.

29. See Hagendahl, *Augustine and the Latin Classics*.

30. "Illi interpretati sunt ante adventum Christi et quod nesciebant dubiis protulere sententiis, nos post passionem et resurrectionem eius non tam prophetiam quam historiam scribimus." "Prologus," ll.35–38; *Confessions*, book 7.

31. See, for example, letters 28, 40, 102, 71, 112, 115, 82 in *The Correspondence (394–419)* and in Jérôme, *Lettres* 2–6. Jerome often argues with Augustine vehemently about interpretations on the grounds that Augustine cannot understand the meaning of the words. See particularly letter 112 in *Lettres* 6, 18–43.

32. See Eugene F. Rice, Jr., *Saint Jerome in the Renaissance* (Baltimore: Johns Hopkins University Press, 1985), 1–83, for an overview of the respect accorded Jerome for his philological studies.

33. S. Hieronymi Presbyteri, *Commentary on Ezekiel XIII*, 42.13, in *Corpus Christianorum Series Latina* 75 (Turnhout: Typographi Brepols Editores Pontificii, 1954), 615–16.

34. Origen, *On First Principles*, trans. G. W. Butterworth and intro. Henri de Lubac (New York: Harper Torchbooks, 1966).

35. "[N]on autem omnis res etiam signum est" (1.2.2).

36. "[S]ine ulla scientia litterrum scripturas divinas et memoriter audiendo tenuisse et prudenter cogitando intellexisse praedicatur" (4).

37. "Quicquid enim aliis exercitatio et cotidiana in lege meditatio tribuere solet, illis Spiritus sanctus suggerebat." *Lettres* 3, 12 (8–25). My translation.

38. Mark D. Jordan's essay "Words and Word: Incarnation and Signification in Augustine's *De Doctrina Christiana*," *Augustinian Studies* 11 (1980): 177–96, deals with this contrast between the unmediated Word and human words. Also, on Augustine's theory of knowledge and language, see Marcia L. Colish, "Augustine: The Expression of the Word," in *The Mirror of Language: A Study of the Medieval Theory of Knowledge*, rev. ed. (Lincoln: University of Nebraska Press, 1983), 7–54. Eugene Vance discusses the difference between unmediated knowledge and the interpretation of words as suggested by Augustine in "Saint Augustine: Language as Temporality," in John D. Lyons and Stephen G. Nichols, Jr., eds., *Mimesis: From Mirror to Method, Augustine to Descartes* (Hanover: University Press of New England, 1982), 20–35.

39. "[Q]uisquis se nullis praeceptis instructum divino munere, quaecumque in scripturis obscura sunt intellegere gloriatur, bene quidem credit, et verum est, non esse

illam suam facultatem quasi a se ipso existentem, sed divinitus traditam; ita enim dei gloriam quaerit et non suam; sed cum legit et nullo sibi hominum exponente intellegit, cur ipse aliis affectat exponere" (Prooemium, 8).

40. "[H]abet nescio quid latentis *energeías* viva vox et in aures discipuli de auctoris ore transfusa fortius insonat" (53, 10).

41. "[A]ut aliter de hisdem libris per Septuaginta interpretes, aliter per Apostolos Spiritus Sanctus testimonia texuit, ut quod illi tacuerunt. . . . Damnamus veteres? Minime; sed post priorum studia in domo Domini quod possumus laboramus. Illi interpretati sunt ante adventum Christi" ("Prologus," ll.32–36).

42. "Sola scripturarum ars est, quam sibi omnes passim vindicent . . . hanc garrula anus, hanc delirus senex, hanc soloecista verbosus, hanc universi praesumunt, lacerant, docent, antequam adiscant." *Lettres* 3, 53, 15. (My translation.)

43. See Gadamer, *Truth and Method,* 238. When I use terms such as *prejudice, immediacy,* and *preconceptions,* I am deferring to Gadamer's vocabulary for discussing hermeneutical issues and methods.

44. "Taceo de meis similibus, qui si forte ad scripturas sanctas post saeculares litteras venerint et sermone conposito aurem populi mulserint, quicquid dixerint, hoc legem Dei putant, nec scire dignantur quid prophetae, quid apostoli senserint, sed ad sensum suum incongrua aptant testimonia, quasi grande sit et non vitiosissimum dicendi genus depravare sententias, et ad voluntatem suam scripturam trahere repugnantem" (letter 53, 15). (My translation.)

45. "Mollis cera et ad formandum facilis, etiamsi artificis et plastae cesset manus, tamen *dunámei* totum est quidquid esse potest" (ibid., 10–11).

46. "[Q]uae in scripturis intellegit, exponit audientibus tamquam litteras, quas agnoscit, pronuntiat lectoris officio; qui autem praecipit, quomodo intellegendum sit, similis est tradenti litteras, hoc est praecipienti, quomodo legendum sit" (Prooemium 9, 5).

47. I am indebted to Brian Stock, whose book *Augustine the Reader: Meditation, Self-Knowledge, and the Ethics of Interpretation* argues that Augustine's innovative theory of reading sets the stage for the intellectual life of the Middle Ages.

48. Jordan, "Words and Word," 177.

49. "Sed quisquis in scripturis aliud sentit quam ille, qui scripsit, illis non mentientibus fallitur" (1.36.41).

50. "[Q]ua aedificet *caritatem,* quae *finis praecepti est,* ita fallitur, ac si quisquam errore deserens viam eo tamen per agrum pergat, quo etiam via illa perducit" (ibid.).

51. See Derrida, *De la grammatologie.*

52. Jordan, "Words and Word," 189.

53. "Tales igitur distinctionum ambiguitates in potestate legentis sunt" (3.2.5).

54. Kenneth Burke, *The Rhetoric of Religion: Studies in Logology* (Boston: Beacon Press, 1961), 50–51.

55. "Nec ulla causa est nobis significandi, id est signi dandi, nisi ad depromendum et traiciendum in alterius animum id, quod animo gerit, qui signum dat. Horum igitur signorum genus, quantum ad homines attinet, considerare atque tractare statuimus, quia et signa divinitus data, quae scripturis sanctis continentur, per homines nobis indicata sunt, qui ea conscripserunt" (2.2.3).

56. "Nihil enim fere de illis obscuritatibus ervitur, quod non planissime dictum alibi reperiatur" (2.6.8).

57. "Si enim Latinis exemplaribus fides est adhibenda, respondeant quibus: tot sunt paene quot codices. Sin autem veritas est quaerenda de pluribus, cur non ad graecam originem revertentes ea quae vel a vitiosis interpretibus male edita vel a praesumptoribus imperitis emendata perversius vel a librariis dormitantibus aut addita sunt aut mutata corrigimus?" ("Praefatio"). "For if we are to pin our faith on the Latin texts, it is for our opponents to tell us which; for there are almost as many forms of the texts as there are copies. If, on the other hand we are to glean the truth from a comparison of many, why not go back to the original Greek and correct the mistakes introduced by inaccurate translators, and the blundering alterations of confident but ignorant critics, and, further, all that has been inserted or changed by copyists more asleep than awake?" (*The Church Fathers and the Bible*, 199). Also, Augustine notes, "We can enumerate those who have translated the Scriptures from Hebrew into Greek, but those who have translated them into Latin are innumerable. In the early times of the faith when anyone found a Greek codex, and he thought that he had some facility in both languages, he attempted to translate it" (*On Christian Doctrine*, 2.11, 44). "Qui enim Scripturas ex hebraea in graecam verterunt, numerari possunt, latini autem interpretes nullo modo. Ut enim cuique primis fidei temporibus in manus venit codex graecus, et aliquantum facultatis sibi utriusque linguae habere videbatur, ausus est interpretari" (*De Doctrina*, 2.11.16).

58. See letter 122 (Jerome to Augustine) and letter 82 (Augustine to Jerome) in *The Correspondence (394–419); Lettres* 4 and 7.

59. "Nam nonnullas obscuriores sententias plurium codicum saepe manifestavit inspectio" (2.12.17).

60. "Cum enim figurate dictum sic accipitur, tamquam proprie dictum sit, carnaliter sapitur" (3.5.9).

61. "Textual community" is an important concept developed by Brian Stock for "microsocieties organized around the common understanding of a script." See his essay "History, Literature, and Textuality," 22–24; and "Textual Communities: Judaism, Christianity, and the Definitional Problem," in *Listening for the Text: On the Uses of the Past* (Baltimore: Johns Hopkins University Press, 1990), 140–58; and *The Implications of Literacy: Written Language and Models of Interpretation in the Eleventh and Twelfth Centuries* (Princeton: Princeton University Press, 1983). I use this term more broadly to designate texts that are in a social, religious, or cultural relationship with one another.

62. "Nemo enim utitur verbis, nisi aliquid significandi gratia. Ex quo intellegitur, quid appellem signa, res eas videlicet, quae ad significandum aliquid adhibentur" (1.2.2).

63. "Hoc unde scio, nisi quia deus ineffabilis est? quod autem a me dictum est, si ineffabile esset, dictum non esset. Ac per hoc ne ineffabilis quidem dicendus est deus, quia et hoc cum dicitur, aliquid dicitur et fit nescio qua pugna verborum, quoniam si illud est ineffabile, quod dici non potest, non est ineffabile, quod vel ineffabile dici potest" (1.6.6).

64. In a roundtable discussion with Derrida, recorded in *The Ear of the Other: Otobiography, Transference, Translation*, ed. Christie V. McDonald, trans. Peggy Kamuf

(New York: Schocken Books, 1985), discussing Augustine's *Confessions*, Eugene Vance presented a similar observation. All language, for Augustine, whether written, spoken, Latin, Greek, etc., Vance refers to as "This estrangement from the ultimate meaning of everything, this exile in the external shell of language" (82).

65. "Horum igitur signorum genus, quantum ad homines attinet, considerare atque tractare statuimus, quia et signa divinitus data, quae scripturis sanctis continentur, per homines nobis indicata sunt, qui ea conscripserunt" (2.2.3).

66. "*[E]sse dilectio* rei, qua fruendum est, et rei, quae nobiscum ea re frui potest" (1.35.39).

67. "[U]t ea quibus ferimur, propter illud, ad quod ferimur, diligamus" (ibid.).

68. "Quae mihi ardenter confitenti, deus meus, lumen oculorum meorum in occulto, quid mihi obest, cum diversa in his verbis intellegi possint, quae tamen vera sint? Quid, inquam, mihi obest, si aliud ego sensero, quam sensit alius eum sensisse, qui scripsit? Omnes quidem, qui legimus, nitimur hoc indagare atque comprehendere, quod voluit ille quem legimus, et cum eum veridicum credimus, nihil, quod falsum esse vel novimus vel putamus, audemus eum existimare dixisse. Dum ergo quisque conatur id sentire in scripturis sanctis, quod in eis sensit ille qui scripsit quid mali est, si hoc sentiat, quod tu, lux omnium veridicarum mentium, ostendis verum esse, etiamsi non hoc sensit ille, quem legit, cum et ille verum nec tamen hoc senserit?" (*Confessionum,* 12.18).

Dante, Boncompagno da Signa, Eberhard the German, and the Rhetoric of the Maternal Body

G A R Y   P.   C E S T A R O

FOR MANY MEDIEVAL thinkers, grammar harbored within her menacingly open borders irksome and even frightening associations with primal chaos and the nurturing female body. Understandably, rhetoricians—whose very discipline promoted the cause of civil society—felt grammar's asocial threat with particular anguish.[1] This essay briefly examines the deprecation of grammar explicit or implicit in three grammatical/rhetorical texts from the thirteenth and early fourteenth centuries: Boncompagno da Signa's *Rhetorica novissima* (1235), Eberhard the German's *Laborintus* (after 1218, before 1280), and Dante's *De vulgari eloquentia* (c. 1304). My somewhat ambiguous classification of the texts as grammatical/rhetorical reflects a confusion between these two branches of the trivium that dates back at least to Quintilian and provides an important background for the present discussion.

Although grammar had always focused primarily on elementary Latin language instruction, even the earliest grammarians considered linguistic analysis of literary texts their bailiwick.[2] While it is true that Donatus confined himself to the eight parts of speech in the *Ars minor*, the *Ars maior* included an ample discussion of barbarisms, solecisms, metaplasms, *schemata*, and tropes.[3] In addition to his monumental *Institutiones grammaticae* (which included chapters on *constructiones*), Priscian authored a lengthy, detailed analysis of the first twelve lines of the *Aeneid*.[4] Here grammar encroached upon the literary provinces of her more fabulous sister.

The situation grew more complex with the reconstitution of grammar/rhetoric toward the close of the twelfth century into various subdisciplines, not least of which was the field of poetics and the composition of *artes*

175

poetriae. Here we find Eberhard's sole effort amidst a cluster of rather more celebrated offerings.[5]

But is this grammar or rhetoric? The taxonomical detail may seem unimportant today; it was significant for at least some medieval theorists. For although the authors of the three texts under consideration identify themselves variously as *rhetor* (Boncompagno), *grammaticus* (Eberhard), and both or neither (Dante), all three communicate a glorification of rhetoric predicated upon a denigration of grammar. Explicit and full-throated in Boncompagno, rhetoric's scorn for grammar requires a more nuanced articulation in Eberhard and certainly in Dante. Yet all three texts betray a similar psychology: because of grammar's proximity to primal chaos—commonly metaphorized by the maternal body—the first art struck fear in the hearts of those personally invested in the rational regulation of language and the consequent power of language to control human behavior.

The statement may seem paradoxical. After all, grammar constituted the very foundation of linguistic regulation. Nonetheless, allegorical and iconographic treatments of grammar throughout the Middle Ages emphasized the first discipline's intimacy with the unregulated mother tongue. Just as the infant appeared to absorb the vernacular with drafts of mother's milk, so the grammar student suckled the elementary principles of Latin composition at the breasts of Lady Grammar. While it is true that all of the arts were allegorized as female figures, none revealed the preoccupation with nurturing, female anatomy so evident in depictions of grammar.[6]

The medieval imagination thus frequently resisted aligning grammar with discipline pure and simple; rather, for many, grammar straddled the fence between pleasure and discipline. She negotiated the passage from maternal nurturing to patriarchal law. Indeed, among the most intriguing allegorizations of Lady Grammar from the later Middle Ages are those that cast her as both mother and, as it were, father: she offered one breast for suck while prohibiting access to the other with a rod or whip.[7] Contemporary psychoanalytic theory suggests a number of fruitful interpretive strategies for this primal scenario, though such investigations would carry us beyond the scope of the present essay.[8] Even without resorting to psychoanalytic paradigms, however, the historical record alone provides a fascinating picture of grammar as a site of potential instability. Grammar's indeterminate status somewhere between nature and art threatened rhetoric, which thus distanced itself to avoid contamination.

The three texts under consideration reflect this phenomenon from different perspectives and in widely divergent manners. Boncompagno, proud *rhetor,* scoffs at the *puerilia* of the first art. Eberhard, sad *magister,* wallows in self-loathing and self-pity while espying the higher arts, rhetoric included, with desperate envy. Somewhat more problematically, Dante moves back and forth between an assured rhetorical self-confidence and a troubling grammatical self-consciousness only to truncate his discourse well before its proposed end.

Boncompagno da Signa (c. 1170–1240)

DR. CARL SUTTER collected and collated the data regarding Boncompagno's life at the close of the previous century.[9] Ronald Witt has sorted through and adjusted these more recently, but precise details remain sketchy.[10] It seems fair to conclude that Boncompagno gained a degree of fame (not to say notoriety) during a celebrated (at least by himself) and tempestuous tenure at the University of Bologna during the first quarter of the thirteenth century. James Murphy roils at the *rhetor*'s outsized ego and insistent claims of radical novelty while concluding that Boncompagno's lasting impact on the history of rhetorical theory was negligible or none.[11] It is precisely Boncompagno's colorful, self-interested style, however, that allows for the kinds of fantastic cultural detail about grammar and rhetoric that interest our study.

Although Boncompagno appears to have authored some seventeen works (nearly all dealing with the *ars dictaminis* in one form or another), he remains best known for his two most comprehensive treatments of rhetoric, the *Rhetorica antiqua* or *Boncompagnus* (1215, 1226/7) and the *Rhetorica novissima* (1235).[12] Both are consistent in their condemnation of grammar as maternal and infantile, and exaltation of rhetoric as the basis for social order.

Witt has characterized Boncompagno's dislike for grammar in terms of the contrasting schools of Bologna and Orléans. He argues correctly that Boncompagno's scorn reflects the rhetorical ambience in which he taught. His students at Bologna were pursuing the eminently pragmatic goal of effective forensic oratory or official letter writing, whence his contempt for the more literary, humanistic grammar of France and of Orléans in particular. Boncompagno sought a clear, useful rhetorical instruction free of servile dependence on the *auctores* and purged of obscure ornamentation.

While it is surely true that Boncompagno often identifies "grammatica" with the belles lettres of Orléans, he elsewhere acknowledges grammar as a necessary first course in basic language principles remote from *exornatio* and *imitatio*.[13] Yet his disdain for grammar in these passages is no less vehement. In this sense, Witt's generally accurate reading seems incomplete, for there where Boncompagno ridicules the "nudi grammantes," he is not thinking exclusively of Orléans, rather also of the primal threat posed by the first art that I articulated above.

Boncompagno proclaims the supremacy of rhetoric from the first. We need only look to the *Rhetorica antiqua*'s alternative title, *Boncompagnus*, to perceive just how intimately the author aligns his ego with that art. In the opening paragraphs, he announces his intention to leave a rhetorical last will and testament; he designates his work as male heir and commands that

Sister Rhetoric come forth from the chamber of philosophy to be decorated as sacred temple. "Rhetorica," the *Boncompagnus,* and Boncompagno tend to merge here. As in the later *Rhetorica novissima,* Boncompago declares rhetoric empress of the arts and daughter of civil and canon law; she is closely identified with the public weal.[14] The *Rhetorica novissima* also instructs that "eloquentia" proceeds from rhetoric as effect from cause, indeed that eloquence and rhetoric are at times synonymous.[15]

In book 9, chapter 3 of the later work, Boncompagno demonstrates how each of the liberal arts along with other disciplines can be metaphorized (*transumuntur*) as a series of interconnected large and small wheels. Although rhetoric takes its place among the other wheels, Boncompagno leaves no room to overlook the discipline's vastly inflated stature:

> Tertia vitam et mortem in se continebat et habebat capitella nature tam rotis quam rotulis illis infixa, nec aliqua illarum poterat sine auxilio illius moveri. Erat etiam propter defectum artificium incompleta.

> The third contained within itself life and death and it had natural rods connected to both the larger and smaller wheels, and so without its assistance no wheel was able to turn. On account of a defect in its construction, it was, however, incomplete.

Rhetoric holds dominion over life and death; no other science can hope to function without her. The sly allusion to the discipline's incompleteness is aimed at the Ciceronian tradition to date. Boncompagno's radically new (*novissima*) rewriting will thankfully remedy the situation.

As Boncompagno's egomania is general, it perhaps comes as no great surprise that he glorifies rhetoric to such extremes. Nevertheless, the metaphorical choices he makes to condemn that which is less than rhetoric are intriguing, for Boncompagno repeatedly depicts undeveloped or incompetent verbal ability as a crisis of weaning, the pain of the teething infant struggling to detach himself from the mother's body.[16]

In that section of the *Rhetorica novissima* that portrays the arts as wheels, grammar is naturally the first:

> Prima quidem volvebatur laborioso impulsu, sed procedebat ex ea lac quod dabatur his qui erant in dentium plantativa.[17]

> The first was turning with great difficulty, but it came forth from that milk which was given to those who were still teething.

Two chapters later, Boncompagno demonstrates the important strategy of argument *pro et contra* (*disputatio in utramque partem*) using the practitioners of the arts and other disciplines as rhetorical guinea pigs. *Pro grammatico* he briefly adduces the traditional definition of grammar as foundation of learning.[18] The *contra* response, however, inspires a longer-winded, more personally engaged advocate:

> Primum membrum tue diffinitionis est falsum, quia grammatica non
> est scientia recte loquendi: immo dicere debeas recte construendi, unde
> necessaria est in principio cuilibet erudiendo. Verumtamen quemlibet
> grammaticum assimilo illi qui est in dentium plantativa, qui lac sugit,
> recitat sicut puer, et cum dicit a, e, i, o, u tamquam infantulus vagire
> videtur. Iudicat enim de solis vocibus, quia bene sustinet et defendit
> regulariter esse dictum "musca parit leonem" et "angelus est cimera."[19]

> The first member of your definition is false, because grammar is not
> the science "of speaking correctly": on the contrary, you should rather
> say "of constructing correctly," wherefore it is necessary to anyone at the
> beginning of their education. Nevertheless I liken all grammarians to the
> infant whose teeth have just come in, who sucks milk, who recites like
> the school boy, and when he says a, e, i, o, u looks just like a crying little
> baby. Moreover, he can only judge physical sounds, for he maintains that
> it is fine and in line with the rules to say, "the fly gives birth to the lion"
> and "an angel is a fire-breathing monster."

Despite the rhetorical trappings, Boncompagno's disdain could hardly sound
more heartfelt. His comparison of the grammarian's tedious vowel recitation
to the anguished birth cry of the infant will find a curious parallel in Eberhard,
as we shall see.

Significantly, Boncompagno's distaste for grammar here would appear
to have little or nothing to do with the belletristic preciosity of the Orléans
school discussed by Witt.[20] Rather, he strikes out against grammar for its
infantile preoccupation with elementary matters of form over and against
content. As the *grammaticus* is concerned only with the surface constructions
of language (pronunciation, syntax) without regard for reference or truth value,
it is perfectly regular for him to pronounce the nonsensical phrases cited above.

The rhetorician by contrast deals in value by putting language to persuasive use in the service of society and its laws. Whence an invective against
the linguistically inept (grammarian) in the following book of the *Rhetorica
novissima:*

> Nudi grammantes, qui non de iure sed de sola vocis prolatione confidunt,
> lingue lubricum intuentur, credentes quod iura civilia subiacent regulis
> Prisciani.[21]

> The naked grammar mongers, who have little knowledge of law but know
> only about pronunciation, are concerned that the tongue be well oiled and
> believe that the laws of society give way to the rules of Priscian.

The final clause subtly elevates rhetoric to the status of Holy Scripture by
echoing a long tradition of Christian defenses of the sometime agrammati-
cality of the Vulgate. This tradition began with an oft-cited letter of Gregory
the Great and carried easily through to grammatical and rhetorical texts of
Boncompagno's day.[22]

When the subject of his own grammatical preparation arises in the introduction to the *Rhetorica antiqua,* Boncompagno confesses somewhat grudgingly that he, too, had acquired the basics of the "primitive" art at the breasts of Lady Grammar in Florence. He immediately adds that this grammatical apprenticeship lasted no longer than sixteen months:

> LIBER: Ubi didiceris
> AUCTOR: Licet ad rem non pertineat, referre ubi didicerim, et quis meus doctor fuerit, tamen te certificio, quod inter floride civitatis Florentiae ubera primitive scientie lac suscepi, sed totum studendi spatium sub doctore sedecim mensium terminum non excessit.[23]

> BOOK: Where did you study?
> AUTHOR: Although it is not really pertinent to the matter at hand to relate where I studied and who my teacher was, I nevertheles assure you that I drank in the milk of the first science amidst the breasts of the florid city of Florence, but my entire period of study with a teacher did not exceed the limit of sixteen months.

Loath to admit even the most short-lived exposure to the florid fertility of Mother Florence, Boncompagno prefers to remember his almost immediate advance to the higher, drier ground of Bologna and rhetoric.[24] More than mere rhetorical formulas, his metaphorical distancing of Lady Grammar's body betrays a deeply rooted aversion.[25]

Indeed, for Boncompagno the very concept of an adult grammarian suggests something of a ridiculous oxymoronic perversion, an old goat at the udders of a young nanny:

> Miror quod tantum in arte gramatica permansisti, non attendens quod propter hoc de ingenii duritie infamaris. Dicet enim aliquis: "O si quis videret hyrcum annosum ubera capre sugentem non rideret? Ecce senex elementarius octo regna orationis et sex provincias casuum perlustravit, et ita cum interiectione dolentis sepelietur in tumulo ablativo."[26]

> I marvel that you dallied at such length in the art of grammar without realizing that you would gain a reputation as a blockhead because of it. For someone will say: "If you were to see an old goat sucking at the breasts of a young nanny, would you not laugh? Well take a look: the old grammar student traveled many years through the eight kingdoms of speech and the six provinces of case, and so with the interjection of pain upon his lips he will be buried in an ablative tomb."

Grammar thus threatens agenerational behavior and, more seriously, the risk of death while still having made no real headway against one's fallen nature and the chaos of human existence.

For Boncompagno this *interiectio dolentis*—the squalling of the new infant—bespeaks the suffering of original sin. There is a sense in which the lifelong grammarian dies with the anguished birth cry, the *vagitus* that

Boncompagno has elsewhere associated with grammar, still on his lips.[27] Much like Dante in the *De vulgari,* in the first book Boncompagno provides his new rhetoric with a megacosmic frame that traces the discipline's origins back through Eden to heavenly paradise. Rhetoric was born of law, and law originated first in response to the fallen angels and then the sin of Eve. Boncompagno reminds us of Eve's just legacy: "Et mulieri dixit: 'In dolore paries.'"[28] Childbirth is suffering for all involved and a continual reminder of originary disorder. At this point in the treatise, Boncompagno begins his formal treatment of rhetoric: for Boncompagno, rhetoric follows original sin as in the medieval trivium it followed grammar. The metaphorical and structural detail of Boncompagno's text links grammar to original sin and postlapsarian woe. By contrast, rhetoric holds out the only real hope to counter primal confusion by promoting law and civil society.

While he allows that God in his invisible essence will be reapprehended only through faith, Boncompagno soundly rejects the kind of fundamentalist mind/body dualism that condemns fallen humanity to total darkness while yet in the flesh. Strategic use of memory—an important component of rhetoric—will enable one to recover some part of the lost Edenic order.[29] While speaking to Adam in the garden, God became the first to employ *transumptiones,* the first inventor.[30] In this context, all of human existence—Augustinian yearning for an essentially invisible truth—becomes a rhetorical act. In the context of such noble striving, grammar offers only constant reference to original suffering, a bawling infant, desire and loss in the mother's body.

Eberhard the German (fl. thirteenth century)

FOR AN INTIMATE, quasi-autobiographical portrait of the *grammaticus* so scorned by Boncompagno, we need only turn to Eberhard the German's roughly contemporaneous *Laborintus.*[31] Although next to nothing is known of Eberhard's life and career, the author of the *Laborintus* clearly considers himself a grammarian, not a rhetorician. The bulk of his treatise consists of basic instruction in the art of poetry and treats the standard array of grammatico-rhetorical figures, the importance of the various *auctores,* and principles of metrics and versification. With regard to technical content, Eberhard's work is largely derivative of the better-known (and, in our day, better-studied) tracts of Geoffrey of Vinsauf and Matthew of Vendôme.

But the *Laborintus* is unique among the *artes poetriae* for its cosmological approach and the elegiac tone of its author's voice, which insists throughout on the sorry plight of the *magister* among the children of Adam. Although unoriginal in basic content, Eberhard excels at larger matters of fantasy and invention, matters generally extraneous to the specific rhetorical project. Thus, the very eccentricity that has earned for the *Laborintus* scant scholarly attention among modern-day historians of rhetoric places it center stage in our more metaphorically minded investigation of grammar and rhetoric in the thirteenth-century cultural imagination.

Eberhard chooses to introduce his teachings with a lengthy preamble on the creation and difficult destiny of the *magister* (1–252). Borrowing heavily for its creational and physiological detail from Bernardus Sylvestris,[32] the *Laborintus* traces a great chain of command from Nature (11–82) and Dame Fortune (83–118) to Philosophy and the seven sister Arts (119–75), including, of course, Lady Grammar, the formation of the *grammaticus* (175–252), and, finally, Grammar's handmaiden Poetry, who at last delivers the rhetorical information normally expected of such a treatise (253–1005).

But while it may seem clear from such an outline that Eberhard files poetry under grammar, a close reading reveals that Poetry and her rhetorical tropes and figures enjoy, at least in Eberhard's conception, an extraordinary fantastic freedom from the miseries of Grammar. In verses 267–68, Poetry announces her dominion over Philosophy and the entire universe: *Est mihi materia quidquid capit ambitus orbis; / Ludit in obsequio Philosophia meo.* ("Whatsoever is contained in the sphere of the universe belongs to me; Philosophy prances about in my service.") Poetry appears to have suffered little in Eberhard's mind from the sorts of grammatical misery with which the first section of the *Laborintus* is obsessively concerned.

Boncompagno was able to attack grammar on two fronts: for the impractical literary pretensions the discipline had absorbed at places like Orléans and, somewhat more colorfully, for the puerile simplicity of the first art as yet barely removed from primal confusion. A similar duality would seem to adhere in the *Laborintus*. Eberhard draws a stark contrast between the tedious, day-to-day realities of the *magister* among his students (with their lack of discipline, loyalty, talent, and parents willing to pay [835–991]) and a loftier, literary conception of grammar as practiced in Paris and Orléans, but for him only a remote memory:

> Cor tibi decoxit curae studiique caminus,
>   Afflixit corpus Parisiana fames.
> Sicut Parisius est divitibus paradisus,
>   Sic est pauperibus insatiata palus.
> Deinde tibi fornax fuit Aurilianis, alumna
>   Auctorum, Musae fons, Heliconis apex.
> Unde reversus eras nudatus veste, lacerna,
>   Pallidus, exilis corpore, rebus inops.
> Sed nunc cura gregis te mancipat, urit et artat
>   Officii jure, sedulitate, metu (vv. 943–52).

The furnace of worry and study brought your heart to boil, Parisian hunger afflicted your body. Just as Paris is a paradise for the wealthy, so it is a bottomless swampland for the poor. Whereafter Orléans became your furnace, nursemaid of the Authors, source of the Muses, pinnacle of Helicon. From which place you were turned away without cloak or mantle, pale, wasting away and without a cent. But now care of the student herd enslaves you, it consumes you and locks you away in a cell of daily duties, painstaking labor and fear.

Just as Eberhard reveals that Paris's mythical fame conceals the hunger and poverty of students, so his formulaic rehearsal of Orléans's glory (*alumna Auctorum, Musae fons, Heliconis apex*) from the perspective of his present misery (overworked, underappreciated, and destitute) resonates with more than a touch of irony. This passage goes on to bewail the tediousness of the master's daily routine, along with the intellectual obduracy and general unruliness of his students.

Eberhard's conception of long-suffering grammar focuses on instruction in basic principles: the alphabet, parts of speech, gender, syntax, and at the most advanced extreme the number and types of rhetorical figures (135–44, 175–92). As for study of the *auctores,* he limits grammar to Donatus and Cato.[33] By contrast and despite his structural hierarchy, Eberhard allows Poetry utter freedom from such abjection. Poetry promotes the analysis of subtle rhetorical distinctions and revels in the study of a wide range of classical and medieval authors (253–84, 992–1005). Although instructed in these arts, the *grammaticus* could put them to use only to bemoan his situation (835–990). Poetry thus enjoys some of the glory of Boncompagno's *Rhetoric.*

As *grammaticus,* Eberhard's admiration for rhetoric amounts to self-loathing. If rhetoric is "a flower," grammar is work (95); grammar knows none of the fame of the greater arts, the florid texts of Ciceronian rhetoric included (53–54); nor can grammar begin to share in rhetoric's important civic function (161–62). Eberhard makes it clear from the very start of his work that grammar means suffering. What is more, within the cosmological frame of the treatise, the equation between grammar and woe initially inspired by real-life conditions soon takes on existential connotations. The analogy—seriously contemplated by Augustine[34]—between the difficulties of grammar and the anguish of the postlapsarian human condition becomes in Eberhard's hands an elaborate conceit, almost to the point of absurdity.

Having foreseen that the developing fetus is destined to become a *magister,* Natura recoils in horror and hopes to abort her handiwork in short order. Bound by Fate, however, she is forced to bring the creature to term, even though the stars portend nothing but sorrow:

> Nasceris ergo, miser; misero tibi signa figurant
> > Sidereusque vigor officiale malum. (25–26)
> Est caeli virtus tibi tota propheta laboris,
> > In quo ditari non tua cura potest. (39–40)

You will thus be born, poor wretch; the constellations and their astral power portend for you, wretched thing, only duty-bound woe. . . . The heavens command nothing but suffering for you, and your labors will never lead to wealth.

Nature proceeds to depict images of the *magister*'s various tribulations to his mother (*Dicit et impingit matri simulacra laborum* [41]). He will spend long nights poring over Donatus, as noted, utterly cut off from the more interesting texts of sexier disciplines. Eberhard goes to great lengths to detail what will not be his: theology, astrology, geometry, arithmetic, rhetoric, dialectic, medicine, canon, and civil law (43–72).

Dame Fortune merely echoes Nature's predictions in the following section: *Vaticinor tibi perduros instare labores, / Quos vilis cathedrae progenerabit honor* ("I prophesy for you difficult inborn sufferings, which the wretched honor of the *cathedra* will multiply" [103–4]). It should be apparent by now that Eberhard chose his title with care to reflect the important recurring motif of grammar as a kind of internal suffering, as concisely explicated by the *glossator* of MS Bibliothèque Nationale 18570 (1349): "Titulus est Laborintus, quasi laborem habens intus."[35] Eberhard then explicitly links the inborn suffering of grammatical toil to the torment of childbirth, the legacy of Eve.[36] At last, the star-crossed *grammaticus* sees light:

> Nascitur hic plorans. Licet hoc generale sit omen,
> > Ploratus tamen hic particulare tenet:
> Iste genas lacrimis oneratas saepe videbit,
> > Nec fiet lacrima prosiliente pius.
> Masculus "a" profert omnis dum prodit ad auras:
> > Ex radice trahit primi parentis Adae:
> Hic cum vagitu speciali ructuat "alpha!"
> > Quod rudibus pueris syllabicando legit. (73–80)

> He is born crying. Although this is a general phenomenon, he will nevertheless have a special cry. For he will often see his cheeks flooded with tears without becoming any more devoted as a result. Now every little boy screams "Ah!" as he comes forth to light: he derives this from the root of our first parent Adam: But this little boy belches forth an extraordinary "alpha!" which he will rehearse while reciting syllables to his unlearned pupils.

Here Eberhard not only casts the nascent grammarian's anticipated sorrow as the fate of postlapsarian humanity. His unique sense of invention compels him to find for the future *magister* a special *vagitus:* not merely "ah!" (the standard human birth cry that echoed the name of Adam), rather the extraordinary "alpha!" (harbinger of the grammarian's particular misery and sign of future anguish in the classroom, where he would waste a lifetime reciting the alphabet with his *pueri*).

Like Boncompagno, then, Eberhard makes of the *vagitus*—already closely associated in the thirteenth-century mind with the sorrowful human condition after Adam—an emblem for the dull life of the grammarian. What was mere suggestion in Boncompagno, born of generalized scorn for the infant not yet in control of his faculties (linguistic and otherwise), becomes in Eberhard a full-blown (and perhaps overly elaborate) construct that casts grammatical labor as a mark of postlapsarian woe. Perhaps most significantly, both thinkers react with fear and loathing to a tradition that had long associated grammar with the nurturing female body.

Eberhard, like Boncompagno, is particularly attracted to the *magister*'s quasi perverse dependence on the breasts of Lady Grammar. In the *Laborintus,* Lady Philosophy presents Grammar to her sister Arts while pointing out her most conspicuous physical feature: *Inter vos gradus est soror in limine prima / Primo, quae lactis ubera plena gerit* ("Among your ranks on the very first level stands your eldest sister with breasts full of milk" [135–36]). Eberhard thus captures centuries of thinking about Grammar in two succinct verses. She is both lacteal and liminal. She at once signifies the presence and absence (presence as absence) of the primal object of desire. On the threshold of learning and culture, between infancy and speech, unregulated idiolect and standard, Lady Grammar recalls as loss early semiotic experience in the mother's body. She occupies a space where corporeal desire has always already begun a process of symbolization.[37] Both the source of higher learning and a threat to that learning, she masks a perilous contradiction.

Just as Boncompagno belittles his apprenticeship at the breasts of Lady Grammar, so Eberhard (as *grammaticus*) can only wallow in milky misery. For Eberhard, the future *magister* suckles all grammatical knowledge from the mother's body (*mater radixque loquelae* [193]) during what appears to be a lengthy instruction:

> Gremium subit iste prioris
> > Germanae, lactis primitiasque trahit.
> Imprimit "a"[38] menti sugens ex ubere primo:
> > Consequitur numero turba vocata suo;
> Sugit quot constet elementis sillaba, partes
> > Quot sint sermonis, quae genus omen creant;
> Sugit quid proprium sit cuique, quid accidit illi,
> > Et quid simpliciter significando notet;
> Sugit quae partes sint prima sede locatae,
> > Quae sint quae sede posteriore sedent;
> Ubere de reliquo bibit uberiore, maritet
> > Dictio se sociae qua ratione suae;
> Quae sit festiva, quae non constructio vocum,
> > Et quot sint species illius inde bibit;
> Quae sit congruitas sensus et vocis, utramque
> > Quae teneat, quae non, synthesis, inde bibit;
> Quis modus excuset vitium, quot quaeque figura
> > Distinctas species continet, inde bibit. (175–92)

he submits to the bosom of the first sister, he draws the first drops of milk. He imprints an "a" on his mind while sucking the first breast: the entire grammatical herd is summoned and follows each in its proper place. He sucks out how many types of syllables there are, how many are the parts of speech, which create each gender; he sucks out what is proper and to what, and what is accidental; and he will note what designates through simple signification; he sucks out which parts are located in the anterior brain, and which in the posterior; he drinks from the remaining breast (which offers even greater nourishment) through what meaning each word may take a bride, which verbal constructs are pleasing and which are not, and how many types are there of each that he drinks; what is congruity of sense and word, and which constructs that he drinks have both in synthesis, and which do not; which mode can license error, how many and which figures that he drinks have distinct subspecies.

Eberhard balances his list between suckling and drinking (*sugit/sugit/sugit . . . inde bibit/inde bibit/inde bibit*); all else is milk and Grammar's overflowing breasts (*lactis primitias trahit . . . sugens ex ubere primo . . . ubere de reliquo bibit uberiore*).[39]

He goes on to describe at length Grammar's watch over the gradual transition from milk to solid foods, such as bread crumbs. Lady Grammar instructs the *magister* to be gentle when violating the virgin wax with its first seal, to increase thumb pressure only as resistance is met (195–202). Students of greater, harder age are to be dealt with more firmly and offered less easily assimilated, liquid forms of nourishment: *Asperius debet tractari firmior aetas / Uteturque meo consolidante cibo* ("A more solid age must be dealt with more firmly and more solid food must be used" [203–4]). It would eventually (after Donatus) fall to the *magister* to grind up and offer to his students morsels from the body of Priscian: *Doctoris Prisci gemino de corpore micas / Extrahe discipulis, contere, sparge tuis* ("Pick bread crumbs from the twofold body of the learned Priscian, grind them up and feed them to your pupils" [209–10]). Eberhard thus nicely details Grammar's surveillance of the individual's passage from milk to bread crumbs and more solid foods to young adult verbal (and sometimes physical) discipline.[40] But the *magister* is forever destined to return to the start; he will never move beyond his eternal, diluvial infancy.

Dante (1265–1321)

THE REPRESSION OF the nurturing body of Lady Grammar evident in Dante's *De vulgari eloquentia* (written in the years immediately following the poet's exile, probably c. 1304) at once acknowledges and undercuts the clean duality of the paradigm established by Eberhard and Boncompagno. The metaphorical moment of weaning resonates deeply with Dante: it is intimately bound up with contemporary political confusion, the poet's recent exile from Florence, Eden, Babel, and the history of language, self, and the universe. I have elsewhere begun to articulate in appropriate detail the centrality of the mother's (absent) body to Dante's thinking.[41] As complement to my readings of Boncompagno and Eberhard, I can here only briefly suggest what is at stake in Dante's treatise before returning in conclusion to the issue of categorization of poetry (grammar or rhetoric?), with which I began.

Now Dante's project to define an "illustrious" Italian vernacular involves a paradox from the start, for the very qualities that draw him to the vernacular, that cause him to praise the mother tongue over Latin (grammar) at the opening of the treatise, are its universal ease of acquisition, lack of regularization (read "grammaticalization"), and, in short, the physical immediacy of its relation to primal human nature, the nurturing maternal body:

> vulgarem locutionem appelamus eam qua infantes assuefiunt ab assis-
> tentibus cum primitus distinguere voces incipiunt; vel, quod brevius dici
> potest, vulgarem locutionem asserimus quam sine omni regula nutricem
> imitantes accipimus . . .
>   Harum quoque duarum nobilior est vulgaris: tum quia prima fuit
> humano generi usitata; tum quia totus orbis ipsa perfruitur . . . ; tum
> quia naturalis est nobis, cum illa [gramatica] potius artificialis existat.
> (1.1.2/4)[42]

> what I call "vernacular speech" is that which babies become accustomed
> to from those around them when they first begin to articulate speech;
> or, as it could be put more succinctly, I would claim as vernacular speech
> that which we learn without any rules in imitating our nurse. . . . Of
> these two, then, the vernacular is the nobler; both because it is enjoyed
> by the whole world . . . and because it is natural to us, while the other is
> more an artificial product.[43]

Grammar, by contrast, is secondary, rational, artificial, and only attained by a very few through long, difficult study.[44] It is a rational principle that potentially counters vernacular diversity through space and time: *gramatica nichil aliud est quam quedam inalterabilis locutionis ydemptitas diversibus temporibus atque locis* ("grammar being indeed nothing other than a certain uniformity of language which does not change in different times and places" [1.9.11]). Given this conceptual frame, to the extent that Dante would regulate and rationalize the vernacular, he is simultaneously subtracting from its worthiness as an object of study: he is dematernalizing it, denaturing it, and thus undoing its very reason for being. It is, in the end, this paradox that will bring the treatise to a grinding premature halt at mid- paragraph in the fourteenth chapter of the second book. Dante could no longer ignore the paradox of Lady Grammar, who at once veils and reveals the attempt to fulfill a primal desire with a thoroughly inadequate, symbolized, fallen object.

And the poet's metaphors can leave no doubt that as he moves toward a regularized vernacular, he is abandoning the primal attraction of the veracular in the mother's body. In the global historical approach to his problem, Dante emulates the language of Adam, *vir sine matre, vir sine lacte* (1.6.1). The exile waxes sentimental about the necessity to turn his back on the mother tongue, nurturing Mother Florence, and sensual pleasure in order to embrace a greater language, universal citizenship, and reasoned judgment.[45] He summarily bans from the new illustrious vernacular (which he conceives as a kind of "paterfamilias" [1.18.1]) the feminine (*muliebria*) and baby-talk (*puerilia*) words so closely linked to the nurturing mother's body, *mamma, babbo, mate, pate* (2.7.4). More dramatically, he rejects even those urbane words that are oily and unrefined (*urbana lubrica et reburra*); as examples, he can only come up with *femina* and *corpo* (2.7.4): the female body.

But where do the categories of grammar and rhetoric fit into this treacherous scheme? Here again, Dante's text conveys a mentality that regards grammar as a liminal, ambiguous space still too close to formless nature to represent the security of pure reason. While he in places, as in the above definitions, espouses *gramatica* as an intellectual course of study and abstract principle of linguistic unity, he elsewhere identifies grammar with Latin (which, he recognizes, can vary through space and time)[46] or, in his only true allegorization of the discipline, the waxing and waning moon: an endlessly divisible and elusive body whose potential wholeness will forever be veiled to human sight.[47] *Gramatica* becomes the conceptual battleground for Dante's conflicting criteria: the maternal affection associated with individual desire and the rational discipline necessary for universal linguistic unity. It is within and through the space of *gramatica* that Dante moves from one to the other while hoping somehow to synthesize the two.

But this synthesis never comes about, at least not within the confines of the *De vulgari eloquentia*. Dante moves from abstract speculation and the possibility of a new language at once maternal and universal in book 1 to the kinds of prescriptive detail worthy of Matthew of Vendôme or Geoffrey of Vinsauf and their *artes poetriae* in book 2. In doing so, he to a significant degree abandons the exciting speculative possibilities held out by the category of grammar. That is to say, he moves from grammar to rhetoric.

The moment Dante begins to identify his new illustrious vernacular with the highly restricted idiom of a handful of vernacular poets, he has betrayed his initial promise for an idiom both maternal (spontaneous, natural) and regulated. The vernacular poetic language he admires is by his own admission a product of those who have turned their backs on the mother.[48] Forced to supply linguistic particulars for his new tongue, Dante embraces an increasingly rhetorical definition of the illustrious vernacular to the clear detriment of grammar and her threatening liminality.

Already toward the close of book 1, he exalts the illustrious vernacular for its persuasive, specifically political, power:

Quod autem exaltatum sit potestate, videtur. Et quid maioris potestatis est quam quod humana corda versare potest, ita ut nolentem volentem et volentem nolentem faciat, velut ipsum et fecit et facit? Quod autem honore sublimet, in promptu est. Nonne domestici sui reges, marchiones, comites et magnates quoslibet fama vincunt? (1.17.4–5)[49]

And that it is exalted by power is evident. For what has greater power than something which can change the human heart, making the unwilling willing and the willing unwilling, as this vernacular has done and continues to do? Then, that it exalts in honor is quite clear. For do not those of its household surpass in fame kings, marquises, counts, and magnates?

Again at 2.6.5, Dante equates the illustrious vernacular both with his coterie of the most celebrated poets and with hard-edged political discourse.[50] What is more, he specifically attributes the failure to attain this highest level of discourse to an inadequate and superficial knowledge of rhetoric (*quorundam superficietenus rethoricam aurientium*). By clear implication, the illustrious vernacular has now become the domain of those élite few who hold a sophisticated command of rhetoric.

Book 2 generally treats the illustrious vernacular in terms of vernacular poetry, and a severely limited selection of vernacular poetry at that. But is grammar not also, at least potentially, a component of poetry? Dante's response is telling. In the second treatise of the *Convivio*, he explicitly includes grammar—alongside rhetoric and music—among the constituents of poetry, there where he invites the reader to admire the formal beauty of his canzone, "Voi che 'ntendendo il terzo ciel movete":

> ma ponete mente la sua bellezza, ch'è grande sì per construzione, la quale si pertiene a li gramatici, sì per l'ordine del sermone, che si pertiene a li rettorici, sì per lo numero de le sue parti, che si pertiene a li musici. (*Convivio* 2.11.9)

But he is no less explicit about his definition of vernacular poetry in book 2 of the *De vulgari: nichil aliud est quam fictio rethorica musicaque poita* ("nothing other than a fiction expressed in verse according to rhetoric and music" [2.4.2]). What has become of *gramatica* here? She has been conveniently, dramatically excised. There is no longer any room in the rhetorician's master plan for the grammarian's unsettling truths.

Dante thus speaks with the confident voice of the *rhetor* in book 2. For all his apparent faith in the power of rational human constructs to control language, states, hearts, and minds, however, he cannot in the end easily forget the lessons proffered by the more daring *grammaticus* in book 1: that linguistic difference is a necessary condition of postlapsarian existence, the immediate expression of human desire, one with the flow of history and time; that human

189

efforts to regulate this flow grow out of, and must always exist in relation to, primal desire as experienced by the infant in the nurturing mother's body; that any rational system is thus always, already inadequate and subject to decay. In this sense, the *grammaticus* plagues the *rhetor*. Boncompagno cannot leave Eberhard behind: Dante falls silent.

In conclusion, I suggest that grammar came to occupy a perilous space in the medieval imagination over the course of several centuries. While ostensibly the very source of linguistic law, we have seen that in more personal metaphorical representations, grammar was significantly open—by the mere fact of its proximity—to the very forces the discipline would counter. The prevalence of the nurturing mother's body in depictions of grammar betray the primal anxieties that the discipline evoked in medieval thinkers. Both nurturing and disciplinary, grammar held out the possibility of symbolic thought while simultaneously recalling the origins of same in the chaotic flow of natural life. She thus constructed and deconstructed with a single gesture.

Medieval anxieties toward grammar are particularly apparent when viewed from the perspective of rhetoric, the more advanced language course. Deeply invested in the construct of the *civis,* rhetoric necessarily boasted its superiority by underscoring the safe distance it held from grammar's primal chaos. Boncompagno and Eberhard illustrate this dynamic with particular force. Dante will attempt to embrace and reconcile, unsuccessfully (at least in the *De vulgari*), both terms of a difficult dialectic that had grown up in grammatical and rhetorical thinking since Quintilian. Intricately caught up in the details of Dante's own mental and political life, the *De vulgari* stages— perhaps unwittingly—a drama of confrontation with the mother's body, whose final act (though not necessarily resolution) will be played out in later, even more ambitious texts.

Notes

1. At least among those rhetoricians who paid her any heed whatsoever. Most of the *artes poetriae* published by Faral, for instance, barely mention the first art; *Les arts poétiques du XII et du XIII siècle: Recherches et documents sur la technique littéraire du moyen âge,* ed. E. Faral (Paris: E. Champion, 1924; rpt. 1958). For the idea of rhetoric in the Middle Ages as a civic-minded art in the service of the state, such classic texts as Cicero's *De inventione* and the Pseudo-Cicero's *Rhetorica ad Herennium* remained influential; see Brunetto Latini, *La Rettorica,* ed. F. Maggini (Florence: Felice Le Monnier, 1968). My discussion of the early confusion and conflict between grammar and rhetoric is based largely on James J. Murphy, *Rhetoric in the Middle Ages: A History of Rhetorical Theory from St. Augustine to the Renaissance* (Berkeley: University of California Press, 1974); see 3–42. See also Jeffrey F. Huntsman, "Grammar," in David L. Wagner, ed., *The Seven Liberal Arts in the Middle Ages* (Bloomington: Indiana University Press, 1983), 58–95.

2. Indeed, Quintilian and Augustine both seem to require basic Latin language competence as a prerequisite to grammar. See Quintilian, *Institutio oratoria*, ed. and trans. H. E. Butler (Cambridge, Mass.: Harvard University Press, 1920; rpt. 1989), 1.4.1–2: *Primus in eo, qui scribendi legendique adeptus erit facultatem, grammatici est locus. . . . Haec igitur professio, cum brevissime in duas parte dividitur, recte loquendi scientiam et poetarum enarrationem, plus habet in recessu quam fronte promittit* (As soon as the boy has learned to read and write without difficulty, it is the turn for the teacher of literature [*grammaticus*]. . . . This profession may be most briefly considered under two heads, the art of speaking correctly and the interpretation of the poets; but there is more beneath the surface than meets the eye); and Murphy, *Rhetoric in the Middle Ages*, 23–26. Augustine makes a distinction between *primi magistri* and the more literary *grammatici* in the *Confessiones*, 1.13. On grammar instruction in Dante's Florence, see the wonderfully informative Paul F. Gehl, *A Moral Art: Grammar, Society, and Culture in Trecento Florence* (Ithaca: Cornell University Press, 1993), esp. 20–42 and 99, where Gehl notes that in Trecento Florence, instruction in composition (*dictamen*) was claimed by both grammarians and rhetoricians.

3. For the complete text of Donatus, see *Donat et la tradition de l'enseignement grammatical: Étude et édition critique*, ed. L. Holtz (Paris: Centre National de la Recherche Scientifique, 1981).

4. Both works are published in *Grammatici latini*, ed. H. Keil, 2–3 (Leipzig: B. G. Teubner, 1853–80).

5. In addition to Eberhard's *Laborintus*, the texts published by Faral include Matthew of Vendôme, *Ars versificatoria;* Geoffrey of Vinsauf, *Poetria nova* and *Documentum de modo et arte dictandi et versificandi;* as well as summaries of John of Garland, *De arte prosayca, metrica, et rithmica*, and Gervase of Melkley, *Ars versificaria.*

6. For a thorough discussion of verbal and visual allegories of grammar in the Middle Ages (and further bibliography), see my unpublished doctoral dissertation, "The Whip and the Wet Nurse: The Psychology of Grammar in the Middle Ages" (Harvard University, 1990), 158–250; see also G. Cestaro, " ' . . . quanquam Sarnum biberimus ante dentes . . .': The Primal Scene of Suckling in Dante's *De vulgari eloquentia*," *Dante Studies* 109 (1991): 119–47.

7. See, for instance, Alan of Lille, *Anticlaudianus* 2.380–513, or the several illuminated manuscripts of Bartolomeo di Bartoli da Bologna's *Canzone delle virtù e delle scienze* studied by Leone Dorez (Bergamo: Istituto Italiano d'Arti Grafiche Editore, 1904).

8. I have begun to analyze this imagery in the light of Julia Kristeva's distinction between semiotic and symbolic in the construction of subjectivity both in my dissertation and in " . . . quanquam Sarnum"; it will be the focus of my forthcoming book.

9. Carl Sutter, *Aus Leben und Schriften des Magisters Boncompagno* (Freiburg and Leipzig: Mohr, 1894).

10. Ronald G. Witt, "Boncompagno and the Defense of Rhetoric," *The Journal of Medieval and Renaissance Studies* 16, 1 (Spring 1986): 1–31.

11. Murphy, *Rhetoric in the Middle Ages*, 253–55.

12. Selections from the *Rhetorica antiqua* or *Boncompagnus* have been edited by L. Rockinger in *Briefsteller und Formelbücher des elften bis vierzehnten Jahrhunderts*

[*Quellen und Erörterungen zur bayerischen und deutschen Geschichte* 9] (Munich: Franz, 1863). Virgilio Pini has also edited much of the first book of the *Boncompagnus* in *Testi riguardanti la vita degli studenti a Bologna nel sec. XIII* (Bologna: Biblioteca di "Quadrivium," 1968); *Rhetorica novissima* [*Bibliotheca iuridica medii aevi: scripta anecdota glossatorum* II], ed. A. Gaudenzi (Bologna: Treves, 1892). For a complete list of Boncompagno's works, see Sutter, *Aus Leben,* 24.

13. See, for instance, the definition discussed below, where grammar teaches the recitation of vowels and construction of the most elementary syntax.

14. It is through Dame Rhetoric that the *Boncompagnus* lords it over the ineffective (i.e., non-civic-minded) mass of precept-laden orators: *illa namque dominabilias imperabit, et imponet silentium oratoribus qui sine comuni profectu ediderunt multitudinem preceptorum* ("through her it will rule over those in need of rule and will impose silence on those orators who issued a great multitude of rules without consideration for the common good" [Rockinger, *Briefsteller,* 129]).

15. *Eloquentia est rivulus a fonte rhetorice derivatus, qui potest ipsius artis effectus probabiliter nominari. . . . Item ponitur aliquando eloquentia pro arte ipsa; unde rhetorica et eloquentia synonima esse videntur* ("Eloquence is a stream that flows forth from the spring rhetoric and can probably be designated as the effect of this art. . . . Likewise, eloquence is sometimes used to designate the art itself; wherefore rhetoric and eloquence appear to be synonymous" [*Rhetorica novissima,* 1.1, 254]).

16. The employment of teething as metaphor for the arduous acquisition of language skills has a long history. See, for instance, Pliny the Elder, *Historia naturalis* 7.15; Martianus Cappella on Lady Grammar's file in the *De nuptiis philologiae et Mercurii* 3; Boncompagno, *Rhetorica novissima,* 2.3, 255; and in particular *Boncompagnus,* 1.23.3, 48, on Jerome's grammatico-rhetorical education: *Item Ieronimus sibi dentes fecit acui et limari, ad hoc quod Hebreorum et Chaldeorum ydioma rectius pronuntiare valeret* ("Likewise Jerome had his teeth filed down and sharpened so that he could correctly pronounce the language of the Hebrews and the Chaldeans"). Thus, well-ordered teeth were a prerequisite to good speech; see Bartholomaeus Anglicus, *De rerum proprietatibus* (written c. 1230; Frankfurt: Richter, 1601; rpt. Frankfurt: Minerva, 1964), 6.1: *Et dicitur 'infans quasi non fans,' eo quod fari non potest, neque exprimere sermonem, dentibus nondum bene ordinatis* ("And he is called 'infant' from 'non fans,' because he cannot yet speak or form words, because his teeth are not yet well ordered"). The nurse—Lady Grammar's archetype—governed this teething process.

17. *Rhetorica novissima,* 9.3, 285; see *Boncompagnus,* 1.5.1–2, 12; see also Boncompagno's suggested *exordium* for the inexperienced orator in the *Rhetorica novissima,* 5.5.5, 267. For the phrase *in dentium plantativa* to refer to the life stage of *infantia,* see Bartholomaeus, *De rerum proprietatibus,* 6.1.

18. *Rhetorica novissima,* 9.5, 287: *Proponit grammaticus quod grammatica est scientia recte loquendi recteque scribendi, omniumque artium fundamentum, unde admonet ut arti grammatice opera impendatur* ("The grammarian claims that grammar is the science of speaking correctly and writing correctly, the foundation of all the arts, wherefore he urges that your efforts be devoted to the art of grammar"). See Quintilian's definition of grammar as quoted above and Isidore of Seville, *Etymologiae,* ed. W. M. Lindsay (Oxford: Clarendon, 1911), 1.5.1: *Grammatica*

est scientia recte loquendi, et origo et fundamentum liberalium litterarum ("Grammar is the science of speaking correctly, and the source and foundation of liberal letters").

19. *Rhetorica novissima,* 9.5, 287. It is interesting to note that just a few paragraphs later, Boncompagno appropriates grammar's traditional function of teaching correct speech (*scientia recte loquendi*) for rhetoric; see 9.5, 288: *nemo potest in aliquo recte loqui . . . sine documento rhetorice facultatis* ("no one can speak correctly in any matter . . . without instruction in the faculty of rhetoric").

20. In the *Poetria nova* (c. 1200–1202), 1010, Geoffrey of Vinsauf brings together what, for Boncompagno, are the two negative aspects of grammar by using the nursing motif (traditionally reserved to portray grammar as basic language instruction) to describe literary grammar as practiced in Orléans: *Parisius dispensat in artibus illos / Panes unde cibat robustos. Aurelianis / Educat in cunis autorum lacte tenellos.* ("Paris, in the arts, dispenses bread to feed the strong. Orleans, in its cradle, rears tender youth on the milk of the authors" [*The Poetria Nova of Geoffrey of Vinsauf,* trans. M. Nims (Toronto: Pontifical Institute of Mediaeval Studies, 1967)]).

21. *Rhetorica novissima* 10, 293. See Witt, "Boncompagno and the Defense of Rhetoric," 10–12, esp. n. 25; also *Boncompagnus* 1.17, 138, where the *nudi grammantes* cannot recognize the distinction between a common and a proper noun. Only in the *Palma* does Boncompagno explicitly link the *grammantes* to Orléans; see Sutter, *Aus Leben,* 113–14; see Witt, "Boncompagno and the Defense of Rhetoric," 9; see also John Ahern, "Nudi Grammantes: The Grammar and Rhetoric of Deviation in *Inferno* XV," *Romanic Review* 82, 4 (November 1990): 466–86.

22. Gregory the Great, *Epistula missoria ad Leandrum Hispalensem,* 75, 516B: *indignum vehementer existimo ut verba caelestis oraculi restringam sub regulis Donati* ("I vehemently deem it shameful that the words of the celestial oracle be bound under the rules of Donatus"). See Petrus Helias in the twelfth century as cited by Charles Thurot, *Notices et extraits de divers manuscrits latins pour servir à l'histoire des doctrines grammaticales au moyen âge* [*Notices et extraits des manuscrits de la Bibliothèque Nationale* 22, 2] (Paris: Imprimerie Imperiale, 1869; rpt. Frankfurt: Minerva, 1964), 204: *dicemus divinam paginam non subiacere regulis huius artis* ("we will respond that the divine page is not subject to the rules of this art"); and John of Garland in the thirteenth century as cited by Thurot, *Notices et extraits,* 526: *Pagina divina non vult se subdere legi / Grammatices, nec vult illius arte regi* ("The divine page does not wish to subject itself to the law of grammar, nor does it wish to be governed by this art").

23. Rockinger, *Briefsteller,* 131.

24. See, for instance, the passage from the *Liber de obsidione Anconae* cited by Sutter, *Aus Leben,* 31: *Cui Florentia dedit initium, et Bononia, nullo praeeunte doctore, celebre incrementum* ("To whom Florence gave a start, and then Bologna—without the guidance of any teacher—notable advance"). Sutter comments: "Aus diesen vielversprechenden Anfängen ist dann in Bologna ein 'celebre incrementum' geworden. Hier vervollkommnete er seine rhetorische Bildung wohl besonders nach der juristischen Seite hin, ohne jedoch die Jurisprudenz oder eine andere Wissenschaft als Fachstudium zu betreiben." Boncompagno's impatience with grammar and hasty

graduation to a more advanced professional discipline was typical of Florentine students of the following century; see Gehl, *A Moral Art,* 20–42.

25. Boncompagno is not beyond recommending that the student on the brink of starvation for lack of money appeal to his biological origins in the mother's body, but only in the extreme case of having tried and been rejected by the father; see *Boncompagnus,* 1.15.6, 41: *LITTERE SPECIALES AD MATREM: Ad vos, reverenda mater, sicut ad specialem portum recurro supplicans vestre lacrimabiliter pietati ut filium quem in corpore vestro portastis, lactastis uberibus, laboribus et exercitiis nutrivistis, non dimittatis fame ac nuditate perire. Nam pater meus, immo non pater sed vitricus, non recordatur mei nec michi procurat in aliquo subvenire* ("EMERGENCY LETTER TO MOTHER: Appealing to your mercy with many tears, o mother worthy of great honor, in you I seek shelter as a foundering ship makes port in an unscheduled harbor, so that you not abandon to death by hunger or cold the son whom you carried in your body, whom you nursed with your breasts, whom you nurtured with great effort and labor. For my father—nay not a father but an evil stepfather—remembers me not nor moves to assist me in any way").

26. *Boncompagnus,* 1.3.3, 12, under the rubric *DE ILLO QUI REPREHENDIT ALIQUEM EX EO QUOD NIMIUM STUDUIT IN GRAMMATICA* ("ON HE WHO WOULD REPROACH SOMEONE FOR HAVING SPENT TOO MUCH TIME STUDYING GRAMMAR").

27. See the passage cited above from *Rhetorica novissima,* 9.5, 287, which compares the grammarian to a squalling infant (*tamquam infantulus vagire videtur*).

28. Boncompagno, *Rhetorica novissima,* 1, 254.

29. See book 8 of the *Rhetorica novissima,* "De memoria," 275–80; see esp. the paragraphs entitled *De unione angelice ac humane nature et quomodo et ubi pati cepit defectum memoria naturalis* ("On the union of angelic and human nature and how and where natural memory began to fail" [275]); and *De memoria paradisi* ("On the memory of paradise" [278]).

30. *Rhetorica novissima,* 9.2–3, 281–86, and esp. the rubric *Quis primus fuit inventor* ("Who was the first inventor?" [281]).

31. On the date of Eberhard's treatise, see Faral, *Les arts poétiques,* 39, who can place the treatise only in the broad period after 1212 and before 1280.

32. Faral has duly noted these passages in his edition; however, he does not mention the importance of the wet nurse in Bernardus's text as a figure for primal chaos. For Bernard, Silva, formless matter, is both womb and wet nurse; the nascent universe is a squawling infant (*infantia Mundi vagit*); see *Cosmographia,* ed. P. Dronke (Leiden: E. J. Brill, 1978); *Megacosmus,* 1.37–42. Indeed, this is somewhat of a Neoplatonic commonplace; see, for instance, Plato's conception of the *chora* ("the wet nurse of becoming") in the second book of the *Timaeus* and Chalcidius, *Timaeus a calcidio translatus commentarioque instructus,* ed. J. H. Waszink [*Plato latinus* 4, ed. R. Klibansky] (Leiden and London: E. J. Brill and Warburg Institute, 1962), 2.40. Clearly, Eberhard's portrait of the grammarian draws heavily on this tradition.

33. See 67–72: *Primi versiculi sed cernit grammata, primam / Quae sibi turba viam discipularis habet; / Donatos vertit, lacrimarum fonte fluentes, / Qui dantur pueris post elementa novis; / Ille tenet parvos lacerata fronte Cathones: / Illos discipuli per metra*

194

bina legunt ("But he discerns the lines of the first little verse, which the throng of students will follow as their first course; he confronts the Donatus, flowing fountain of tears, which is given to new students after the elementary principles; with great anguish he will take by the hand little Cato, whom students read in binary meter")

34. See *Confessiones* (Cambridge, Mass., and London: Harvard University Press and Heinemann, 1912; rpt. 1989), 1.13–15 and esp. the following passage, which equates grammatical discipline to the martyr's torment. Augustine sees both as manifestations of God's law and signs of the fallen human condition that should lead us toward truth: *sed illius fluxum haec restringit legibus tuis, deus, legibus tuis a magistrorum ferulis usque ad temptationes martyrum, valentibus legibus tuis miscere salubres amaritudines revocantes nos ad te a iucunditate pestifera, qua recessimus a te* ("But your law, o God, permits the free flow of curiosity to be stemmed by force. From the schoolmaster's cane to the ordeals of martyrdom, your law prescribes bitter medicine to retrieve us from the noxious pleasures which cause us to desert you" [*Confessions,* trans. R. S. Pine-Coffin (New York: Penguin Books, 1961)]).

35. Faral, *Les arts poétiques*, 38; see 39: "Le titre de son ouvrage est expliqué comme voulant dire 'labor habens intus.' Ce sens figuré du mot *laborintus*, signifiant 'misère, fléau,' se retrouve dans Gautier de Saint-Victor, qui appelait Pierre Abélard, Gilbert de la Porree, Pierre Lombard et Pierre de Poitiers les 'quatre labyrinthes de la France.' Sans aucune doute, c'est le mot *labyrinthus* des anciens. Mais on a mis ordinairement sa signification dérivée en rapport avec le mot *labor,* qu'on a considéré comme la forme d'ou il provenait."

36. Eberhard thus renders narratively explicit what was in Boncompagno merely a subtle, structural analogy between the pain of childbirth and grammar; see above. In this context, perhaps the most appropriate gloss for Eberhard's title is Genesis 3:16–17: *Mulieri dixit: "Multiplicabo aerumnas tuas et conceptos tuos: in dolore paries filios. . . ." Homini vero dixit: "Quia audisti vocem uxoris tuae et comedisti de ligno, ex quo praeceperam tibi, ne comederes, maledicta humus propter te! In laboribus comedes ex ea cunctis diebus vitae tuae"* (*Nova Vulgata Bibliorum Sacrorum Editio* (Vatican City: Libreria Editrice Vaticana, 1979). "To the woman he said: I will multiply thy sorrows, and thy conceptions: *in sorrow* shalt thou bring forth children. . . . And to Adam he said: Because thou hast hearkened to the voice of thy wife, and hast eaten of the tree, whereof I commanded thee that thou shouldst not eat, cursed is the earth in thy work; *with labor* and toil shalt thou eat thereof all the days of thy life" (Confraternity-Douay Version of *The Holy Bible* (New York: P. J. Kenedy, 1961). Emphasis added.

37. She thus in many ways "embodies" the dialectic between semiotic and symbolic that Julia Kristeva has located at the base of all language and subjectivity; for an introduction to Kristeva's terms, see *Revolution in Poetic Language*, ed. L. Roudiez and trans. M. Waller (New York: Columbia University Press, 1984), 19–106.

38. Again, this "a" must be glossed with the *a/alpha vagitus* of the nascent grammarian discussed above; see 77–79.

39. It is interesting to note that Philosophy advises moderation in drinking from Lady Grammar's breasts in 171–74: *Vester sic praeco, qui fati lege vocatur, / Ubera grammaticae sobrietate bibat. / Si de lacte satur fuerit, contemnet alumnos / Nec stomacho*

pascet esuriente rudes ("Let your herald, who is summoned by the law of fate, drink with moderation from the breasts of grammar. If he becomes sated with milk, he will have contempt for his pupils, and yet he will be unable to nourish the ignorant on an empty stomach"). Implicit in her warning is the same fear of overexposure to the nurturing female body that motivates Boncompagno's disdain for the *senex elementarius*; see above. Philosophy's warning would seem to be intended more for the *magister*'s pupils, who (like Boncompagno) after an acceptable, limited period of grammatical instruction could move on to intellectual maturity and the higher arts; the *magister* himself, as we have seen, is forever in thrall to the body of his mistress and thus a lifetime of misery.

40. See esp. 231–32: *Corrige delicta verbis et verbere, verbis / Asperius, virgis conveniente modo* ("Correct transgressions with both words and beatings, more harshly through words, in proper measure with the rod"). Grammar thus thoroughly plays the role of the wet nurse as defined by Bartholomaeus, *De rerum proprietatibus*, 6.9: *ad loquendum instruit puerum nescientem, balbutit nutrix et quasi frangit linguam, ut sic facilius instruat loquentem . . . cibum primo masticat, & masticando puero edentulo praeparat, ut facilius transglutiat cibum* ("in order to teach the ignorant boy to speak the nurse stutters and mumbles and, as it were, fractures her tongue and thus she more easily prepares the speaker . . . she first chews the food and by chewing she prepares it for the toothless child so that he can more easily swallow it"). We recall in this context the elaborate controlling metaphor constructed by Dante in the opening pages of the *Convivio:* Dante will prepare and administer the crumbs fallen from the table of the professional philosophers so that those equipped with the necessary physiological apparatus (teeth, tongue, palate), but unable to devote full time to learning, will be able to digest them; see *Convivio,* ed. G. Busnelli e G. Vandelli (Florence: Felice Le Monnier, 1954), 2 vols., 1.1.

41. See esp. Cestaro, " . . . quanquam Sarnum"; see also Gary P. Cestaro, "Irony of the Narrator in the *De vulgari eloquentia,*" *Italian Culture* 9 (1991): 15–27.

42. *De vulgari eloquentia,* ed. Pier Vincenzo Mengaldo, in *Opere Minori* 2 (Milan and Naples: Ricciardi, 1979).

43. English translations of Dante's treatise are from *Literary Criticism of Dante Alighieri,* ed. and trans. R. S. Haller (Lincoln: University of Nebraska Press, 1973), 3–60.

44. See 1.1.3: *Est inde alia locutio secundaria nobis, quam Romani gramaticam vocaverunt. Hanc quidem secundariam Greci habent et alii, sed non omnes: ad habitum vero huius pauci perveniunt, quia non nisi per spatium temporis et studii assiduitatem regulamur et doctrinamur in illa* ("We can also acquire another speech which is dependent on this one called by the Romans 'grammar.' The Greeks and other peoples, but not all peoples, have this sort of secondary speech; and furthermore, very few people attain fluency in this speech because we do not adapt ourselves to its rules and teachings without concentrated attention over a long period of time").

45. See 1.6.2–3 and esp.: *Nos autem, cui mundus est patria velut piscibus equor, quanquam Sarnum biberimus ante dentes et Florentiam adeo diligamus ut, quia dileximus, exilium patiamur iniuste, rationi magis quam sensui spatulas nostri iudicii podiamus* ("I, on the other hand, have the world as my native land, as a fish has the sea; and although I drank of the Arno before I had teeth, and although I have loved Florence so

much that I have suffered exile unjustly for my love, I support the shoulders of my judgment on reason rather than on sense impressions"). See *Convivio*, 1.3.3–4 and 4.24.14: *Onde, si come lo figlio a la tetta de la madre s'apprende, così tosto, come alcuno lume d'animo in esso appare, si dee volgere a la correzione del padre, e lo padre lui ammaestrare.*

46. See *De vulgari*, 1.10.1–2, 1.11.7, 2.7.6; and *Convivio*, 3.2.18, 4.6.3.

47. See *Convivio*, 2.13.9–10; for a close reading of Dante's uses of "gramatica," see Cestaro, " . . . quanquam Sarnum." For a solid general introduction to Dante's "rhetorical" education, see G. Nencioni, "Dante e la Retorica," in *Dante e Bologna nei Tempi di Dante*, ed. Facoltà di lettere e filosofia dell'Università di Bologna. (Bologna: Commissione per i Testi di Lingua, 1967).

48. See, for instance, his praise for Aldobrandino of Padova at 1.14.7: *Inter quos omnes unum audivimus nitentem divertere a materno et ad curiale vulgare intendere, videlicet Ildebrandinum Paduanum* ("Among all the Venetians I have heard only one who has made an effort to separate himself from his mother and to strive for the curial vernacular, and that is Aldobrandino of Padua"). See other such formulations at 1.12.9, 1.13.5, 1.14.3, 1.15.6.

49. Appropriately, Mengaldo here cites the classical (and subsequently medieval) Ciceronian conception of rhetoric as persuasive oratory in the service of the state.

50. *[E]st sapidus et venustus etiam et excelsus, qui est dictatorum illustrium, ut "Eiecta maxima parte florum de sinu tuo, Florentia, nequicquam Trinacriam Totila secundus adivit"* ("And then there is that construction which is both flavorful and charming, and, in addition, elevated, which is used by illustrious writers, as in 'The greatest part of the flower having been thrown out from your breast, Florence, in vain a second Totila will go to Sicily' ").

Never-ending Dispute:
A Proposal of Marriage

Thomas O. Sloane

O NE OF ERASMUS's most famous letters was written, he claimed, simply for the amusement of his young pupil and patron, his "Maecenas," he called him,[1] Lord Mountjoy. The letter urges the young Englishman to marry, for all the stock reasons—companionship of a woman, perpetuation of the family name, fulfillment of God's command. Allegedly designed for scholarly amusement, this advisory epistle is also highly disputatious—although not unusually so, for its time. But in its disputatiousness, the letter became both famous and notorious. To certain eyes, it told tales out of school, and Erasmus's claim about his intentions seemed all too characteristically disingenuous.

The storm the letter caused was intensified by its eventual publication. Even modern readers cannot fail to notice Erasmus's frequent use of prolepsis, anticipatory refutation, a sign that he was perhaps aiming at some larger target than this young man's vow to live a single life. Mountjoy, Erasmus notes at the outset of the letter, had reportedly made the vow either out of grief (his parents had recently died) or for the sake of religion (his sister, apparently out of the same grief, had entered a nunnery). It was, of course, Erasmus's attack upon the latter reason that caused the most trouble. When the letter was published in 1518, it outraged a large group of theologians who claimed that Erasmus had virtually mounted a public platform to attack some of their most cherished beliefs. Intellectual amusement, the letter's purported genre, was beside the point. And the author's vaunted ambition, his sought-after role as humanist educator, and his own monkish vows were not enough.[2] Or perhaps they were too much, for they seemed to become the very rationale and center of churchly furor.

Yet the title Erasmus used for the published letter might seem innocuous enough: *Declamatio in genere suasoria de laude matrimonii*—he called it "a declamation of the suasory kind, affirming matrimony." The *declamatio* was a set piece in traditional rhetoric with two major forms or genres. Of these, the *suasoria* was overtly and literally the less controversial. Unlike the *controversia*, which was adversarial and legalistic, the *suasoria* was intended to be a gentler, advice-giving form of declamation. Thus, the title might affirm Erasmus's stated intentions: the piece was nominally at least no more than a rhetorical tour de force, an almost nugatory essay prepared by a master for the instruction of a neophyte.

But theologians of the time found the letter intentionally threatening and censured it heavily. Almost immediately upon its publication, the vice-chancellor of the University of Louvain judged it a weighty attack on the blessedness of celibacy. Nonetheless, the infamous letter was to reappear several times, usually under its more popular and more pointed title, the *Encomium matrimonii,* and for at least a decade it enjoyed not only considerable vogue but also continued, formal condemnation by the Church.[3]

Let us note, too, that the encomium is another traditional rhetorical genre, one that like other types displays its intention: whereas *suasoria* signifies only general advice-giving, *encomium* always signifies praise, as in *Encomium moriae,* to mention another of Erasmus's most notorious discourses, "The Praise of Folly" (first published 1511, the *Moria,* Erasmus called it informally). Thus, the letter's contemporary reception plus its more pointed title might confirm impressions that he had indeed a veiled or at least collateral intention: if the Church was not Erasmus's "true" audience, this troublesome monk clearly had seized the opportunity once more to needle ecclesiastical authority. But these conjectures obscure the real point at issue.

Erasmus's response to his critics gives us yet another view of the debate his letter sought to enter and thus another view of the actual marriage his letter proposes. Against his severest critics, his contemporary theologians, Erasmus always had a singular defense: they were consistently unreliable interpreters, he argued, because they were ignorant of and unsympathetic to the classical world and its rhetoric. These flaws were apparent in their work, he argued, whether they were reading his orations, his letters, or even the Holy Bible. Erasmus's defense—which, obviously, thrusts as well as parries—appears in his apologies for the *Encomium moriae,* for his Paraphrases of Paul, among other pieces, and in his 1519 *apologia* for his encomium on matrimony. The epistle to Mountjoy was, he claimed again, simply a rhetorical exercise (indeed, one of the most popular schoolroom exercises for boys was to argue pro and con on the subject of marriage).[4] He noted that, as proper in such exercises, he had also written a counterargument against matrimony. Finally, pressing the point once more against a seemingly impenetrable obtuseness, he advised that one should always get down to cases and understand arguments in terms of their contexts: consider, he said, not simply the speech but the speaker, the audience, the occasion, and the examples.[5] So considered, he seemed to insist, his letter loses the sting certain readers had found in it. Marriage may be best for Mountjoy, the very crux of his argument, but not necessarily for all people.

However, as many of his readers well knew, this is not a simple defense. Nor are its implications simple, particularly in regard to that profession dear to the heart of Erasmus, the education of the young. In most important respects, save one, Erasmus's defense is not unlike ones used by his humanist epistolary predecessors Petrarch, Augustine, and Jerome. The exception is that the controversy in this case centers in a master-pupil relation, a centering that makes salient exactly what it was that Erasmus was in fact offering young students. It was, I shall argue, precisely what he usually counterpoises against his attackers, a rhetorical cast of mind. Some of its chief elements we have already noted: an abhorrence of depersonalized argument, an insistence that one get down to cases, a contextual view of meaning and intention, and a willingness (a lawyerly willingness, to be exact, as I shall explain later) to argue both sides of a question. Constituted of these elements, the preferred if not habitual discourse of this cast of mind is by nature ironic or, better, duplex in tone, in intention, and even in audience—like Erasmus's letter. The very reception of the letter reveals its propensity to cast a wide net in the troubled waters of what our own students would call real-world disputes. Such is the propensity of Erasmian instruction in rhetoric. His actual proposal of marriage is aimed, here as elsewhere, at the union of rhetoric and educational disputation, a union to be blessed by the birth of the rhetorical cast of mind.

It is significant that when Erasmus himself republished his letter to Mountjoy in 1522 in his manual on letter writing, *De conscribendis epistolis,* he also published his counterargument immediately following it. The significance of this prime example of two-sided argument does not lie in any effort to moderate past troubles; it lies rather in its revelation of exactly what Erasmus means by "rhetorical exercises." Here, in his widely read work on letter writing, the refutation of the Mountjoy letter is designed not so much to retract the arguments in favor of marriage (or of renouncing celibacy) as to inculcate in the minds of his pupils the habits of rhetorical debating. Such inculcation, he argues, is the way to achieve richness in *inventio:* one is meant to learn not how to "deconstruct" meaning and intention but how to invent discourse through a kind of dialectical split focus. In simplest terms, one matter, one statement, one argument always presupposes its opposite, as in dialectic. However, "dialecticians," as he says in his famous work on rhetoric, *De copia,* "confuse the different significations of words"—not only because their Latin is bad but also because they ignore—again—speakers, audiences, and occasions. They ignore, that is, that meaning is not formalist or presumptive but context-driven. Otherwise, the two arts—dialectic and rhetoric—are coordinate arts of disputation, and by that Erasmus means two-sided argument, with rhetoric in particular centered on two-sided arguments about ideas that matter in the real world.

201

Thomas O. Sloane

We shall return several times to the *De conscribendis* with its significant lessons about *inventio,* but first some definitions seem in order. Let us define *dialectic* simply as "logical debate," which places an emphasis on forms of reasoning. (In Erasmus's age, *dialectic* was synonymous with *logic.*) Its chief venue, throughout the history of Western education, was formal disputation. Let us also note that *rhetoric,* too, may be defined as another kind of debate. Unlike dialectic (or logic), rhetoric places an emphasis not simply on forms of reasoning but also on speaker, audience, and occasion—not simply on unembellished evidence but also on circumstance and motive. There were thus two arts of argument, the one as loftily recondite as the other was lowly and corporeal. But each was equally centered on two-sided argument. The prize Erasmus sought for rhetoric was the one dialectic already had, the hand of public, particularly curricular disputation. With that prize, rhetoric would replace dialectic in its long-honored union with disputation and so enter into a marriage that, among other effects, would reform traditional education, dominated for years by the churchly elevation of dialectic as the queen of the curriculum. Thereby the students would be moved into a life of constant inquiry, of skeptical questioning and never-ending dispute, a life in which their academic debating would train them to become like "academics" in the most ancient sense, Folly's friends, "the least arrogant of the philosophers."[6] It is this challenge to philosophical or educational arrogance, and not skepticism per se, that is the true aim of Erasmus's proposal.

Erasmus believed that training in rhetoric would by its nature counteract dialectical formalism by putting an emphasis on personality and circumstance. For it is the nature of rhetoric to confront real people on real issues, as opposed to the abstract, formalist nature of dialectic. Should a man marry? is a dialectical question. Should Lord Mountjoy marry? is a rhetorical one.[7] In its engagement with specificity, rhetoric necessarily acknowledges that meaning is context-driven, and the outcome of the dispute is often provisional and local, with a lingering modesty and dubiousness—closely akin to what we might call critical thinking—as its ultimate effect.

But Erasmus could begin, as we cannot, with the assumption that students come to rhetoric already trained in dialectic and used to disputation. He could therefore commence inculcating a rhetorical cast of mind by changing the dialectical willingness to argue both sides of the question into a lawyerly one: what matters, however much abstract questions may be involved, is what finally happens when one gets down to specific cases. Centering thus on a revival of the classical world and its rhetoric, the Erasmian educational reform was indeed controversial. But, in fact, it was actually less revolutionary in his age than in ours. For Erasmus lived in an age suffused with disputation, both in school and out—a highly fractious age, in which almost every statement initiated or responded to a debate, and virtually no statement was neutral. The New Philosophy as well as the New Politics were calling all into doubt. My

202

point remains: that is the sort of age in which rhetoric flourishes, and revivals of rhetoric, particularly in America, have done little to acknowledge its life-giving linkage to fractiousness and turmoil, even the fractiousness and turmoil of our own age. Further, given our professed interest in critical thinking, surely our age, too, no less than Erasmus's, can profit from an educational practice so clearly aimed as humanist rhetoric was, toward a loosening of intellectual strictures. Dogmatics and authoritarians, whether of the intellectual or the religious kind, are not unique to either age. But, to put my central point quite simply, just as Erasmus's age saw rhetoric as an interloper in the union of dialectic and disputation, we are now more likely to see disputation itself as a strange interloper in our sporadic obsession with rhetoric in education.

"In practice," Richard Lanham has reminded us, "rhetorical education is education in two-sided argument, argument where the truth is decided by the judge or jury, where truth is a dramatic criticism handed down on the forensic drama which has been played out according to the rules laid down, finally, by a rhetorical education."[8] This is one of the great traditions in education, as Erasmus well knew, extending from his Roman forebears if not from the Greeks. But this tradition has been largely abandoned in America, leaving behind an acknowledged and bewildering impoverishment in our theories of *inventio*—to say nothing for the moment, at least, of the impoverishment of what passes for public debate in America—leaving behind, too, very little of the humanist sense of rhetoric as a means of critical inquiry. Nor has that sense been fully revived in the revised rhetoric proposed in our own age by such major theorists as Kenneth Burke or Chaim Perelman,[9] simply because neither is wedded to disputation: Burke is married to symbolic action, Perelman to the epideictic with its universal audience. However, it is not Burke or Perelman that I would do battle with. It is, rather, those theorists and historians who are merely synecdochists of our long tradition—who, like the Ramists in the sixteenth century or Brian Vickers in our own, identify the whole of rhetoric with an archaic vocabulary that does little more than name stylistic fragments in the speaker's own mind and thereby short-circuit the intellectual excitement of the discipline.[10] We have forgotten the wellsprings of what our forebears meant by "eloquence."

The ancient alliance of rhetoric and two-sided argument, now in practice largely annulled, is historically unmistakable. When the humanists revived Ciceronianism—even though their preferred mode of argument was *suasoria*, advice-giving, and their preferred manner of writing was the easy conversational style known as *sermo*—they revived a rhetoric whose conceptual model is the criminal trial with its two sides, prosecution and defense, forming a triangle with the third point, the judge.[11] It is this kind of triangulation that best illustrates the use of rhetoric as a means of critical inquiry: disputation refined through personality and social context into a multiplex argument, aimed at judgment but predicated less on the immutability of truth than on

203

the possibility of human concord, that possibility Gilmore calls "the essential heritage of Erasmian thought in the sixteenth century."[12] It is something of this optimistic skepticism—this critical thinking with a good will—that constitutes the goal of Erasmus's educational reform.

However, we must also acknowledge, in our effort to understand Erasmian rhetoric, that the master's professed love of concord seldom prevented him from exploiting controversy and fractiousness—and not always in the interest of curricular reform. Thanks in part to the work of Lisa Jardine, we may now go even farther in our view of Erasmus as a thoroughgoing rhetorician. Not only was he an educator sans classroom. He was also a successful self-promoter, the soi-disant leader of a complex educational and intellectual reform, aimed ultimately at changing society's manner of thought. In exploring some of the deep involvement of rhetoric in that protocol, one will find Erasmus's most meaningful instruction not so much in his theories as in his actual practice. And in that practice, perhaps the most notable exemplars are his letters—"rhetorical exercises" indeed, as Jardine has pointed out, "intended to make a particular point of view compelling."[13] His own success in making a point of view compelling in his letter to Mountjoy is patent: he let the chips fall where they might do him and his ideas the most good.

Let us go farther into these ideas, using as our keywords *two-sided argument* and *disputation*. Our goal will be not simply to find other means of understanding humanist discourse but also to discover pedagogical instruments that we have perhaps overlooked in reconstructing rhetorical invention for our own students. Having searched these ideas, we shall return once more to Erasmus's letter. I shall conclude by leveling my charges against rhetoric as it is currently taught in the American classroom.

I

I HAVE SUGGESTED that the alliance of rhetoric with two-sided argument is an ancient one. Irregularly, from earliest times through the Renaissance, rhetoric cohabited with dialectic in the domicile of educational disputation. At its inception, however, this menage-a-trois (rhetoric, dialectic, and two-sided argument) usually held an honored place deep within that initial, creative process rhetoricians called invention.

According to Aristotle (*Rhetoric*, 1.1), a prime similarity between rhetoric and dialectic is that each generates arguments indifferently on both sides of the question; these two artistic "counterparts," as the philosopher called them, are unique among the arts, for only rhetoric and dialectic "reason in opposite directions."[14] In the antecedent tradition, even before there were two arts known as rhetoric and dialectic, two-sided argument already had been popularized by those early educators and self-promoters known as Sophists.[15]

That first great critic of "sophistry," Plato, constructed his famous work on rhetoric, the *Phaedrus,* as a dramatic demonstration of two-sided argument— as Erasmus well realized, when he advised boys to construct letters modeled on the opposing views of Socrates and Lysias (to be quoted below). Cicero's own practical masterpiece was a conscious imitation of the *Phaedrus,* his *De oratore,* in which it is assumed that pro and con argumentation is at the heart of rhetoric, a matter never in dispute by either Crassus or Antonius.

Of these three major documents, the most important one for identifying the spirit and intellectual method of Erasmian humanism is *De oratore.* At the beginning of the Renaissance, it was the first book printed in Italy; later it became the work "most frequently referred to by English writers of the sixteenth century."[16] Centering in a debate between two lawyer-statesmen, the dialogue is a veritable demonstration that *controversia*—the forensic battle of attack and defense—is the conceptual model of rhetorical invention.[17]

Further, in the tradition descending from Cicero, Seneca, and Aphthonius, *controversia* and *suasoria* overlapped—not the result, I would argue, of a theoretical laxity on the part of the classical rhetoricians but, rather, a reflection that two-sided argument inheres in both and generates either. Battle lines are more neatly drawn, of course, in *controversia,* where two sides are targeted, as in a case at law. But even in the advisory *suasoria,* when no opponent is manifest, the speaker must still refute unspoken objections in his hearers' minds—and rhetorical education trained him to do that by training him to play his own opponent's role, requiring him to give voice to those objections through arguing the other side of the case in a *dissuasoria.*[18] This centrality of *disputatio in utramque partem* ("arguing both sides") is made abundantly clear by Quintilian, who claims that there is only one almost exclusively inventive activity, debate.[19] It was made equally clear centuries later by Erasmus in his treatise on letter writing, *De conscribendis epistolis:* "The students' skill in invention will be improved if they practice recantations, arguing against what they have just proposed; what you have previously lauded to the skies, you dash down to the depths with violent denunciation; or first advocate something, then urge its avoidance" (*Collected Works of Erasmus,* 25: 43). In the intervening period, between Quintilian and Erasmus, disputation continued to be practiced, but on rather different grounds and with rather different questions. Medieval disputation was preeminently dialectical, the grounds were formalist, and the questions were theological and scientific. The discipline of choice was dialectic, not rhetoric. But, as noted, *disputatio in utramque partem* remained the chief educational enterprise.

Among the many ways of describing the passage of Western culture from the Middle Ages to the Renaissance—such as the philosophical shift from a view of God as the *conditio sine qua non* of epistemology to an obsession with that being who was supposedly created in God's image and likeness[20]—a crucial one for rhetoric may be the semantic shift described by Waswo, from the "referential," which regarded language as a "transparent vehicle," to the "relational," which regarded language "as a creative agent that constructs its own protean meanings."[21] For that matter, however, both shifts, the philosophical as well as the semantic, seem correlative to the attempted rise in prominence of rhetoric as a mode of thought. And for that rise in the Renaissance, one need look only at the abundant evidence provided by modern literary scholars. But since our interests here are primarily curricular, let us look at two renovated and deeply twined professions in the Renaissance, law and pedagogy.

Many humanists, including those most active in educational reform, had received training in civil law. Although the relation between humanists and the universities was at the outset embattled, the history of universities is often traced to the founding of the law curriculum at Bologna in the Trecento. Indeed, a virtual *conditio sine qua non* of humanism itself could well be the establishment of law as a major career pursuit along with medicine and theology. At the upper reaches of the curriculum, this new career pursuit, itself an appendage of rhetoric, was either a precursor or fellow traveler of humanism as it spread from Italy to Germany to France to England.[22] As such, it necessarily conditioned the very foundations of humanist reform in education, curriculum, and pedagogy.

A recent observation, concerning humanism's initial base in centers of power—that as it spread northward from Italy to Germany, France, and England, it "gained acceptance first in secular courts and bourgeois urban centers, then gradually in the universities"—pertains mostly to the Kristeller view of humanism, as a movement that revived the *studia humanitatis* (grammar, rhetoric, history, poetry, and moral philosophy).[23] But if one actually centers humanism in rhetoric as a kind of surrogate philosophy or *paideia*,[24] and above all if one links humanism with the rising profession of law, then another kind of curricular gradualism must be taken into account: the attempted liberation of disputation, for centuries held in thrall to dialectic, that is, to formalized procedures and highly speculative, especially theological, questions. A common thread in humanism is not so much the revival of the liberal arts, a thread that gets easily interwoven into that doubtfully humanist fabric known as the Age of Enlightenment, but the abhorrence of scholastic disputation and its displacement by rhetorical—that is to say, personalized—debate.[25] In this view, humanist pedagogical reform centered on making disputation less clerical and more lawyerly.

Valla struck a theoretical keynote of this effort in his early attempt actually to incorporate dialectic into rhetoric.[26] A correlative movement, aimed at rhetoricizing dialectic—if only to give its *inventio* the primacy it has in rhetorical composition—was carried on by such distinguished pedagogues in humanism's northward sweep as Vives, Sturm, Melanchthon, and Agricola. To this movement, Erasmus, too, belongs. He did less, I would argue, to revive the *studia humanitatis* than to rhetoricize *inventio,* including dialectical *inventio,* as part of his larger effort to create a new epistemology and hermeneutic. For that matter, Jardine's recent work suggests that Erasmus and his circle had a major role not simply in the publication but in the actual reconstruction, or perhaps even construction, of Agricola's dialectic, one of the most influential of the rhetorically oriented textbooks of disputation. At root, a rhetoricized *inventio* allows a subject to be inquired into and disputed not simply according to the rule of reason (or even, *pace* Augustine, the rule of charity) but according to the rule of reason *and* the moving of the will. Thus, Erasmus in *De ratione studii* would have schoolboys understand that rhetoric is a kind of logic, too, whose "chief points" are not only rational ones, such as "propositions" and "the grounds of proof," but also emotional ones, such as "figures of speech" and "amplifications" (*Collected Works,* 24: 670).

"Histories make men wise," Bacon wrote in his essay on the learned arts, but logic and rhetoric together make them "able to contend." By the time of Bacon, the tradition had been reborn and established, thanks largely to the efforts of Erasmus and his circle: rhetoric was not merely ornamental logic but a coordinate art of *contentio,* of inquiry and disputation. The instrument had come easily to hand for the pedagogues of England, who among all northern Europeans gave Erasmus his greatest reception: "In the treatise *De ratione studii* by Erasmus is the fundamental philosophy of the grammar school in England. On these general principles it was organized and by these methods it was taught. What is more, the strategic textbooks in the system were suggested, prepared, or approved by Erasmus."[27] Thus, whether the English student was guided by regulations based on *De ratione studii* or simply by his own desire to enter law, medicine, theology, or the arts, he seldom escaped the explicit commingling of rhetoric and dialectic, and he never escaped trial by disputation.

Disputation—a lingering medieval practice whose implications for rhetoric we have slighted—was unquestionably the major instrument of Renaissance pedagogy.[28] The ineluctable prominence of educational disputation was, as I am trying to suggest, a most significant context within which Erasmian humanists revived Ciceronian rhetoric.

In the grammar schools, the disputations were on the subject of grammar. Formally, they were less like debates than catechisms, or, better, that type of oral combat once prevalent in American education, the spelling bee. Although correctness was the point, winning was the supreme point.[29] On the highest levels, the temper of the age, particularly at Cambridge, was well captured in Master Holdsworth's "directions" for his students at Emmanuel College in the early seventeenth century: controversies (that is, private, in-house disputations) in the first year centered on logic and in the second year on logic, ethics, and physics; these gradually opened up to allow in the third and fourth years "controversies of all kinds"; meanwhile, his students, already grounded in logic, got progressively heavy doses of Cicero's letters and, among other writings, *De oratore, De officiis, De finibus,* and finally the orations. "Logic without oratory is dry and unpleasing," Holdsworth wrote, "and oratory without logic is but empty babbling."[30] Logic, that is, dialectic, continued to be taught but along with rhetoric; together they fulfilled *inventio,* by making it a mode of inquiry actively applied in educational disputation.[31]

In the universities, besides partaking in frequent "controversies," the student beyond his second year became a "sophister" and was required to take part in a stated number of disputations, both in college and in public, as a means of demonstrating not simply mastery of subject matter but also skill in dialectic and rhetoric. Undergraduates in their third or fourth year and for their baccalaureate degrees often treated philosophical questions. For the M.A., the questions could become no less philosophical but increasingly timely: "whether a college education will get you ahead in politics . . . whether women should have a liberal education . . . whether there is any certain knowledge of things . . . [whether] the power of the sword is the prince's alone . . . [whether] all change in the commonwealth is dangerous."[32] The list of questions is tonally similar to those Erasmus suggests in his manual on letter writing:

> in support of love, as Socrates and many others argue in Plato's dialogue, and against love, as does Lysias in the same author; for and against learning, wealth, the monastic life, languages, matrimony, and monarchy. Similar to these are themes handled by comparison or contrast. Which life is superior, the active life which the Greeks call practical, or the contemplative, which they call theoretical? Is celibacy better, or wedlock? Does art or natural ability contribute more to speaking? Is the modern kind of theology superior to the older one? Is military service or the study of literature more useful for the acquiring of reputation? Is jurisprudence or the study of medicine more profitable for the securing of wealth? (*Collected Works,* 25: 44)

Both lists bear interesting comparisons with the "dunsical" but actual list of disputational questions Folly pokes fun of in the *Moria,* a list Erasmus knows is overwhelming in its irrelevance: for example, "Whether there is any instant in the generation of the divine persons? Whether there is more than one filial relationship in Christ? Whether the following proposition is possible: God the Father hates the Son."[33]

When Elizabeth I visited Cambridge in 1564, she heard public disputations on propositions that may have been philosophical, even dialectical in appearance, but that were at the same time topical, current, indeed quite close to Elizabeth herself: whether the authority of Scripture is better than the authority of the Church, and whether the civil magistrate has authority in matters ecclesiastical.[34] A decision for the affirmative may have been expected; but if the debates were to be anything other than farcical, before a monarch who herself had been schooled by Roger Ascham, one of her country's leading humanists, opposing arguments had to be rigorous and attended to with respect. Moreover, Elizabeth, as we know, was subjected to all sorts of entertainment as she made her famous "progresses" through the countryside. But that debaters would be trotted out and required to perform for a grave and powerful head of state must strike us as curious indeed. At the very least, it is a reminder that disputation was a prominent educational activity in that year of Shakespeare's birth—and remained so, at least through the age of Milton. As I have noted, given this prominence, the humanists' challenge was not, as in our age, to encourage further use of disputation in *inventio* but to veer its course toward the rhetorical.

The form of educational disputation was variable, but it usually included only one proposer and several opposers, thereby complicating the simple binary divisions of pro/con analysis or of the affirmative/negative split. Procedures consisted of cross-examinations, refutations, and rebuttals. Sometimes the form became overtly triangular and included a moderator, who resolved the dispute.[35] Sometimes, too, the form included a "varier" or "prevaricator." Not exactly one of the disputants, the varier took the fool's part in public debates by playing verbally upon the question under dispute. One varier, for example, in a dispute on whether celestial bodies are the causes of human actions, averred that all dons present may be called stars: after all, stars are the denser parts of the heavens, and dons are the denser parts of the academic world. As Costello has shown in his study of Cambridge in the early seventeenth century, variers had a field day in disputes on such medieval-sounding questions as whether gold can be produced by chemical art or—the question disputed before James in his 1614 visit—whether dogs can make syllogisms (24–31). This fun-loving "prevaricating" spirit, exercising something of that virtuosity the humanists called wit, bears interesting and favorable comparisons with certain present-day Oxford debates and even with modern American "off-topic" debating. Finally, public debates were usually marked with elaborate ceremony and occasionally with fights and riots.[36]

Educational disputation, moreover, was oral. I shall return to this point later, but for the present I wish to emphasize a certain irony: it was most likely the humanists who gradually undercut the importance of orality in education—who in placing a new premium on literacy gave us textbooks, term papers, and, in place of disputations, written finals.[37] It was, in short, most likely the humanists who—all inadvertently—lessened the likelihood that their own revived rhetoric would succeed by weakening its most natural habitat, oral modes of composition and communication, a natural habitat particularly congenial to the insistence that all arguments should be attached to sources and purposes, to speakers and occasions.

Indeed, as a classical scholar has recently defined it, rhetoric itself may be thought of as "the written word attempting to do the work of the spoken word."[38] For the original nature of rhetoric was to institute conscious attention—the sort of conscious attention possible only with the advent of written texts—to linguistic strategies in the creation of oral or mock-oral performances. By the time of Cicero, the humanists' chief exemplar, lawyerliness had somewhat refashioned rhetoric's ancient nature, without any lessening of its orality: if *controversia* was now clearly the conceptual model of rhetorical *inventio*, the *rhetor* remained (as Cato the Younger put it) *vir bonus dicendi peritus*, the good man skilled in speaking. Therefore, the true irony in the ultimate overthrow of Ciceronian rhetoric may lie in humanist efforts to bring rhetoric itself to a new, heightened level of critical and educational consciousness, where reading and writing necessarily took precedence.

But at the outset, orality pervaded humanist instruction, with no consideration that writing and speaking may be disparate skills. Even letter writing, as the humanists taught it, was a kind of oral performance, one that could draw upon the inventive dexterity of disputation.

Again, Erasmus is a superb example. Like other humanist epistolographers, he challenged the formalist approaches of the medieval *dictatores* by moving oral disputation to the center of the inventional process. Speaking on both sides of a question, he believed, is precisely the way to perform that pedagogically invaluable function of making the student a rhetorical virtuoso, the goal sought by humanist pedagogues in teaching two-sided argument: never to be at a loss even under the pressure of oral composition. Erasmus is specific in his advice, as well as in his practice, as in this passage from his textbook on epistolography that not only conflates writing with speaking but, not surprisingly, advocates sophistry, echoing advice we have heard him give earlier:

> The teacher should . . . criticize [the pupils'] arguments, and then tell them to write a recantation. Sometimes, to sharpen their wits, he should propose disagreeable subjects. One might be asked, for instance, to defend poverty, exile, ingratitude, illness, contempt of study, neglect of language, or tyranny, or to argue that an old man should marry an old woman, or bring home a lewd wife. For nothing is so inherently good that it cannot be made to seem bad by a gifted speaker. By such practice both fluency and readiness in speaking on any topic will be acquired.[39]

Not only was letter writing a form of oral performance, but, as I have suggested from the beginning, it was also a slice of disputation, which for the humanists almost invariably veered off into their preferred mode of argument, the *suasoria,* and into their preferred manner of composition, the *sermo.* Both mode and manner, however, as I have also suggested, were profoundly oral and equally profoundly disputatious—as was the Ciceronian rhetoric the humanists revived, with its emphasis on lawyerly virtuosity. Thus, the chief characteristics of humanist writing might best be revealed through keeping these points in mind: to listen, that is, for the sounds of disputation in the lively flow of conversational writing, and above all to recognize that the discourse bespeaks a rhetorical cast of mind. Let us return to my initial example.

II

THE TRADITION IN which Erasmus composed his letter on marriage, sub-sequently published as an *encomium,* was a standard *suasoria,* based on a conventional question offered for schoolboy disputation: *an ducenda sit uxor* ("whether a man should marry"). One could center an entire history of two-sided debate on this question and find a host of examples, extending from the *suasoria* of Seneca and the classroom exercises of Aphthonius down to dense relics of the tradition, such as Ben Franklin's well-known letter on the advantages of having a mistress rather than a wife.[40]

Erasmus's rhetorical skill in this long tradition is shown in his adaptation to context: he bends stock arguments, the perpetuation of the family, for example, to fit the case at hand, such as the urgency for Lord Mountjoy to marry and not follow his sister into the religious life. On the other side, the argument against marriage, which he published along with this letter in his textbook on epistolography, becomes one of devoting one's life to learning and so finding one's "sons" through teaching, not through procreation. Alas, dogmatics—in this case, the theologians—apparently can take only one argument at a time and imagine only one context, not specific to the intention or purposes of the rhetor. Thus, because their interpretation is dialectical and not rhetorical, they cannot fully understand the letter. Nor, of course, are they content to admire Erasmus's virtuosity, his skill in argumentation. Any isolated argument against celibacy, viewed abstractly, becomes a potential threat.

Such, at least, was the Erasmian defense. On the other hand, Erasmus (as I have suggested, with a nod toward Jardine's most recent book), like any skillful *rhetor,* was surely aware of the extratextual confrontation his letter would provoke when first published and just as surely enjoyed it, not so much because the letter attacked priestly celibacy but because it challenged intellectual strictures, the bête noire of humanist educational reform and, for that matter, chief obstacle to Erasmian concord. The letter, that is, furthered Erasmus's cause and enhanced his publicity. Those rhetoricians who followed in his wake, with much the same cast of mind, often had to provoke their readers in somewhat different ways.

When the Englishman Thomas Wilson, for example, translated and reprinted Erasmus's letter in his famous *Arte of Rhetorique* in 1553, there could be little doubt that he was aware of its anticlerical thrusts. Although these thrusts suited well Wilson's own brand of dogmatism, he put the letter to a different use. In his companion volume on dialectic, *The Rule of Reason,* published two years earlier, he had used many of the letter's stock arguments in favor of marriage as examples of syllogisms in order to poke incidental fun at clerical celibacy. But in the rhetoric book, Wilson used Erasmus's letter neither to further his own brand of dogmatic anticlericalism nor to challenge intellectual strictures. He used it, rather, to show his Protestant and newly arrived middle-class audience what a well-written "oration" looks like and, implicatively, how such a letter can be an important access to the rich and powerful.

Nonetheless, Wilson's Protestant dogmatism to the contrary notwithstanding, he was a Renaissance humanist par excellence. In his book on rhetoric, Erasmus's letter is very much at home. For the book is pervaded by that humanist impulse I have sought to describe: rhetorical disputation. To begin with, although he published separate books on the two arts (the first to appear in English), Wilson, like most humanists, found rhetoric overlapping dialectic. And, although he shows that dialectic always moves toward general application, while rhetoric moves toward specific circumstance, he also shows that what makes an argument effective in dialectic is exactly what makes any "oration"—such as a letter—rhetorically efficacious: one should always keep the opposition in view, including any opposing or unfavorable emotion. "Wariness" Wilson calls it and insists that it is ever thought great wisdom.[41] His traditional-appearing book on rhetoric, too easily read today as a schoolbook, is more nearly a demonstration of wary eloquence as an avenue to power—as taught and exemplified by a successful practitioner, one whose eloquence propelled his rise from the newly mobile middle class through a highly successful political career. In this respect, Wilson sheds light on my prime example, whose own career is a case study in the use of eloquence as an instrument of power and whose retrospective view of his work as an educator was simple: "Erasmus," he once said of himself, "taught nothing except eloquence."[42]

It is an eloquence that Erasmus shows and Wilson tells that arises from wariness, and in such wariness lies the doubleness or duplexity I have touched on here. Therein, too, as I have suggested, lies an important principle: rhetorical *inventio* in the humanist tradition I am discussing relies not simply on processing ideas through the topics but on generating arguments with one eye on the opposition—and, in educational practice, on actually developing ideas on both sides of the question. Thus, schoolboys in Elizabethan England, immersed in disputation, were advised by their humanist schoolmasters to prepare "copybooks" listing arguments pro and con. Erasmus upholds the practice in his *De copia*, and Francis Bacon shows very clearly how it was done.

Bacon brings me back to that ancient schoolroom debate on whether a man should marry. Bacon's famous essay "Of Marriage and Single Life" begins, "He that hath *Wife* and *Children*, hath giuen Hostages to Fortune."[43] In the "copy" or "promptuary" book among Bacon's writings,[44] that very statement is listed on the *con* side. The next statement in the essay begins, somewhat grudgingly, to move toward the *pro* side: "For they are Impediments to great Enterprises, either of Vertue, or Mischief." The essay proceeds through a thicket of prolepses, in which pro and con arguments are lifted directly out of the copybook and strung, sometimes violently, together, all leading to a nonconclusion and producing the effect of a preliminary brief that could take the debate in either direction.[45] But even in its ambivalence, the essay is an affront to absolutism.

I am never comfortable with calling Bacon a humanist. There is a certain meanness of spirit and, in many of his writings, a drive toward indisputable certainty, better suited to inquisitions than to the kind of pursuits most humanists engaged in.[46] Nonetheless, structurally his essays reveal those characteristics I associate with humanism, Erasmian humanism particularly. Irony, duplexity, and ambivalence, I've suggested, are effects coincident with the split focus of two-sided argument. So is the effect of keeping two or more audiences in mind. Like triangulation, these effects are born of humanist optimism: readers and hearers have minds capable of entertaining a range of possibilities. The author's purpose is always to engage those minds, either, as Bacon does, in a demonstration of rhetoric as a mode of two-sided, skeptical inquiry or, as Erasmus does in his letter to Mountjoy, in a move actually to secure collaboration and assent or at least to make a certain and in some cases highly troublesome point of view compelling.

I am convinced, too, that it was the commingling of *sermo* and *disputatio* which produced the distinctive characteristics of humanist writing.[47] *Sermo,* the easy ebb and flow of good conversation, the preferred humanist genre, was reflected in the written dialogues so popular with humanists; and it was also, not surprisingly, the category within which humanists fit their epistolography.[48] As a consequence of its commingling of *sermo* and disputation, most humanist prose is often desultory but always many-voiced, as if the author were casting a wide net for truth[49] while at the same time attempting to preserve "the integral validity of each point of view."[50] Like good conversation, the discourse can be irresolute: it does not necessarily move toward closure.[51] It can end in a volteface, or display an ostensible and at times even baffling inconsistency or, better, Erasmian irony that readers have found in such pieces as *De contemptu mundi* and the *Moria.*[52] Nonetheless, the practice allows us to grasp a certain ideal: the best communication, in this view, though conversational, remains as rhetorically complex as a two-sided debate in which the reader sits in judgment. And often that "triangulated" reader must sort through a smooth tangle of widely ranging issues and questions. Thus, Ascham (*Toxophilus,* 1545) demonstrates pedagogy and rhetoric while his two personae talk about archery. George Puttenham (*The Arte of English Poesie,* 1589) shows courtiers how to dissemble while teaching them poetry. Wilson demonstrates middle-class mobility and access to power while Englishing the theory of rhetoric. And Erasmus impugns churchly dogmatism while advising an English aristocrat to marry. John Donne makes the strategy explicit, opening one of his sermons by talking about how the epideictic oration of praise may be used to blame—to chastise and correct—a person in power. Donne, who as sermonizer and theologian never abandoned his law-school training, calls the strategy by an appropriately legalistic term, "collaterall increpation."[53] The point is to capture an audience, or an opponent for that matter, and it is—like the enriched *inventio* on which it is based—a legacy of the marriage of rhetoric and disputation, sanctioned by antiquity and blessed by the motives of skeptical inquiry.

III

But this marriage of rhetoric and disputation, so familiar in humanist education, has become gradually dissolved, particularly in America. There are undoubtedly a host of causes—Ramism, the new science, even Romanticism with its emphasis on "sincerity," on being true to one's inner self.[54] There is another cause I shall propose, though the result remains the same: debate has gradually retreated from a central position in rhetorical *inventio*.

The revival of rhetoric in America is now more than half a century old. But the context in which it was revived had had at least three centuries to solidify. As Stephen Toulmin has argued, seventeenth-century philosophers banished the "oral," along with the "particular," the "local," and the "timely," in order to privilege arguments that no longer rested on "human facts": "From the 1630s on," Toulmin states, "Formal Logic was In, Rhetoric was Out."[55] Earlier, I suggested that the humanists themselves may have participated in the demise of oral composition, perhaps even of Ciceronian rhetoric itself. Whether the philosophers were at fault, as in Toulmin's analysis, or the humanists as in my suggestion, or both or neither, the outcome is observably the same: rhetoric was out. When it returned, it had to reclaim its ground from dominant modes of reasoning—this time largely silent but, as before, utterly formalist. Currently, the topics of invention are called "heuristics" in American rhetoric. But because we have not fully restored "the oral," we continue to slight the greatest heuristic of all: debate, the use of the topics as, in Nancy Struever's happy phrase, "argumentative wrestling holds" on an opponent.[56]

Toulmin's description of modern philosophy recalls humanist efforts to liberate dialectic. I find most insightful his listing of the "oral" first among those items banished by seventeenth-century philosophers. For the oral is of the very essence in rhetoric—and the recovery of practical philosophy, which Toulmin advocates, is the recovery of forms of reasoning that are, as he puts it, "rhetorical, not geometrical." In oral argumentation, Toulmin notes, the soundness of propositions depends less on the formal relations among them than on raising the question, "*Who* addressed this argument *to whom*, in what *forum,* and using what *examples?*" This, of course, is the "realm of rhetoric"— the realm where Erasmus sought to place the understanding of discourse, including, above all, Scripture; it was also where he placed the education of the young. But if this realm was banished from the modern philosophy that arose in the seventeenth century, it is a realm that remains severely fragmented in American education.

Once "elocution" disappeared and new specialties began proliferating in letters and sciences, American educationists seldom knew what to do about instruction in speaking.[57] Ultimately, in 1913, a union that should have been indissoluble experienced divorce: the teaching of composition was distributed into two disciplines—one for writing, one for speaking, each with its own professional society. However, since that time, the speech profession has itself grown increasingly bewildered about how to identify its own specialty. Substantive elements of what Toulmin means by "the oral" have undergone interdisciplinary revival in the restoration of rhetoric as a mode of composition and analysis. But what to do about the remainder of the oral, actual instruction in speaking—including, above all, practice in oral composition before a "live" audience—this remains an open question, a perplexity reflected in part by the changing titles of the speech teacher's professional organization. Originally called the National Association of Academic Teachers of Public Speaking, the organization changed its name to the Speech Association of America in 1956, then to the Speech Communication Association in 1970, and now, perhaps in the ultimate expression of their ongoing uncertainty, the association periodically considers the proposal to drop "Speech" altogether from its title.[58]

The history of debating in America, especially on the university level, follows the pattern I've just described. Initially, debating was confined to the various, largely extracurricular "literary societies" of the nineteenth century. But as speech became a specialty and a discipline apart from English, debating began to be taught and studied as a kind of unique craft. A host of debating textbooks flooded the market. Debating tournaments swept the country, abetted by the new speech profession, and in some small schools the debate teams hold a position of honor second only to athletic teams. National tournaments were—and still are—held, the most famous ones at the military academies. Resolutions for these tournaments are decided nationally each year. Though the contests are called forensic, the questions themselves are largely deliberative—("Resolved that the federal government should abolish the death penalty") a conflation of *controversia* and *suasoria* which seems to me natural when debating itself is given such prominence, whether in humanist education or in American extracurricular activities. Inevitably, business got into the act, churning out debate manuals, books of evidence pro and con on each year's national question.

Inevitably, too, ancient charges of sophistry recurred. Just thirty years ago, at the very peak of debating activity in America, a senior member of

215

the speech profession protested the practice of making debaters argue both sides of the question. His argument was based on the premise that "a public utterance is a public commitment" and that therefore it's unethical to follow the "anachronistic" practice of overthrowing a commitment to one side in merely mouthing a commitment to the other—so certain was he that students walk in to any debate with their ethical commitments already worked out. The practice was "anachronistic," he believed, because it belongs to the older sophistic disputation of our forefathers—finding fault where I find sanction.[59]

Moreover, though I am gratified that the argument went nowhere, I would bring a different kind of charge against American collegiate debating, especially the so-called spread debating. It is simply not rhetorical. If anything, it is rather more like dialectic, or the scholastic disputation that provided a target for humanist reform. American debaters speak to judges, not juries. Abandoned to eristic, American debaters do not even practice good speaking, using rather a rapid-fire delivery which challenges even the judge's comprehension. Above all, American collegiate debaters have abandoned the broadly humanistic nature of rhetorical *inventio*.

Teachers of writing, set free in 1913 from the responsibility to teach oral composition, pursued a course that equally abandoned most attention to rhetorical *inventio*. Their approach, so claim two recent historians of rhetoric, was a residue of high Victorianism with its positivistic view of sure knowledge: since all that was important to know came from the sciences and from observation, "[i]nvention, in the classical sense of discovering probabilistic arguments, was rarely studied," and it became the job of rhetoric merely "to record and transmit this knowledge with a minimum of distortion."[60] Just as for teachers of speech, so for teachers of writing, disputation became a discrete specialty, if even more attenuated. Specifically, it became vaguely conflated with the argumentative genre, which was located with two other types (description and narration) in the hinterlands somewhere beyond the all-important expository.

Little wonder, then, that of all the elements of rhetoric, *inventio* remains the most impoverished in the American revival. The point has been forcefully made in a recent book on the subject.[61] No recent book on rhetoric, however, urges a restoration of debate, or even the practice of two-sided argument and the writing of recantations, let alone the virtuosity of oral composition. Indeed, American rhetoric is notably silent on the matter of disputation, whether oral or written. But this is the very matter I would urge my colleagues to bring back into the composition classroom, not simply because I find it an essential feature of the classical tradition but more importantly because I find it, as Erasmus did, a possible way of enriching *inventio* in all genres. Recent American efforts to revive stasis theory in the absence of a strong disputational practice in the classroom offer only further evidence of my point.[62] Stasis can never be a fully operational instrument unless actively applied in two-sided argument. We have lost one of the greatest innovations of the Renaissance, the use of rhetorical *inventio* in generating arguments pro and con, because we no longer honor the marriage of rhetoric and disputation—or, for that matter, the equally hallowed union of writing and speaking.[63]

The metaphor I have used—marriage—though I have borrowed it from my primary example, may seem far-fetched. After all, the union I propose is linked neither by harmony nor by eros but by an interest in division and argument. The metaphor, however, is the sort Renaissance rhetoricians loved, the sort they called *catachresis,* a joining together of ostensibly disparate elements—itself the difficult pursuit of an age that, like ours, was trying to resist easy, authoritarian answers in the midst of a deepening awareness that knowledge and experience are fragmentary and that there are perplexing gaps between language and thought, words and things, what the rhetoricians then called *verba* and *res.* Fractiousness as well as irony were virtually unavoidable. That long and complex disquisition Erasmus eventually created in which he argued that marriage is as blessed a choice as celibacy, the *Institutio christiani matrimonii* (1526), was regarded as being suspiciously Lutheran. But it was history, in collusion with the initially innocent author, which gave that work its final and thoroughly Erasmian irony: it was dedicated to Catherine of Aragon.

Erasmus's lesson about words—not simply that they can be deconstructed but that they are wrapped in their own historicity and circumstance, that their meaning arises functionally from person, situation, and motive, and in effect inheres not so much in the things they represent as in the kind of story they tell—is a lesson that, a modern novelist has suggested, is in need of rebirth:

> a perfect *word,* a necessary WORD, is like a dream: once it is said or written, nothing can be added, and what it describes disappears forever: the palace, the desert, the mirror, the library, the compass pass: when they are identical to their word, they disappear forever, they dream forever, they die forever. We must never find the exact identification of words with things—a mystery, a divorce, a dissonance must remain. Then a poem will be written to close the separation, never achieving the re-union. A story will be told.

The passage is from a remarkable encomium, Carlos Fuentes's tribute to Borges upon the death of the Argentinean master.[64] The encomium is in the form of a narrative, a story is told, in which an imaginary Borges encounters an imaginary Erasmus, along with an imaginary Fuentes. Brilliant with insight, the piece calls for, among other qualities, a renaissance of "the desolate Erasmian irony" and for a voice insisting that the world is "made of realities, not of shadows."

Thus, I begin and end with encomia. Both center in the uneasy marriage of language to a world of realities, a marriage made a little less uneasy,

Erasmus believed, through linguistic virtuosity, or copiousness, and through an imagination stretched over both sides of almost every argument. The lesson of or in each encomium is utterly humanist and was reborn in the Renaissance union of rhetoric and disputation: language is first and foremost centered in personality and social context, and is instrumental, evanescent, quotidian—that is to say, oral—its meaning the provisional outcome of a never-ending dispute.

Notes

This essay is an expanded and revised version of "Rhetorical Education and Two-Sided Argument," in Heinrich F. Plett, ed., *Renaissance-Rhetorik/Renaissance Rhetoric* (Berlin and New York: De Gruyter, 1993), 163–178. Reprinted with permission of the publisher.

1. See *Collected Works of Erasmus*, 4: *The Correspondence of Erasmus*, trans. R. A. B. Mynors and D. F. S. Thomson, annot. James K. McConica (Toronto: University of Toronto Press, 1977), 249.
2. For Erasmus's ambition, see Lisa Jardine, *Erasmus, Man of Letters* (Princeton: Princeton University Press, 1993). In correspondence with Budé (*Collected Works*, 4: 103), Erasmus has an amusing remark about his own chastity, confessing to marriage with only one "wife," poverty.
3. For a brief review of the conflict, see Charles Fantazzi's note to his translation of the epistle in *Collected Works*, 26: 528–29.
4. Adding to the force of Erasmus's argument, though not formally a part of it, is that the letter incorporates an earlier encomium on matrimony (c. 1498); see Craig R. Thompson, *The Colloquies of Erasmus* (Chicago: University of Chicago Press, 1965), 99–100. The popularity of the subject as a rhetorical exercise is further indicated in *De copia;* see *Collected Works*, 24: 598. See also note 40 below.
5. Our ongoing failure to grasp this key Erasmian doctrine is a source of our misunderstanding of John Colet's character: we mistook as objective biography Erasmus's use of Colet as an argumentative example. See John B. Gleason, *John Colet* (Berkeley: University of California Press, 1988), 4–5. It is also, as Jardine has argued, a possible source of our misunderstanding of Erasmus's letters; *Erasmus, Man of Letters*, esp. chapter 6.
6. Clarence H. Miller, trans. *The Praise of Folly* (New Haven: Yale University Press, 1979), 71.
7. Quintilian poses a similar distinction in terms of "infinite" and "finite" questions: "Quod ut exemplo pateat, infinita est, *an uxor ducenda?* finita, *an Catoni ducenda?* ideoque esse suasoria potest" (3.5.8). The two types, as Quintilian—and, for that matter, Cicero and their followers in the Renaissance—insisted, must always be linked in argument, whether that argument was to be in a *suasoria* or in a *controversia*.
8. Richard A. Lanham, "The 'Q' Question," *South Atlantic Quarterly* 87 (1988): 600.
9. Kenneth Burke, *A Rhetoric of Motives* (Berkeley: University of California Press, 1969); for symbolic action, see esp. his *Attitudes toward History* (Berkeley: University of California Press, 1984). Chaim Perelman and L. Olbrechts-Tyteca, *The*

New Rhetoric: A Treatise on Argumentation, trans. John Wilkinson (Notre Dame: University of Notre Dame Press, 1969); see also Perelman's *The Realm of Rhetoric*, trans. William Kluback (Notre Dame: University of Notre Dame Press, 1982).

10. Ramists are surely well known now, thanks to Walter J. Ong's comprehensive *Ramus, Method, and the Decay of Dialogue* (Cambridge, Mass.: Harvard University Press, 1958). Brian Vickers's curious lamentations about the attenuation of the rhetorical tradition need to be weighed in the light of what he actually does as a reader of discourse, whether of Cicero (36) or Joyce (387), in his *In Defense of Rhetoric* (Oxford: Oxford University Press, 1988); see also the review by Arthur Quinn in *Rhetorica* 7 (1989): 291–94.

11. Vico, perhaps the last great humanist, offers an extreme instance. Vico defined "jurisprudence" as "the knowledge of all things human and divine"—and in doing so he believed he was following his master Cicero. See Michael Mooney, *Vico in the Tradition of Rhetoric* (Princeton: Princeton University Press, 1985), 159. As Mooney notes, "for Vico, as for Cicero, the forensic is paradigmatic" (71). I shall return to this point later. The process of triangulation in judgment is described by Arthur F. Kinney, "Rhetoric as Poetic: Humanist Fiction in the Renaissance," *ELH* 43 (1976): 413–43.

12. Myron Gilmore in his study of Erasmus's *apologiae*, "Methodus Disputandi: The Apologetic Works of Erasmus," in *Florilegium Historiale: Essays Presented to Wallace K. Ferguson*, ed. J. G. Rowe and W. H. Stockdale (Toronto: University of Toronto Press, 1971), 82. See also John W. O'Malley, "Erasmus and Luther, Continuity and Discontinuity as Key to Their Conflict," *Sixteenth Century Journal* 5 (October 1974): "Much that on the surface seems contradictory is ultimately reconcilable. Life's great truths, after all, should be more or less accessible to all, and it is the purpose of good literature to convey them. The radically concordistic nature of Erasmus' enterprise derives in large measure from this conviction" (50).

13. Jardine argues that with Jerome as his model and mentor, we are invited to read Erasmus's own letters in the very way he himself invites us to read Jerome's; *Erasmus, Man of Letters*, 173.

14. George A. Kennedy, trans., *Aristotle on Rhetoric* (Oxford: Oxford University Press, 1991), 34.

15. See G. B. Kerferd, *The Sophistic Movement* (Cambridge: Cambridge University Press, 1981). I offer no contention about the origins of rhetoric in two-sided argument; my point is only that rhetoric was ab initio associated with disputation, a contention further substantiated by Thomas Cole, *The Origins of Rhetoric in Ancient Greece* (Baltimore: Johns Hopkins University Press, 1991), esp. 99–100.

16. T. W. Baldwin, *William Shakspere's Small Latine and Less Greeke* (Urbana: University of Illinois Press, 1944), 2.62.

17. See *De oratore*, 1.158, 2.102–4, 3.69–74, 3.80. This point is pursued in my "Reinventing Inventio," *College English* 51 (1989): 461–73. In addition, as Stanley Fish has argued, Plato and Aristotle were far more concerned about eristic, about quibbling, about Protagoras and what he represented, than were Cicero and the humanists in his direct line of influence; "Rhetoric," in *Doing What Comes Naturally* (Durham: Duke University Press, 1988), esp. 478–85, in which Fish, coincidentally, controverts his earlier mistaken observation (472) that Aristotle

was opposed to making arguments on either side of the question. Furthermore, it is dismaying, in light of the high regard in which humanists held Cicero's dialogue, to encounter Vickers's nugatory view: "A critical evaluation of the dialogue form of De Oratore reveals it to be cumbersome, inefficient in exposition, and frequently breaking its own supposed distinction between the personae" (34); "In De Oratore, we may feel, content is obscured by form, as if somewhere inside the dialogue a rhetorical handbook was trying to get out" (36). Vickers's first insubstantial remark is outweighed by the gross inaccuracy of the second; Cicero purposely avoided producing a handbook as a mature rhetorician.

18. On this point, with specific reference to the tradition Erasmus inherited, see Roland H. Bainton, *Erasmus of Christendom* (New York: Scribner, 1969), 16.

19. 6.4.1. Little wonder that he urges students to attend criminal trials and prepare speeches of their own on both sides of actual cases (see 10.5.19–20).

20. For the former, see Marcia L. Colish, *The Mirror of Language: A Study in the Medieval Theory of Knowledge*, rev. ed. (Lincoln: University of Nebraska Press, 1983). For the latter, see Charles Trinkaus, *In Our Image and Likeness: Humanity and Divinity in Italian Humanist Thought* (Chicago: University of Chicago Press, 1970).

21. Richard Waswo, *Language and Meaning in the Renaissance* (Princeton: Princeton University Press, 1987), 21–22.

22. See in particular William J. Bouwsma, "Lawyers and Early Modern Culture," *American Historical Review* 78 (1973): 303–27; and R. J. Schoeck, "Lawyers and Rhetoric," in James J. Murphy, ed., *Renaissance Eloquence* (Berkeley: University of California Press, 1983), 274–91. Other studies by Schoeck include "The Elizabethan Society of Antiquaries and Men of Law," *Notes & Queries* n.s. 1 (1954): 417–21; "Early Anglo-Saxon Studies and Legal Scholarship," *Studies in the Renaissance* 5 (1958): 102–10; "Sir Thomas More, Humanist and Lawyer," *University of Toronto Quarterly* 26 (1964): 1–14. Some important studies by other authors include F. W. Maitland, *English Law and the Renaissance* (Cambridge: Cambridge University Press, 1901); Guido Kisch, *Humanismus und Jurisprudenz: Der Kampf zwischen mos italicus und mos gallicus an der Universität Basel* (Basel: Helbing & Lichtenhahn, 1955); M. P. Gilmore, *Humanists and Jurists* (Cambridge, Mass.: Belknap, 1963). That English humanists preferred law over medicine as a career pursuit has been interpreted by one writer as a preference for man's social over his physical well-being: Mark H. Curtis, *Oxford and Cambridge in Transition 1558–1642* (Oxford: Clarendon, 1959), 156.

23. The quotation is from Bruce A. Kimball, *Orators and Philosophers: A History of the Idea of Liberal Education* (New York: Teachers College Columbia University Press, 1986), 85. See Paul Oskar Kristeller, *Renaissance Thought: The Classic, Scholastic, and Humanist Strains* (New York: Columbia University Press, 1961), esp. "The Humanist Movement," which ends with the argument that Renaissance humanism "in its substance was not philosophical, but had important philosophical implications and consequences" (22).

24. See Ernesto Grassi, *Rhetoric as Philosophy* (University Park: Pennsylvania State University Press, 1980). Lanham discusses the "rhetorical paideia" in "The 'Q' Question."

25. John F. Tinkler has a succinct discussion of humanist versus scholastic dialogue, with implications for similar distinctions in disputation, in "Humanism and Dialogue," *Parergon*, n.s. 6 (1988): 197–214. The importance of ethos in Ciceronian disputation is well discussed by James M. May, *Trials of Character: The Eloquence of Ciceronian Ethos* (Chapel Hill: University of North Carolina Press, 1988).

26. See John Monfasani, "Humanism and Rhetoric," in Albert Rabil, Jr., ed., *Renaissance Humanism: Foundations, Forms, and Legacy* 3 (Philadelphia: University of Pennsylvania Press, 1988), 191.

27. Baldwin, *William Shakspere's Small Latine* 1: 94. The observation has been confirmed most recently by Richard J. Schoeck, *Erasmus Grandescens* (Nieuwkoop: De Graaf, 1988): "the teaching of Erasmus is the underpinning of the Tudor public schools" (121).

28. Among the other works I have consulted, in addition to those cited throughout this study, are such primary sources as Roger Ascham, *The Scholemaster* (1570) and *Toxophilus* (1545); John Brinsley, *Ludus Literarius* (1612); Francis Clement, *The Petie Schole with an English Orthographie* (1587); Thomas Elyot, trans. (Plutarch), *The Education or Bringing Up of Children* (1533); Gabriel Harvey, *Ciceronianus* (1577) and *Rhetor* (1577); Richard Mulcaster, *The first part of the Elementary* (1582); Richard Rainolde, *The Foundacion of Rhetorike* (1563)—and such secondary sources as Donald Lemen Clark, *John Milton at St. Paul's School* (New York: Columbia University Press, 1948) and "The Rise and Fall of Progymnasmata in Sixteenth and Seventeenth Century Grammar Schools," *Speech Monographs* 19 (1952): 259–63; William T. Costello, S.J., *The Scholastic Curriculum at Early Seventeenth-Century Cambridge* (Cambridge, Mass.: Harvard University Press, 1958); Harris Fletcher, *The Intellectual Development of John Milton* (Urbana: University of Illinois Press, 1961); Joseph S. Freedman, "Cicero in Sixteenth- and Seventeenth-Century Rhetoric Instruction," *Rhetorica* 4 (1986): 227–54; Anthony Grafton and Lisa Jardine, *From Humanism to the Humanities* (Cambridge, Mass.: Harvard University Press, 1986); Paul F. Grendler, *Schooling in Renaissance Italy: Literacy and Learning, 1300–1600* (Baltimore: Johns Hopkins University Press, 1989); M. B. Hackett, *The Original Statutes of Cambridge University* (Cambridge: Cambridge University Press, 1970); Jo Ann Hoeppner Moran, *The Growth of English Schooling 1340–1548* (Princeton: Princeton University Press, 1985); John Mulder, *The Temple of the Mind* (New York: Pegasus, 1969); Ray Nadeau, "The Progymnasmata of Aphthonius," *Speech Monographs* 19 (1952): 264–85; Nicholas Orme, *English Schools in the Middle Ages* (London: Methuen, 1973), and "An Early-Tudor Oxford Schoolbook," *RQ* 34 (1981): 11–39; Joan Simon, *Education and Society in Tudor England* (London: Cambridge University Press, 1966); Bromley Smith, "Extracurricular Disputations: 1400–1650," *QJS* 34 (1948): 473–76; Craig R. Thompson, *Schools in Tudor England* (Washington, D.C.: Folger Shakespeare Library, 1959); Karl R. Wallace, "Rhetorical Exercises in Tudor Education, *QJS*, 22 (1936): 28–51; Foster Watson, *The English Grammar Schools to 1660: Their Curriculum and Practice* (Cambridge: Cambridge University Press, 1908).

29. Hoole, for example, describes the practice in the following way, suggesting each Friday as the best time for disputations: "Each Form has two 'sides,' which face

one another. Each boy propounds to the boy opposite him points of difficulty in the week's work—'which if the other cannot answer readily before he count six, or ten (in Latin) let him be *captus,* and the question be passed to the next boy on the other side.' The lowest boy is to begin the questions. Account to be kept of those who are '*capt,* and how often.'" Charles Hoole, *A New Discovery of the Old Art of Teaching School* (1660); quoted in Watson, *The English Grammar Schools,* 95. On such verbal combativeness, higher disputation was built.

30. Eugene E. White, "Master Holdsworth and 'A Knowledge Very Useful and Necessary,'" *QJS* 53 (1967): 6.
31. In this respect, an especially useful study is Lisa Jardine's "The Place of Dialectic Teaching in Sixteenth-Century Cambridge," *SR* 21 (1974): 31–62, which shows that dialectic moved into the center of the curriculum at Cambridge from 1560–1590 and that this central dialectic was humanist: it was the study of practical argumentation, drawing widely on literary materials, and it was virtually identical with rhetorical *inventio* with the possible exception that rhetoric seemed to go farther in its insistence upon circumstance.
32. Craig R. Thompson, *Universities in Tudor England* (Washington, D.C.: Folger Shakespeare Library, 1959), 27.
33. See Miller, *The Praise of Folly,* 88–89. Folly, of course, gives not only the clergy but lawyers a drubbing, too (see 85). Almost the only professional group she lets off the hook at all are the rhetoricians, mainly because they love jokes (81–82).
34. See Curtis, *Oxford and Cambridge,* 169.
35. On form, see esp. Thompson, *Universities in Tudor England,* 26; and Curtis, *Oxford and Cambridge,* 88. See, too, Thomas Wilson on the duties of the speakers in *Rule of Reason,* 1551, ed. Richard S. Sprague (Northridge, Calif.: San Fernando Valley State College, 1972), 153–56. See Abraham Fraunce, *Lawiers Logike* (1588), 101, for an attempt to bring Ramist orderliness to disputation. Note, too, Sidney's question, "Nowe, whom shall wee finde (sith the question standeth for the highest forme in the Schoole of learning) to bee Moderator [between the claims of history on the one hand and philosophy on the other]?"; "An Apologie for Poetrie," in *English Literary Criticism: The Renaissance,* ed. O. B. Hardison, Jr. (New York: Appleton-Century-Crofts, 1963), 110.
36. For a vivid glimpse of the elaborateness of ceremony, see Costello, *The Scholastic Curriculum,* 15–17; and for an amusing review of the violence often attendant upon public disputation, see Bromley Smith, "Extracurricular Disputations: 1400–1650," *QJS* 34 (1948): 473–76.
37. See Ong, *Ramus,* 155; Curtis, *Oxford and Cambridge,* 110.
38. Cole, *The Origins of Rhetoric,* 1.
39. "Deinde illorum inventa castiget, mox palinodiam scribere jubeat. Nonnunquam etiam acuendi ingenii gratia, infames materias proponat. Veluti si quis suadeat paupertatem, exilium, ingratitudinem, aegrotationem, contemptum studiorum, neglectum linguarum, tyrannidem, ut vetulus vetulam ducat, ut domum ducat uxorem improbam. Nihil enim est ita natura bonum, quin ab ingenioso Oratore depravari possit. Hac exercitatione tum copia, tum promptitudo quaedam, quavis de re dicendi parabitur" (Cap. 48: De Genere Dissuasorio). The excellent translation is by Fantazzi; *Collected Works,* 25: 145–46. The relation of the practice

Erasmus advocates to the period's absorption with paradox should be noted; my own view would add a pedagogical emphasis to the history so well traced by Rosalie L. Colie, *Paradoxia Epidemica* (Princeton: Princeton University Press, 1966). For example, Anthony Munday's translation of Ortensio Lando's *Paradossi* (*The Defence of Contraries*, 1593) is offered not simply to make "truth" more apparent through opposition but also to "exercise" the reader's "witte" (A4v)— and he offers brief disquisitions on "That it is better to be poore than Rich," "That it is better to be fowle than faire," "That ignorance is better than knowledge."

40. Following is a suggestion of how this history might proceed: *An ducenda sit uxor?* The question was Latinized in the tradition extending from Priscian (sixth century c.e.), who in effect Latinized Hermogenes (second century c.e.). Aphthonius, who also follows Hermogenes closely, wrote the most widely used *Progymnasmata* in European education (Clark, "The Rise and Fall of Progymnasmata"). The exercise lay in propounding a deliberative thesis and arguing for or against a general question. Both Quintilian (3.5.8) and Cicero describe the use of the thesis in education, the latter (*Orator*, 14.46) tracking its use back to Aristotle. According to Watson (*The English Grammar Schools*, 430–34), "declamations" on theses (called "themes" by Watson) were divided into three types: affirmative, *uxor est ducenda;* negative, *uxor non est ducenda;* and a third "moderating" between the two. He cites Richard Brinsley's consideration (in *Ludus Literarius*) that the declamation properly belongs in the university, not in the grammar school. Richard Rainolde, who Englished the *progymnasmata* traditions in his *Foundacion of Rhetorike* (1563), offers a comprehensive view of the deliberative thesis ("Tully's *propositum*"), "Whether is it best to marie a wife," and offers an oration on the subject (53–59) structured by means of "objections" and "answers." But surely one of the cleverest contributions to the long tradition is Alberti's "Dinner Pieces" (c. 1430); see "Maritus" and "Uxoria." One of the most delightful *dissasoriae* is Walter Map's epistle (c. 1182) "Valerius to Rufinus," and one of the most pointed (and therefore rhetorical) is Petrarch's letter to Pandolfo Malatesta. Ben Franklin's famous letter takes on added dimensions when seen in light of this history.

41. Wilson, *The Rule of Reason*, 153; see also *The Art of Rhetorique* (1553), 35.

42. In his letter to John Botzheim, Jan. 30, 1523, *Opus Epistolarum* (Oxford: Clarendon, 1906–57), 1:30.1–3.

43. Edward Arber, ed., *A Harmony of the Essays, etc., of Francis Bacon* (London: English Reprints 271, 1871), 265.

44. *De augumentis scientarum*, in *Works*, ed. James Spedding et al. (1858–75), 4: 472–92.

45. "The effect," Joel Altman states, "is that of a circumnavigation of the topic, which ends not offering a 'stand' on marriage at all, but simply exploring its significance in the wide universe in which it exists. This accounts for its disjunctive quality: many eyes are seeing and reporting." *Tudor Play of Mind* (Berkeley: University of California Press, 1978), 42.

46. Another way of putting my point is to note the thoroughly anti-Erasmian reform of language in which Bacon was engaged; see Waswo, *Language and Meaning*, 50–51.

47. In *De officiis*, 1.132, Cicero makes *sermo* and *contentio* equally at home in debates. For an excellent discussion of this passage and the place of *sermo* in humanist writing, see John F. Tinkler, "Renaissance Humanism and the *Genera Eloquentiae*," *Rhetorica* 5 (1987): 279–309.

48. On dialogue in Erasmus, see Schoeck, *Erasmus Grandescens:* "In the 1490s to write a dialogue was in itself to take a stand against scholasticism, with its favorite forms of disputation and *Quodlibets (disputationes quodlibetales,* or 'free' as distinguished from disputations with announced topics)" (95). See, too, Walter Ruegg, *Cicero und der Humanismus* (Zurich: Rheinverlag, 1946): "im Dialog findet er [Erasmus] seine innere Freiheit, seine Form. Die Komposition ist, wie wir uns gewohnt sind, ganz associativ, unsystematisch, und unproportionert" (121). David Marsh has discussed dialogic precursors in his *Quattrocento Dialogue: Classical Tradition and Humanist Innovation* (Cambridge, Mass.: Harvard University Press, 1980). See, too, Kenneth Wilson, *Incomplete Fictions: The Formation of English Renaissance Dialogue* (Washington, D.C.: Catholic University Press, 1985), and Tinkler, "Renaissance Humanism." On epistolography, see Judith Rice Henderson, "Erasmus on the Art of Letter-Writing," in Murphy, ed., *Renaissance Eloquence*, 331–55.

49. As Cicero advised in his *multiplex ratio disputandi*. An excellent discussion of this point is in Michael J. Buckley, S.J., *Motion and Motion's God: Thematic Variations in Aristotle, Cicero, Newton, and Hegel* (Princeton: Princeton University Press, 1971), esp. 93.

50. Wilson, *Incomplete Fictions*, 29. Wilson describes the characteristics of Ciceronian dialogue as used by the humanists, in which "voice" was often dependent on the "autonomy" of characters in the dialogue.

51. Altman, *Tudor Play of Mind*, links this irresoluteness in Tudor drama to *in utramque partem* disputation.

52. A reading of *De contemptu mundi* in terms of two-sided debate is offered by Bainton, *Erasmus of Christendom*, 14–17. Miller's introduction to his translation of *The Praise of Folly* comments on that work's inconsistencies and bafflements; throughout his translation, he shows, too, skillfully, how to read the work for the kind of irony Erasmus surely intended.

53. *Sermons*, ed. George R. Potter and Evelyn M. Simpson (Berkeley: University of California Press, 1962), 5: 200. As O'Malley has shown, Aurelio Brandolini makes much the same point about the doubleness of epideictic oratory. John W. O'Malley, *Praise and Blame in Renaissance Rome* (Durham: Duke University Press, 1979), 192.

54. That American institutions owe their origins and thereby much of their cultural nature to Ramism was proposed a half century ago by Perry Miller in *The New England Mind: the Seventeenth Century* (New York: The Seventeenth Century, 1939). It would be too simple, of course, to cast all the ills of American education on the Ramists. But Ramism, or whatever it represents in its complex connections with the scientific revolution and with Romanticism, is surely a cause of at least one major affliction: the overweening drive to categorize, to specialize, to claim that one discipline must not overlap another. The Ramists called the drive the *lex sapientia,* the law of wisdom. It found practical application in divorcing silent logic from oral rhetoric and, ultimately, in reducing rhetoric itself to simply style

and oral delivery. An interesting argument, in new terms, concerning Western man's ongoing absorption with Romanticism is Richard Lanham's *The Motives of Eloquence* (New Haven: Yale University Press, 1976), with its positing of "homo rhetoricus" and "homo seriosus" as diametrical opposites. Moreover, an ability to speak on either side of a question as well as the skill to make an audience believe in an apparent truth are exactly the qualities in Cicero that most troubled late Romantics and high Victorians; see Mary Rosner, "The Two Faces of Cicero: Trollope's *Life* in the Nineteenth Century," *Rhetoric Society Quarterly* 18 (1988): 252–58.

55. Stephen Toulmin, "The Recovery of Practical Philosophy," *American Scholar* (August 1988): 339. Toulmin's discussion of "orality" has philosophical implications not directly addressed by Gerald Graff in his insightful discussion of the disappearance of America's "oratorical culture" in the nineteenth century, *Professing Literature* (Chicago: University of Chicago Press, 1987), esp. chapter 3. Moreover, as Toulmin shows in *The Abuse of Casuistry: A History of Moral Reasoning*, coauthored with Albert R. Johnson (Berkeley: University of California Press, 1988), indispensable to the recovery of practical reasoning is the long-abused method of casuistry (see esp. 34–35), itself rooted in case law and orality.

56. Nancy Streuver, "Lorenzo Valla: Humanist Rhetoric and the Critique of the Classical Languages of Morality," in Murphy, ed., *Renaissance Eloquence,* 195. The phrase, moreover, is similarly used by both Erasmus and Cicero, though Erasmus talks about strife, Cicero about gracefulness in strife. Erasmus compares his "brief rules" to "wrestling holds": "Conabimur autem breviter regulas quasdam quasi nexus quosdam palaestricos tradere" (Cap. 8, *Enchiridion militis christiani;* the edition I have used is the one edited by Jean LeClerc [Leiden, 1703]; see 20E). Cicero compares conscious training in oratorical style to training in wrestling: "cognitus quasi quandam palaestram et extrema liniamenta orationi attulit" (*Orator,* 187). It is nonetheless very clear in the *Orator* that the function of the "topics" is to assist in the strife of pro-and-con argumentation (46–50).

57. On our shores, the peculiar discipline known as "elocution" achieved a prominence unknown in France and England, where it originated. The standard work on the subject remains Karl R. Wallace, ed., *A History of Speech Education in America* (New York: Appleton Century Crofts, 1954), esp. chapters 7, 8, 9.

58. This history appears in *Spectra,* published March 1989 by the Speech Communication Association. The proposition to change the association's name to Communication Association narrowly lost in 1989.

59. Richard Murphy, "The Ethics of Debating Both Sides," *Speech Teacher* 6 (1957): 1–9.

60. Patricia Bizzell and Bruce Herzberg, *The Rhetorical Tradition* (Boston: St. Martin's Press, 1990), 903.

61. Jean Dietz, ed., *Rhetoric and Praxis* (Washington, D.C.: Catholic University Press, 1986). See, too, James J. Murphy, "Implications of the 'Renaissance of Rhetoric' in English Departments," *QJS* 9 (1989): 335–43. The flurry of publication on the subject of rhetoric, which Murphy discusses, would seem to indicate an attempt to seek an identity for rhetoric/composition as an academic field. It is not too much to suggest that the nature of rhetoric as an academic discipline depends on some clear ideas about the nature of its *inventio.*

62. Kathryn Rosser Raign provides an excellent review in "Stasis Theory Revisited: An Inventional *Techne* for Empowering Students," *Focuses* 2 (1989): 19–26. See also Antoine Braet's "The Classical Doctrine of *Status* and the Rhetorical Theory of Argumentation," *Philosophy and Rhetoric* 20 (1987): 79–93. For an incisive review of classical stasis theory and an argument that modern rhetoric (assuming an identification of rhetoric with pro and con argument, or conflict) necessitates a privileging of the "fourth" stasis, "objection" (an interesting translation of *rectene factum sit; De oratore*, 2.113), see David Goodwin, "Controversiae Meta-Asystatae and the New Rhetoric," *RSQ* 19 (1989): 205–16.

63. To George A. Kennedy's now famous division, in *Classical Rhetoric and Its Christian and Secular Traditions from Ancient to Modern Times* (Chapel Hill: University of North Carolina Press, 1980), 4–5, of traditional rhetoric into "primary" (speech-making) and "secondary" (all written, especially literary genres), Ronald G. Witt has added a third: "a way of thought that seeks conclusions by inference rather than by demonstration, whose weapon is more often the enthymeme than the syllogism." "Medieval Italian Culture and the Origins of Humanism as a Stylistic Ideal," in Rabil, ed., *Renaissance Humanism*, 32. Debate, I am arguing, is an important way whereby this "way of thought" is systematized and learned (see Witt, 31: rhetoricians taught students "to declaim, to debate, and to deliver orations of their own making"). Vico's critique of education provided a similar solution to a similar set of problems: let students learn the topics, he argued in the early eighteenth century, let them learn how to fashion arguments before they go on to the study of criticism—"And let them develop skill in debating on either side of any proposed argument." *On the Study Methods of Our Time,* trans. Elio Gianturco (Ithaca: Cornell University Press, 1990), 19).

64. Carlos Fuentes, "Borges in Action: A Narrative Homage," *PMLA* 101 (1986): 778–87.

BIBLIOGRAPHY

Primary Texts

Ancient

Aristotle. *Aristotle on Rhetoric*. Trans. George A. Kennedy. Oxford: Oxford University Press, 1991.

———. *Categories and De Interpretatione*. Trans. J. L. Ackrill. Oxford: Clarendon, 1963; rpt. 1978.

———. *Nicomachean Ethics*. Trans. Terence Irwin. Indianapolis: Hackett Publishing Co., 1985.

———. *Poetics*. Trans. W. Hamilton Fyfe. London: Heinemann, 1927.

———. *Poetics*. Trans. Gerald F. Else. Ann Arbor: University of Michigan Press, 1969.

———. *Rhetoric*. Trans. John Henry Freese. London: Heinemann, 1926.

———. *Rhétorique*. 3 volumes. Ed. M. Dufour and A. Wartelle. Paris: Societé d'Édition "Les Belles Lettres," 1932–73.

———. *Sophistical Refutations*. Trans. E. S. Forster. London: Heinemann, 1965.

Augustine, St. *Confessions*. Trans. R. S. Pine-Coffin. New York: Penguin Books, 1961.

———. *Confessionum Libri XIII*. Ed. Lucas Verheijen. Turnhout: Brepols, 1981.

———. "De Doctrina Christiana." Ed. Joseph Martin. In *Corpus Christianorum Series Latina* of *Aurelii Augustini Opera* in *Corpus Christianorum* 32. Turnhout: Brepols, 1962. 1–167.

———. *De Doctrina Christiana, On Christian Doctrine*. Trans. D. W. Robertson. New York: Macmillan, 1958.

Biblia Sacra: Iuxta Vulgatam Versionem II. Stuttgart: Württembergische Bibelanstalt, 1975.

Catullus, Tibullus, and *Pervigilium Veneris, Works*. Trans. F. W. Cornish. London: Heinemann, 1913.

Chalcidius, *Timaeus a calcidio translatus commentarioque instructus*. Ed. J. H. Waszink [*Plato latinus*. Ed. R. Klibansky, 4]. Leiden and London: E. J. Brill and Warburg Institute, 1962.

Cicero. *De Inventione, De Optimo Genere Oratorum, Topica*. Trans. H. M. Hubbell. London: Heinemann, 1949.

———. *De Oratore*. Trans. H. M. Hubbell. London: Heinemann, 1939.

Demetrius. *On Style.* Trans. W. Rhys Roberts. London: Heinemann, 1927.

The Holy Bible. Douay Version. New York: P. J. Kenedy, 1961.

Homer. *Opera.* 5 volumes. Ed. David Munro and Thomas W. Allen. Oxford: Clarendon, 1902–12.

Horace. "The Ars Poetica," in *Horace on Poetry.* Ed. C. O. Brink. Cambridge: Cambridge University Press, 1971.

Isocrates 2. Trans. George Norlin. London: Heinemann, 1929.

Jerome, St. *Commentary on Ezekiel XIII,* 42.13 in *Corpus Christianorum Series Latina* 75. Turnhout: Brepols Editores Pontificii, 1954.

———. *Lettres* 1–8. Trans. into French and ed. Jérôme-Labourt. Paris: Societé d'Édition Les Belles Lettres, 1949–63.

Longinus. *On the Sublime.* Trans. W. Hamilton Fyfe. London: Heinemann, 1927.

Nadeau, Ray. "Hermogenes' On Stases: A Translation with an Introduction and Notes." *Speech Monographs* 31 (1964): 361–424.

Origen, *On First Principles.* Trans. G. W. Butterworth and intro. Henri de Lubac. New York: Harper Torchbooks, 1966.

Plato. *Cratylus.* Trans. H. N. Fowler. London: Heinemann, 1926.

———. *Euthyphro, Apology, Crito, Phaedo, Phaedrus.* Trans Harold North Fowler. Cambridge, Mass.: Harvard University Press, 1914.

———. *Gorgias.* Ed. E. R. Dodds. Oxford: Clarendon, 1959.

———. *Ion.* Trans. W. R. M. Lamb. London: Heinemann, 1925.

———. *Opera.* Volume 1. Ed. J. Burnet. Oxford: Clarendon, 1900.

———. *Protagoras.* Trans. W. R. M. Lamb. London: Heinemann, 1924.

———. *Republic.* Trans. Paul Shorey. London: Heinemann, 1930.

Pliny the Elder. *Historia naturalis.* Ed. and trans. H. Rackham et al. Cambridge: Harvard University Press, 1940–63.

Pseudo-Cicero. *Rhetorica ad Herennium.* Trans. H. Caplan. Cambridge, Mass.: Harvard University Press, 1961.

Quintilian, *Institutio oratoria.* Ed. and trans. H. E. Butler. Cambridge, Mass.: Harvard University Press 1920; rpt. 1989.

Sadowski, Frank, ed. and trans. *The Church Fathers and the Bible.* New York: Alba House, 1987.

Seneca. *Ad Lucilium Epistulae Morales.* Trans. Richard M. Gummere. London: Heinemann, 1917.

Tacitus. *Dialogus, Agricola, Germania.* Cambridge, Mass.: Harvard University Press, 1958.

Virgil. *Opera.* Ed. R. A. B. Mynors. Oxford: Clarendon, 1969.

White, Carolinne. *The Correspondence (394–419) between Jerome and Augustine of Hippo.* Lewiston, N.Y.: Edward Mellen, 1990.

Early Modern (or Medieval to Eighteenth Century)

Alain de Lille. *Anticlaudianus.* Trans. James J. Sheridan. Toronto: Pontifical Institute for Medieval Studies, 1973.

Alighieri, Dante. *Convivio.* Ed. G. Busnelli and G. Vandelli. Florence: Felice le Monnier, 1954.

————. *De vulgari eloquentia.* Ed. Pier Vincenzo Mengaldo. In *Opere Minori* 2. Milan and Naples: Ricciardi, 1979.

————. *Literary Criticism of Dante Alighieri.* Ed. and trans. R. S. Haller. Lincoln: University of Nebraska Press, 1973.

Anglicus, Bartholomaeus. *De rerum proprietatibus.* Frankfurt: Richter, 1601; rpt. Frankfurt: Minerva, 1964.

Ascham, Roger. *English Works of Roger Ascham.* London: R. & J. Dodsley, 1761.

————. *The Scholemaster* (1570). Cambridge: Cambridge University Press, 1904.

————. *Toxophilus.* 1545.

Bacon, Francis. *A Harmony of the Essays, etc., of Francis Bacon.* Ed. Edward Arber. London: English Reprints 271, 1875.

————. *Works.* Ed. James Spedding, Robert Leslie Ellis, and Douglas Dennon Heath. London: Longman, 1858–74.

Boileau Despreaux, Nicolas. *Oeuvres diverses du sieur D***: Avec le traité du sublime, ou du merveilleux dans le discours.* Amsterdam: Chez Abraham Wolfganz, 1683.

Boncompagno. *Boncompagnus.* In *Testi riguardanti la vita degli studenti a Bologna nel sec. XIII.* Ed. Virgilio Pini. Bologna: Bibliòteca di "Quadrivium," 1968.

————. *Rhetorica antiqua.* Ed. L. Rockinger, in *Briefsteller und Formelbücher des elften bis vierzehnten Jahrhunderts* [*Quellen und Erörterungen zur bayerischen und deutschen Geschichte* 9]. Munich: Franz, 1863.

————. *Rhetorica novissima* [*Bibliotheca iuridica medii aevi: Scripta anecdota glossatorum* 2]. Ed. A. Gaudenzi. Bologna: Treves, 1892.

Brinsley, John. *Ludus Literarius* (1612). Menston, Yorkshire: Scolar Press, 1968.

————. *Ludus Literarius.* Ed. E. T. Compagnac. Liverpool: Liverpool University Press, 1917.

Cappella, Martianus. *De Nuptiis Philologiae et Mercurii* Liber 9. Intro., trans. in Italian, and comm. Lucio Cristante. Padova: Antenore, 1987.

Clement, Francis. *The Petie Schole with an English Orthographie.* 1587.

Donatus. *Donat et la tradition de l'enseignement grammatical: Étude et édition critique.* Ed. L. Holtz. Paris: Centre National de la Recherche Scientifique, 1981.

Donne, John. *Sermons.* Ed. George Potter and Evelyn Simpson. Berkeley: University of California Press, 1962.

Elyot, Thomas, trans. [Plutarch] *The Education or Bringinge Up of Children* (1533). New York: Da Capo Press, 1969.

Erasmus. *Collected Works of Erasmus.* Vol. 4: *The Correspondence of Erasmus.* Trans. R. A. B. Mynors and D. F. S. Thomson, annot. James K. McConica. Toronto: University of Toronto Press, 1977.

————. *The Colloquies of Erasmus.* Trans. Craig R. Thompson. Chicago: University of Chicago Press, 1965.

————. *The Enchiridion.* Trans. and ed. Raymond Himelick. Bloomington: Indiana University Press, 1963.

————. *The Praise of Folly.* Trans. Clarence H. Miller. New Haven: Yale University Press, 1979.

Fraunce, Abraham. *Lawiers Logike.* London: W. How, for T. Grubbin and T. Newman, 1588.

Geoffrey of Vinsauf. *The Poetria Nova of Geoffrey of Vinsauf.* Trans. M. Nims. Toronto: Pontifical Institute of Mediaeval Studies, 1967.

Grammatici Latini. Ed. H. Keil. Leipzig: B. G. Teubner, 1853.

Gregory the Great. *Epistula missoria ad Leandrum Hispalensem,* PL 75, 516B.

Harvey, Gabriel. *Ciceronianus* (1577). Intro. and notes by Harold S. Wilson. Trans. Clarence A. Forbes. Lincoln: University of Nebraska Press, 1945.

———. *Rhetor* (1577). London: Henrici Binneman, 1577.

Hoole, Charles. *A New Discovery of the Old Art of Teaching School* (1660). Syracuse, N.Y.: C. W. Bardeen, 1912.

Isidore of Seville. *Etymologiae.* Ed. W. M. Lindsay. Oxford: Clarendon, 1911.

———. *Etymologiae II.* Ed. and trans. P. K. Marshall. Paris: Les Belles Lettres, 1983.

Kant, Immanuel. *Critique of Judgment.* Trans. J. H. Bernard. New York: Hafner-Macmillan, 1951.

———. *Werke.* Ed. Wilhelm Weischedel. Wiesbaden: Insel, 1957.

Keil, H., ed. *Grammatici Latini.* Leipzig: B. G. Teubner, 1853.

La canzone delle virtù e delle scienze di Bartolomeo di Bartoli da Bologna. Ed. Leone Dorez. Bergamo: Istituto Italiano d'Arti Grafiche Editore, 1904.

Latini, Brunetto. *La Rettorica.* Ed. F. Maggini. Florence: Felice Le Monnier, 1968.

Les arts poétiques du XII et du XIII siècle: Recherches et documents sur la technique littéraire du moyen âge. Ed. E. Faral. Paris: E. Champion, 1924; rpt. 1958.

Mulcaster, Richard. *The first part of the Elementary* (1582). Menston, England: Scolar Press, 1970.

Munday, Anthony. *The defence of contraries.* Amsterdam: Theatrum Orbis Terrarum, 1969.

Puttenham, George. *The Arte of English Poesie* (1589). Ed. Edward Arber. London: A. Murray and Son, 1869.

Rainolde, Richard. *The Foundacion of Rhetorike* (1563). Intro. Francis R. Johnson. New York: Scholars Facsimiles and Reprints, 1945.

Sidney, Sir Philip. *An apologie for poetrie.* In *English Literary Criticism: The Renaissance.* Ed. O. B. Hardison. New York: Appleton-Century-Crofts, 1963.

Sylvestris, Bernardus. *Cosmographia.* Ed. P. Dronke. Leiden: E. J. Brill, 1978.

Thurot, Charles. *Notices et extraits de divers manuscrits latins pour servir à l'histoire des doctrines grammaticales au moyen âge* [*Notices et extraits des manuscrits de la Bibliothèque Nationale* 22, 2]. Paris: Imprimerie Imperiale, 1869; rpt. Frankfurt, 1964.

Vico, G. B. *De Antiquissima Italorum Sapientia ex Linguae Originibus Eruenda.* Naples: Mosca, 1710.

———. *On the Study Methods of Our Time.* Trans. Elio Gianturco. Ithaca, 1990.

Wilson, Thomas. *The Art of Rhetoric.* Ed. Peter E. Medine. University Park: Pennsylvania State University Press, 1994.

———. *The Rule of Reason.* Ed. Richard S. Sprague. Northridge, Calif.: San Fernando Valley State College, 1972.

Modern Criticism and Rhetoric

Adorno, Theodor. *Aesthetic Theory.* Trans. C. Lenhardt. London: Routledge & Kegan Paul, 1984.

————. *Notes to Literature.* Ed. Rolf Tiedemann. Trans. Shierry Weber Nicholsen. New York: Columbia University Press, 1991.

Bakhtin, M. M. *The Dialogic Imagination.* Ed. M. Holquist. Trans. C. Emerson and M. Holquist. Austin: University of Texas Press, 1991.

Barthes, Roland. *S/Z.* Paris: Seuil, 1970.

————. "Theory of the Text." In *Untying the Text: A Post-Structuralist Reader.* Ed. Robert Young. Boston: Routledge & Kegan Paul, 1981.

Berman, Russell A. *Modern Culture and Critical Theory.* Madison: University of Wisconsin Press, 1989.

Brown, Richard Harvey. *Society as Text: Essays on Rhetoric, Reason, and Reality.* Chicago: University of Chicago Press, 1987.

Burke, Kenneth. *Attitudes toward History.* Berkeley: University of California Press, 1984; first pub. 1937.

————. *Counter-Statement.* Berkeley: University of California Press, 1931.

————. *Language as Symbolic Action: Essays on Life, Literature, and Method.* Berkeley: University of California Press; London: Cambridge University Press, 1968.

————. "Methodological Repression and/or Strategies of Containment." *Critical Inquiry* 5 (1978): 401–16.

————. *The Philosophy of Literary Form: Studies in Symbolic Action.* Baton Rouge: Louisiana State University Press, 1941.

————. *A Rhetoric of Motives.* Berkeley: University of California Press, 1950.

————. *The Rhetoric of Religion: Studies in Logology.* Boston: Beacon Press, 1961.

Chomsky, Noam, and Edward S. Herman. *Manufacturing Consent: The Political Economy of the Mass Media.* New York: Pantheon, 1988.

De Man, Paul. "The Epistemology of Metaphor." *Critical Inquiry* 5 (1978): 13–30.

Derrida, Jacques. *De la grammatologie.* Paris: Les Éditions de Minuit, 1967.

————. *Dissemination.* Chicago: Chicago University Press, 1981.

————. *The Ear of the Other: Otobiography, Transference, Translation.* Ed. Christie V. McDonald, trans. Peggy Kamuf. New York: Schocken Books, 1985.

————. *Of Grammatology.* Baltimore: Johns Hopkins University Press, 1976.

Eagleton, T. *The Function of Criticism.* London: Verso Editions, 1984.

————. *Ideology: An Introduction.* London/New York: Verso Press, 1991.

————. *Literary Theory: An Introduction.* Minneapolis: University of Minnesota Press, 1983.

Eco, Umberto. *A Theory of Semiotics.* Bloomington: Indiana University Press, 1976.

Fish, Stanley. *Doing What Comes Naturally.* Durham: Duke University Press, 1989.

Foucault, Michel. *The Archaeology of Knowledge and the Discourse on Language.* New York: Pantheon Books, 1982.

————. *Madness and Civilization: A History of Insanity in the Age of Reason.* New York: Pantheon Books, 1965.

————. *The Order of Things: An Archaeology of the Human Sciences.* New York: Pantheon Books, 1971.

Fowler, Roger. *Linguistic Criticism.* New York: Oxford University Press, 1986.

————. *Literature as Social Discourse.* Bloomington: Indiana University Press, 1981.

Gadamer, Hans-Georg. "The Expressive Power of Language." *PMLA* 107 (1992): 345–52.

———. *Reason in the Age of Science.* Trans. Frederick G. Lawrence. Cambridge: MIT Press, 1981.

———. *Rhetorik und Hermeneutik.* Göttingen: Vandenhoeck, 1976.

———. *Truth and Method.* New York: Crossroad, 1986.

Geertz, Clifford. *The Interpretation of Cultures.* New York: Basic Books, 1973.

———. *Local Knowledge: Further Essays in Interpretive Anthropology.* New York: Basic Books, 1983.

Genette, Gérard. *Palimpsestes: La littérature au second degré.* Paris: Seuil, 1982.

Grassi, Ernesto. *Rhetoric as Philosophy: The Humanist Tradition.* University Park: Pennsylvania State University Press, 1980.

Greenblatt, Stephen. "Culture." In *Critical Terms for Literary Study.* Ed. Frank Lentricchia and Thomas McLaughlin. Chicago: University of Chicago Press, 1990.

Hock, Ronald F., and Edward N. O'Neil. *The Chreia in Ancient Rhetoric.* 1: *The Progymnasmata.* Atlanta: Scholars Press, 1986.

Hollander, John. *The Figure of Echo: A Mode of Allusion in Milton and After.* Berkeley: University of California Press, 1981.

Huyssen, Andreas. *After the Great Divide: Modernism, Mass Culture, Postmodernism.* Bloomington: Indiana University Press, 1986.

Jameson, Frederic. *The Political Unconscious: Narrative as a Socially Symbolic Act.* Ithaca: Cornell University Press, 1981.

König, Ed. *Stilistik, Rhetorik, und Poetik in Bezug auf die biblische Litteratur.* Leipzig: Dieterich, 1900.

Kraftchick, Steven J. "Why Do the Rhetoricians Rage?" In *Text and Logos: The Humanistic Interpretation of the New Testament.* Ed. T. W. Jennings, Jr. Atlanta: Scholars Press, 1990.

Krentz, Edgar. *The Historical-Critical Method.* Philadelphia: Fortress Press, 1975.

Krieger, Murray. *The New Apologists for Poetry.* Bloomington: Indiana University Press, 1963.

———. *The Play and Place of Criticism.* Baltimore: Johns Hopkins University Press, 1967.

———. *The Tragic Vision.* New York: Holt, Rinehart, and Winston, 1960.

———. *A Window to Criticism.* Princeton: Princeton University Press, 1964.

Kristeva, Julia. *La Révolution du langage poétique.* Paris: Seuil, 1974.

———. *Revolution in Poetic Language.* Ed. L. Roudiez and trans. M. Waller. New York: Columbia University Press, 1984.

———. *Semiotik.* Paris: Seuil, 1969.

Kuhn, T. S. *The Structure of Scientific Revolutions,* 2nd ed. Chicago: University of Chicago Press, 1970.

Lausberg, Heinrich. *Handbuch der literarischen Rhetorik.* München: Max Hueber, 1960.

Lentricchia, Frank, and Thomas McLaughlin, eds. *Critical Terms for Literary Study.* Chicago: University of Chicago Press, 1990.

Lippmann, Walter. *Public Opinion.* New York: Harcourt Brace Jovanovich, 1922.

MacIntyre, A. *Whose Justice? Which Rationality?* Notre Dame: University of Notre Dame Press, 1988.

Ong, Walter, S.J. *Fighting for Life.* Ithaca: Cornell University Press, 1981.

Bibliography

———. *Ramus, Method, and the Decay of Dialogue*. Cambridge, Mass.: Harvard University Press, 1958.

———. *Rhetoric, Romance, and Technology*. Ithaca: Cornell University Press, 1971.

Perelman, Chaim. *The Realm of Rhetoric*. Trans. William Kluback. Notre Dame: University of Notre Dame Press, 1982.

Perelman, Chaim, and L. Olbrechts-Tyteca. *The New Rhetoric: A Treatise on Argumentation*. Trans. John Wilkinson. Notre Dame: University of Notre Dame Press, 1969.

Richards, I. A. *The Philosophy of Rhetoric*. Oxford: Oxford University Press, 1936.

Ricoeur, Paul. "La structure, le mot, l'événement." In *Le conflit des interprétations*. Paris: Éditions du Seuil, 1969.

———. "New Developments in Phenomenology in France: The Phenomenology of Language." *Social Research* 34 (1967): 1–30.

———. "The Problem of the Double-Sense as Hermeneutic Problem and as Semantic Problem." In *Myths and Symbols: Studies in Honor of Mircea Eliade*. Ed. J. M. Kitagawa and C. H. Long. Chicago: University of Chicago Press, 1969.

———. "Qu'est-ce qu'un texte? Expliquer et comprendre." In *Hermeneutik und Dialektik*. Ed. R. Bubner, K. Cramer, and R. Wiehl. Tübingen: J. C. B. Mohr, 1970.

———. *The Rule of Metaphor*. Trans. Robert Czerny, Kathleen McLaughlin, and John Costello. Toronto: University of Toronto Press, 1977.

———. *The Symbolism of Evil*. New York: Harper & Row, 1967.

Rorty, Richard. *Philosophy and the Mirror of Nature*. Princeton: Princeton University Press, 1979.

Schleiermacher, Friedrich. "The *Hermeneutics:* Outline for 1819 Lectures." Trans. Jan Wojcik and Roland Haas. *New Literary History* 10 (1978): 1–16.

Stock, Brian. *Augustine the Reader: Meditation, Self-Knowledge, and the Ethics of Interpretation*. Cambridge, Mass.: Harvard University Press, 1996.

———. *The Implications of Literacy: Written Language and Models of Interpretation in the Eleventh and Twelfth Centuries*. Princeton: Princeton University Press, 1983.

———. *Listening for the Text: On the Uses of the Past*. Baltimore: Johns Hopkins University Press, 1990.

Toulmin, Stephen. "The Recovery of Practical Philosophy." *American Scholar* (August 1988): 337–52.

Toulmin, Stephen, and Albert R. Johnson. *The Abuse of Casuistry: A History of Moral Reasoning*. Berkeley: University of California Press, 1988.

Vickers, Brian. *In Defense of Rhetoric*. Oxford: Oxford University Press, 1988.

Wheelwright, Philip. *The Burning Fountain*, rev. ed. Bloomington: Indiana University Press, 1954.

———. *Metaphor and Reality*. Bloomington: Indiana University Press, 1962.

Secondary Bibliography

Ahern, John. "Nudi Grammantes: The Grammar and Rhetoric of Deviation in Inferno XV." *Romanic Review* 82, 4 (November 1990): 466–86.

Alonso-Schkel, Luis. *Estudios de Poetica Hebraea*. Barcelona: Juan Flors, 1963.

BIBLIOGRAPHY

Altman, Joel. *Tudor Play of Mind.* Berkeley: University of California Press, 1978.

Auerbach, Erich. "Figura." In *Scenes from the Drama of European Literature.* Minneapolis: University of Minnesota Press, 1984. 25–28.

———. *Literary Language and Its Public in Late Latin Antiquity and in the Middle Ages.* Trans. R. Mannheim. Princeton: Princeton University Press, 1965.

Bainton, Roland H. *Erasmus of Christendom.* New York: Scribner, 1969.

Baldwin, T. W. *William Shakspere's Small Latine and Less Greeke* Urbana: University of Illinois Press, 1944.

Banniard, Michel. "Jérôme et l'elegantia d'après le *De optimo genere interpretandi.*" In *Jérôme entre l'Occident et l'Orient.* Ed. Yves-Marie Duval. Paris: Études Augustiniennes, 1988. 305–22.

Baynes, N. H. "Isocrates." In *Byzantine Studies and Other Essays.* London: Athlone, 1960. 144–67.

Bestor, T. W. "Plato's Semantics and Plato's Cratylus." *Phronesis* 25 (1980): 306–30.

Binns, J. W., ed. *Latin Literature in the 4th Century.* London: Routledge & Kegan Paul, 1974.

Bitzer, Lloyd F. "The Rhetorical Situation." *Philosophy and Rhetoric* 1 (1968): 1–14.

Bizzell, Patricia and Bruce Herzberg. *The Rhetorical Tradition: Readings from Classical Times to the Present.* Boston: Bedford Books/St. Martin's Press, 1990.

Black, E. *Rhetorical Criticism: A Study in Method.* New York: Macmillan, 1965.

Boisacq, E. *Dictionnaire etymologique de la langue grecque.* 4th ed. Heidelberg/Paris: Carl Winter/C. Klincksieck, 1986.

Bostock, David. *Plato's Phaedo.* Oxford: Clarendon Press, 1986.

Bouwsma, William J. "Lawyers and Early Modern Culture." *American Historical Review* 78 (1973): 303–27.

Braet, Antoine. "The Classical Doctrine of Status and the Rhetorical Theory of Argumentation." *Philosophy and Rhetoric* 20 (1987): 79–93.

Brandt, William J. *The Rhetoric of Argumentation.* New York: Bobbs-Merrill, 1970.

Brickhouse, Thomas C., and Nicholas D. Smith. *Plato's Socrates.* Oxford: Oxford University Press, 1994.

Brown, Peter. *Power and Persuasion in Late Antiquity: Towards a Christian Empire.* Madison: University of Wisconsin Press, 1992.

Buckley, Michael J., S.J. *Motion and Motion's God: Thematic Variations in Aristotle, Cicero, Newton, and Hegel.* Princeton: Princeton University Press, 1971.

Cameron, Averil. *Christianity and the Rhetoric of Empire: The Development of Christian Discourse.* Berkeley: University of California Press, 1991.

Cestaro, Gary. "Irony of the Narrator in the *De vulgari eloquentia.*" *Italian Culture* 9 (1991): 15–27.

———. " ' . . . quanquam Sarnum biberimus ante dentes . . .': The Primal Scene of Suckling in Dante's *De vulgari eloquentia,*" *Dante Studies* 109 (1991): 119–47.

Clark, Donald Lemen. *John Milton at St. Paul's School.* New York: Columbia University Press, 1948.

———. "The Rise and Fall of Progymnasmata in Sixteenth and Seventeenth Century Grammar Schools." *Speech Monographs* 19 (1952): 259–63.

Cole, A. T. "Archaic Truth." *Quaderni Urbinati* 42 (1983): 7–28.

234

Bibliography

Cole, Thomas. *The Origins of Rhetoric in Ancient Greece.* Baltimore: Johns Hopkins University Press, 1991.

Colie, Rosalie L. *Paradoxia Epidemica.* Princeton: Princeton University Press, 1966.

Colish, Marcia L. *The Mirror of Language: A Study in the Medieval Theory of Knowledge.* Rev. ed. Lincoln: University of Nebraska Press, 1983.

Commager, Henry Steele. *Horace.* New Haven: Yale University Press, 1962.

Copeland, Rita. *Rhetoric, Hermeneutics and Translation in the Middle Ages.* Cambridge: Cambridge University Press, 1991.

Corbett, Edward P. J. *Classical Rhetoric for the Modern Student.* Oxford: Oxford University Press, 1965.

Corbett, E. P. J., ed. *Rhetorical Analyses of Literary Works.* New York: Oxford University Press, 1969.

Costello, William T., S.J. *The Scholastic Curriculum at Early Seventeenth-Century Cambridge.* Cambridge, Mass.: Harvard University Press, 1958.

Curtis, Mark H. *Oxford and Cambridge in Transition, 1558–1642.* Oxford: Clarendon, 1959.

Dale, A. M. "Ethos and Dianoia: 'Character' and 'Thought' in Aristotle's Poetics." In *Collected Papers of A. M. Dale.* Ed. T. B. L. Webster and E. G. Turner. London: Cambridge University Press, 1969.

Dieter, Otto Alvin Loeb. "Stasis." *Speech Monographs* 17, 4 (1950): 345–69.

Dietz, Jean, ed. *Rhetoric and Praxis.* Washington, D.C.: Catholic University Press, 1986.

Dihle, Albrecht. *The Theory of Will in Classical Antiquity.* Berkeley: University of California Press, 1982.

Ebeling, H., ed. *Lexicon Homericum.* 2 volumes. Hildesheim: Olms, 1963 (rept. of original edition, Leipzig: Teubner, 1885).

Eden, Kathy. *Poetic and Legal Fiction in the Aristotelian Tradition.* Princeton: Princeton University Press, 1986.

Edwards, M. W. *Homer: Poet of the Iliad.* Baltimore: Johns Hopkins University Press, 1987.

Else, G. F. *Aristotle's Poetics: The Argument.* Cambridge, Mass.: Harvard University Press, 1963.

———. *Plato and Aristotle on Poetry.* Chapel Hill: North Carolina University Press, 1986.

Eucken, C. *Isokrates: Seine Positionen in der Auseinandersetzung mit den zeitgenössischen Philosophen.* Berlin and New York: De Gruyter, 1983.

Field, G. C. *Plato and His Contemporaries: A Study in Fourth-Century Life and Thought.* 2nd ed. London: Methuen, 1948.

Fine, G. "Plato on Naming." *Philosophical Quarterly* 27 (1977): 289–301.

Finley, M. I. "The Heritage of Isocrates." In *The Use and Abuse of History.* London: Chatto & Windus, 1975. 193–214.

Fletcher, Harris. *The Intellectual Development of John Milton.* 2 volumes. Urbana: University of Illinois Press, 1961.

Freedman, Joseph S. "Cicero in Sixteenth- and Seventeenth-Century Rhetoric Instruction." *Rhetorica* 4 (1986): 227–54.

Frend, W. H. C. *The Rise of Christianity.* London: Darton, Longman & Todd, 1984.

Frisk, H. *Griechisches Etymologisches Wörterbuch.* 2 volumes. Heidelberg: Carl Winter, 1955–70.

Fry, Paul. *The Reach of Criticism.* New Haven: Yale University Press, 1983.

Fuentes, Carlos. "Borges in Action: A Narrative Homage." *PMLA* 101 (1986): 778–87.

Furley, David, and Alexander Nehamas, eds. *Aristotle's Rhetoric: Philosophical Essays.* Princeton: Princeton University Press, 1994. 211–30.

Gehl, Paul F. *A Moral Art: Grammar, Society, and Culture in Trecento Florence.* Ithaca: Cornell University Press, 1993.

Gilmore, M. P. *Humanists and Jurists.* Cambridge, Mass.: Belknap, 1963.

———. "Methodus Disputandi: The Apologetic Works of Erasmus." In *Florilegium Historiale: Essays Presented to Wallace K. Ferguson.* Ed. J. G. Rowe and W. H. Stockdale. Toronto: University of Toronto Press, 1971.

Gleason, John B. *John Colet.* Berkeley: University of California Press, 1988.

Goodwin, David. "Controversiae Meta-Asystatae and the New Rhetoric." *Rhetoric Society Quarterly* 19 (1989): 205–16.

Graff, Gerald. *Professing Literature.* Chicago: University of Chicago Press, 1987.

Grafton, Anthony, and Lisa Jardine. *From Humanism to the Humanities.* Cambridge, Mass.: Harvard University Press, 1986.

Greene, Thomas M. *The Light in Troy.* New Haven: Yale University Press, 1982.

Grendler, Paul F. *Schooling in Renaissance Italy: Literacy and Learning, 1300–1600.* Baltimore: Johns Hopkins University Press, 1989.

Grube, G. M. A. *A Greek Critic: Demetrius on Style.* Toronto: University of Toronto Press, 1961.

Gundert, Hermann. "Die Simonides-Interpretation in Platons Protagoras," *EPMH-NEIA: Festschrift Otto Regenbogen.* Heidelberg: C. Winter, 1952. 71–93.

Guyer, Paul. *Kant and the Claims of Taste.* Cambridge, Mass.: Harvard University Press, 1979.

Hackett, M. B. *The Original Statutes of Cambridge University.* Cambridge: Cambridge University Press, 1970.

Hagendahl, Harald. *Augustine and the Latin Classics.* 2: Testimonia. Stockholm: Almquist & Wiksell, 1967.

Halliwell, Stephen. "Philosophy and Rhetoric." In *Persuasion: Greek Rhetoric in Action.* Ed. I. Worthington. London: Routledge, 1994. 222–43.

———. "Popular Morality, Philosophical Ethics, and the Rhetoric." In *Aristotle's Rhetoric: Philosophical Essays.* Ed. David Furley and Alexander Nehamas. Princeton: Princeton University Press, 1994. 211–30. Reprinted as "The Challenge of Rhetoric to Political and Ethical Theory in Aristotle." In *Essays on Aristotle's Rhetoric.* Ed. A. O. Rorty. Berkeley: University of California Press, 1996. 175–90.

Hefele, Charles Joseph. *Histoire des Conciles II.* Paris: Letouzey et Ané, 1908.

Heilbrunn, Gunther. "Isocrates on Rhetoric and Power." *Hermes* 103 (1975): 153–78.

Henderson, Judith Rice. "Erasmus on the Art of Letter-Writing." In *Renaissance Eloquence.* Ed. James Murphy. Berkeley: University of California Press, 1983. 331–355.

Bibliography

Hendrickson, G. L. "The Origin and Meaning of the Ancient Characters of Style." *AJP* 26 (1905): 249–90.

———. "The Peripatetic Mean of Style and the Three Stylistic Characters." *AJP* 25 (1904): 125–46.

Henrich, Dieter. *Aesthetic Judgment and the Moral Image of the World.* Stanford: Stanford University Press, 1992.

Hofmann, J. B. *Etymologisches Wörterbuch.* Munich: Oldenbourg, 1949.

Irwin, T. H. "Aristotle's concept of signification." *Language and Logos: Studies in Ancient Greek Philosophy Presented to G. E. L. Owen.* Ed. Malcolm Schofield and Martha Craven Nussbaum. Cambridge: Cambridge University Press, 1982. 241–66.

———. "Plato: The Intellectual Background." In *The Cambridge Companion to Plato.* Ed. R. Kraut. Cambridge: Cambridge University Press, 1992.

Jaeger, W. *Paideia: Die formung des griechischen mensch.* Berlin: De Gruyter, 1934.

———. *Paideia: The Ideals of Greek Culture.* Trans. Gilbert Highet. Oxford: Oxford University Press, 1943–45.

Jardine, Lisa. *Erasmus, Man of Letters.* Princeton: Princeton University Press, 1993.

———. "The Place of Dialectic Teaching in Sixteenth-Century Cambridge." *SR* 21 (1974): 31–62.

Jordan, Mark D. "Words and Word: Incarnation and Signification in Augustine's *De Doctrina Christiana.*" *Augustinian Studies* 11 (1980): 177–96.

Jüthner, J. "Isokrates und die Menschheitsidee." *Wiener Studien* 47 (1929): 26–31. Reprinted in *Isokrates.* Ed. F. Seck. Darmstadt, 1976. 122–27.

Kaster, Robert A. *Guardians of Language: The Grammarian and Society in Late Antiquity.* Berkeley: University of California Press, 1988.

Kemal, Salim. *Kant and Fine Art.* Oxford: Clarendon Press, 1986.

Kennedy, George A. *The Art of Persuasion in Greece.* Princeton: Princeton University Press, 1963.

———. *The Art of Rhetoric in the Roman World.* Princeton: Princeton University Press, 1972.

———. *Classical Rhetoric and Its Christian and Secular Traditions from Ancient to Modern Times.* Chapel Hill: University of North Carolina Press, 1980.

Kerferd, G. B. *The Sophistic Movement.* Cambridge: Cambridge University Press, 1981.

Ketchum, R. J. "Names, Forms and Conventionalism: Cratylus 383–95." *Phronesis* 24 (1979): 133–47.

Kimball, Bruce A. *Orators and Philosophers: A History of the Idea of Liberal Education.* New York: Teachers College Columbia University Press, 1986.

Kinney, Arthur F. "Rhetoric as Poetic: Humanist Fiction in the Renaissance." *ELH* 43 (1976): 413–43.

Kisch, Guido. *Humanismus und Jurisprudenz: Der Kampf zwischen mos italicus und mos gallicus an der Universität Basel.* Basel: Helbing & Lichtenhahn, 1955.

Kraut, R., ed. *The Cambridge Companion to Plato.* Cambridge: Cambridge University Press, 1992.

Kretzmann, Norman. "The History of Semantics." *The Encyclopedia of Philosophy.* Ed. Paul Edwards. New York: Macmillan, 1967. 7:359–62.

Kristeller, Paul Oskar. *Renaissance Thought: The Classic, Scholastic, and Humanist Strains.* New York: Columbia University Press, 1961.

Kroner, Hans-Otto. "Dialog und Rede: Zur Deutung des Isokrateischen Panathen-aikos." *Antike und Abendland* 14 (1968): 102–21.

Kustas, George L. *Studies in Byzantine Rhetoric.* Thessaloniki, 1973.

Laborderie, Jean. *Le dialogue platonicien de la maturité.* Paris: Les Belles Lettres, 1978.

Lanham, Richard A. *The Motives of Eloquence.* New Haven: Yale University Press, 1976.

———. "The Q Question." *South Atlantic Quarterly* 87 (1988): 653–700.

Lausberg, Heinrich. *Handbuch der Literarischen Rhetorik.* Munich: M. Hueber, 1960.

Leeman, A. D. "Gloria." Ph.D. diss., Rotterdam, 1949.

Lefèvre, Eckard. *Monumentum Chiloniense: Studien zur augusteischen zeit: Kieler Fest-schrift fur Erich Burck zum 70.* Amsterdam: Adolf M. Hakkert, 1975.

Levine, P. "The Original Design and Publication of the *De Natura Deorum.*" *HSCP* 62 (1957): 20–22.

Maitland, F. W. *English Law and the Renaissance.* Cambridge: Cambridge University Press, 1901.

Makkreel, Rudolf A. *Imagination and Interpretation in Kant.* Chicago: University of Chicago Press, 1990.

Markus, R. A. "Pagans, Christians and the Latin Classics." In *Latin Literature in the 4th Century.* Ed. J. W. Binns. London: Routledge & Kegan Paul, 1974.

Marrou, Henri-Irénée. *A History of Education in Antiquity.* Trans. George Lamb. New York: Sheed and Ward, 1964.

Marsh, David. *Quattrocento Dialogue: Classical Tradition and Humanist Innovation.* Cambridge, Mass.: Harvard University Press, 1980.

May, James M. *Trials of Character: The Eloquence of Ciceronian Ethos.* Chapel Hill: University of North Carolina Press, 1988.

Mazzeo, Joseph. "St. Augustine's Rhetoric of Silence: Truth vs. Eloquence and Things vs. Signs." In *Renaissance and Seventeenth-Century Studies.* New York: Columbia University Press and London: Routledge & Kegan Paul, 1964. 1–28.

McKeon, Richard. "Aristotle's Conception of Language and the Arts of Language." In *Critics and Criticism.* Ed. R. S. Crane. Chicago: University of Chicago Press, 1952. 176–231.

Metzger, Bruce M. *The Canon of the New Testament.* Oxford: Clarendon Press, 1987.

Miller, Perry. *The New England Mind: The Seventeenth Century.* New York: The Seventeenth Century, 1939.

Monfasani, John. "Humanism and Rhetoric." In *Renaissance Humanism: Foundations, Forms, and Legacy.* Ed. Albert Rabil, Jr. Philadelphia: University of Pennsylvania Press, 1988. 191–227.

Mooney, Michael. *Vico in the Tradition of Rhetoric.* Princeton: Princeton University Press, 1985.

Moran, Jo Ann Hoeppner. *The Growth of English Schooling 1340–1548.* Princeton: Princeton University Press, 1985.

Most, Glenn. "Canon Fathers: Literacy, Morality, Power," *Arion Third Series* I 3rd series 1 (1990).

Mulder, John. *The Temple of the Mind.* New York: Pegasus, 1969.

Murphy, James J. "Implications of the 'Renaissance of Rhetoric' in English Depart-ments." *Quarterly Journal of Speech* 9 (1989): 335–43.

Bibliography

————. *Rhetoric in the Middle Ages: A History of Rhetorical Theory from St. Augustine to the Renaissance.* Berkeley: University of California Press, 1974.

Murphy, James J., ed. *Renaissance Eloquence.* Berkeley: University of California Press, 1983.

Murphy, Richard. "The Ethics of Debating Both Sides." *Speech Teacher* 6 (1957): 1–9.

Nadeau, Ray. "Classical Systems of Stases in Greek: Hermagoras to Hermogenes." *Greek, Roman and Byzantine Studies* 2, 1 (1959): 51–71.

————. "The Progymnasmata of Aphthonius." *Speech Monographs* 19 (1952): 264–85.

Nagy, G. *The Best of the Achaeans: Concepts of the Hero in Archaic Greek Poetry.* Baltimore: Johns Hopkins University Press, 1979.

————. *Greek Mythology and Poetics.* Ithaca: Cornell University Press, 1990.

————. *Pindar's Homer: The Lyric Possession of an Epic Past.* Baltimore: Johns Hopkins University Press, 1990.

Nehamas, Alexander. "Eristic, Antilogic, Sophistic, Dialectic: Plato's Demarcation of Philosophy from Sophistry." *History of Philosophy Quarterly* 7 (1990): 3–16.

Nelson, Lowry, Jr. *Poetic Configurations.* University Park: Pennsylvania State University Press, 1991.

Nencioni, G. "Dante e la Retorica." In *Dante e Bologna nei Tempi di Dante.* Ed. Facoltà di lettere e filosofia dell'Università di Bologna. Bologna: Commissione per i Test di Lingua, 1967.

Nightingale, Andrea. "Plato's *Gorgias* and Euripides' *Antiope*: A Study in Generic Transformation." *Classical Antiquity* 11.1 (1992): 121–40.

O'Malley, John W. "Erasmus and Luther: Continuity and Discontinuity as Key to Their Conflict," *Sixteenth Century Journal* 5 (October 1974): 47–65.

————. *Praise and Blame in Renaissance Rome.* Durham: Duke University Press, 1979.

O'Sullivan, N. "Plato and Kaloumene—Rhetorike (Comments on Recent Works by Schiappa and Cole)." *Mnemosyne* 46 (1993): 87–89.

Orme, Nicholas. "An Early-Tudor Oxford Schoolbook." *RQ* 34 (1981): 11–39.

————. *English Schools in the Middle Ages.* London: Methuen, 1973.

Otto, W. F. *Die Gestalt und das Sein: Gesammelte Abhandlungen uber den Mythos und seine Bedeutung fur die Menschheit.* Tübingen: Eugen Diederich, 1955.

Owen, G. *Language and Logos.* New York: Columbia University Press, 1982.

Parry, Milman. *The Making of Homeric Verse: The Collected Papers of Milman Parry.* Ed. Adam Parry. Oxford: Oxford University Press, 1971.

Penner, Terry. *The Ascent from Nominalism: Some Existence Arguments in Plato's Middle Dialogues.* Dordrecht: D. Reidel, 1987.

Press, Gerald A. "The Subject and Structure of Augustine's *De Doctrina Christiana*." *Augustinian Studies* 11 (1980): 99–124.

Prier, R. A. *Archaic Logic: Symbol and Structure in Heraclitus, Parmenides, and Euripides.* The Hague and Paris: Mouton, 1976.

————. *Thauma Idesthai: The Phenomenology of Sight and Appearance in Archaic Greek.* Tallahassee: Florida State University Press, 1989.

Pucci, P. *Hesiod and the Language of Poetry.* Baltimore: Johns Hopkins University Press, 1977.

Quinn, Arthur. "Brian Vickers, *In Defense of Rhetoric*." *Rhetorica* 7 (1989): 291–94.

Rabil, Albert, Jr., ed. *Renaissance Humanism: Foundations, Forms and Legacy*. Philadelphia: University of Pennsylvania Press, 1988.

Race, William H. "Panathenaicus 74–90: The Rhetoric of Isocrates' Digression on Agamemnon." *TAPA* 108 (1978): 175–85.

Raign, Kathryn Rosser. "Stasis Theory Revisited: An Inventional Techne for Empowering Students." *Focuses* 2 (1989): 19–26.

Reiss, Timothy J. *The Meaning of Literature*. Ithaca: Cornell University Press, 1992.

Rice, Eugene F., Jr. *Saint Jerome in the Renaissance*. Baltimore: Johns Hopkins University Press, 1985.

Roberts, W. Rhys. *Greek Rhetoric and Literary Criticism*. New York: Longmans Green, 1963. 48–70.

———. "The Greek Words for 'Style.'" *Classical Review* 15 (1901): 252–55.

Rorty, A. O., ed. *Essays on Aristotle's Rhetoric*. Berkeley: University of California Press, 1996.

Rosenstock, Bruce. "Socrates as Revenant: A Reading of the Menexenus." *Phoenix* 48 (1994): 331–47.

Rosner, Mary. "The Two Faces of Cicero: Trollope's Life in the Nineteenth Century." *Rhetoric Society Quarterly* 18 (1988): 252–58.

Ruegg, Walter. *Cicero und der Humanismus*. Zurich: Rheinverlag, 1946.

Schäublin, Christoph. "Selbstinterpretation im 'Panathenaikos' des Isokrates?" *Museum Helveticum* 39 (1982): 165–78.

Schenkeveld, Dirk Marie. *Studies in Demetrius on Style*. Amsterdam: A. M. Hakkert, 1964.

Schildgen, Brenda. "Jerome's Prefatory Epistles to the Bible and the *Canterbury Tales*." *Studies in the Age of Chaucer* 15 (1993): 111–30.

———. "Petrarch's Defense of Secular Letters, the Latin Fathers, and Ancient Roman Rhetoric." *Rhetorica* 11, 2 (Spring 1993): 119–34.

———. "St. Augustine's Answer to Jacques Derrida in the *De Doctrina Christiana*." *New Literary History* 25, 2 (Spring 1994): 383–97.

Schmidt, P. L. "Die Anfänge der institutionellen Rhetorik in Rom." In *Monumentum Chilonense*. Ed. E. Lefevre. Amsterdam, 1975.

Schoeck, Richard J. "Early Anglo-Saxon Studies and Legal Scholarship." *Studies in the Renaissance* 5 (1958): 102–10.

———. "The Elizabethan Society of Antiquaries and Men of Law." *Notes & Queries*, n.s. 1 (1954): 417–21.

———. *Erasmus Grandescens*. Nieuwkoop: De Graaf, 1988.

———. "Lawyers and Rhetoric." In *Renaissance Eloquence*. Ed. James J. Murphy. Berkeley: University of California Press, 1983. 274–91.

———. "Sir Thomas More, Humanist and Lawyer." *University of Toronto Quarterly* 26 (1964): 1–14.

Simon, Joan. *Education and Society in Tudor England*. London: Cambridge University Press, 1966.

Sloane, Thomas. "Reinventing Inventio." *College English* 51 (1989): 461–73.

———. "Rhetorical Education and Two-Sided Argument." In *Renaissance-Rhetorik/Renaissance Rhetoric*. Ed. Heinrich F. Plett. Berlin and New York: De Gruyter, 1993. 163–78.

Bibliography

Smith, Bromley. "Extracurricular Disputations: 1400–1650." *Quarterly Journal of Speech* 34 (1948): 473–76.

Snell, B. "ALETHEIA." In *Festschrift Ernst Siegmann*. Würzberg: Schoningh, 1975. 9–17.

———. *Der Weg zum Denken und zur Wahrheit: Studien zur fruhgriechischen Sprache*. Gottingen: Vandenhoeck & Ruprecht, 1978.

———. *Die Entdeckung des Geistes*, 4th ed. Gottingen: Vandenhoeck & Ruprecht, 1975.

Spariosu, Mihai. *God of Many Names*. Durham: Duke University Press, 1991.

Stern, Paul. *Socratic Rationalism and Political Philosophy: An Interpretation of Plato's Phaedo*. Albany: State University of New York Press, 1993.

Streuver, Nancy. "Lorenzo Valla: Humanist Rhetoric and the Critique of the Classical Languages of Morality." In *Renaissance Eloquence*. Ed. James J. Murphy. Berkeley: University of California Press, 1983. 191–206.

Sutter, Carl. *Aus Leben und Schriften des Magisters Boncompagno*. Freiburg and Leipzig: Mohr, 1894.

Swearingen, C. Jan. *Rhetoric and Irony: Western Literacy and Western Lies*. New York: Oxford University Press, 1991.

Thesleff, Holger. *Studies in the Styles of Plato*. Helsinki: Suomolaisen Kirjalisuunden Kirjapaino, 1967.

Thompson, Craig R. *Schools in Tudor England*. Washington, D.C.: Folger Shakespeare Library, 1959.

———. *Universities in Tudor England*. Washington, D.C.: Folger Shakespeare Library, 1959.

Thomson, Wayne N. "Stasis in Aristotle's Rhetoric." *Quarterly Journal of Speech* 58 (1972): 134–41.

Tinkler, John F. "Humanism and Dialogue." *Parergon*, n.s. 6 (1988): 197–214.

———. "Renaissance Humanism and the *Genera Eloquentiae*." *Rhetorica* 5 (1987): 279–309.

Trimpi, Wesley. *Muses of One Mind: The Literary Analysis of Experience and Its Continuity*. Princeton: Princeton University Press, 1983.

Trinkaus, Charles. *In Our Image and Likeness: Humanity and Divinity in Italian Humanist Thought*. Chicago: University of Chicago Press, 1970.

Vance, Eugene. "Saint Augustine: Language as Temporality." In *Mimesis: From Mirror to Method, Augustine to Descartes*. Ed. John D. Lyons and Stephen G. Nichols, Jr. Hanover: University Press of New England, 1982. 20–35.

Vickers, Brian. *In Defense of Rhetoric*. Oxford: Oxford University Press, 1988.

———. *Rhetoric Revalued*. Medieval & Renaissance Texts and Studies 19. Ed. B. Vickers. Binghamton, N.Y.: Center for Medieval & Renaissance Studies, 1982.

Vlastos, Gregory. "Elenchus and Mathematics: A Turning Point in Plato's Development." *American Journal of Philology* 109 (1988): 362–96. Reprinted as chapter 4 in Gregory Vlastos, *Socrates: Ironist and Moral Philosopher*. Ithaca: Cornell University Press, 1991.

———. *Socrates: Ironist and Moral Philosopher*. Ithaca: Cornell University Press, 1991.

———. "The Socratic Elenchus." *Oxford Studies in Ancient Philosophy* 1 (1983): 27–58.

Voloshinov, V. N. *Marxism and the Philosophy of Language*. Cambridge, Mass.: Harvard University Press, 1973.

Wagner, David L., ed. *Seven Liberal Arts in the Middle Ages*. Bloomington: Indiana University Press, 1983.

Wallace, Karl R., ed. *A History of Speech Education in America*. New York: Appleton Century Crofts, 1954.

———. "Rhetorical Exercises in Tudor Education." *Quarterly Journal of Speech* 22 (1936): 28–51.

Waswo, Richard. *Language and Meaning in the Renaissance*. Princeton: Princeton University Press, 1987.

Watson, Foster. *The English Grammar Schools to 1660: Their Curriculum and Practice*. Cambridge: Cambridge University Press, 1908.

Wellek, René. *A History of Modern Criticism*. 8 volumes. New Haven: Yale University Press, 1955.

———. *Immanuel Kant in England, 1793–1838*. Princeton: Princeton University Press, 1931.

White, Eugene E. "Master Holdsworth and 'A Knowledge Very Useful and Necessary.'" *Quarterly Journal of Speech* 53 (1967): 1–16.

White, James Boyd. *When Words Lose Their Meaning: Constitutions and Reconstitutions of Language, Character, and Community*. Chicago: University of Chicago Press, 1984.

Wilson, Kenneth. *Incomplete Fictions: The Formation of English Renaissance Dialogue*. Washington, D.C.: Catholic University Press, 1985.

Witt, Ronald G. "Boncompagno and the Defense of Rhetoric." *Journal of Medieval and Renaissance Studies* 16, 1 (Spring 1986): 1–31.

———. "Medieval Italian Culture and the Origins of Humanism as a Stylistic Ideal." In *Renaissance Humanism*, 3. Ed. Albert Rabil, Jr. Philadelphia: University of Pennsylvania Press, 1988.

Worthington, I. *Persuasion: Greek Rhetoric in Action*. London: Routledge, 1994.

Yinger, J. Milton. "Contraculture and Subculture." *American Sociological Review* 25 (1960): 625–35.

———. *Countercultures: The Promise and the Peril of a World Turned Upside Down*. New York: Free Press, 1982.

Zammito, John H. *The Genesis of Kant's Critique of Judgment*. Chicago: University of Chicago Press, 1992.

INDEX

Index

Index